A Short Guide to the History of South Africa 1902-1989

By

Damian P.O'Connor

I0425776

Also by the Author

Non-Fiction

A Short Guide to the History of South Africa 1652-1902

Imperial Defence and the Commitment to Empire

The Zulu and the Raj: The Life of Sir Bartle Frere

Between Peace and War: The History of the Royal United Services Institute 1831-2010

Africana Fiction

The If Conspiracy

Pelly's Quest

Kruger's Millions

Veldt Ozymandias

The Oshadangwa Murders

The Capinga Questions

Contents

*

Introduction

*

Intellectual Health Warning

*

The Growing Importance of the Background.

*

Smuts and Bosman

*

The Native Question

*

Poor Whites, the Economy and the Expanding Government

*

The Long Rise of the Purified National Party

*

South Africa at War 1939-45

*

Fagan and Sauer: A Tale of Two Commissions.

*

The National Party Coup d'Etat and The Vision of Utopia 1948-58

*

The Background moves to the Foreground.

*

The Point of No Return

*

Apartheid Triumphant 1964-76

*

Foreign Affairs

*

Rhodesia

*

The Carnation Revolution

*

The Angolan War 1975-87

*

The Total Strategy

*

Mozambique Revisited

*

Rhodesia/Zimbabwe

*

The ANC in Exile 1960-84

*

Apartheid at Home

*

P.W. Botha: Brutality and Reform

*

Crossing the Rubicon, Drowning in the Tiber 1985-89

*

Conclusions

There are those who, in the absolute conviction of their own rectitude, resent the fact that anyone should hold an opinion different from their own. When that does happen they ascribe it not to intellectual conviction, but to some form of moral turpitude. So they become impatient of the free expression of opinion – they want to put restraints on opposition and criticism – they desire to see created in support of their views and policies, that servile, standardised mass-mentality which is one of the instruments of dictatorship.

J.H. Hofmeyr, 1939.[1]

*

Do these thick-headed people in Equity not know or care that apartheid in South Africa was introduced by white, English trade unionists protecting their jobs against black immigrant labour from the countryside or abroad?

The Spectator's view of a boycott of South African artists performing in London by actor's union, Equity, 1977.[2]

*

From the late 1960s and 1970s, the Black Consciousness Movement campaigned for the use of the word black to describe all those defined as other than white. However, this was by no means universally accepted and many members of the so-called black group still prefer to be described as coloured, Indian and so on. Another debate arises around the term African. Does this or can this refer only to black Africans? The debate is not really capable of being resolved.... No disrespect is intended to any group.... It is simply impossible to write a History of South Africa without erring on one side or another of the argument.

Final Report of the Truth and Reconciliation Commission 1998.

---

[1] Quoted in A. Paton, *South African Tragedy. The Life and Times of Jan Hofmeyr* (New York, 1965) p.250
[22] 'Racial Art, *The Spectator* 8th October, 1977.

4

*

Introduction

Don't Skip It. It's Important.

First of all, this is Volume II. You can read it as a stand-alone, but it will make more sense if you read Volume I first (*A Short Guide to the History of South Africa 1652-1902*).

A quick gallop through History; hold on tight and don't fall off. I have been studying South African History all my life and I've visited the country many times over the past two decades. I've read just about everything - fact or fiction - I could get my hands on about the subject, pored over countless documents in plenty of archives, trod the red earth of battlefields, driven long, long miles over black top, tracks and the corrugated, plain old dirt of South Africa's back roads. I've eaten *biltong*, drunk *Castle*, necked *Springboks*, been through those quintessential 21st Century South African experiences, armed robbery and being shaken down by the Joburg traffic police (before I got out of the airport even!); and I've got an MA and a Ph.D in African and Imperial History, published academic books and articles, given talks and lectures, got awards from Chief Buthelezi, Nelson Mandela and the Oppenheimers through the Brenthurst Foundation/Royal United Services Institute and have done a bit of work on African development issues. I'm telling you this just so that you know I'm not someone just off the boat. I'm writing this History because - make no mistake – things in the great country known as the Republic of South Africa *can* go the way of Zimbabwe, but only if a false narrative of South African History can be created to justify the destruction of property rights, the abandonment of the rule of law and the dispossession and expulsion of white South Africans. And, yes, that false narrative has been under construction for a very long time, has gained a currency in politics and academia that it simply does not deserve and has now (2019) worked itself into the official policy of the ANC under the guise of *Expropriation without Compensation*. It is a narrative that claims that white people ripped off the land and wealth that properly belonged to indigenous Africans in an orgy of capitalist, imperialist exploitation resisted only by the heroic efforts of the ANC; this narrative is untrue, yet even to voice that opinion is to invite vitriol from those on the Left who are responsible for constructing that false narrative.

You should not expect much detached objectivity in this book simply because a lot of the aforementioned garbage has been shovelled down my throat under the cloak of a 'detached objectivity' that was anything but and, frankly, I'm fed up with it. Be prepared to be offended. That said, it is an accurate and reliable broad brush account and all the better for being openly and honestly subjective. The style I've adopted is on the 'Gonzo' side, which means that I am going to employ all the black arts of sarcasm, subjectivity, hyperbole, splenetic polemic and humour to pour scorn on a lot of the garbage that I've been asked to believe over the years. *That said*, although a certain amount of gruesome flippancy is acceptable when dealing with incidents and people long gone, the closer one gets to the present, the more raw the wounds and the more careful we have to be. This doesn't mean that I'm going to spare the rod when necessary.

There is no reason to fall out over questions or interpretations of historical events. If you are the sort of person who thinks that it's worth issuing death threats over the internet because I don't agree with your version of events or you think I'm (*insert your favourite epithet here*) then please confine your activities to buying several thousand copies of this book and holding a celebratory book burning. The only reason to get hot under the collar about History is when someone is using it to persuade you to vote, think or behave in a way that is harmful to you or your neighbours. Admittedly, that does happen a lot but the answer to it is not to throw your teddy out of the cot and Tweet something pithy but to read up on the subject, do your own thinking and, most importantly, assess the motivations of the person selling you the pony. Having your own point of view does not make you a bad person. Not questioning the guff that you are being fed does.

Finally, this book cannot be comprehensive and a lot of events, people and places have been left out – sorry Bambatha, Delville Wood and the Flu - but I think I've made a fair selection and I hope that you'll know a bit more about South Africa when you have finished the book than you did before you started it. If you think that's a modest ambition for an author, well, I've read books on this subject that are so bad that I've had to reach for the mind bleach before I've got more than half way in to them. Believe me, there are plenty of people out there who seem to have made an effort to so distort the record that we have to call their output 'anti-History'.

Unlike the first volume, I'm going to put a few more footnotes in mainly because this is an area that, paradoxically, isn't as well served by readily available sources as the earlier period but which does have a wider variety of sources to choose from, if you get my drift. Generally speaking, the period between the end of the Anglo-Boer war and the coming of Apartheid has been pretty much left to academics who have produced much good research but it tends to be written in prose that is often interminable, impenetrable and unreadable. Hopefully, this tome won't be. I'm leaving out the index and bibliography again though. There are enough references to books in the text to provide you with some next steps if your interest is particularly sparked and if you have an electronic version, the text is probably searchable; if you have a paper copy, be happy that it's cheaper as a result and the rainforest has a few extra leaves left in it.

*

Mea Culpa

In the first volume, I put Kruger at Blood River. He wasn't, but he was at Vegkop and so the main point stands. Also, Professor Fransjohan Pretorius didn't give Chis Ash's book a one star rating on Amazon. This was done by someone else, who then padded out his review with a review by Fransjohan Pretorius which amounted to much the same thing.

Intellectual Health Warning.

Now it might seem odd to start a History of 20th Century South Africa with a discussion of a book about 19th Century Britain but the last volume started with the story of King Arthur so bear with me and all will be revealed. Righty ho. There was a time back in the 1970s when the History taught in British schools started to change from 'dates and battles' (aka Political History) to 'strikes and steam engines' (aka Social and Economic History). Fortunately, Political History wasn't completely scotched because, of course, it deals with the important stuff like war and peace, government and legislation but there was enough of the social and economic stuff to put it under threat for a little while; things could have been worse – there were some dimwits who wanted to replace History with Sociology, God 'elp us. As a way of looking at the past, Social and Economic History has its place – indeed, a very valuable place, especially in 20th Century South African History – but the problem was that it tended to be written mainly by socialists and Marxists so instead of 'The History of the Working Man' you got 'The Making of the English Working Class' which of course is not the same thing at all; there are some quite hard working men who are not, never will be and never wanted to be, part of what the Marxists call the 'Working Class'. This is an obvious point but the obvious is so often ignored, skated over or obscured by Historians that I thought it best to restate it. My favourite work of this kind, *A Social and Economic History of Britain 1760-1950,* was written by Pauline Gregg, a committed socialist, who put forward the perfectly neat view that the mid-19th Century saw two great class battles in which the rising middle class gave the feudal aristocracy a damn good thrashing and established their dominance. These battles were over the 1832 Reform Act and the 1846 Repeal of the Corn Laws in which, she claimed, the Reform Act gave the middle class the vote while the repeal of the Corn Laws cleared the way for free trade and rampant capitalism. I loved that book; I used it whenever I wrote my 'A' Level essays. It answered all my questions very simply and I never needed to think about the issue again.

Later on, however, I found out that just about everything she said was unfounded on anything resembling reality. The middle class in 1832 *already had the vote;* what happened was a clear up of hilariously corrupt rotten boroughs and the redistribution of seats to industrial areas; Old Sarum had been abandoned when New Sarum was built, had only three houses and seven inhabitants but still sent two MPs to parliament while the thriving mill town of Bolton had no MPs at all; Dunwich in Suffolk had fallen into the sea but still had an MP; you get the picture. As far as the Corn Laws went, she was also *completely wrong*: the feudal aristocracy were not swept away but adapted remarkably well, engaging in extremely profitable 'high farming' and investing in industry. As for political power being wrested from their weakened grasp, well…. There were only two non-aristocratic Prime Ministers between 1830 and 1900 (and one of those was made an Earl), no non-aristocrats at the Foreign Office and only six out of thirty-five at the Colonial Office. The *parvenus* did rather better at the Home Office and as Chancellor of the Exchequer it is true, but the idea that the top hat replaced the coronet is nonsense.

Indeed, I quickly began to realise that the appellations of 'Middle Class' and 'Feudal Aristocracy' were rather poor stereotypes and not really descriptive of anything resembling the reality of 19th Century Britain. The 16th Earl of Derby invested heavily in Liverpool docks, as a cabinet minister opposed the expansion of the empire and worked tirelessly to improve the lot of the working man – not the complete CV for a Middle Class Capitalist Bastard or an Upper Class Feudal Throwback either, I think. Joseph Chamberlain, the wealthy scion of a Birmingham industrialist dynasty was philanthropist, imperialist, municipal socialist, brilliantly successful capitalist, educational reformer and with his wing-collar, monocle and orchid in his buttonhole, the complete model of an aristocrat, but refused all offers of a title. The Prime Minister at the end of the century was the *Earl* of Salisbury, also not noted for his bourgeois origins or status, while the rising star was a bloke from the back end of Wales who was brought up without a pot to piss in and ended up an Earl by way of being Prime Minister; David Lloyd George. So the so-called 'triumph of the Middle Classes' seemed to have turned out to be a bit of a damp squib; at any rate, it was a poor tool to describe what was really a much more complex process of interaction between the interests of Town and Country, Rich and Poor as described by the brilliant but much neglected E.J. Feuchtwanger in his 1985 work *Democracy and Empire; Britain 1865-1914.* (That fine man even put my old pal Sir Bartle Frere on the cover).

What Pauline Gregg was doing, of course, was taking some square pegs, giving them a good sanding down and then hammering them into some good old Marxist round holes and this is why we have to be careful about Social and Economic History. Like I said elsewhere, Marxism is very simple because it divides people up into two opposing groups – the 'workers' who earn their living by their labour and the 'capitalists' who earn their living by investing their money. It's simple to understand and this is the reason why so many simpletons embrace it. The problem is that the moment a 'worker' opens a savings account or starts to save for a pension, he becomes in part a 'capitalist' because he is investing his money and earning interest or being paid dividends from the shares that his pension is invested in. Similarly, the moment the 'capitalist' goes in to the office to manage the company, he becomes a 'worker' because he is earning a living by his labour. The reality is that there is a continuum between 'worker' and 'capitalist' that includes extremes of both, but also consists largely of those who earn from both labour and capital and this continuum is complicated and constantly shifting. As people get older, work part-time, retire earlier and get a part-time job while drawing their pensions they change the mix of labour and capital in their incomes. They might even make a loan to their children, which muddies up the picture further, or their children might inherit greater or lesser amounts which they then save, spend or invest as they choose while still working. It's obvious to any but the most blinkered, therefore, that the simpleton Marxist analysis is so fundamentally flawed that it is very little use as a tool to describe reality and ought to be discarded. What it is useful for though is in mobilising people for violent purposes, usually involving the dispossession of 'capitalists' by 'workers', which has the observable result in every case of destroying both capital and labour and making the wealth built up by the sweat and thrift of generations disappear like a snowball in a blast furnace. These obvious and readily observable phenomena are simply brushed aside by Marxists whose scholarship is thus so often suspect. On top of that, being at the same time richly inventive and fearsomely stupid, too often they are so blinded by socialist assumptions that their research is done on the Witchfinder-General principle, i.e., if you pay a person to find witches, then witches will be found; if your university tutor or Head of Department is convinced of the overwhelming importance of class divisions, then important class divisions will be found. Truly, when reason destroyed religion, the devil needed another tool and he found it in Marx.

We have to be doubly careful when we are looking at the Social and Economic History of South Africa because it has been written almost exclusively by Marxists and almost exclusively in the language of class and race conflict, often with the laudable aim of undermining the legitimacy of the Apartheid state but more recently being used to *promote* class and race conflict. If you doubt this, then I would refer you to the 2017 row about the dominance of 'white monopoly capital', a term that is straight out of the spittle-flecked mouth of the Loony Left Handbook and which was used by President Zuma of South Africa to bolster his corrupt regime by raising up popular anger against the white minority and usher in as his prospective successor, a female paragon of African revolutionary virtue, firmly in the mould of Grace Mugabe and Winnie Mandela, his ex-wife Nosazana Dlamini-Zuma.[3] He even hired a PR company, Bell Pottinger, to run this fake news in order to divert attention from his corrupt association with the Gupta family[4] and the fact that he was wanted on no fewer than 783 charges of corruption.

Now, it is quite clear that the usual swivel-eyed Leftie Loons were not involved in this scandal (though a fair few leaped on the bandwagon), but the fact that their theories, research and writings has prepared the ground for the acceptance of such charges as apparently credible, means that they do bear some responsibility for such toxic and dangerous racism. And it *is* toxic and it does permeate into the public consciousness; set up to heal the divisions caused by Apartheid, the 1998 Truth and Reconciliation Commission, in a fit of utter cant, declared that 'Racism came to South Africa in 1652'[5] which, by overtly implying that racism and white people were synonymous was a very odd way to start a search for reconciliation; they could never have made this statement without the distortions of Marxist historians to back it up. What all this means is that we have to be very, *very* careful indeed about reading their stuff and accepting it without question because, rather than the study of History, the encouragement of class and race conflict was – *is* - at bottom, what they were aiming for because that's how they thought Apartheid would be overthrown and the socialist Nirvana ushered in. The

---

[3] 'Nice one, Cyril,' *The Economist*, 23rd December 2017.
[4] https://www.biznews.com/guptaleaks/2017/06/09/bell-pottinger-white-monopoly-capital/
[5] Final Report TRC Vol. 1. Ch1. Para 65.

thought (fact) that capitalism is colour blind and Apartheid was getting in the way of its proper operation used to make them come out in hives; actually, it still does.

One of the other really dismal things about reading Marxist Social and Economic History is actually having to put up with the language that they use; Shakespeare and Milton it ain't; rather more, it resembles an over-promoted corporal attempting to sound clever to an audience of barristers. 'Giving someone a job' becomes *mobilising a labour supply*; buying some land or getting together enough money to pay *lobola* for a bride becomes *acquiring rural assets*; 'farming' becomes a *system of agricultural and pastoral production* and most depressing of all (all these are from William Beinart's 1994 *Twentieth Century South Africa)*, 'having kids and raising a family' becomes *the reproduction of labour*. One of my favourites from the 1970s is *Bosses' Street Army* – which is 'the Police', to you and me – as well as the oxymoronic *wage slavery* (N.B. slaves don't get wages; it's one of the defining characteristics of slavery) but there is also the *Final Crisis of Capitalism* (we've had a few of these over the years) which is more accurately rendered as 'the normal operation of the business cycle' and the *Final and Inevitable Crisis of Capitalism* which is akin to what Fundamentalist Christians call 'the Rapture'; much prophesised but still appearing as unlikely as ever. One academic I came across described the massive expansion of trade, commerce, employment, material well-being – everything from Bentham to Crapper – that the British Empire brought to Africa as 'a continent-wide system of exploitation.' What a miserable bastard! Someone ought to tell 'em to cheer up, really; but then again, Marxism is full of such linguistic military atrocities; *strike, picket line, struggle, mobilise, vanguard party, long march, front, worker brigades, agitprop, dialectic materialism, proletarian resistance, democratic socialism, dictatorship of the proletariat, bourgeois capitalism*; they're used to them by now and their thought processes are duly imprisoned by them.

That said, these chaps did do some very good work in rootling about in the undergrowth and digging up some useful information. The trick to using it is to accept the raw data (with the usual provisos of course) but not the assumptions or the conclusions. So, for example, when the aforementioned William Beinart decided to 'begin with African people' he was making the conscious assumption that they - and he meant black Africans - were the most important factor in driving developments in South Africa. It's a point of view, but clearly one that I don't accept; the people driving South Africa right up until (say) the 1980s were also Africans – they just happened to be white ones, rather than black. This doesn't mean that black people were not important (DID YOU GET THAT? DO I HAVE TO REPEAT IT?), just that they were not making the big decisions that led South Africa into its particular groove. Similarly, when he referred to the white South Africans as 'settlers' he was deliberately using a term associated with the 'opening and closing of the frontier' that we looked at in relation to the clash between the Xhosa and the Trekboers in Volume I; it was a term widely used by the Left to undermine the claims of white South Africans to be equally 'African' and one that the Truth and Reconciliation Commission only just stopped short of calling a term of racist abuse.[6] More importantly, it was used to open up the possibility of dispossessing the land holdings of white commercial farmers in favour of black peasants (in theory, at any rate; everyone knows who gets the goodies when dispossession happens and it isn't your average, poor, black farm worker) and has given rise to the (2019) ANC policy of 'Expropriation without Compensation' (translation for non-Marxists: 'stealing from white people'). As we have seen, just about everyone, black, white, brown and all the gradations in between, in South Africa is the descendant of a 'settler' or a 'colonist'.

*

In addition to these strictures, the other thing that we have to bear in mind when discussing the History of Southern Africa in this period is that there was a great debate rumbling on about the worth of empire within the British establishment. As we have seen in Volume I, Gladstone and the Liberals were opposed to the idea of empire as a concept and went out of their way to prevent, repudiate and divest themselves of imperial advances. When this resulted in the disasters of the 1880s, a separate trend known as 'Liberal Imperialism' opened up whose embodiment was Joseph Chamberlain. This school of thought held to the idea that the empire might become a loose collection of self-governing states, sovereign in all but name, and held together by mutual regard, mutual interests and family ties. Becoming the dominant idea after the First World War, under the 1931

---

[6] Final Report TRC Vol. 1. Ch. 4, para.128

Statute of Westminster, the empire was duly reconstituted as the Commonwealth whereby Australia, Canada, New Zealand and South Africa became self-governing in all but name. This went for India too where the British Raj was actively transforming itself into a unified, independent India; by the 1937 Government of India Act, India became self-governing in virtually all aspects excepting foreign policy. Although the empire expanded territorially after the First World War, the Treasury demanded empire on the cheap and successive governments actively looked for ways in which commitments might be reduced; during the late 1920s and early 1930s a number of reports recommended that the interests of native Kenyans ought to be given priority over those of the European colonists; in 1936, the British occupation of Egypt was reduced to occupation of the Suez Canal Zone while in 1937, the Irish Free State was allowed to slip off into its sullen, virulently anti-English independence (a political stance not entirely shared by all the Irish people, it has to be said). Perhaps the only large exception to this trend towards divestment was the creation of the naval base at Singapore, which was meant to reassure India, Australia and New Zealand about the rise of Japan.

After the Second World War and the independence of India in 1947, Britain was anxious to get out of Africa as quickly as possible because the old logic of the route to India had gone the way of the small boy in the rope trick. It was also the case that although colonial produce and manpower had been important during the war, the Treasury logic reasserted itself in the face of the financial realities of post-war Britain. Whatever the rantings of the Left over 'imperialism and colonialism', the fact is that the British Treasury made a loss on its occupation of most of the empire – India was the one great exception – because it cost far more to conquer, develop and administer than it ever produced in revenue. Trade, went the logic, could still be had without the expense of keeping the flag flying over the Customs House.

What this means for our purposes is that from 1906 onwards, Britain was predisposed to leave South Africans alone to get on with their own affairs in the way that they thought best. 'The people of South Africa have a liberal franchise and complete liberty in using it,' said *The Spectator* summing things up nicely in 1914. 'If, then, the majority on the spot like to govern themselves on reactionary lines, we have no right to prevent them. We cannot ram our ideas of liberty down their throats against their will.'[7] Though uncomfortable with the racial policies that were being promulgated there and eager to see a better solution to the problem than segregation and Apartheid, the government in London felt constrained to influence rather than interfere directly in case a Third Anglo-Boer War was the result. This fear was real; rebellion against British rule happened once in 1914 and almost once more in 1939-41. When South Africa became a Republic in 1961, the last vestige of British political direction evaporated until Margaret Thatcher gave P.W. Botha his marching orders in 1985. What this means is that the direction that South Africa chose after 1906 was the choice of South Africans and *not* Britain or the British people. South Africans made their own History and are solely responsible for it. The same can be said for Zimbabwe after 1980.

I make this point because there is a strain of South African historiography that attempts to excuse Apartheid on the principle of 'blame it on the Brits'; indeed during the strained negotiations that brought Apartheid to an end, there was an attempt to build a new united South African identity on that very principle. It failed, mainly because it wouldn't stand up to even the briefest scrutiny but that hasn't stopped the more rabid Afrikaaner nationalists (or, for that matter, the dimmer end of the ANC) from hanging on to it. If you want an example of this, I would point to that beautifully written but poisonous apologia for Afrikaanerdom, *White Tribe Dreaming*, written by Marq de Villiers in 1987, which laid out a version of Afrikaaner History taken straight from Reitz and Smuts' nasty little shocker *A Century of Wrong,* but whipped up like spun sugar and thoroughly dipped in Pakenham's *Boer War* treacle. This was needed to cover the taste of the fatal arsenic of the argument that all would have been well had it not been for the nasty British forcing the Afrikaaners to become bastards; the Afrikaaners, it seems, are the real victims and it was the British who brought Afrikaaner nationalism into existence and twisted it into its fatal shape. Really, the sjambok wouldn't melt in his mouth. The book is also full of historical howlers, such as the claim that Andries Stockenstrom was killed by the Xhosa (bronchitis actually, in London), the Jameson Raiders surrendered without firing a shot (they were shot down and shelled) and some even wilder assertions that anglicising the Boers and 'cultural genocide' was actually British policy; Gandhi barely gets a mention, nor any of the Xhosa or Tswana, and the coverage of the great Boer expansion

---

[7] 'The South African Indemnity Bill', *The Spectator* 7th February 1914.

after 1881 is, to make a charitable judgement, inadequate in the extreme. Mind you, Allister Sparks' 1990 work, *The Mind of South Africa* which echoes de Villiers' theme,[8] isn't much better. There is much to admire in the Afrikaaner character – toughness, independence, hospitality, openness – but there is also a strain of wounded self-pity which makes it difficult for them to face up to hard truths sometimes; de Villiers' book played to those flaws in a masterpiece of seductive and selective prose. There is also something that might be interpreted as distinctly un-Afrikaaner about the book in the way that de Villiers spends rather a lot of time buffing up his liberal credentials and distancing himself from the Afrikaaner nationalism of Apartheid; someone less charitable than myself might fairly wonder if the book was an attempt to hedge his bets against the revenge of black South Africans should the feared apocalyptic future materialise. It's also notable that like many other South Africans who maintain a simmering dislike for Britain, he managed to swallow it for long enough to study at the London School of Economics. Still, the last chapter is worth a read, if only to enjoy the stamping of little feet at the unfairness of the world's revulsion towards Apartheid which, apparently, it didn't understand and how unjust the sanctions imposed were and how hypocritical the West was and...oh, the list is almost endless; and, of course, there is no mention of the fact that it was Margaret Thatcher's Britain that was doing the most to save the Afrikaaners from annihilation and find a workable way to end Apartheid without the outbreak of a race war and economic collapse by resisting the imposition of those sanctions. Perhaps a better title for the book should have been *White Tribe Whining*, or perhaps, *White Man Fuming*. Ho hum. As for Allister Sparks, well, I'd bet the farm that when he wrote *The Mind of South Africa* he had his future in a black majority South Africa firmly in mind too; when the ANC took over, he got his reward with a plum job at the SABC. Much of this book will be devoted to debunking this nonsense. The essence of political Afrikaanerdom remained the same from the beginning of the British occupation in 1806 to the end of Apartheid – a refusal to accept that black people were the equal of white people and no amount of wriggling, special pleading or whataboutery will cast that hook.

One last thing; because social and economic trends are often slow moving, it isn't practical to take a strictly chronological approach to a subject in the way that it is for Political or Military History. This means that the narrative can sometimes appear disjointed or disconnected from other events, but there really isn't any way around this. It's part and parcel of the approach that one has to jump back and forth across the chronology in order to make sense of what's going on.

Right, now we are properly primed we can stop digressing and get on with some Social and Economic History.

*

---

[8] Allister Sparks, *The Mind of South Africa* (London, 1990) p.111

The Growing Importance of the Background.

The 1905 Report

Native family life is undergoing a great change; in some parts, owing to various causes, more rapidly than in others. Contact with Europeans, with their mode of life, their industries, their Christianising influences, their business dealings; the laws and forms of government, facilities for travelling, exchange of ideas, and a number of other factors appertaining peculiarly to civilised races, are slowly but surely transforming the whole social system and life of the Natives. European influence and example have variously impressed and operated upon them, and not in all cases for their good.

Report of the South African Native Affairs Commission, 1905, para.269.

*

I will leave out of account altogether the unwise and hard things said by reckless and unthinking white men about natives; I will only ask white men to consider whether they have ever calculated the cumulative effect on the natives of what I may call the policy of pin-pricks? In some places a native, however personally clean, or however hard he may have striven to civilise himself, is not allowed to walk on the pavement of the public streets; in others he is not allowed to go into a public park or to pay for the privilege of watching a game of cricket; in others he is not allowed to ride on the top of a tramcar even in specified seats set apart for him; in others he is not allowed to ride in a railway-carriage except in a sort of dog-kennel; in others he is unfeelingly and ungraciously treated by white officials; in others he may not stir without a pass, and if, for instance, he comes, as thousands of natives do, from the farm on which he resides to work in a labour district -(an act which is highly beneficial to the State and commendable in the eyes of all white men) - he does not meet with facilities, but with elaborate impediments. In the course of his absence from home he may have to take out at least eight different passes, for several of which he has the additional pleasure of paying, though he would be much happier without them; and it is possible that, in an extreme case, he may have to conform to no fewer than 20 different pass regulations! Now, let a white man put himself in the position of a black man, and see how he would like it....

Lord Selbourne, British High Commissioner for Southern Africa 1905-10, addressing Cape of Good Hope University in 1909.

*

Chronology

1902-1906 Lord Milner's British government controls the four provinces of Cape Colony, Natal, Orange River Colony and the Transvaal, which make up South Africa.

1906 General election in Britain establishes a pro-Boer, anti-imperialist Liberal government in office.

1908 Self-governing provincial governments are established in South Africa. Afrikaaner majority governments are elected in the Cape Colony, Orange River Colony and the Transvaal.

1910 Union of South Africa is proclaimed. South Africa becomes self-governing under the British Crown.

*

Although black Africans were not calling the shots, they were still part of the picture and it is important that their place in the background is kept in mind because that background is growing in importance. We know this because the government were acutely aware of the changes that were happening in the lives of black people because a series of reports were produced that both documented the changes and put forward proposals to

13

alleviate dislocations, improve living conditions and address the questions of wealth, education and political representation. On top of this, dedicated Native Affairs Departments produced annual reports for their provinces that gave detailed information on a wide range of issues. By and large, these and other government reports, provide really good, convincing guides to contemporary thinking on social, economic and race issues and, as the period from the end of the Boer War to the beginning of Apartheid is quite badly covered by sources untainted by Afrikaaner Nationalism or Marxism, I put a lot of store by them. The usual attempts have been made to dismiss their findings as being created by (insert your favourite epithet here) white people for a white dominated government, but this ignores the reality that many of the people who produced these reports were of determinedly liberal disposition and the reports themselves were often issued with strong dissenting opinions included when agreement could not be reached. It also defies logic that governments of whatever hue were so intent on oppressing black people that they would go to such lengths as to set up whole departments and expend vast sums of money on the production of reports which were, by and large, overwhelmingly concerned with improving the lot of black people. That said, the fact that quite a few Afrikaaner governments *were* intent on oppressing black people means that many of the recommendations contained in these reports were never acted upon.

Reading through these reports, therefore, is beneficial in all sorts of ways but there are two main trends that run through them. The first is the one that Marxists spend their time enthusing over and this is the growth of a black urban working class that is distinct from the rural tribal societies from which they emerge. The second is one that they tend to ignore and that is the explosion in population brought about by the *Pax Britannica*, which is just as important.

Between the destruction of the power of the chiefs in the 1880s and the Union of South Africa in 1910 the land reserved for black farmers in the Eastern Cape and along the coastal strip up and beyond Zululand added up to about 20% of the total land area. This was better than it sounds because some individual chiefdoms retained much more than others, and because the land there was well watered, generally productive and miles better than the arid regions to the north and west but also because there were only three million people who needed to use it. The total population of South Africa was around 5 million in 1904 divided into roughly 67% black, 21% white, 9% coloured and 3% Asian. Today there are roughly 45 million South Africans. In Natal, the average landholding worked out at 9.5 acres per person.[9] On top of this, many black Africans occupied land through acquired customary rights or had retained traditional usage even though the land was officially owned by someone else; others were 'squatters' renting land for money or labour. Many others – perhaps as many as a million - lived on white owned farmlands but were effectively left to get on with life as normal by absentee landlords. There were also plenty of labourers who were given parcels of land to farm in lieu of wages, sharecroppers and tenant farmers too; probably around 85% of black Africans, including those migrant labourers who spent some time in the mines, lived on the land in communities that would have been recognisable to their forefathers.

This does not mean that the world had passed them by; traders opened stores bringing useful things like textiles, iron cooking pots and a wider variety of household furniture and utensils; European clothing, eminently more practical than a skin kaross and a loin cloth, rapidly grew in popularity. Christianity brought not just religion but also education, medicine and a broader outlook on life; smelling out might still occur from time to time but if the magistrate got word of it there would be trouble. Many black people took advantage of the new professions that commerce and industry brought to Africa, especially in the matter of transport riding where their expertise in managing animals was put to good and profitable use, but also in supplying food to the cities. Whole new industries such as forestry were introduced, especially in northern Natal and Swaziland where huge forestry blocks are still to be found. Many peasants took advantage of new technology – iron ploughs, prickly pear for fruit and animal feed, bluegums and wattles for firewood – to improve the productivity of the land, while still more raised mortgages, bought their own land individually or in syndicates and sub-let it to their own tenants. The great disaster of these years (apart from the Anglo-Boer War) was rinderpest and other animal epidemics which repeatedly wiped out whole herds.

---

[9] Report of the South African Native Affairs Commission 1905 para.93

Democracy had also come to the African village and there were several constituencies in the Eastern Cape where the black vote was an important factor; in the Cape as a whole, coloureds made up around 15% of the electorate. And again, we ought to remind ourselves that this was how British Victorian and Edwardian democracy was supposed to work; the vote was only to be trusted to men of property and education, rather than handed out willy-nilly to any old scrounger, lounger, loafer or joker who happened to be in possession of a pulse. There was also *Imvo Zabantsundu*, the first Xhosa language newspaper, run by John Tengo Jabavu (and financed by white businessmen) which was a vocal and respected journal known throughout the Cape.

The emergence of labourers who chose to stay in Joburg and take their chances as independent people rather than return to the village was an important development. Much of the labour employed in Joburg was actually sourced from Mozambique and came up the Delagoa Bay railway but probably 10% of black migrant labour (almost all of it male) were permanent urban residents by 1900. When they went home for a visit, pockets jangling with filthy lucre and tongues wagging with tall tales of the city, they provided a potent example of an alternative way of life and were rather less inclined to accept the ever-weakening authority of the chiefs. All these things meant that black Africans were beginning to adopt a lifestyle that was, on the surface, ever more 'Western' or 'civilised' and which thus entitled them to the same rights, responsibilities and opportunities as white people.

And there's the rub. One of the major themes of the years between 1902 and 1960 is the way in which Afrikaaner nationalism reasserted itself and effectively discarded the British philosophy which Lord Milner and other imperialists had hoped would take root in South Africa. The essence of that philosophy was that people ought to be free to go about their daily business as they saw fit, taking responsibility for their failures and credit for their successes; that all should acknowledge the rule of Law and be equal in its sight; that all should be represented one way or another in parliament and that the role of government should be limited to maintaining the peace, defending the realm and running essential infrastructure where private capital couldn't; that capitalism was the way to generate wealth; that society would evolve from the bottom, from the millions of decisions and choices taken daily according to the wishes, interests and desires of those individuals; most importantly, that there should be no grand visions imposed on the general public from the top and that dissent should always be tolerated. The logical end to this was that at some stage, black, coloured and Indian people would have to be treated as fully equal to white ones. At the time it was expressed in the maxim of 'equal rights for all civilised men'. This did not mean that practices of segregation would cease overnight, but it did mean that the direction of travel was set and that only the pace and mode of achieving this was in question.[10]

Afrikaaner nationalism accepted very little of this, preferring to hold to a racial hierarchy and strict segregation rooted in a Calvinist religion which pre-dated even Social Darwinism; which rejected capitalism in favour of a brand of feudalism; which held that the unity of the *Volk* was more important than the right to dissent; which was as much a totalitarian view of the world as that of Socialism, Nazism, Fascism and Communism. Underlying much of this was a deep bitterness born of the sour taste of defeat in war; the impoverishment of Afrikaaners who could not or would not compete in an industrial economy; a realisation that many black people were adapting fast to the new situation and prospering; fear of the uncertainties of life beyond the laager and a desperate need for a new sense of self-respect; 'If you aren't better than a kaffir', so the saying went. 'What are you better than?' To all this was welded a stubbornness and a refusal to think deeply about the reasons for their defeat in the Anglo-Boer War 1899-1902, beyond the comforting, maudlin excuse of 'overwhelming force'. What this meant in practice was, at worst, a refusal to accept the fact that black people were 'progressing in civilisation' to the point where they were nigh on indistinguishable from white and, at best, a deep ambivalence to what this meant for the survival of the *Volk*. Whereas both the British and English-speaking South Africans were equipped with a History that taught that culture, both political and otherwise, was dynamic and independent of race the Afrikaaners were equipped only with one that emphasised the values of the laager, fixed and unchanging, in a dangerous world. This difference may be illustrated simply by comparing Kipling's 1906 *Puck of Pook's Hill* with Reitz and Smuts' *Century of Wrong*. The first shows how Britain emerged from Roman, Saxon, Danish and Norman roots (among others), the second is one long appeal to victimhood.

---

[10] Ivan Evans, *Bureaucracy and Race: Native Administration in South Africa* (Berkeley, 1997).

Once the Anglo-Boer War 1899-1902 was over and the Transvaal and Orange Free State annexed to the British Crown the task that the High Commissioner, Lord Milner, set out to achieve was, in essence, quite simple (though the details were a bugger); conciliate the Afrikaaners, reconstruct the war damage and then federate the different colonies into one British Confederation of South Africa. The question of what to do with black Africans was rather more of a problem. Despite conquest and dispossession they had not gone away; they existed as a political fact that could not be ignored because the Afrikaaners could admit no equality with them while the Cape British saw them as potential future partners, once they were educated and developed. To square this circle, in 1903, Milner opened an investigation to look into the whole subject and what emerged two years later was the *Report of the South African Native Affairs Commission* – the first really comprehensive attempt to look at African conditions on a 'national' level. It really was a remarkable document because it took a fresh and dispassionate view of how life was changing for black Africans in both town and countryside.

Running through this document were the assumptions of Social Darwinism which had become steadily more prevalent during the last two decades of the 19th Century. As we have seen in Volume I, this was the idea that as species of animals compete for existence and so evolve into higher forms from lower ones, so too do the races of Humanity. This was never really codified into any sort of formal, recognisable, convincing scientific theory and whenever anyone looked deeper than the surface, all sorts of oddities made an appearance; there were supposed to be 'Martial races' in India (Sikhs, Gurkhas, Pathans etc) who had taken the evolutionary path of the soldier – did that mean the Zulus were also a 'Martial race'?; Italians, Chinese and Indian 'Coolies' were all regarded as existing on some equal level;[11] *The Spectator* rather slyly noted that there were an awful lot of Boers who would not pass a very strict definition of what constituted 'white' if an admixture of blood was the determining factor.[12] Nationality and race were often confused into meaning the same thing and it wasn't unusual for people to refer to the 'British race' while simultaneously referring to the Celtic bits of it as being distinct. Sometimes there was a bit of primitive genetics thrown in; 'blue blood', 'young blood', 'good breeding' were all in some way related to stock management; Lord Mountbatten traced his royal family tree on cattle-breeding principles; *pedigree* was applicable to more than just dogs. Sometimes – actually, almost always - the 'scientific' claims regarding race were so bizarre as to be comical. Check out *Professor* Lyde's 1931 application of Darwinian natural selection; the 'gaping nostrils of a Negro' had evolved because;

> 'In the rarefied air of the tropics - with its relatively small percentage of oxygen, and that, too, of an inelastic quality - every possible facility was, and is, needed for giving the air easy access to the lungs, e.g., wide and everted nostrils in a short and concave nose above a huge and protruding mouth. Even amongst White women the only type that can at all count on good health - or even on being habitually good-tempered!- in the tropics, is the snub-nosed brunette.'[13]

'Caste' too was sometimes used as a marker which by betraying its Indian origins confused the picture further; no-one in the British Raj ever refused an invitation from the Maharajah whatever his skin colour, but this did not stop complicated rules of precedence, both official and social, producing a level of snobbery that everyone who wasn't English found appalling. And on top of this, in 1903, Britain concluded an alliance with Japan – later on, after the establishment of Apartheid in 1948, the Japanese were classed as 'white' while Chinese were classed as 'Asiatics', a designation which in turn led to problems when South Africa developed relations with friendly Taiwan. The Eugenics movement so favoured by Left wing social reformers was heavily indebted to Social Darwinism for its ideas of breeding out the deficiencies in the working class. 'Natural' aptitudes and defects were considered to be the property of particular nationalities too; Jews were crafty and conniving, Scotsmen were canny and thrifty, Pathans were wily, Germans were ape-like brutes etc etc. The practical problems of actually applying the concept of race in law added another layer of complexity: 'Even if the exact tincture that constituted colour were fixed, the disqualification thus created would have to be applied in practice,' declared *The Spectator*. 'But this would mean that the Revision Courts would be choked with pedigree cases as complicated as peerage claims.'[14] The net result of all this though was the assumption that the 'white' races had

---

[11] *Amery* Vol.VI p.104
[12] 'The Coloured Vote in the Transvaal'. *The Spectator* 14th July 1906.
[13] "Concomitants of Colour,' Prof. L.W. Lyde. *The Spectator* 22nd August 1931.

floated to the top of the gene soup and black Africans were lagging behind a bit but could be brought up to speed through education, sanitation, Christianity and general Europeanisation; through 'civilisation' – and from this point on, I shall drop the inverted comas. Perhaps the best example of this way of thinking can be seen in Lord Selbourne's address to the University of the Cape of Good Hope in 1909, quotes from which I have liberally laced this book with.[15] Until that happened, however, a degree of segregation was both necessary and desirable because neither side could really tolerate or understand the habits and practices of the other.

The other theme was one of Tory paternalism. This was a development of the old idea of *noblesse oblige*, that being wealthy, educated and further up the social status tree than those less fortunate than you meant that you incurred moral responsibilities to those people. It was your duty to see to the welfare of the peasantry, the toiling masses, the poor and uneducated and so sit on all sorts of committees and charities, serve as Justices of Peace, Yeomanry officers and enter public life with a view to serving your country rather than yourself. The conservative philosophy held that this duty was sacred. The philosophical bedrock of conservatism was the idea that the nation was a compact between the dead, the living and the unborn and it was a person's duty to build upon what was already there rather than tear it down in bloody revolution; if something wasn't working anymore, the idea was to reform and improve it or if necessary, replace it with something that was of practical use, relying on custom, compromise and experience rather than untried, high fallutin' theory; and then hand it on intact and working to the next generation rather than leaving them a pile of smoking ruins. To use an analogy; imagine a fruit orchard in need of management; the conservative approach would be to let well alone beyond the necessary spraying and normal pruning and then pick such fruit as it produced in the belief that there was a reason the orchard had grown up like this and though nature, custom and tradition might turn up apparent anomalies and strange deviations, those reasons, however mysterious or undiscovered, were still *reasons* and thus to be respected. A Liberal would be inclined to experiment with more vigorous pruning, the lopping off of a branch here or there and the laying of pathways to make things a bit more logical and regular and perhaps improve the crop that way; a socialist radical would look at the orchard, decide that it was no bloody good, chop the whole lot down and start again – and starve in the ignorance that fruit trees need years and years before they produce a crop. Conservatism is a theory based on humility; conservatives don't believe they know all the answers, just some of them; neither do they believe in imposing untried and unwanted doctrinal gibberish or grand social and economic theories while wiping away established custom and practice by fiat. The 19th Century conservatives knew what worked – capitalism, property rights, parliamentary democracy and the law – and adapted it to local circumstances and accepted the compromises that this entailed.

Land, Segregation and Civilisation.

The Report started by looking at land rights and surveyed the different conditions under which black Africans held title to land. In the Transvaal, lands were held in Trust for Africans by the government which too often meant, in practice, that an African paid for the land but the Native Commissioner decided when to sell it and pocketed the profits.[16] Nor was it unheard of for the deeds to a piece of land to be made out in the name of a particular Boer, rather than the chief to whom the land actually did belong.[17] In the Free State (or Orange River Colony), Africans were forbidden to own or lease land outside one or two specified areas; in Natal and the Cape, there was no restriction based on race and it was felt by the government that, of the alternatives on offer, this was the way forward. In particular, the Commission noted the increasing desire for individuals to own their own land rather than accept their place in tribal communal ownership schemes and wanted to encourage it for the obvious reasons that individual ownership meant greater efficiency. It was also felt that the creation of a sturdy, independent yeomanry was a good thing and represented a good, long stride towards civilisation; a series of proclamations during the 1890s had already spread the idea of individual ownership into the Transkei, so it was not an entirely new suggestion.[18] At the same time, being true to the conservative belief that 'if it ain't broken, don't fix it', the Commission also considered that if people were happy owning land communally then

---

[14] 'The Coloured Vote in the Transvaal'. *The Spectator* 14th July 1906.
[15] Address delivered by Lord Selbourne Before the Congregation of the University of the Cape of Good Hope, on Saturday, 27th Feb., 1909. https://archive.org/details/addressdelivered00selb/page/4

[16] Rev J.H. Bovril, *Natives under the Transvaal Flag* (London 1900) p.14.
[17] Sol Plaatje, *Native Life in South Africa*.
[18] CO 633/32 Native Affairs Department Report 1912.

they should be allowed to carry on as they so pleased; it was no business of government to tell people how they should organise their lives as long as they remained within the law and reasonable bounds. What the government would not do, however, was to increase the amount of land reserved or held in Trust for African usage.

Where the Commission ran into difficulties was on the issue of admixture of the races. They noted that the European farmers generally disliked having to live too close to black farmers and though they were quite happy to employ them or do business with them, they were insistent on living separately from them. Different customs had already resulted in a great deal of segregation in the towns throughout South Africa, with certain areas being designated, formally or informally, as areas where one or another race predominated and although this had not hardened up into forms so rigid they could not be avoided, they *were* hardening. The process had begun decades ago, usually with ordinances making Africans forego their near nakedness and wear trousers in town, had taken great strides when Joburg was formally segregated, and was now starting to be recognised in law. Attitudes were harder in the ex-Boer Republics than in Natal and the Cape but in many cases, the restrictions were aimed at *reducing* racial tensions by removing points of friction. In the towns the frictions were often due to alcoholism; in rural areas these tended to be related to stock theft but there was also the ever-present fear of an African uprising. The practice of reserving land for African usage was also long established, it having been introduced after too many cases of Africans unsure of what property rights entailed had been swindled out of their landholdings by unscrupulous carpetbaggers; ditto the stricture that Europeans should not be allowed to buy land in reserved areas. Unfortunately, this well meant practice set a precedent; the Commission recommended that as Europeans should keep out of African areas, black Africans should, in general, not be allowed to buy land in predominantly European areas.

This was a contentious issue that split the Commission and resulted in dissenting opinions being included in the Report. There was a strong body of opinion that held that both coloured and Africans were 'progressing in civilisation' and that they should be encouraged; segregation was a barrier to progress and would tend to undermine the trust that was the basis of loyalty to British rule; it would also be costly and virtually impossible to administer. In addition to these objections, the Natal representatives complained that this was against the vital 'right of free trade possessed by every other subject of the British Empire'.[19] As far as they were concerned, as long as an African had given up polygamy and possessed the necessary degree of civilisation, he should be allowed to buy and sell land howsoever he pleased. Unfortunately, this thoroughly sensible British conservative outlook clashed with the naked refusal of the Bitter-enders of the Orange Free State and the Transvaal backveldt Boers to countenance any thought of progress and advancement for black people and forcing through such a measure would be no easy task for a government aiming at the conciliation of Boer opinion. There can be no doubt that this was an opportunity missed though.

Law, Ladies and the Condition of the People.

On the issue of tribal customary law, the Commission was inclined to leave things alone. Generally speaking, when the Cape government had gathered up the various decayed polities of the Eastern Cape during the 1890s, they had left tribal leaders to their own devices as long as they accepted the authority of the magistrates set above them. So as far as customary law was concerned, as long as it was accepted by those who lived under it and as long as it was overseen by magistrates and the government as Paramount Chief, there seemed no reason to do anything but tinker around the edges and let time and the advance of civilisation erode it until it was replaced by ordinary Colonial law; it was an established principle in Natal that a person might apply for exemption from it and come under Colonial law and a trickle of people - 28 in 1912 – took it up.[20] The tinkering was limited to practical matters; recommendations that chiefs exercising judicial authority should be paid directly rather than keeping the fines they levied on malefactors; that Wills should be made more widespread to ensure the orderly transfer of inherited property; that debts should not be collected from anyone other than the person who contracted them – under Native Law there was a collective responsibility on all the family; and the number of magistrates should be increased; and although Natives were not considered ready for

---

[19] Report of the South African Native Affairs Commission 1905 para.199
[20] CO 633/32 Native Affairs Department Report 1912

18

jury service yet, it was recommended that those of intelligence or education start to attend court in order to learn about the legal system.

What was quite revolutionary was the insistence on female emancipation. It isn't necessary to accept the gibberish written by 'Grievance Studies' feminists about an oppressive patriarchy to accept that the position of African women in village life was restricted by the 'separate spheres' view of gender to vital supportive roles but which tended to exclude them from direct influence on decision making – although certainly they wielded indirect influence. The fact that this was changing as new jobs, challenges and technologies were drawing women into different roles was noticed by the Commission and acted upon. This was in keeping with the conservative idea of responding to changes in society by admitting that change was indeed happening and so managing it that grievances could be settled and accommodations made to reasonable demands; it was Disraeli's Conservative government that had passed the 1870 Married Woman's Property Act which gave British women a legal status independent from their husbands for the first time since the 17th Century and the concomitant agitation by female Suffragists in Britain no doubt encouraged the Commissioners to accept a more dynamic view of a woman's situation. In the Cape Colony and the Free State, black women gained their majority at twenty-one and were thus free to leave the village, take up jobs – often as teachers – or move with their husbands to his place of work, all of which was thought desirable, to be insisted upon and to be extended.

> ...by recognition of a Native woman's right to attain majority, she is placed in a position to emancipate herself from a condition which may have become distasteful to her and be free to choose her own path in life. As Christianity and education spread, a woman's endeavours towards a higher and more self-respecting position than that appointed to her by ordinary kraal life should not be thwarted by perpetual tutelage unsuited to present-day conditions.[21]

Such changes were taking place rapidly even in those areas of the Transkei that had little contact with either government or Europeans. In 1912, it was noted that there was 'a distinct movement among Native women towards greater freedom...they come freely to the Magistrates on business or with complaints whereas a few years previously they would not have come unless accompanied by the men...until recently, they were practically looked upon as "property"... they are asserting themselves in many minor ways.'[22] Nevertheless, even though it was becoming rarer, that odd marker of female subordination, polygamy, remained a widespread practice in rural areas, as indeed it does today.

The British believed in the power of the Law to protect and extend liberty, check abuses and alleviate grievances probably above anything else and the Report carried a strong recommendation that inter-colonial conferences should be held to extend the more egalitarian view of Cape law across the whole of South Africa. The British tradition was that the law was there to protect the people and it should be fair, seen to be fair and applied in an even-handed manner. Ever since Robin Hood and the Sheriff of Nottingham had slugged it out in Ye Olde Merrie England, police forces had been expected to abide by this creed but upon enquiry the Commission found plenty of evidence that practices common up in Joburg – it did not explicitly mention the Transvaal but the evidence points to it – were oppressive and degrading to African workers.

> It was disclosed to the Commission that in various parts of the country inspections of municipal and other locations in urban areas were sometimes carried out in a harsh and injudicious manner, respectable Natives and their families being turned out of their dwellings at night time, and subjected to objectionable personal handling. Conduct of this sort is extremely harmful, and rankles long in the minds of the people.[23]

This was unacceptable according to British legal principles and notions of fair play, never mind counter-productive to the creation of happy workers advancing in material comfort and civilisation and it had to stop.

Like other Victorian and Edwardian social reformers, the Commission was genuinely interested in the 'Condition of the People' and was scathing about the accommodation provided for workers. They were

---

[21] *The 1905 Report.* Para.239
[22] CO 633/32 Native Affairs Department Report 1912.
[23] *The 1905 Report* para.247

perfectly happy with segregated 'locations' in or near the cities but those locations ought to be of a good standard. This could have been written by Joe Chamberlain himself, who as mayor of Birmingham in the late 19th Century had done much to alleviate the conditions under which working people lived.

> The Natives who reside in or frequent these locations are in the main working people. As such there is every reason why they should be encouraged to stay as useful members of the community. The tendency of inadequate accommodation is to make them dissatisfied and restless; the standard of comfort is low and they are liable to be over-crowded and over-charged.[24]

The answer to the problem was all Joe Chamberlain too; cheap ownership where possible, Local Authority housing where it wasn't; sanitation, street lighting and cheap public transport provided and all of it attractive enough to encourage wives and families to accompany the individual worker to the city. All this would be under superintendents who would protect 'the respectable, industrious Natives'[25] from the idle, drunks, vagrants, crooks and prostitutes who had also gravitated in one way or another towards the Urban Dream.

The Demon Drink.

The scourge of booze was also gone into in much the same terms as the demon drink was discussed in 19th Century Britain. That beer was seen as a wholesome addition to the diet was agreed – and in the absence of clean water, an awful lot safer. 'Kaffir' beer was brewed from millet and was rarely more than 2% alcohol; in the mines it was issued as an anti-scorbutic because greens were not a big part of the African diet. The problem arose when Square-Face Gin, *mampoer* and other spirits were issued; many Africans had no genetic resistance to these stronger brews and drunkenness and alcoholism in the mine compounds resulted. Absentee rates could be as high as 10% and all attempts to curb the supply of illegal rotgut only stimulated the illicit trade that was already such a feature of pre-war Joburg. Many employers issued booze in lieu of wages – the *dop* system - and many claimed that it was so customary that labour could not be had without it. Those who saw the deleterious effects on Africans were convinced that there should be a total prohibition on liquor sales to them but this came up against the same libertarian arguments (and vested interests) that are bandied around about the drugs trade today. Respectable men who had the vote should surely be allowed to drink whisky? What right had the government to interfere in a working man's Friday night pint? Whose business was it but the individual's if he wanted to get bladdered on a Saturday afternoon? The Commission, full of the confidence that enabled Edwardian gentlemen to make a decision rather than tip-toe around it, came down heavily in favour of prohibition of spirits but in favour of beer, home brewed, 'in moderate quantities and under due control'[26] and never for sale; in effect, properly enforced Licencing Laws. It was much the same in the countryside where, in 1912, the Magistrate of one Transkei district overwhelmed by smuggling remarked drily that 'the 1889 gallons of brandy imported into this district are not consumed by the handful of Europeans'.[27]

Passes, Education and Politics

The Pass Laws were also looked at and declared to be essential, but it was agreed that the workings of the system should be made less onerous. During the Boer war, the Chairman of the Commission, Godfrey Langdon, had been given the job of getting African labourers back to the mines and to encourage this had simplified the pass system, rooted out a lot of corruption and sharp practice among labour recruiters, appointed inspectors to ensure that workers understood the terms of their contracts and dealt with their grievances.[28] He also abolished flogging for breaches of the Pass Laws, exempted the more educated Africans from carrying them at all and was particularly concerned to see that fair treatment, decent boarding houses and sanitary arrangements replaced 'needless and vexatious' treatment; the Pretoria station officials were famous for robbing departing workers.[29] Segregated carriages on trains were the norm but, said the Commission, there ought to be black conductors to assist the black travelling public and, in tones reminiscent of the travelling public's experience of British Rail during the 1970s, added;

---

[24] *The 1905 Report* para.248
[25] *The 1905 Report* para.252.
[26] *The 1905 Report* para. 349+
[27] CO 633/32 Native Affairs Department Report 1912.
[28] *Amery* Vol VI, p.27.
[29] Rev J.H. Bovril, *Natives under the Transvaal Flag* (London 1900) p.25.

That railway officials should be instructed to remember that the travelling Natives are paying passengers and are entitled to reasonable attention.[30]

Entitled to reasonable attention; rather than the depressing vocabulary of Marxists, this was the real language of Empire; *sympathetic recognition*; *legitimate aspirations*; *assistance in any well-regulated plans*. Among all the verbiage about capitalist exploitation, oppression of the workers, racist imperialism etc, the Marxists forgot that the Empire rested on the acquiescence of those who were ruled over. Without this essential acquiescence it could never have survived; it could never have raised from India the largest volunteer army in History during the Second World War (despite two decades of Gandhi) nor reinforced it with regiments from East, West and South Africa. A large part of creating that essential acquiescence lay in the Empire's ability and desire to give everyone a fair shake as far as it was possible to do so; *reasonable attention, legitimate aspirations*, *sympathetic recognition*, *civilised ways* (by which they meant, of course, *modern* or *developed*). It's all here in the Report.[31]

In discussing the question of education, the Commission took a great deal of evidence claiming that all that an African needed was a simple, technical education that gave him just enough know-how to do an unskilled or semi-skilled job and that anything else just made him uppity and discontented. They rejected this completely and set out a strong case that;

> Apart from the consideration that there is a moral obligation upon the State to provide for the intellectual development of all classes of its subjects, there appear to be very sound reasons of policy for the adoption of a liberal and sympathetic attitude towards the subject of Native education. The Native, in common with the rest of mankind, does not live by bread alone, and possesses certain mental impulses and aspirations which demand satisfaction.... No policy can be complete or sound which is limited to political or economical considerations only, and which takes no account of the irrepressible forces within each individual. And it is evident that there is among the people themselves a growing desire for education, which cannot and need not be suppressed.[32]

It comes as an agreeable surprise to note that black students were already attending higher education facilities in Britain and America but this number was probably too small to be significant; only around 3% of Africans were in school at this time when the normal figure should be roughly 25% of the population. What the Commission wanted was for every colony to start spending a lot more money on education and getting a lot more Africans into school. This was to be done by supporting the Mission schools, expanding technical education but also by setting up teacher training colleges, higher level technical institutes and a Native College to act as a university (the result was Fort Hare, Mandela's *alma mater*).

What about political opposition? The Commission was generally in favour of it, which is proof positive of the strong streak of benevolence in the Imperial philosophy, but they were not to be fooled into according any loudmouth a political credibility that they didn't deserve. This was the case of the Ethiopian Churches movement – not actually Ethiopian but just plain old South African with an impressive latin-ish name - which some writers have taken as evidence of early political opposition. A movement to separate from the Anglican and Methodist organisations run by Europeans and so constitute independent African churches, the Commission came quickly to the conclusion that it was all something of a scam and moved to protect the duly constituted Churches. This was done not by 'any measure capable of being misrepresented as religious persecution' by refusing to allow these men of 'restless ambition' unlikely to provide 'ennobling examples of personal self-sacrifice and piety' to issue marriage licences. They dismissed the idea that there was anything political about this movement out of hand and confessed themselves ready to consider an 'Ethiopian' church just as soon as the men running them proved themselves to be more than an early version of Steve Martin in *Leap of Faith* or the good Pastors of Nigeria who, when I lived there, advertised revival meetings with the alluring promise of *Nights of Bliss*.[33] One such chap, the leader of the 'Saints of Christ and Church of God' was run out of town on a rail in 1912 when he tried to push an early version of Free Love on his unwilling congregation.[34]

---

[30] *The 1905 Report* para. 266
[31] *The 1905 Report* para.276.
[32] *The 1905 Report* para.329
[33] *The 1905 Report* para. 320
[34] CO 633/32 Native Affairs Department Report 1912.

The Native press *did* constitute a political opposition but this was seen as entirely positive. It was taken as proof that educational advancement was going well, that the thoroughly British habits of free speech and liberty of thought were developing and that, on the whole, it was a fairly accurate chronicler of life in South Africa. It wasn't perfect in that it was felt to be immature, rather excitable and guilty sometimes of 'the unripe judgement of would-be political writers'[35]; but you would say the same thing about *The Guardian*. A question was raised as to the possibility of censorship, but this was slapped down: 'freedom of thought and speech within lawful limits is not lightly to be assailed'[36] - a sentiment which is, at the time of writing (2019), probably not something that you would find in *The Guardian*. This approach was replicated in the case of Political Association; as long as they were public and constitutional, they were to be encouraged, 'public expression being better than discontented silence'.[37]

The Workers.

The Labour Question was also addressed by the Report. For Apartheid-era Marxist historians, Africans were only interesting in so far as they provided the 'labour' in the struggle against 'capital' or in providing a living example of a proletariat emerging from 'feudal modes of production' into the 'wage slavery' of capitalism and so proving Marx's pseudo-scientific prophesy. This led whole hordes of them to focus on the labour question to the exclusion of almost everything else. Here is our old friend from Volume I Shula Marks's judgement on the subject.

> ...the demand for indigenous labour – in the greatest possible numbers at the lowest possible cost – was to become the predominant concern of every colonial interest – imperial officials, Cape liberals, Natal segregationists as much as Afrikaner farmers and 'cosmopolitan' capitalists and Chartered Company directors.[38]

Every colonial interest? What? All of them? Even those tearing their hair out about imperial defence and the routes to India? No: this is a gross exaggeration. If rounding up 'indigenous labour' – what you and I call 'offering people job opportunities' – was the 'predominant concern' you would expect it to feature as Item No.1 in the Report, no? It is actually down at No.12 of 14 headings, just after Liquor and before Taxation. And it was such a 'predominant concern' that, the Commission reported, no-one had bothered to collect any reliable statistics about it and so was reduced to guesstimating the demand and supply of workers. It wasn't until 1914 that the government decided to start collecting statistics and not until 1919 that anything meaningful was produced in the annual *Year Book*.[39] What the government *did* collect was statistics regarding death rates among workers employed on the mines and public works due to disease, so that something could be done to make the work healthier and safer, which tells you something different to what the Marxists would have you believe.[40]

What the Commission was prepared to say about the Labour Question was that demand far outstripped supply largely because African workers tended not to be continuously employed. The general pattern was a sort of transhumance where a man might migrate to the mines or farms for part of the year, collect up as much money as he thought he needed and then go back to the village. This was a practical way of life because most Africans lived on communal land in reserves where rents and taxes were low, their needs were small and their crops and cattle sufficient to meet them - the Commission reckoned that Africans were sitting on £114 million worth of rent-free land. Those who didn't live on communal land enjoyed similarly favourable situations renting from private landlords or the Crown; it was all rather eco-friendly and sustainable. Dismissing any notion of 'South African Natives being hopelessly indolent'[41], 'living at his own village a lazy and luxurious life, supported by his wife or wives'[42], they stated quite simply that industrialisation and the mineral revolution had raised the

---

[35] The 1905 Report para.323.
[36] The 1905 Report para. 322
[37] The 1905 Report para. 324
[38] A. Atmore and S. Marks, 'The Imperial factor in South Africa in the Nineteenth Century: Towards a reassessment', in *European Imperialism and the Partition of Africa*, (London, 1975).
[39] Nicoli Nattrass and Jeremy Seekings, *The Economy and Poverty in Twentieth Century South Africa*, Centre for Social Science Research UCT July 2010.
[40] CO 633/32 Native Affairs Department Report 1912.
[41] The 1905 Report para.373

demand for labour far beyond what could be supplied. The combination of these factors and the fact that so much damage had been done to the mines and the mining companies by three years of war and lost production meant that the usual solution – higher wages to tempt more people into taking the available jobs – was either not an option for the cash-strapped industry or not working.

The Commission sensibly decided not to get involved in wage fixing; that was a job for the market and any attempt to regulate the private contract between the worker and the employer would simply lead to distortions elsewhere. Farmers complained already that higher wages at the ports and mines made recruiting difficult, even though farm work was nearer to the skills that African workers possessed and involved none of the inconveniences of the mine compound. They also came out firmly against compulsory labour or taxes payable in labour. What the Commission did recommend was the introduction of 'push' factors in the shape of more economic rents, better industrial training and the enforcement of vagrancy laws, combined with 'pull' factors of better conditions for workers at the mines and when travelling to and from them. The employment of women as domestic servants was also recommended, especially if it could displace male workers who would then be more inclined to work at the mines. These mild measures could only tinker with the situation though; the labour shortage in Joburg and the Rand was in the process of being solved by the importation of Chinese workers who, though expensive to bring in, were industrious and worked on a permanent basis.

The 1905 Report was a remarkable document and provided a basis for much of what came after the Chinese workers left and the problem reasserted itself. The Director of Native Labour began to encourage recruitment by properly licencing the labour recruiters, doing what he could to curb sharp practice (such as poaching workers to whom advances had already been paid) and generally improve the conditions of the miners with the Native Labour Regulation Act of 1911, which was intended to apply across the Union. The new Native Recruiting Corporation Ltd aimed to centralise and regulate the labour supply by allowing recruitment only in those areas with a surplus of labour so as not to disrupt farming and other businesses while further attempts were made to improve the facilities in the compounds. Still, the death rates remained horrendous. In 1911, they were as high as 30 per thousand in the deep gold mines and 40 per thousand in the diamond mines, mainly from pneumonia, phthisis (silicosis) and TB but also from the smallpox, leprosy and other diseases which the miners brought from their home districts, especially if they came from Mozambique or other regions where tropical diseases were prevalent – the death rate among these workers was roughly double that of those recruited in the Union; 60 per thousand broke contract and deserted. Many applicants were immediately rejected as being physically unfit to work underground; out of 109,000 men recruited in 1911, 3,000 were rejected immediately, 59 were sent to the leper hospital, 2,300 were given permission to seek surface work and 3,400 were sent home injured or unfit.[43] Of those left, roughly 5000 died of disease and 100 from accidents; of thirty-three Transvaal deep mines, only two got through 1912 without a fatal accident; of sixty-two of the considerably safer outcrop mines, the number was nineteen; by comparison, for surface work in steel, brick, chemicals and the like, sixteen out of nineteen business in the Transvaal got through the year without a fatality and of the fourteen who did die, eleven were due to an explosion in a dynamite factory.

Such a wastage rate led in turn to the Director coming down hard on the mine owners when contractual grievances and complaints of ill-treatment were made. In 1912, where withholding of wages was concerned 66% of cases were decided in favour of the workers, and roughly a third in cases of claims of ill-treatment or contractual violation. A further regulation forbade the deduction of monies from a worker's wages to pay off store debts without the written permission of the Director himself. Inspectors also carried out more than 5,000 visits to compounds to enforce minimum standards (220cu ft. per person) and hospital facilities, levied £2700 in fines for more than 5000[44] violations and worked to reduce intimidation by making it the responsibility of compound managers to report incidences where black workers had been assaulted by white ones.[45] Remitting wages home was also made easier by the abolition of fees charged for the service, so that the Native Affairs Department managed upwards of £70,000 in 1912 alone; the practice was adopted by the Native Recruiting Corporation. No one can ever pretend that conditions in the mines were anything but horrendous, but this was

---

[42] The 1905 Report para.373
[43] CO 633/32 Native Affairs Department Report 1912. Appendices.
[44] CO 633/32 Native Affairs Department Report 1912. Appendices.
[45] CO 633/32 Native Affairs Department Report 1912. Report of the Director of Native Labour.

due to the nature of the work and was common to mines the world over from Cornwall to Chile. If you doubt this, try a quick squizz through Upton Sinclair's description of industrial work in contemporary America in his 1906 work *The Jungle* or George Orwell's description of Lancashire miners during the 1930s in *The Road to Wigan Pier*. What is remarkable is the extent to which the government got involved to try to protect workers within the constraints of what was accepted as best practice for the times; in 1911, £8,272 was paid out in compensation to the families of those killed in accidents, £6740 paid out for injuries sustained and, under the terms of the Miners Phthisis Act of 1912, £776 was paid out to 66 sufferers of phthisis.

Taxation and Representation.

Yet another of the great canards peddled by the Left is that Africans were conquered for the taxes that could then be levied on them and handed over to evil, grasping imperialists. The truth is, as always, very different largely because believers in big government and lavish spending on the public sector i.e., Left wing academics, find it very difficult to understand that before the arrival of Attlee's disastrous spendthrifts in 1945, low taxation was the virtuous norm. What is often regarded as heartless, Victorian penny-pinching was actually sensible restraint and an insistence on value for money. Taxation would be levied where it was required for some demonstrable and desirable purpose but idiocies such as punitive wealth redistribution aimed at 'equality', welfare dependency on easy terms and the nationalisation of industry were simply not countenanced. Taxation was also suspended in times of hardship, as during the 1912 drought.[46] It was also the case that work was seen as being morally uplifting as well as economically necessary; both of these ideas cause an involuntary shudder to run up the spine of your average Leftist and their latest wheeze (2018), the concept of the Universal Basic Income, is designed to break the link between work and income and so free them from the curse of work altogether; really, they rail against the Curse of God on Adam, against the concept of economic 'scarcity' (a subject on which they claim special expertise), against the whole human condition and just as futilely as Adam did. So taxation was, for the Victorians and Edwardians, a necessary evil rather than a social scientists' Jacuzzi. That it was nowhere near central to the thinking of Rapacious Imperialists and Complete Capitalist Bastards in South Africa is pretty much proved by the fact that no-one seems to have collected any statistics on what was being paid and who was paying it.

> This is a matter in which an accurate knowledge of the actual existing facts would be of the greatest service in considering what changes, if any, should be made in the amount of taxation to be borne by the Natives and in the manner of levying or collecting it. Definite information in clear and reliable figures covering the whole ground is difficult, if not impossible, to get at present, and in this connection the Commission takes the opportunity of suggesting to the Governments concerned that more attention might be given to the continuous collection of complete data and the creation of full and reliable records on many questions of fact touching the Native population : their numbers, their movements going to and returning from work, their marriages, their birth and death rate, their consumption of dutiable goods, and their other contributions to the revenue, the amount fairly chargeable to them for police and administration purposes, the amount spent on them for education, and so forth.[47]

What was needed, of course, was a new Domesday Book.

The average wage for a black miner on the Rand between 1903-5 was roughly 40 shillings or £2 per month. The amounts collected in sales taxes, the Commission guesstimated on a per head basis, were less than a shilling a year for Natal, two shillings in the Bechuanaland Protectorate, and a bit more in the Orange River Colony (two shillings and fourpence) – there were no figures for the Transkei but two shillings per annum was reckoned about right. In terms of poll or hut taxes, the average per head was under four shillings a year (in the Cape it was 10s and in Natal 14s per hut). So, taking five shillings a year as a rule of thumb average, a man with one wife and four children might expect to pay thirty shillings per annum in taxes, a rate of 6.25%. I'd settle for that; the Commission didn't and demanded that the hut tax should go up to a minimum of £1pa. I'd still settle for it, especially as the Commissioners from Natal recommended the abolition of compulsory labour as a *quid*

---

[46] CO 633/32 Native Affairs Department Report 1912.
[47] The 1905 Report para. 387

pro quo; if you resided in a town or lived and worked on a farm on a permanent basis, you would be exempt the hut tax. They also came out against making those still living on lands conquered and annexed - officially, Crown lands – pay rent. So much for imperialist exploitation.

The final heading of the Report was 'Representation' and this issue laid out all the contradictions of an empire that was liberal, democratic, paternalistic and authoritarian all at the same time. Britain had just fought the Boers to establish supremacy in South Africa and guarantee the security of the routes to India, but it was quite conceivable that a democratically elected parliament of the Union of South Africa might be stuffed full of Afrikaaners willing to vote for independence; certainly during the war, the Schreiner ministry at the Cape had come so close to actual treason that martial law had had to be proclaimed. That wasn't the end to the possibilities either; representation of the interests of all people was seen as both desirable, expedient and essentially right but a black majority might vote to expel the whites; this might seem unlikely in 1905 but what about 1915 or 1925? The colour-blind constitution of the Cape Colony had extended the vote to all who were literate and could meet a reasonable property qualification and although non-European voters made up only around 20% of the electorate their influence was growing. As wages were increasing, education was doing its job and good, settled British administration was increasing the general wealth of the colony, the prospect of non-Europeans holding the balance of power in elections was one that could not be ignored. For many, this was something to be celebrated as a triumph of the British civilising mission but the Commission feared that substantial elements within the colony were simply not ready to admit a preponderating non-European influence in the politics of the colony. They feared that the majority of Europeans, never mind the Boers, would indeed rebel at the prospect and all the nightmares of a race war would result. Squaring this circle would be difficult to say the least. As *The Spectator* was to say in 1909; 'Much as we regret a disqualification which excludes even the most highly educated natives [from the franchise], we cannot blink the obvious fact that if it were removed … the Union would vanish into thin air. There can be no doubt about that.'[48]

At this point we should also deal with one of the common charges laid against Britain in the historiography, namely, that British imperialists sold out the blacks by denying them the franchise during the period between the end of the Anglo-Boer War and the Act of Union in 1910. We can dispense with this charge on several grounds. Firstly, the British government was not run by imperialists 1906-1910 but by pro-Boer anti-imperialists of the Gladstone stamp; as we have seen in Volume I, the British people who really foul things up in South Africa are never the imperialists but the *anti-* imperialists and this is a fact that continued to plague British policy in southern Africa throughout the 20th Century. The real damage done to contemporary Africa by Britain was because of too rapid decolonisation, by Harold Wilson's bungling in Rhodesia and by Tony Blair's disastrous rejection of the Lancaster House Agreement on Rhodesia which ushered in Mugabe's land grab. Secondly, the promises made at the Vereeniging peace talks that the issue of the franchise would be postponed until after peace were then hardened up into a promise that the question would wait until self-government had been granted; that the government of anti-imperialist pro-Boers led by Henry Campbell-Bannerman after 1906 chose not to pursue the issue was entirely their responsibility, despite the fact that their man on the spot, Lord Selbourne, was entirely in favour of extending the franchise to civilised natives.[49] Besides which, any attempt to extend the Cape franchise to the ex-Boer Republics would, as the ever sympathetic Transvaal Commissioner for Native Affairs, Godfrey Lagdon, stated, be 'bitterly resented'[50] and likely to ignite the war again. So, although there is some substance to the charge against Britain, you would need to be a real idealist to think that there was any chance that a British government however sympathetic would be successful in achieving this. All that could be done was to prevent the coming Union from incorporating the three protectorates of Basutoland, Bechuanaland and Swaziland into it – which Selbourne recognised was no small thing and worked hard to achieve.[51]

---

[48] 'The Wonderful Issue', *The Spectator* 21st August 1909.
[49] Selbourne to Secretary of State, 14th November 1908. CO 879/106 Secret Correspondence Relating to Affairs in South Africa.
[50] Also CO 879/106 (Secret) Report of the Committee appointed to enquire and report upon certain matters connected with the future constitutions of the Transvaal and Orange River Colony, July 1906.
[51] CO 879/106 Secret Correspondence Relating to Affairs in South Africa. CO Comments on Lord Selbourne's telegram of 3rd July 1908. Also Selbourne to Sir Henry de Villiers 17th November 1908.

At the cost of labouring the point, 'democracy' in 1905 did not mean Universal Suffrage. British democracy was supposed to represent *interests* and parliament was the place to balance them to the general benefit of the community. Although parliament had its fair share of eccentrics, most parliamentarians were acutely aware of the plain fact that handing the vote to large numbers of people without education or something to lose – the working classes mainly - was like handing a chimp a maxim gun and the question of who should actually get the vote was often tied up with practical questions of how to represent the views of, for example, trade unions or female suffragists. If anyone was in doubt about the disadvantages of universal suffrage, they need only look across the English Channel and see the dog's breakfast of the French Third Republic at work – on average, one government per year 1870-1909. Indeed, universal suffrage did not come to Britain until 1928.

In addressing this vexed question, the Commission began from the standpoint that everyone ought to be represented in some way or other in parliament and made the point strongly that this had to happen in fact, rather than just in theory. In Natal, the franchise was open to non-European voters in theory but in practice only two Africans had ever bothered to register and out of 18,600 voters only 250 were non-European. In the Transvaal and the Free State, the mere suggestion of handing the vote to non-whites would have started eyeballs from sockets; *Brits* couldn't get the vote in the Transvaal Republic. This had to change. No-one was to lose their right to representation and those who had no rights would gain them, but this had to be done in a way that did not threaten the dominant position of the European voter.

> ...in those parts where the Natives have not in the past had any vote or any form of elected representation in the Legislatures, it is likely to be advantageous to the State and conducive to their contentment to give them the same privileges as elsewhere in South Africa ; provided that this can be done without conferring on them political power in any aggressive sense, or weakening in any way the unchallenged supremacy and authority of the ruling race, which is responsible for the country and bears the burden of its government.[52]

The solution offered was to segregate the vote. Europeans and non-Europeans would have the same property and educational qualifications but vote separately for separate candidates and the number of non-European candidates who sat in the legislature would be fixed in some proportion that would allow them influence but never a majority or even the balance of power. This was, of course, a classic fudge but it is difficult to dispute the logic of it if we make our judgement from the standpoint of the times. The facts were that a substantial number of Boers, perhaps a majority of them, would never accept substantial black political influence and would fight beyond the bitter end to prevent it and in this they would be aided by substantial numbers of Cape Dutch and Natal English; if a race war did erupt then the black people would probably lose it and end up in a worse position than the one they presently occupied; and when the race war was over, British rule would be replaced by a hostile white South African polity and the route to India would be compromised and thus another British invasion would be required and God alone knew what the consequences of that would be for world peace, given the state of the opposing alliances in Europe at that time.

Nor should we be so quick to jump on this as a step on the road to Apartheid; that's a slippery slope argument which presumes that the future is fixed and it never is. As we have seen, segregation was a growing part of South African life but it was not an insurmountable one and there were plenty of people crossing those boundaries; legislation was necessary to stop white prostitutes taking the hard earned pay of black men and we can imagine that they were very pleased to use the added risk to raise their prices as a result (in the 1970s the white Cape Town hookers were all bottle blondes because that's what the trawlermen from the Japanese fleet landing their catch there preferred). Racial prejudice is not fixed in the DNA of white people and there was plenty of mixing in the post-Boer war world of urban renewal, expansion and immigration from Britain. Out in the remoter rural areas, it was not unusual for a European trader or digger to have a black wife whether legally married or not.[53] Racism was something that would need to be taught. And it would be, in due course.

The Native Affairs Department at Work.

---

[52] The 1905 Report para. 442.
[53] CO 633/32 Native Affairs Department Report 1912.

In the meantime, the Native Affairs Department got on with its work and the 1912 Report gives a good flavour of its activities. In the field of Public Health, it was particularly aggressive in reporting on outbreaks of common diseases like measles, leprosy, TB, malaria and smallpox, conducting campaigns against syphilis and advancing sanitation and vaccination programmes – in some cases, enforcing vaccinations by the employment of the Cape Mounted Police[54] but generally insisting that anyone who came to town would have to be vaccinated. Among the many health challenges faced, pneumonia contracted in the mining industry was a particular scourge, alongside Miner's phthisis and other diseases caused by working in dusty environments, which the NAD did much to quantify and notify. In 1912, it was partly due to the NAD that compensation was paid to families of workers who died from phthisis, while those who were incapacitated by it were entitled to compensation on a sliding scale.[55] They also encouraged bodies such as the South African Anti-Malarial Association in their work of educating Africans on reducing the risk from breeding grounds, dispensing free quinine and other medicines and erecting placards in the vernacular languages. The campaign against spitting in order to reduce the incidence of TB was also encouraged. Very often the lack of adequate medical facilities in the rural areas was deplored but this went for virtually everyone in South Africa and although the dependence on traditional healers and *sangomas* was much reduced, in the absence of anything else they were still widely consulted – as indeed they are today. In one case, a *muti* killing was recorded for the purpose of rain-making – again, something that is not unknown in modern South Africa.[56]

One of the causes of the increase in the black rural population was undoubtedly the public health and sanitation work of the NAD. Another one was the famine relief programmes, especially important in 1912 when a terrible drought hit, which the NAD monitored and in many cases used as an opportunity to aggressively promote beneficial agricultural reforms such as increased irrigation, livestock dipping against common animal diseases such as East Coast and Redwater fever, encouraging the use of modern tools and the introduction of better seed varieties. The planting of fruit trees, previously neglected in many parts, was also instituted in order to lessen the dependence of the population on a limited range of crops.[57] It really is startling to realise just how primitive African farming methods were at the beginning of the 20th Century. Despite the advances made by copying the example of the European farmers, there were still large areas where hoes were used rather than ploughs; there was almost no mechanisation, cattle breeds were inferior, manure was used as fuel rather than fertiliser, while fish and fowl were neglected as foodstuffs – many tribes regarded fish as unwholesome; in many cases crops were limited to maize, millet and squashes; little or no use was made of storage dams or irrigation. All these problems had been overcome in most other cultures centuries ago and the failure to address them meant that famine was an ever present danger to a growing population. It was already being noticed in the Cape Province that the land available for small holdings was insufficient to meet the demand for them and that as a result encroachment on pasturage was beginning to happen, the number of boundary and inheritance disputes was increasing, largely due to unfamiliarity with the concept of Title Deeds. In the Transkei, it was the lack of sanitation for a growing population that worried Chief Magistrate Stanford the most, and he feared that some terrible epidemic of Typhoid could not be far off as a result.[58]

Education in the Transkei also came under the remit of the NAD and it was again aggressive in pushing for a greater measure of education for Africans, even though the debates as to what should actually be taught and for what purpose tended to bog progress down. Should black African children be taught the History of England from 1066 – 1485? It seems absurd that this might even be considered – I taught the geography of North Sea oil to Arab children in the Gulf during the 1990s - but the underlying issues were whether black children should receive the same education as white ones and whether poorer black people should be taxed to provide a more expensive, higher level of education for the children of better off black people. In both cases, the opinion of the Chief Magistrate in this year was that the standard of education provided was so poor anyway that taxes to pay for a higher standard would simply be wasting money that could be spent on practical agricultural improvements.

---

[54] CO 633/32 Native Affairs Department Report 1912.
[55] CO 633/32 Native Affairs Department Report 1912. Report of the Director of Native Labour.
[56] CO 633/32 Native Affairs Department Report 1912.
[57] CO 633/32 Native Affairs Department Report 1912.
[58] CO 633/32 Native Affairs Department Report 1912.

To sum up; during the period 1902-14, the black African population was undergoing something of a transformation as it accommodated itself to the new order and though this had brought with it much that was onerous, there were very many tangible benefits. Generally speaking, it seems fair to say that much of the government was paternal, benevolent and genuinely interested in the welfare of black Africans as long as it was a *British* government, but this is not to ignore the reality that there were also some sinister undercurrents at work in these years, especially after 1910 when the government became dominated by Afrikaaners (of which more later). And the most sinister of these was without a doubt the 1913 Native Land Act.

*

> *...if a native has the capacity and force of character to become a farmer or a mechanic or a professional man, the law should put no obstacle in his way. Every avenue of honest livelihood should be open to him as to the white man under the law....*

> *...I do not think it would be just... to put legal impediments to individual ownership of land in the rest of South Africa in the way of civilised natives struggling to escape from tribal influences.*

> Lord Selbourne, British High Commissioner for Southern Africa 1905-10, addressing Cape of Good Hope University in 1909.

*

Sol Plaatje and the 1913 Native Land Act.

The workings of the 1913 Native Land Act have been much debated and, indeed, became a *cause celebre* with the ANC. Quite rightly so; it was an outrageous act of sheer spite aimed at preventing black people from enjoying the material benefits and empowerment provided by capitalism. The issue gained prominence mainly because the founder of the ANC, Sol Plaatje, wrote his fine (if exhausting) polemic *Native Life in South Africa* as an attack on the Land Act and thus it became not just required reading for activists but an Article of Faith for the ANC. As we have seen, roughly 20% of *good* land was in African ownership in 1913 and few Africans were short of enough for their needs but after the Act, this figure was in almost continuous decline because the main provision of that notorious Act was that no black man could buy or rent land from a white man in a 'white' area; the area reserved for black farmers only covered 7% of the land (doubled to 14% in 1936). Among its other aims were the eviction of black squatters and sharecroppers from farms in the hope that they would be replaced by poor whites; where this failed then black farmers would become tenants paying in labour rather than sharecropping. Also, to advance a general policy of segregation, especially in the Free State where legislation was already draconian but mostly, and most appallingly, it aimed at stopping African farmers buying up or renting more land in order to prevent them competing with European ones.

In order not to tar all Afrikaaners with the same brush, we should note here that, according to Plaatje, the legislation was driven by Afrikaaners in the Free State and Transvaal but widely resisted by many Afrikaaner and English farmers who were quite happy with the existing arrangements and held firm to the distinction made between civilised natives and the raw barbarian expressed in the formula of 'equal rights for all civilised men regardless of colour'. The Act was therefore not applied in the Cape Colony. There were also plenty of objections to the legislation on the simpler grounds that it was simply unfair and unworkable, an imposition and a straightforward betrayal of natural justice. There was much well-voiced concern that this was a measure guaranteed to alienate Africans from the existing order and encourage rebellion. What it was *not* was an act of capitalist exploitation. For the Afrikaaners, capitalism was something alien and best confined to Joburg; right from the beginning *Het Volk* formed an alliance with the Labour party against 'money power';[59] when Solomon Maritz went into rebellion in 1914 he did so to regain Boer independence from 'the Jews and financiers of England'.[60] Indeed, the Land Act was an *anti-capitalist* measure aimed at preserving a semi-feudal relationship between white land owners and black serfs; *serfs* was exactly the term that was used at the time to criticise the Act because now black farmers were tied to the land without having a measure of ownership of it.

---

[59] CO 879/106 (Secret) Report of the Committee appointed to enquire and report upon certain matters connected with the future constitutions of the Transvaal and Orange River Colony, July 1906.
[60] Tim Couzens, *The Great Silence*, (South Africa, 2014) p.40

Rushed through parliament, the law came into operation before any assessment or preparation for its impact had been made and resulted in an immediate crisis in the contractual relations of sharecroppers and squatters. To begin with, the law now prevented any black person residing on a farm who was not a labourer. This led to a large number of African squatters and sharecroppers deciding not to renew their contracts with the landowner and taking to the roads in search of a better deal. Unfortunately, the law ensured that no better deal could be had and the cattle wealth that had been accumulated quickly evaporated for without a place on a farm, there could be no grazing. The rapacious and unscrupulous among the landowning community took full advantage of the imbalance in the contractual relations and in many cases demanded that both the labour of the farmer and his family, *and his cattle*, should be the price of employment; in essence, the African farmer was *buying* his job with his cattle and then accepting a wage that was well below what he might expect to earn under the previous conditions. For the many honest landowners, longstanding mutually beneficial relationships with African sharecroppers were disrupted for no good reason at all and in many cases their reaction to the law was one of incredulity, but there was little that could be done. The old contracts were now illegal – and the landowner (however much he might object to the new law) was liable for a substantial fine if the contract was honoured - and independent sharecroppers must, therefore, be evicted along with their livestock if they chose not to be employees. In truth, this looked like an attempt to force them back into the bondage of the 'apprentice' system and the resultant grief, financial loss and dislocation was all the more searing for being so utterly unexpected. The Land Act was robbing African farmers not just of their wealth and livelihood, but also their future advancement.

Plaatje raised a rather ineffectual campaign – the first of very many ineffectual campaigns by the ANC - against the Act and getting nowhere decided to go off to London to plead with the Imperial government to intercede but despite widespread support from the public and the press nothing was achieved. This was for several reasons; the first was that the overwhelming importance of the Cape lay in its position on the route to India, a fact that had not changed since Van Riebeeck's time and would not change until Indian independence in 1947. In order to protect this route the principle threat to it had to be neutralised and as that threat was the Afrikaaner government, their views outweighed those of Plaatje and the ANC. The second reason was that the Liberal government of the day contained many, many 'pro-Boers' who had made their careers in supporting the Boers during the South African War, and had then been elected on a racist ticket of 'Chinese Slavery' and a commitment to a South African self-governing Union under Afrikaaner leadership. The terms of that Union effectively excluded Africans from political representation outside the Cape and thus allowed Afrikaaner notions to drive the Land Act. Sending out a man called Gladstone as the first Governor of the Union of South Africa simply because he carried the disreputable name of his father was thus a reassuring reminder to the Afrikaaners that there were still plenty of Liberal dimwits in Britain who were all too willing to appease them whenever they required; sending out Lord Gladstone was as clear a signal that the Imperial government had no intention whatsoever of standing in the way of whatever the new self-governing colony thought right and proper in its own backyard. The third reason was that the First World War and the 1914 Boer rebellion broke out while Plaatje was in London and thus the problems of black Africans dropped well down the list of priorities; he was reduced to translating the marching song 'It's a long way to Tipperary' into Zulu in the hope of gaining attention. When he did finally get an interview with Lloyd George in 1919, Smuts intervened to ensure that his account was regarded as full of 'startling inaccuracies' and '*suggestio falsi*'[61] but even then, it was out of the Imperial government's remit to do much about the situation anyway.

There were still plenty of white people opposed to the Act, especially in Natal, and as the prime mover behind the legislation, P. Grobbler, was in jail following his participation in the 1914 rebellion, a Land Commission was conceded to look into the workings of the Act. This duly reported in 1916 and Plaatje again appealed to the Imperial government to step in and prevent the legislation going forward; but this was the year of the Somme and though his representations were once again kindly received by the press and the public, there was absolutely no chance that resources were going to be devoted to the issue during the ongoing crisis. The Act remained; the economic development of African agricultural entrepreneurs was stopped dead in its tracks.

---

[61] CO 537/1198 Comments on the Minutes of the South African Native Deputation to Lloyd George 21st November 1919.

This then is the situation of the African background in the period 1902-1914. Firstly, it is expanding in numbers as the benefits of the *Pax Britannica* reveal themselves in better nutrition, medicine and reduced conflict. Secondly, it is changing as an increasing number of black Africans begin to choose the city over the rural life and start to learn how to live, work and compete in a capitalist economy. Thirdly, it is facing the fact that while many of the British have a benevolent attitude towards them, they rate the concerns of the Afrikaaners above theirs; and most of the Afrikaaners have no intention of letting them compete on anything like equal terms in any field, endeavour or forum. In short, the Afrikaaner South African government had abandoned the cardinal English virtues of personal liberty, representation for all in a parliamentary government and the freedom to make your own wealth in a capitalist system.

*

Smuts and Bosman

Why can it not go forward in a straight line like other lands? Brilliant men come here to solve its problems and go away defeated.

Jan Smuts, speaking of South Africa.[62]

One of the curious things about History is that the subject isn't really very old. It isn't too far off the mark to say that before the 19th Century it was almost a branch of the Law or an extension of Philosophy. Herodotus is usually accorded the title 'Father of History' for his 440BC *Histories* and Thucydides' 431BC *Peloponnesian War* are classics. There is also the Venerable Bede and the *Anglo-Saxon Chronicles* but these, and other such works, tended to be attempts to record events and did not always distinguish between verifiable fact and literary fiction. During the reign of Charles I of England (1625-49), much of the dispute between him and Parliament over their relative powers orbited around 'ancient rights' which led all sorts of lawyers, clerks and scholars to start digging through the mountains of scrolls and old parchment stored away here and there in search of historical precedents that would support their respective cases. What was generally absent was not a desire to know about the past or to ponder on ancient wisdom, but the idea that History could somehow illuminate the path that mankind was taking into the future and so, spotting the gap in the intellectual market, beginning at the time of the 1789 French Revolution or thereabouts, a number of writers accordingly came up with a variety of theories of History.

Roughly speaking, the 'Liberal' school of thought, led by T.B. Macaulay, held that History was the study of how mankind would perfect itself through the gradual improvement of its laws and systems of government; it was often two steps forward and one step back but the general trend was upwards. Karl Marx, in one of his rarer moments of lucidity, said that Historical change occurred as a result of conflict between social classes, which was reasonable enough, but then he went and spoiled it all by saying that the process was 'scientific' and that he had cracked the mystery of the 'Laws of History' and that the future would definitely and inevitably end in Communism; ho hum. Conservative historians said that there were no 'Laws of History' at all and that it was crucial to realise that each historical situation was unique; History did *not* repeat itself. After 1945, hardly surprisingly a school of Historical Pessimists emerged who stated, not without good reason, that progress was an illusion and that mankind was really no more than a barbarous caveman with better weapons and would probably remain so. If this was a depressing outlook the French *Annales* school made things even worse by arguing that geography was more important in determining the future than anything people did; Fernand Braudel managed to write up around half of his 750+ page book *The Mediterranean and the Mediterranean World in the Age of Philip II* before he got round to dealing with the chap in the title. One of the most enduring ideas was Thomas Carlyle's idea that 'Great Men' like Napoleon drove History by enacting laws, winning battles and making generally big decisions. The Marxists challenged this, of course, by saying it was all about economics and then went on to write endless hagiographies of 'Great Men' like Lenin, Stalin and Mao which was all rather

---

[62] Sarah Gertrude Millin, *The South Africans* (London, 1927) p.115.

pointless when Leo Tolstoy and Victor Hugo had already turned the idea on its head. In *War and Peace*, Tolstoy said that the War of 1812 and Napoleon's downfall came about because of small decisions made by small people over a small piece of land called the Duchy of Oldenburg and that all Great Men were cursed by the 'illusion of power' and at the mercy of the millions of little decisions that they barely knew about; it's a sort of historical Chaos Theory. Victor Hugo said in *Les Miserables* (the book, that is, not that ludicrously un-historical musical; Lloyd-Webber shifted the action back from 1832 to 1789 for crying out loud) that Napoleon's defeat at Waterloo was due to a peasant neglecting to tell him that there was a sunken road behind the British lines; he launched his cavalry in a massive charge, they fell into the ditch, and the British shot them down in droves and the rest was ABBA. It's a point of view that commands sympathy; Buller's defeat at Colenso in 1899 was due in no small part to the fact that the chap hired to guide Hart's Brigade to a drift over the Tugela was bluffing, got lost and then decamped at speed when the Boer riflemen opened up. The same thing happened to Gatacre at Stormberg too.

That *said;* it just isn't possible to discount the 'Great Man' theory because it can hardly be denied that *sometimes* individuals do have a decisive influence over events; this is why there is so much interest in figures like Napoleon. Carlyle wasn't just interested in politicians though and included writers like Dante and Shakespeare, religious leaders like Luther (and, curiously, the god Odin) and philosophers such as the appalling cad and hypocrite Rousseau among his subjects. In some way, he thought, the spirit of the age could be encapsulated in such men for it was they who drove forward History and ensured that societies evolved and progressed. And if we apply this idea to South African History then we simply have to look at Jan Christian Smuts.

To balance this out with a bit of Tolstoy and Hugo, we also need to look at someone who is hardly known at all outside South Africa; the thoroughly obnoxious but incredibly talented short story writer, Herman Charles Bosman, who we might equate with Hugo's fateful peasant. Both of them lived through the period when, from the ashes of defeat in the Anglo-Boer War, two competing visions for the future of South Africa vied for control. The first, represented by Smuts, saw the English and Afrikaaner peoples joined together in a new South African identity, linked to the British Empire and drawing on its paternalist traditions to manage the civilisation of the black man. The second, represented by the old Bitter-enders of Herzog, Christian de Wet and the rising star of Afrikaaner Nationalism, Daniel Malan, wanted a Union entirely dominated by a reunited Afrikaaner *Volk*, with the English kept in a subordinate position and the blacks, Asians and coloureds kept well down below them. If the emergence of a black urban class and a population explosion in the countryside was the background to the events of these years then this struggle was the foreground.

Smuts first; for, as his biographer, Sarah Gertrude Millin, concluded, 'he is an inexplicable man to South Africans: their History does not give precedents for men like him'.[63] His upbringing was remarkable. Born in 1870 the son of a Swartland MP, he grew up on what then passed for a prosperous farm in the Cape. In fact, his home was a Spartan farmhouse that would compare very unfavourably with a similar farm in England; Constable's Flatford Mill it ain't and the barn is a fraction of the size of the ones you'll find in Essex; you can visit it today – it's just outside Riebeek-Kasteel, in the middle of a cement factory, oddly. Of modest means, the family didn't think it was necessary to educate him until his elder brother died and created a vacancy for the potential *predikant* they so wanted. At twelve he was packed off to a village school in Riebeek West where some precocious gene seems to have been monstrously triggered; he became a prodigy. 'Of what use will a mind, enlarged and refined in all possible ways, be to me, if my religion be a deserted pilot and morality a wreck?' he wrote, aged 16, in his application to Victoria College in Stellenbosch. Having no interest whatsoever in sport, girls, booze, novels but only in Law, Poetry, Philosophy and Psychology, he won every prize – including one for classical Greek, a language he taught himself in a couple of weeks – in between teaching Bible classes to coloured boys, parading with the Volunteers and learning German. The pictures of him as a student are truly daunting; he has the eyes of the zealot, the brow of the torturer and all the grim, gothic gauntness of the Bates Motel. Winning a scholarship to Cambridge, he went off to study Law rather than Philosophy - South Africa then as now having no shortage of philosophers – won all the prizes, cultivated his passion for solitude and wrote a book psychoanalysing the author Walt Whitman in his spare time; it is quite

[63] Sarah Gertrude Millin, *General Smuts, Vol.1* (London, 1936) p.261

possible that he was up in the top three students that Cambridge University has ever educated. He also began work on his philosophy of Holism, a rather vague idea that somehow all things in the world are connected and the more they could be connected, the better the world would be; this accounts for his interest after the First World War in the League of Nations and, a little later, the idea of transforming the British Empire into the British Commonwealth and then later still, in his work to establish the United Nations. He courted his wife by teaching her Greek; she must have loved him dearly. (Mind you, General Montgomery, a true romantic, courted his wife by teaching her how to lay out a trench system). What was remarkable about him – and what was *noticed* about him – was that his intellect took him beyond knowledge and into the realm of the truly brilliant. As Carlyle himself put it: 'Intellect is not, as some men think, a tool. It is a hand which can handle any tool.' It was this that made him able to fulfil the many different roles that he was called on in life to play. It was this that made him unlike his predecessors in the various Afrikaaner governments; and quite distinct from contemporaries like Herzog, Malan and the architects of Apartheid, who overthrew his legacy.

Beginning work in Cape Town in 1895 as a lawyer, he made little progress in that noble profession so turned increasingly to journalism as a way to supplement his meagre income and from there he stepped into politics almost, one senses, like a man who steps on a dog turd and decides then and there that something has to be done to clean the place up. Quickly marked down by both Rhodes and Hofmeyr as a man of talent, he was in turn a great admirer of them. He had joined the *Bond* and imbibed Hofmeyr and Rhodes' idea that the future was a united white South Africa and publicly defended Rhodes against many of the charges brought against him by scoundrels like Kruger and Olive Schreiner - right up until the Jameson Raid. Smuts, like many other Afrikaaners, felt betrayed by the unsavoury episode of the Raid, but reacted in an extreme manner, almost like a spurned lover, (especially after Shrieky Schreiner lambasted him publicly). Throwing up his British nationality for the limbo of Transvaal second class citizenship, he moved North; he could not abide Johannesburg with all its rough and tumble, industrial grimness and money-grubbing materialism and couldn't wait to move to the more authentically Boer Pretoria. There he quickly won the favour of Kruger through his newly acquired rabid Anglophobia and, more importantly, through the utterly despicable expedient of providing him with legal cover for his undermining of the independence of the Judiciary (see Volume I); every other lawyer on the continent thought Kruger was wrong but 'Slim Jannie' found a bit of sophistry that did very nicely, thank you very much, and Kruger carried the day. His reward was the job of State Attorney, a post which he was not legally qualified to hold but which this fine legal expert despicably accepted anyway. He seems to have needed someone to look up to, someone to follow and his attachment to Kruger was so strong that he allowed himself to excuse the old troll's obvious failings through the oldest and weakest excuse going; Kruger wasn't corrupt, but he was surrounded by corrupt advisors, who kept the truth from him. And when Kruger wanted to harass the Uitlanders, he found Smuts all too willing to help. Still only 29, Smuts 'lean, cadaverous, pugnacious'[64] was among Kruger's advisers at the Bloemfontein conference (Milner treated him like the organ-grinder's monkey) and it seems that there, when brought face to face with Sir Alfred Milner, a light went on inside his head; Kruger *was* prepared to go to war with Britain but had absolutely no idea what he was dealing with. What took him a little longer to realise was that Kruger and the Orange Free State president Reitz had already decided to gamble on an invasion of the Cape and Natal, a prospect that Smuts embraced with a cynical glee; it was he who, along with Reitz of the Orange Free State, wrote the despicable pamphlet *A Century of Wrong* at this time and it was this that made his apparent last minute attempts to stave off war by talking to Conyngham Greene in August 1899 so despicably duplicitous. And it was this quality of despicableness, this curious lack of shame, that led him after the war to tell his biographer that he wished Joe Chamberlain's bedroom to be stacked with the bodies of the dead Tommies of Spion Kop, so that he might know something of the horrors of 'the conflict which he has promoted'[65] as though he, Smuts himself, bore no responsibility for starting it. Despicable too were his outright lies about coloured participation against the Boers during that war that he deployed to discredit the native deputation to Lloyd George in 1919.[66]

Indeed, there was also something disturbing about Smuts' thought processes as a young, moderately successful Commando leader – if we accept 'not being caught' as the primary measure of success. He took things to

---

[64] *Grey Steel* p.56
[65] Sarah Gertrude Millin, *General Smuts, Vol.I* (London, 1936) p.122
[66] Smuts to Lloyd George, 12th May 1920. CO 537/1198

logical extremes, was not above summary execution of informers and bandits, and capable of mass murder, as at Modderfontein in January 1901, where he was responsible for the killing of 200 black people. Similarly, his laying siege to Okiep, a backwater of no importance at a time when the war was beyond lost, is an indication of his capacity for fanatical pointlessness in which the act is the sole justification for itself, rather in the manner of a man taking a peashooter to a tank to demonstrate his commitment to resistance. There was also in his character, the continued stubborn sophistry that had served him so ill in the past - objecting to Kitchener's entirely legal scorched earth tactic while excusing his own, frequent abuses of the laws of war by wearing captured British uniforms, a tactic that had saved his skin on several occasions, was nothing more than the pot calling the kettle black.

War changes some people but for Smuts that change came only slowly and with reflection; initially, he slipped straight back into his old role as lawyer-politician from the moment the 1902 Vereeniging peace conference began and as the war ended, his gothic darkness enveloped him once again. He had shown bravery, seen death, gained weight by the exercise and endurance of near constant flight and then slipped into frustrated depression and a rather spiteful sulk when, having turned down the offer of serving on the Legislative Council to help with reconstruction, he had rejected Milner's magnanimity in favour of carping and harping, moaning, griping and complaining from the sidelines – he truly hated Milner for beating him - and protesting about the Chinese labour now being brought in to work the mines. He retained too the aura of the aesthete, a liking for loneliness and books, an incomprehension of fun and a huge capacity for work; and also the mysticism about the oneness of the world in his philosophy of *Holism*. It was some grim comfort against the battery of malicious allegations from the whipped curs gathering around de Wet and Herzog who blamed the defeat and surrender on him and claimed that without Smuts and Botha, they would have continued the fight. That said, he did have enough of a sense of humour to get one of Kruger's grandsons cleared of a murder charge by having him plead hereditary insanity.[67]

From 1905 he began to get back into politics through his involvement with *Het Volk*, the beginnings of an Afrikaaner political party, and when the Liberals came into office in Britain at the end of that year, he was sent off to London to negotiate with a government that contained more 'pro-Boers' than even the most unreasonable Bitter-ender could hope for. And it was here that Smuts had the second of his Damascene conversions. He had hoped to persuade the new Prime Minister, Henry Campbell-Bannerman, to speed up the timetable for self-government in the conquered colonies but what Campbell-Bannerman offered produced a stunning effect on him. 'Smuts,' said the Prime Minister of the greatest empire the world has ever seen to the lowly emissary of a defeated people. 'You have convinced me.'[68] There would be elected self-government under the British flag as soon as the details could be arranged. This was very convenient of course because the Liberals had lied like Bolsheviks over the issue of bringing in Chinese labour to work in the mines of the Rand (which they attacked as 'Chinese Slavery'; a 'terminological inexactitude', as Churchill put it. See Vol.1) during the election and were now faced with the dilemma of actually admitting to the electorate that they had indeed lied like Bolsheviks; by handing over self-government, they could pat themselves on the back as forward-looking anti-imperialists *and* hand the whole issue over to Smuts with a flourish and a bowl of Pilate's permanganate. (Churchill was of the opinion that if self-government wasn't granted quickly then the Afrikaaners and English-speakers would band together in mutual frustration at what they saw as a distant, dithering and uncaring government and throw off the imperial connection altogether. His opinion was taken seriously, for a week after he made it known a commission for Transvaal self-rule was set up which reported back a mere four months later).[69] Still, it was a generous offer and Smuts saw in it the hope for reconciliation between English-speakers, the Boer National Scouts who had fought for Britain, Bitter-enders and the whole mass of people who lay somewhere along that spectrum. From this point on, he refused to discuss that dreadful pamphlet *A Century of Wrong* and stopped all talk of 'Africa for the Afrikanders' before it began. As Sarah Gertrude Millin put it;

> 'The feeling for the English that swept into him when Campbell-Bannerman so trusted the Boers in 1906 has been the strongest influence in Smuts' life....It linked him forever, he says, in love to

---

[67] *Smuts by his son* p.158
[68] Sarah Gertrude Millin, *General Smuts, Vol.I* (London, 1936) p.213
[69] CO 879/106 (Secret). W.S. Churchill, *Situation in South Africa* 15th March 1906. Also CO 879/106 (Secret) Report of the Committee appointed to enquire and report upon certain matters connected with the future constitutions of the Transvaal and Orange River Colony, July 1906.

England and so set him on his honour that he fought his own countrymen who went against England in 1914.'[70]

Perhaps he shouldn't have been so surprised at the magnanimity; the British Empire rested as much on co-operation and acquiescence as it did on its capacity for decisive force and the British have never been very much in love with arbitrary power and the jackboot of oppression; elections in which the Uitlanders would play a part, security for the routes to India guaranteed by suzerainty and eventual union were what the British had fought the war for. Within a year, elections were held and by the end of 1908 strong, pro-Afrikaaner majorities were returned in the Transvaal, the Orange Free State and the Cape (rather to the surprise of the Colonial Office officials who had tried to ensure that pro-British governments with small majorities that necessitated conciliatory coalitions would be formed).[71] Smuts became King's Counsel, Louis Botha became Transvaal Prime Minister, while in the Free State, Abraham Fischer led a cabinet of Bitter-enders, including Herzog and Christian de Wet into government.

Within two years of self-government, the Union of South Africa was achieved and this too was largely Smuts' work. A driven and imperious man, impatient of opposition and unwilling to suffer fools gladly – and there were very many fools in the *praatfontein* parliament - it was he who turned up at the inter-colonial conference with a fully worked out plan and a secretariat bigger than all the other delegates' combined to push it through and so succeed where Grey, Frere, Rhodes and Kruger had failed. It was he who dangled the profits of the Joburg gold mines in front of the doubters' noses in indebted Cape Colony and Natal; who circumvented the race question by allowing each colony to keep its own franchise but ensured that only white people could sit in the Union parliament; who salved regional pride by allowing for two capital cities, the legislature to be in Cape Town and the executive to be in Pretoria. Botha became the first Prime Minister of the Union of South Africa, Smuts took the Interior, Defence and Finance departments while Herzog was reluctantly handed the Justice ministry; but everyone knew that the whole government was run by Smuts. Botha was popular, chummy and smoked his pipe on the *stoep* like a real Boer, but cold, restless 'Slim Jannie' who lacked the common touch, did the paperwork and set the agendas because Botha had had only two years in a farm school for an education.

It's hard to reconcile the fact that a man with the brains of Smuts could wholly subscribe to Social Darwinist theories of race, yet he did. He believed that there was a natural hierarchy of race and that the white races were at the top of it, the black races were at the bottom of it and the Asians somewhere in the middle and that, further, the picture didn't need complicating by the addition of the Chinese. This was about the depth of his revealed thinking on the subject before 1914 and any reasonable person stood no chance of drowning in it; my best guess is that he thought the question not worth thinking about, equal rights for all races being beyond the realm of anything approaching practical Afrikaaner politics, a fact that *The Spectator* pointed out right from the beginning of the Union.[72] If anything, his primary concern (which he shared with both Louis Botha and Dr Jameson) was the merging of the Afrikaaner and the British race, each of which he believed had particular inherited qualities which, if combined in a new South African identity, would be beneficial to both. It was this curious blindness to what Asians might contribute to a new South Africa that led him into conflict with the Natal Indians; and this blindness was indeed curious because the person standing up for the Natal Indians was that very curious hybrid of Britain and India, at the time known as a 'Brindian' and, somewhat later and more disparagingly, as a 'Brown Sahib', the frock-coated, top-hatted, barrister Mohandas Gandhi.

Indians had come to Natal to work on the sugar plantations during the 1880s and within twenty years had so thoroughly colonised it that they outnumbered the European population there. When Gandhi came from London to fight a case in Pretoria, it is fair to say that he was as ignorant of South African attitudes to 'coolies' as South Africans were ignorant of Indian barristers; both sides got a shock. Gandhi was subjected to all the petty nastiness of Kruger's Transvaal – as an Indian, he wasn't even allowed to sleep over in the Orange Free State – and so decided to do something about it. Serving in a British auxiliary ambulance unit during the Anglo-Boer

---

[70] Sarah Gertrude Millin, *General Smuts, Vol.I* (London, 1936) p.215
[71] CO 879/106 (Secret). W.S. Churchill, *Situation in South Africa* 15th March 1906. Also CO 879/106 (Secret) Report of the Committee appointed to enquire and report upon certain matters connected with the future constitutions of the Transvaal and Orange River Colony, July 1906.
[72] 'The South African Elections', *The Spectator* 27th August 1910.

War, he began to agitate for Indians to receive the same rights as British citizens in the post-war Africa and though Milner was generally in favour of equal rights for men of 'equal civilisation', Smuts absolutely was not. Neither, it should be noted, was Gandhi, who also held to Social Darwinist concepts in his assessment of black Africans as being lower on the scale of development than Indians (and who has subsequently been a victim of the idiocy of removing statues because they somehow give offence to small minded bigots; in 2018, his statue was removed from the University of Ghana).[73] Although this is vehemently contested by the politically correct/intersectionality crowd, the observable fact is that just about every civilisation and culture since the making of the world has held views on the supposed superiority/inferiority of people based on skin colour, language, culture or religion and Indians then, as now, were no different in this respect.

The issue that Gandhi chose to fight on was centred on registration. When immigrants entered South Africa, they were required to register their presence with the local authorities and so receive permission to stay by the simple expedient of sticking a thumb print on a form. All right and reasonable; the problem was that these forms, being valuable items as they bestowed residency, were being forged, bought and sold and routinely abused in every bazaar from Bombay to Durban to Joburg. Natal introduced a 1907 law preventing any more Indians from landing. Smuts then brought in the Asiatic Registration Act which ordered the Indians to re-register with a view to weeding out the illegals only this time, all ten fingerprints would be taken. On such finicky details do barristers feed; Gandhi appealed to London and got the order overturned. When the Transvaal got self-government, Smuts reintroduced the Act and Gandhi opposed it with measures of passive resistance; 10,000 Indians in the Transvaal refused to re-register and dared Smuts to put them all in jail. He put a fair number in and then opened up the sort of tortuous negotiations that only barristers could conduct. In the end, Gandhi agreed to *voluntary* re-registration while Smuts agreed to repeal the law and in 1908 the jails were relieved of their groaning burdens.

And then, in a move of despicable duplicity, Smuts repealed the Asiatic Registration Act…and replaced it with a law forbidding any more Indians to enter the Transvaal. Gandhi began his campaign of passive resistance again, but to no successful purpose because when tested in court, the law backed Smuts and Gandhi being a barrister had to accept this. With the Act of Union came more laws specifically designed to discourage Indian immigration which Gandhi continued to challenge. Bloemfontein jail beckoned but pressure from London sprung him and Smuts was forced to remove any clauses that specifically mentioned Indians in such laws as were passed in the Union parliament. He complied… in 1914 Gandhi patted himself on the back and left South Africa, fully aware that he had been defeated by Smuts because only the form and not the substance of the legislation had changed. But that was always Gandhi's way; a successful protester, he rarely rose to the challenge of leadership; when the terrible massacres that accompanied the 1947 partition of India occurred, he *fasted*, as though missing his breakfast in protest was a sensible course of action, rather than doing something effective like sending in the Indian army to restore order. (Gandhi was also fortunate in having the British for opponents; Hitler's advice for dealing with him, given to former Viceroy of India Lord Halifax, was simple – shoot him).[74] Unlike Gandhi, Smuts looked facts square in the face and knew what their logical consequences were. For him, there was no use kicking against the pricks whatever the protests from both Britain and the Raj. 'We are not based on a system of political equality,' he declared. 'You cannot give political rights to the Indians which you deny to the other coloured citizens of South Africa. If you touch the Indian position you must go the whole length….'[75] In the event, he never put into practice any plans for the deportation or expulsion of Indians from Africa as very many Afrikaaners urged; that was something reserved for newly liberated governments of Kenya and Uganda to do during the 1960s. In the meantime, the Indians of the Raj demanded that pretty much the whole of East Africa be handed over to them for colonisation as 'an Indian Crown Colony', if South Africa was to be denied them.[76]

Politics, it is often stated, is the art of the possible. The hindsight of History is its judge, but in order to understand *why* a particular decision or course was taken, we must look at how things were seen from the standpoint of the times. So we cannot condemn Smuts' judgement as a conscious step towards Apartheid, even

---

[73] 'Statue of 'Racist' Gandhi Removed from University of Ghana', *The Guardian* 14th December 2018.
[74] Julia Boyd, *Travellers in the Third Reich* (London, 2018).
[75] Quoted in Sarah Gertrude Millin, *General Smuts*. Vol II (London, 1936) p.247
[76] 'Indians in East Africa', *The Spectator* 7th September 1918.

though this is essentially what it was, because he had no intention of making such a step. That said, it was *possible* then, even within the framework of Social Darwinism, to have admitted civilised Indians and others into the political life of South Africa as enfranchised citizens along the lines of the Cape constitution. *Difficult*, but not impossible, and the fact that Gandhi stood right there in front of Smuts wearing a top hat and frock-coat, brandishing his Law degree and damning the natives, should have appeared to him as proof positive that it *should* have been attempted. And the organisation that was most vociferous in insisting that it should indeed be attempted was the British government in London and the British Raj in India which attempted on several occasions during the 1920s to get Smuts, Herzog and Malan to stop harassing Indians in Natal, a process that culminated in the Cape Town Agreement on Indian immigration of 1927 (which subsequently failed). As the movement for Indian Independence progressed, so it was obvious to everyone that even if Smuts and the Afrikaaners held to an ever more ragged Social Darwinism, they could not but admit that an increasing number of Indians passed all the tests for 'civilisation' bar the skin-colour one. When the British Raj passed the Government of India Act 1937, handing virtually all matters of internal rule over to Indians, there could not have been a more obvious signal to Smuts that Social Darwinism was on its way to the dustbin of History.

It wasn't attempted because of the opposition of Afrikaaner Nationalists like Herzog and de Wet. Where Botha and Smuts hoped for the fusion of Boer and Briton into a new South African identity, Herzog, with his customary demonic and ungoverned passions, feared that the Afrikaaner language and culture would be swamped by the English whom he roundly and uncompromisingly hated; de Wet, with his ingrained stupidity, hoped for another war with Britain. Increasingly rabid in his denunciation of reconciliation, Herzog precipitated a split in the South Africa Party that he had formed with Botha; de Wet, the original dunghill rooster, did indeed give his support from a dunghill at a pro-Herzog rally in Pretoria in 1912; and after a failed attempt to overthrow Botha's leadership in 1913, they set up the National Party at Bloemfontein in January 1914. (This was the man who, remarkably, Allister Sparks regarded as a 'moderate').[77] Their platform was based on fundamentalist Christian republicanism, Anglophobia, strict segregation of the races and the subordination of black people.

Herzog had split from Botha for many reasons; Herzog's wife had died in the camps while he was being beaten on Commando as one of de Wet's hapless lieutenants; he hated Smuts' idea that in the Transvaal education system, English should be compulsory and Dutch optional and as a minister in the government of the Orange River Colony he had insisted on equal status for the two languages, dismissing English teachers who couldn't speak Dutch (which was most of them) and reinstating republican officials; he felt snubbed by not being offered a more senior position in the 1910 government - but at bottom he suspected that Botha and Smuts were 'soft on the blacks', as the saying went; Herzog was not 'soft on the blacks'. In fact, he was absolutely Bourbon in his determination to learn nothing and forget nothing; in the rest of the world it was 1914, but in his head it was 1814 or perhaps 1614; either way, the Enlightenment had by-passed him completely.

What this meant in practice was that no sort of progress whatsoever or howsoever attempted could be made to bring about any sort of change in the status of non-white Africans. As far as Herzog was concerned, the English were a bad enough threat to the racial purity of the Afrikaaner and as for Indians or blacks... well, the old Free State laws restricting the rights, freedoms and status of non-whites were retained and expanded upon. Botha and Smuts could do nothing about this if they wanted to avoid being booted out altogether at the next election. The 1913 Land Act pretty much buried any sort of liberality towards Africans as a result; black people were labourers as far as Herzog was concerned; they should not be able to buy land in 'white' areas; and that 'when they placed the native in a separate territory they gave him the opportunity of developing'[78]. 'Separate' and 'developing': two fatal words; *separate, development;* in Afrikaans, *Apartheid*. Botha and Smuts were Social Darwinists who believed that black people could be civilised through Christianity, education and capitalism; Herzog and de Wet were racists because they admitted of no prospect that black people could ever be admitted into Afrikaaner society. J.G. Keyler, MP for Ficksburg, summed up the views of those of the Herzog persuasion. 'The laws of the Orange Free State,' he said,

> 'told the coloured people plainly that the OFS was a white man's country, and that they intended to keep it so. They told the coloured people that they were not to be allowed to buy or hire land and they

[77] Allister Sparks, *The Mind of South Africa* (London, 1990) p. 150.
[78] Quoted in Brian Bunting, *The Rise of the South African Reich* (London, 1964) p.22

were not going to tolerate an equality between whites and blacks...that they were not going to tolerate that in the future, and that if an attempt was made to force that on them, they would resist it at any cost to the last for if they did tolerate it, they would very soon find that they were a bastard nation... the native should be treated firmly, kept in his place and dealt with honestly.'[79]

It was said of the 19th Century French Bourbon family, deposed by revolution, that they failed to regain the throne of France even when it was offered to them on a plate, because they learned nothing from and forgot nothing about their experience. Well, de Wet was in one sense even more Bourbon than the Bourbons in the sense that he was incapable of learning very much – his nickname was 'baboon' - but rather less like them in that he was able to forget all sorts of things; principally the fact that he had been beaten constantly during the war but also that German promises of help during 1899-1902 had never materialised. He also forgot that his attempt to overthrow Botha in 1913 had been defeated on a vote of 131 to 90; another fact that slipped his memory was that when the First World War came in 1914, despite Herzog's declaration that this was not South Africa's war, the Union parliament backed Smuts and Botha to the tune of 92 votes to 12 when they declared war on Germany. The one thing he *did not* forget was that he had been fined five shillings by an *English* magistrate for beating up a *black* man; and that, he considered, was unforgiveable on both counts.

The Five Shilling Rebellion of 1914 followed. Furious at the idea of fighting for the Empire against Germany, de la Rey, filled with a 'religious mania [and]...having lost some of his usual mental stability'[80] decided to act on the inspiration of his pet prophet Van Rensburg[81] decided to revolt; Beyers, Commander of the Union Defence Force, joined; Solomon Maritz, who had chosen German service in 1902 before being tempted back by a commission in that same Union Defence Force turned his coat; de Wet joined, of course; all blinded by hate or bought by the Germans in South West Africa, a colony that dangled like gonads awaiting a gelding by the Royal Navy stockman. De la Rey didn't even make it to the assembling rebel camp, being accidentally shot and killed by a policeman chasing bank robbers in September 1914 (a detail of the future that escaped Van Rensberg's gift for prophesy) but Beyers, who was with him, did nothing to quell the rumour that Smuts had had him murdered and in October, the Free State went up in rebellion with de Wet's bands of poor whites taking the opportunity to engage in a looting spree.[82] Maritz declared for the Germans and brought in German troops from South West Africa to aid his gallant six hundred; Smuts and Botha appealed for calm and quietly gathered their forces.

For Smuts, it was a matter of honour; the British had treated the defeated Boers with fairness and generosity and deserved loyalty in return. Botha agreed; so did the forces that were called up to meet the rebellion, two thirds of them being Afrikaaners; 'Regiment after regiment arose as if at the touch of a wizard's wand,'[83] is how Smuts described the result. The rebels' performance was as dismal as it had always been; Beyers drowned while running away and de Wet was captured after being run to earth by troops in motor vehicles that didn't need rest or forage; Maritz surrendered his men and then absconded for Portuguese territory. Smuts and Botha invaded German South West Africa, took it, destroyed the U-boat wireless station there and then offered themselves and South Africa for imperial service.

We might be forgiven for thinking that that was that for the Bitter-Bitter-enders but unfortunately this was not the case. For the next four years, Smuts would be away from South Africa. After the rebellion was put down he took command of the Imperial forces fighting in East Africa where he proved rather unsuccessful as it turned out, it being much harder to catch guerrillas than to be one; he was always a greater general in his own mind than in any reality. From there he went to work for the British War Cabinet where he was a useful organiser and committee man but a rather poor military adviser; he had the cheek to tell Haig what to do – the same Haig who had thrashed him and his ilk repeatedly during the Boer War – and then busied himself about the League of Nations, writing the memo on which it was based. At the Versailles peace conference, he held out for the lenient treatment of Germany but fell some way short of understanding the realities of European diplomacy;

---

[79] Quoted in Sol Plaatje, *Native Life in South Africa before and since the European War and the Boer Rebellion* (London, 1916) p.37
[80] CO 537/564 Governor-General to Colonial Office 1st October 1914.
[81] *Voice of a Prophet* Trans. Adriaan Synman, 1995. I found this in the Internet Archive and make no claims as to the accuracy of this source but apparently he was a man whose prophecies have never been found to be untrue – 'except [by] those ignorant people who have attempted to interpret them in their own way'.
[82] Lindie Korf, *D.F. Malan: a political biography.* University of Stellenbosh Ph.D Thesis, 2010.
[83] Quoted in Sarah Gertrude Millin, *General Smuts*, Vol.II p.322.

there were plenty of attendees, such as the French president Clemenceau, who thought he was no better than a yokel.

And while the cat was away the Nationalist mouse grew into a cane rat.

*

The leader of Afrikaaner Nationalism was JBM Herzog but its rising star was Daniel Francois Malan. It was he who did most to lead the Afrikaaner people on the Great Trek Up The Wrong Road and so we really should look at what formed him and how he came to his remarkable conclusions about the proper way to organise a country. Four years younger than Smuts, he came from the same town, came from the same Cape Dutch, Anglophile gentleman farmer background, went to the same school with the same teacher and followed him to Stellenbosch where he attended the same Victoria College. In other ways they were very much alike, being serious and committed students, overly cerebral and not a little priggish, interested in Theology and Philosophy, preaching to the Cape Coloured, and were enthusiastic members of the debating society. Malan became its secretary and the editor of the student magazine but he was not in the same league intellectually as Smuts, was conscious of it and had developed something of an inferiority complex as a result. He was hesitant in debate, played no sports and being short-sighted, rather reluctant to get involved in student rough and tumble. This sense of inferiority was heightened by the fact that when the Anglo-Boer War broke out, Smuts picked up a gun while Malan went off to study in the Netherlands which subsequently prompted accusations of cowardice that he was never quite able to shake off. It's hard not to wonder whether, when they were both sitting in the schoolroom in Riebeek-Kasteel studying at their mathematics, it ever occurred to them (to mangle a metaphor) that one of them would come to represent the Highest Common Factor among Afrikaaners while the other would sink to become the Lowest Common Denominator; the problem in the equation being the question of how to deal with skin colour.

It's fair to say that he did not particularly enjoy his time in the Netherlands and made heavy weather of gaining his doctorate. What he did learn there though would form much of his later outlook and among the first of those things was a real hatred for the British, a feeling that he imbibed largely from the frenetic propaganda of *Ons Land* and the Dutch penny-dreadfuls, the revelations of Emily Hobhouse about the camps and, we might surmise, a certain amount of guilt about not doing his bit. He was also completely disconcerted by the urban lifestyles of both London and Europe where he was a complete fish out of water and shocked that students seemed to spend more time in the pub than in the library (*plus ça change...*). This was followed up by a bout of hero worship of de Wet, Kruger and de la Rey when they visited Holland after the war and a long association with ex-President of the Orange Free State, Steyn and his family, who were then in Germany seeking treatment for his ailments. It's a commonly observed phenomena that those people who do not experience combat often end up hating the enemy more than those who have actually shot them down and in this, Malan had the classic symptoms. His disdain for General Ben Viljoen, whose tart memoirs were rather more believable and certainly a lot wittier than de Wet's and who painted a more mixed picture of Boer successes and heroism in the war – he described the victory at Spion Kop as 'undoubtedly a fluke,'[84] related how a number of burghers were dismissed for cowardice and recalled that the Piet Retief Commando was known as the Piet *Retreat* Commando - is a case in point.

He also came away with a nationalism that owed much to the German 19th Century Romantic movement which placed an emphasis on emotion rather than reason as the defining element in the Human existence; the heart should rule rather than the head; this point may be simply illustrated by comparing Mozart's mathematical, rational and technical music with Beethoven's massive appeal to emotion in compositions such as the *Moonlight Sonata* and the *Ode to Joy*. The Romantics held that a nation was defined by its language, land, History and culture, something that would become known as 'Blood and Soil' nationalism, rather than a legal framework, military force or particular form of government and that this essentially emotional attachment needed to be passed on to succeeding generations through education.

Romanticism was also to be found in Malan's theological studies; accepting both Darwin and the idea that the Bible was not necessarily to be taken literally in all circumstances, he was still in favour of the notion that the

---

[84] Ben Viljoen, *My Reminiscences of the Anglo-Boer War* (London, 1902).

mystical experience of faith overrode any and all contradictions in the text; in short, though he held to the Calvinistic tradition of his forebears, he was prepared to move with the times. Into this heady mix was added an aversion to capitalism which derived from its manifestations in the dark Satanic mills of Kimberley and Johannesburg as something alien and corrupting to the Afrikaaner people. Indeed, Malan would probably have subscribed to the idea of building the New Jerusalem but it would necessarily have to be relocated from England to Svartland's green and pleasant land. Coming from a prosperous family, he could also afford to rail against the rampant materialism of the industrial society and long for the preservation of the bucolic paradise of Malmesbury, Wellington and Riebeek-Kasteel.

Perhaps the biggest impression made on him came when he attended the World Conference of the Students Christian Association and came across Japanese, Chinese, Syrian, European and Russian Christians.

'To me, this meeting is such a beautiful promise for the future of humanity. Every nation is allowed here, and it is also expected from each to follow its own methods, to preserve its own national peculiarities. No dominance by the stronger, or trampling or denying the rights of the weaker. No imperialism or dead uniformity, but federation and rich variety. In this way, God's kingdom of righteousness and peace will come when every nation is itself and no other, and thereby fulfils its God-given place and calling.'[85]

This is really quite startling: the founder of the Apartheid state is here expressing views that no modern multiculturalist would challenge. What was less admirable was that running through his education was a growing intolerance of other viewpoints. Once he had thought through his conclusions he could not be persuaded to change them, admit they were flawed or concede that another angle might be equally valid. It was this refusal to compromise or seek common ground that led him to reject politics and the law in favour of the Church; like many extremists, he sought absolutes and in his case, he found them in the Bible and the Afrikaaner Nation.

Malan returned to South Africa in 1905, aged thirty, flint-eyed, serious, hard-working, capable of great concentration and took up a post preaching in the Dutch Reformed Church in Heidelberg, an area that was still impoverished and rebuilding after the war. There he quickly slipped into the beginnings of the Afrikaaner Nationalist movement. He read *Die Volkstem*, a newspaper full of lurid tales of stout Piet Retief and the barbarous blacks, and then joined the movement to replace Dutch with Afrikaans as the language of South Africa. On taking over as predikant of Montagu in 1906, virtually his first act was to refuse to conduct church services in English. A year later he became Chairman of the *Afrikaanse Taal Vereeniging* dedicated to promoting Afrikaans as a distinct language complete with spelling and grammar (which at present it lacked, existing only as a spoken dialect) in competition with English. In 1911, he went further and declared that the Union notwithstanding, the Afrikaaner nation had to use its language and religion to unite and strengthen itself, remaining distinct from any Smuts-like notion of a new South African identity forged from both English and Afrikaaner peoples. It was for this reason that he opposed the upgrade of the South African College to Cape Town University in case it drew students away from the pure Afrikaans atmosphere of Victoria College at Stellenbosch and exposed them to the English.

So far, so unremarkable. In 1912, however, he was invited to travel north to view the missionary activity in Rhodesia and points northward and it was here that he was presented with a series of situations that he could not approve of and which sharpened up his thinking on a range of issues that would lead him towards the Apartheid ideal. To begin with, he came into contact with black people in large numbers for the first time, having previously only really mingled with Cape Coloureds, and having met them came to a series of quite remarkable conclusions. His assumptions were those of the Social Darwinist but with a couple of added twists; the first was that black people naturally respected Afrikaaners more than British people; the second was that the racial hierarchy inherent in Social Darwinism was not primarily a scientific concept, but actually a religious one and that it was the God-given duty of the white man to look after the poor benighted heathen. He was also surprised to find that the large Afrikaans-speaking Coloured community in Rhodesia had imbibed the concept of Social Darwinism too and insisted that if they were not the equal of whites they were certainly a long step above the

---

[85] Malan. Quoted in Lindie Korf, *D.F. Malan: a political biography*. University of Stellenbosh Ph.D Thesis, 2010.

local black people. For Malan, this was as it should be but the white Afrikaaners were often so spread out that they had stopped attending Dutch Reformed Churches or, shockingly, were attending the services of other denominations including the dreaded Catholics and, even more shockingly, were marrying both Coloured people and, possibly worse, the English. They were also sending their children to English-speaking schools – if they were sending them at all. The existence of poor whites also posed serious dangers because, Malan concluded, the racial hierarchy could only be maintained if the whites constantly proved themselves to be deserving of the respect that he imagined they were held in by black people; black people could be educated, brought to the Word of God and elevated in civilisation but it was the duty of the white man to out-perform him and so honour God's ordering of the races. The problem of poor whites living Godless, debauched, inter-married lives was, for him, a White Peril much worse than the Black Peril. The answer to all these problems, he concluded, was not just the rebuilding of the Afrikaaner nation based on its language, religion and a renewed self-respect but also a strong interventionist government committed to education, religion, the separation of the races and the alleviation of the condition of poor whites.

On returning from Rhodesia, Malan took up a new position at Graaff-Reinet where he began to put into practice some of the conclusions that his trip had produced. The town was full of poor whites, many of whom lived side by side with Coloured people in an area nicknamed the 'Black Horde', often inter-married and, as Coloured people were not allowed in the Dutch Reformed services, deserted to the Mission church. His answer to this was to persuade the Town Council to bring in segregation by forbidding white people to buy property in that particular area and prevent Coloured people from buying property anywhere else but in it. The plan came to nothing despite the enthusiastic backing of many of the Council members because it was not legal, a fact that Malan drew the relevant conclusions from.

It was the 1914 Rebellion and the execution of the rebel Jopie Fourie that drew Malan into politics. Fourie was an officer in the Union Defence Force who had gone over to the rebels while in uniform, was thus guilty of treason and had been sentenced to execution. Malan objected and came to believe that in allowing the execution, Smuts had substantially abandoned his attachment to Afrikaanerdom; also he had lied to him about his whereabouts when Malan had tried to intercede against Fourie's execution. He also concluded that the Botha-Smuts government was itself responsible for the rebellion by expecting Boers to fight for Britain only twelve years after they had been beaten by her. This was sophistry to cover his Anglophobia and his argument that the Dutch Reformed Church should unite to prevent any divisions within Afrikaanerdom came off the same menu; what he really meant was that any government that didn't put Afrikaaners first was not deserving of Afrikaaner allegiance and that the true allegiance should be reserved for the church not only because it was God that directed the course of nations, not governments, but also because the Dutch Reformed Church was the only Boer institution that had survived British conquest. 'Dual-unity' – the idea that English and Afrikaaners would come together by developing separately (black people were discounted as a nationality) – he served up for desserts as a way to avoid drawing the logical conclusion that for his ideas to work, Malan would have to kick out the English in their entirety (good luck with that one). It was to push these ideas that Malan, not without long thought and much persuasion from prominent Afrikaaners (de Wet wrote to him from jail) gave up the Church and accepted the offer of the editorship of *De Burger* in 1915, with the promise of a seat in parliament shortly afterwards, as part of Herzog's new National Party. His slow but thorough conscience had persuaded him that he could serve God, the Church, the Language and the Nation more effectively in politics than from the parsonage at Graaff-Reinet and *Die Burger* would be the pulpit from where he could preach to the whole of Afrikaanerdom. And once the decision was made, he stuck to it. As his biographer Lindie Korf so brilliantly put it: 'He was in no danger of becoming a pillar of salt.'[86]

*

The Nationalists took the opportunities presented by the absence of Smuts on Imperial service in East Africa and London to press ahead relentlessly. In August 1915, a demonstration of 6000 women was organised to demand the release of de Wet from jail (he served only 18 months of a six year sentence); in September, the Cape branch of the Nationalist Party was founded, with Malan as its titular head and dedicated to following Herzog's lead; in

---

[86] Lindie Korf, *D.F. Malan: a political biography.* University of Stellenbosh Ph.D Thesis, 2010.

October they picked up 27 seats in the elections to the Union parliament despite Malan failing to gain a seat – only a third of what Smuts, Botha and the English Unionists claimed, but still significant, especially, as it seemed to Botha and Smuts, as their own Afrikaaner people had turned on them. In 1917, the Nationalists attempted to get black people removed from the protection of the law altogether under the Native Affairs Administration Bill and expelled from the towns under the Native Urban Areas Bill.[87] Their tactics were vicious, their campaigns respected no decencies and they constantly charged Botha and Smuts with being incompetent, corrupt, traitorous turncoats awash with the blood of their countrymen spilled in the service of an alien British government; the fact that Malan personally did *not* engage with these tactics probably cost him his seat but another one was quickly found for him. He got the Calvinia seat in 1919 because the incumbent could no longer afford to be an MP and look after his twenty-one children at the same time; Calvinia is not known for the variety of its entertainments.

Still, despite the feeling that they had the wind in their sails, the Nationalists weren't having it all their own way; when next Herzog came to Joburg with a Commando, there was a riot and the windows of the National Party Club were patriotically smashed. In 1919, Herzog had the cheek to head up a deputation to London at the end of the First World War (on a Dutch ship as no English crew would carry them; Malan went too) to demand the independence of the republics on the grounds that as President Wilson's Fourteen Points guaranteed the rights of small nations then their rights, as the *old* population of South Africa, should be guaranteed too. Smuts answered this by pointing out that the war had so radically altered the constitution of the British Empire that it was now a Commonwealth of co-equals from which South Africa gained rather more than it contributed; South Africa's signature was on the peace treaty – could the Orange Free State ever expect to be so regarded in the world? Lloyd George, the original pro-Boer, was rather more sarcastic: were not the greater number of ministers in the Union government Dutch? And as to the *old* population, how many black people were in favour of the restitution of the independence of the Orange Free State? When the deputation returned (via Dutch Java, as no English ship would carry them) they were met with rotten eggs and renditions of *God Save the King* – but Herzog's claims that Smuts and Botha were busying themselves in Paris with things which were of neither use nor concern to South Africa hit home. And when Botha died of a heart attack, Smuts, the cold, 'diabolically clever'[88], unapproachable schemer was deprived of both his leader and his interpreter; Slim Jannie did the paperwork but needed Louis Botha to deal with the people. At the 1920 election, the Nationalists (republican Afrikaaners, *mainly*) were returned as the largest party, attracting more Afrikaaner votes than Smuts and forcing him, in 1921, to merge his South Africa Party (unionist Afrikaaners, *mainly*) with the Union Party (English unionists, *mainly*) in order to win his 79-41 majority in a second election. Herzog and Malan's National Party had been outflanked and one might have been justified in thinking that the challenge had been seen off; how then did the racists of Afrikaaner Nationalism ever come to form their first government just a few years later?

With the support of the Labour Party socialists, of course.

*

> It is extremely difficult for a reasonable man to be a Socialist in South Africa. He is faced immediately with a situation which neither precedent nor imagination can overcome. He is brought up against the problem of the Kaffir....If he styles himself a Socialist, he must qualify his attitude to the extent of excluding from his humanity those millions who most desperately need it....the real workers in the land.

Sarah Gertrude Millin, *The South Africans* (1926).

There had been labour trouble in the mines of the Rand ever since the end of the Anglo-Boer War. In order to get the mines back working, the mine owners had found it both necessary and desirable to get labour costs down in order to restore both production and the vital profitability that ensured the investment necessary to repair the extensive damage that the mines had suffered. The problem was that the halving of wages meant that black Africans were unwilling to submit to the humiliations of the compounds and the dangerous work involved for

---

[87] 'The labour Problem in South Africa', *The Spectator* 18th October 1918.
[88] A. Paton, *South African Tragedy. The Life and Times of Jan Hofmeyr* (New York, 1965) p.61

such diminished rewards and while white miners had been employed in increasing numbers, the problem had only been solved by importing Chinese labour. When these men went back home at the end of their contracts and were not replaced, the original problem replicated itself, except that now white miners, many of them with British experience of militant trade unionism behind them, resisted any revived movement to bring in cheaper black labour which they declared would undermine their status and wages. Anyone who lived in Britain during the 1970s would instantly recognise what 'resistance' meant; petty wrangling with managers, the refusal to allow lazy workers to be fired, enforcement of demands by blatant violence and intimidation and utter imperviousness to any argument based on economic reality. That trade unions should bargain for better wages and conditions was (and is) all well and good, as long as the actual managers are allowed to manage, but when the leadership of the union is taken over by revolutionaries whose aim is not the improvement of wages and conditions but the forging of a tool for the illegitimate seizure of political power, then it is not all well and good. In 1913, the miners had gone on strike and had armed themselves to the teeth. When Smuts and Botha went to negotiate with them, they had been covered by trade union pistols and the army had had to be called out; Beyers and de la Rey were particularly eager for a fight because they reckoned that the miners were all English.

By 1922, many things had changed. The first was that the English miners had, by and large, joined the army and had gone off to war leaving their places to be filled by Afrikaaners escaping the rural poverty that was increasingly afflicting their communities. With them came hardened racial attitudes which did nothing to make the Trade unions more amenable to reasonable negotiations, especially when the price of gold fell off a cliff edge and unemployment beckoned. It was the trade unions' restrictive and corrupt practices that played a large part in making the mines uneconomical; a colour bar prevented black workers doing white jobs; black workers were not allowed to work except under white supervision and so spent a large part of the day sitting down waiting for the said white 'worker' to turn up; this was all standard stuff that persisted right into the 1980s in Britain and which earned her the name of 'the sick man of Europe'. Smuts, with that same curious optimism that had allowed him to believe in things like the League of Nations, appealed to reason.

> 'It is one of the most terrible facts that thousands of miners look upon their industry, not as the main interest in their lives, but as their enemy...it seems that they [are] anxious to destroy the industry that keeps them going....'[89]

(He might have said the same words fifty years later, with exactly the same effect – none. During the 1970s, I worked in a factory where the rule was 'one man one lathe', which meant, of course, that each man worked no more than ten minutes in the hour because setting the machine up and replacing the piece being turned only took ten minutes; needless to say, after yet another strike, the factory closed). When the mine managers attempted to keep production going in a manner which did not risk immediate bankruptcy, mass unemployment and starvation by tightening up on working conditions and, crucially, getting rid of 2000 semi-skilled white workers, in January 1922 the miners came out on strike. *The Spectator*, as usual, got to the heart of the problem;

> In many mines gold can no longer be got at a profit under the present conditions, and the employers were faced with the necessity of either closing down the unprofitable mines or reducing their working expenses. They proposed to reduce expenses by employing more coloured men to do unskilled work. It seems pretty plain that the employers were justified. From the point of view of the white miners themselves it was obviously the best thing that the mines should be kept open. The men's leaders, however, acting on the fatal tacit assumption that employers can somehow pay out more money in wages than they actually have, chose to make the dispute turn upon the "colour bar." The Rand, they preached, must be a white man's reef - except, of course, for such 'mean, distasteful and laborious duties as they did not themselves wish to undertake.[90]

This was no ordinary strike though; the unions of the Industrial Federation organised themselves into military units, armed themselves in preparation for a revolution that would see them in charge of the mines and when, in February, the government and the mine owners tried to re-start production, went into overdrive, beating up strike-breakers, attacking their families and lynching black workers for the fun of it. In February, the first shots

---

[89] Millin, *Smuts* Vol.II p.368
[90] 'The Rising on the Rand, *The Spectator*, 18th March 1922.

were fired and in March, a general strike was called amid terrible racial violence; the Red Flag was run up, the *Internationale* sung – right alongside the old Transvaal national anthem, for the National Party were hard at work convincing the Afrikaaner miners that it was all the fault of Smuts, who was soft on blacks, soft on the English and in the pocket of Jewish capitalists. 'Workers of the World Unite,' cried the South African Communist Party. 'And Fight for a White South Africa!' Indeed. It was Bill Andrews, General Secretary of the South African Communist Party and leading trade unionist who was one of the main defenders of the colour bar.

As usual, the blinkered, limited intelligence of the leaders of the revolt led them to overestimate their support (just as in 1984, the Stalinist Arthur Scargill thought he could overthrow the Thatcher government, a government elected largely by working class people who were sick of people like Scargill); many Joburgers wished they had never heard of a trade union: Red Flag? Old Flag? 'You can't live on fried flag,' they heckled.[91] In March, the revolutionaries went the whole hog and seized Joburg in the expectation of being joined by Burgher commandos coming in to help their Afrikaaner relatives. They came, alright, but at Smuts' command and at Smuts' command the rebellion was put down with tanks, aircraft and martial law; the revolutionaries' leaders prepared to make a last stand at Fordsburg, but their ardour was cooled within an hour of the first gun being fired and they surrendered. All in all, the police and troops lost nearly 300 killed and wounded, the revolutionaries around 150, bystanders accounted for another 90 or so while 150 black people were also killed. Herzog, joining hands with the socialists, said that Smuts' footsteps 'dripped with blood'.[92]

Daniel Malan watched these developments with some dismay but also with the opportunism for which he would become famous. His main interest in the first years of his involvement in politics was the problem of poor whites and, in 1923, he attended a conference on the problem. Shocked to find that 70,000 Afrikaaners had left the land for the cities, this touched all the nerves in his anti-capitalism, Blood and Soil Nationalism and Social Darwinist beliefs. Revolted at the sight of troops being deployed to put down strikes in order to preserve the profits of the (English and Jewish) mine owners, like the English Chartists of the mid-19th Century, Malan saw the ideal solution in a 'back to the land' movement based around the establishment of small holdings supported by agricultural co-operatives that were such a feature of North European farming communities. Suspicious of communal ownership schemes, he rejected Communism because he felt that it was not in the nature of the Afrikaaner to be anything other than sturdily independent and that, further, because black people pursued the communal creed of *uBuntu*, whereby things were shared more readily than in more individualistic societies, it was a creed that more naturally suited them than the Afrikaaner. This solution would have to wait, however, because he also believed that poor whites and coloureds were trekking to the cities because they were being displaced by cheaper African labour only to find that when they got to the cities, they were undercut once more by that same cheap African labour. Whites, he concluded, were about to be swamped and it was this combination of fears about capitalism, communism and Black Africans that led him to enthusiastically support segregation, job reservation, nationalisation of mining dividends and the Colour bar. Until such time as black Africans could be educated and civilised, Malan argued, there would have to be separate development. *Die Burger* continued to print cartoons showing Smuts in hock to the fictional stereotypical Jewish Randlord financier, Hoggenheimer, and determined to impoverish the Afrikaaner, while Malan personally came out to attack the 'imperialism, militarism, capitalist-monopolistic domination'[93] that was opposed to worker and burgher alike.

Thus was the intellectual foundation for the alliance of the Communist Party, the Labour Party and the Nationalists laid. When the Rand Revolt was suppressed, a 'United Front' to prevent harsh treatment of the rebels was formed and when elections loomed, they joined together in an anti-Smuts pact. In 1924, they defeated him; the Nationalists gaining 63 seats, Labour 18 and the Smuts' Unionist South Africa Party only 53. Herzog became Prime Minister and Malan became Minister of the Interior, Education and Health, willingly supported by a ragbag collection of racist socialists, communists and trade unionists.

*

[91] Millin, *Smuts* Vol.II p.370
[92] Millin, *Smuts* Vol.II p.380
[93] Quoted in Lindie Korf, *D.F. Malan: a political biography*. University of Stellenbosh Ph.D Thesis, 2010

A contemptible little man who deserved all the contempt that Smuts treated him with, Barry Hertzog was a small-minded third-rate ex-Commando leader who had learned enough at law school to understand just how to manipulate the truth but never to divine it. He possessed the same talent for cronyism as Kruger, the same obstinacy as de Wet in his refusal to face the fact that he had been roundly thrashed by Tommy Atkins and never had the imagination to look forward rather than backwards. He was a republican because Kruger was a republican. He rejected the British connection because Kruger rejected the British connection. He hated the English because Kruger hated the English. He hated the Kaffirs because Kruger hated the Kaffirs. Sometimes you have to wonder if he believed that Kruger was actually dead or if he was just awaiting the right moment for a Second Coming.

Nor was he anything in the way of a leader; he had followed his party rather than led them, had kept his head down during the 1914 revolt and only raised it once it had been quelled. In theory, he stood for the policy of separate development for the Afrikaaner and English-speaking peoples but being an opportunist scoundrel, he had gone into an electoral alliance with the (English) trade unions and when he got into office, buoyed up by an unexpected turn of good luck – the rains came and ended a racking drought – the immediacy of his republicanism faded. He sat back and enjoyed being in charge, handed out some jobs to his pals and pushed bilingualism in the civil service – which meant he sacked some Englishmen and handed their jobs to Afrikaaner cronies. At the behest of his trade union allies, the colour bar was reinforced and nationalist socialist economic measures were introduced; poor whites were protected by a minimum wage, employers could now be forced to sack black workers and replace them with whites, as well as coming under an obligation to hire whites ahead of blacks. Black workers were prevented from joining trade unions and Indians were prevented from occupying skilled jobs in the mining industry. Old Age Pensions were introduced but paid at rates dependent on colour while a Wages Board was set up to regulate the pay rates across a range of industries. In the countryside, subsidies, guaranteed prices and barriers against foreign competition were introduced to keep the rural Afrikaaner base happy in the world's first - but far from the last – example of socialist racism.

*

Bosman was a man, a woman, an angel, a devil, a tenderness, a cruelty, a brave man and a coward, an emasculated satyr, a womaniser, a racist and a liberal. He searched for purity in filth and, like, Wilde, found stars in the gutter.

Gordon Vorster, drinking buddy.[94]

It's too easy to get bogged down in politics, especially when talking about 'Great Men' and it's also too easy to get bogged down in the binary, the versus, the either/or; will it be Smuts or Herzog who wins? Whose vision will prevail? Will they combine together or cancel each other out? So this is where we are going to turn aside from politics just for a moment and look at South Africa from the point of view of a man who was very definitely South African, but hardly concerned with politics at all, Herman Charles Bosman.

Now, again a note of warning; it's easy to make the mistake of believing what 'cultural commentators' say about the past, about how a particular painter or writer summed up the spirit of the age but you only need to compare your own experience with what you read to understand what drivel most of this is. During the 1980s, I lived in Manchester when the achingly trendy Hacienda Club was being splashed across the newspapers and music press as though Mozart and Beethoven had been discovered there; what was entirely ignored was the existence of very visible and much larger queues of hairy bikers with jackets embroidered with the names of Heavy Metal bands outside the rammed to the rafters Jilly's Rock Club a little distance away, a venue that was far more popular with music fans than with hip journalists. The same could be said of the 1970s when disco music outsold punk by several orders of magnitude, but it was the latter that got all the attention; during the 1990s, Maeve Binchy and Ian Rankin were lauded as literary superstars yet both were outsold by the deceased Enid Blyton, the appalling Dan Brown and the comic Terry Pratchett; it's pretty certain that Harry Potter has outsold just about all the literary superstars combined, however defined. So the idea that a set of writers like the Bloomsbury group somehow changed the world is, at the very least, something of a stretch. That said, some

---

[94] Valerie Rosenberg, *Sunflower to the Sun* (Johannesburg, 1976) p.10.

writers are worth reading and some painters worth looking at because they do give us an insight into life as it was lived at that time whether they were successful or not; van Gogh never achieved anything but a passing following until the poor old bugger kicked the bucket. Bosman fits into this group rather well.

Born in the Cape, the son of an Afrikaaner who had fought for the British during the Boer War, Bosman trained as a teacher during the 1920s before being posted to the Groot Marico, the sort of deep backveldt area that really needed teachers. The year that he spent there observing the ways of these most rustic of Transvaalers furnished him with the material for the brilliant series of short stories that he wrote about life in the poor, rural backend of South Africa. *Mafeking Road* (1930), *Makapan's Caves* (1930) and the rest of his Voorkamer Stories are classics of the short story genre. He paints a picture of clever, slow, witty farmers as ready with the cracker-barrel wisdom as with the smuggler's art. In these stories, often narrated by a *stoep* character called Oom Schalk Lourens, the bones of the one horse dorp are laid out for inspection. Some of the stories are ludicrous; *The Bekkersdal Marathon* (1950) is so unbelievable as to be nothing short of hilarious. There are dark moments in *Mafeking Road* and *Drieka and the Moon*. There is complexity too, of relationships across the racial boundary and their consequences and though he admires his subjects he is not above pointing out their absurdities, their frailties and their questionable attitudes to the times; *Unto Dust* (1949) was overtly anti-racist, but *Jim Fish* would probably give a publisher a heart attack today for its mixture of the bizarre, the racist, the strangely noble and hilariously subversive tale of Mletshwa 'a nigger performing a Zulu war dance in a kneading trough'[95] making confectionary dough for white people to eat.

Bosman himself, though immersed in the emerging literary and artistic world of the inter-war Transvaal, was not without complexity himself. He was sentenced to death for the killing of his half-brother in a fit of the selfish rage that he was prone to. His sentence was commuted so that he only served close on four years but the book that emerged from it, *Cold Stone Jug*, is a brilliant prison memoir. Throughout his life he considered himself to be first and foremost a poet but it is his short stories that show his talent. In his writings on Art he anticipated the garbage that became popular in the 1960s, that somehow anything that an artist creates is actually 'Art', that an artist must live his 'Art' without regard to the human cost on those caught up in his egotism and that nothing was more important than 'Art' itself; the subtext of this nonsense being, of course, that the 'artist' should be paid more than the mere painter and decorator because of his heightened sensibilities. For him the Second World War was a complete irrelevance and though he had no time for either Communists or Nazis he gradually slipped into an Afrikaaner Nationalism that, though soft, and in many ways admirable in its determination to shake off European influences and create something specifically African, made no great challenge to the emerging Apartheid. At the same time, he could also be scathing about the more ludicrous aspects of an already segregated society. Adding further complexity to his outlook, it is also the case that his third wife was a willing member of the Nationalist Party organisation, the *Ossewabrandwag,* and he himself was dedicated to a sort of Afrikaaner literary nationalism and so forfeited the international recognition that Olive Schreiner, Doris Lessing (who worked for him for a while) and Alan Paton all craved; he was unknown – and, pretty much, remains to this day unknown – outside South Africa.

He was, in short, capable of real brilliance but also, in his excessive posing, petty money-making schemes that verged on the criminal, wanton blasphemy and procuring (and performance) of back street abortions, the sort of boorish lout that would be worshipped at the Tate Modern for, rather than suffering for his 'Art', he preferred to make others suffer for it instead; he treated each of his three wives appallingly. It was also the case that when he stayed on the familiar ground of his short stories he showed skill, judgement and the ability to produce works that were pleasing to his audience; the moment he went outside these boundaries, as in his work of literary criticism *A Cask of Jeripigo,* he slipped into gibberish. During his lifetime, his works were popular but never really popular enough to be a properly paying prospect and it was only after 1947 that the collection *Mafeking Road* allowed him anything more than a bohemian existence. As with many artists, the ground he broke only bore a decent crop after his death in 1951, when by the 1980s, he was on every bookshelf in South Africa, Oom Schalk Lourens being the voice of an Afrikaaner tradition that was both nostalgic and strangely contemporary.

---

[95] H.C. Bosman, *Jim Fish* (First published, 1980)

And this was the problem with his work. Bosman claimed that he was never political but his work proved the worth of the adage that while you might not be interested in politics, politics is interested in *you*. His work made it possible for an average reader to misunderstand his jovial treatment of black people being mistreated as legitimising that mistreatment; of making it normal, routine and so acceptable, rather in the way that many people took the questionable views of the character of Alf Garnett in *Till Death Us Do Part* seriously, rather than as satire. His work is brilliant, but its potential for misuse was high. Bosman reported the prevailing racial attitudes and satirised them, but he also made those attitudes comfortable, homely and jokey; no more serious than an *Englishman, Irishman, Scotsman go into a bar* joke; and like Hugo's peasant at Waterloo, he sent Smuts' people charging like the French cavalry into the concealed ditch.

Much as Bosman would have loved it, it is doubtful if anyone mistook him for an intellectual but Sarah Gertrude Millin was one, and she too might happily fill the role of Hugo's fateful peasant. Born in 1889 of Lithuanian Jewish stock she had been brought up in Kimberley and though qualifying for university, she turned down the bursaries offered to concentrate on a writing career. In 1912, she married a rising young lawyer who would go on to be a Supreme Court judge and moved to Johannesburg where she established herself during the 1920s as South Africa's literary doyen – and earned herself a continuous stream of barbs from Bosman after she had dared to criticise one of his execrable poems about shagging. We have already met her as the biographer of Smuts, but she also carried on in South Africa's tradition of producing excellent amateur historians (Moodie, Theal, Ash: somehow it seems that South Africa's problems with History start only when the pros get involved) with a biography of Rhodes. She also wrote a string of novels and became increasingly concerned about the rise of the National Socialists in Germany before endorsing the Apartheid policies of the post-war National Party government. This, I found quite surprising when I first came across the info because *The South Africans* is generally sympathetic to the problems of black Africans and as she revised it several times between 1926-31 and reissued it in 1951, it would seem fair to say that she meant what she wrote. If anything, her first novel *The Dark River* was rather feminist in approach, being scathing of men in general and poor, white men in particular, but she held the firm idea that miscegenation leads to the degradation of both the races involved – not an unusual conclusion among racial theorists.[96] In some strange way, she saw the existence of Coloured or mixed-race people as a symptom of Adam's Fall and the expulsion from Eden and how she managed to accept this sort of racial theory at the same time as opposing Hitler is suggestive of intellectual confusion at the very least: 'he had squandered the best years of his life,' she states of one of her characters. 'On a drunken, coloured woman that was little removed, judging by any mental or moral standard, from a beast....'[97] Perhaps, old Gertie having thought long and hard about the Social Darwinist 'race of civilisations',[98] came to the conclusion that she ought not to pussy foot around but make sure she was on the winning (white, or perhaps, Jewish) team. She certainly enjoyed befriending powerful figures and during the later 1930s was careful to cultivate J.H. Hofmeyr, a liberal whom many had tipped for Prime Minister. Hedging? I think so. All that can be said of her for certain, I suppose, is that she remains a mystery in all but one way; like very many intellectuals, she spotted a theme that was extremely marketable and followed the money. Would her husband have risen so high if she had denounced Social Darwinism (she lobbied shamelessly for his promotion)? Would she have been able to count Mr and Mrs Smuts among her friends, meet Woodrow Wilson and be a house guest of the Roosevelts in America, hang out with George Bernard Shaw and D.H. Lawrence in London? Get an honorary doctorate from the University of Witwatersrand for 'explaining South Africa to the English speaking world'? I doubt it; she was, after all, only qualified to be a piano teacher. What Millin did was give intellectual permission to other members of the wealthy, *faux*-liberal intelligentsia to accept and endorse an Apartheid theory that was ludicrous and sinister and objectionable but something that could be lived with if it did not threaten their own positions in the arts, society or government. It's a very familiar story.

*

The Native Question

---

[96] 'Mixed marriages and the Colour bar,' *The Spectator* 18th July 1931.
[97] S.G. Millin, *The Dark River*.
[98] S.G. Millin, *The Dark River*.

We suggest that a...clause should be embodied in the new constitution namely that all slavery or labour "partaking of slavery"...should be prohibited....[99]

The British Government reveals its suspicions of South African labour practices.

*

Here, then, is an impasse. The white man has awakened the native, and, like a dream, the old savage life is ended. He has been called. He has arisen. He is on the road - travelling in the shadow of the white man, carrying his chattels. The white man looks around at this being he has himself aroused....He begins to distrust him, to fear him....'You'd better leave me,' says the white man. 'You'd better go back home.'

'Go back?' says the native. 'Home? But the road has fallen in behind us. And.... I am carrying your load.'

They face one another unable to move forward or back.

'And I wish to God I never had called you,' mutters the white man.

Sarah Gertrude Millin, *The South Africans*, 1926.

*

It should be a recognised principle of Government that Natives – men, women and children – should only be permitted within municipal areas in so far and for so long as their presence is demanded by the wants of the white population and should depart therefrom when they cease to minister to the needs of the white man.

Report of the (Stallard) Transvaal Local Government Commission, 1922.

*

...it seems to us Natives that you want our labour, but as soon as you have finished with us you want us removed so far away from you that you do not want to see us until certain hours when you again want our labour. We are just so many horses that have to be stabled after they have been working - just as though we are not human beings.

Rev. John L. Dube giving evidence to the Native Economic Commission, 1932.

Segregation had begun as a natural clustering of different groups and had then hardened up into the geographical segregation of 'Locations' and 'Zones', each of which had appeared on the scene as a reaction to local circumstances and emphatically not as part of any plan. Pretty much the same thing happened in the USA when the government flung open its borders to the European and Russian poor and welcomed them through Ellis Island on the proviso that they should have some contacts to receive them and prevent them becoming a charge on the state; Irish-American, Italian-American and Jewish-American neighbourhoods resulted. In Natal, the existing situation of Locations had been undermined by the unrestricted immigration of Indians brought in as indentured labour for the sugar plantations and the predominantly English population (numerically speaking after black Africans, of course) suddenly faced being outnumbered and reacted defensively by hardening up segregation into a legislative policy even before the Boer War. It was post-Boer war Johannesburg that was the real driver behind segregation, however. Here a truly toxic mix of Afrikaaner backveldt attitudes coalesced with British trade union socialism to produce not just segregation and ghettoization, but economic segregation in the form of the Colour bar.

---

[99] CO 879/106 (Secret) Report of the Committee appointed to enquire and report upon certain matters connected with the future constitutions of the Transvaal and Orange River Colony, July 1906.

Even before the reconstruction period, it had been noticed that large numbers of poorer, white Afrikaaners were being driven off the land by a Roman-Dutch legal system which enforced the progressive subdivision of family farms into uneconomic plots (the same process that had led to the potato famine in Ireland) and this process continued through both reconstruction and the First World War so that by 1918, roughly half the miners employed on the Rand were white; previously the figure had been around 10%. Black labour was cheaper by several orders of magnitude and capital being colour blind and the gold market in depression, the Randlords sought to do the obvious and were, by and large, successful in doing it. With the failure of the 1922 Rand Revolt, the percentage of white miners dropped back to 10% and the whole question of what to do about the now unemployed whites cropped up. The answer was 'job reservation' whereby the trade unions, backed up by both the Smuts and Herzog governments, enacted a colour bar across a range of government, transport and mining jobs which was designed to maintain stable employment for poor whites but also to maintain wage differentials between whites and blacks - the white trade unions seemed to make a point of *not* supporting strikes by black workers. That such restrictive practices would only make everyone poorer in the long term was beyond the understanding of the trade unionists whose understanding of economics was sketchy (or indeed 'socialist') at best but they were supported by the backveldt Afrikaaner's traditional suspicion of capitalists, who they understood very often to be the equivalent of usurers. This was re-reinforced by the traditional anti-Semitism of the Left who, to this day, equate Jews with the skulduggery of high finance; Smuts was often portrayed as being in hock to 'Hoggenheimer'. During the 1920s, Keynesian arguments were made for labour to be free of trade union and colour bar restrictions because greater competition and rising wages for black labour would increase demand and thus grow the economy, but they fell on deaf ears; the Randlords knew that any attempt to push this sanity through the alliance of cloth caps and cloth ears of British trade unionism and Afrikaaner racial attitudes was impractical on both political and business grounds.

Segregation was also powered by the very thing that the Social Darwinists, missionaries and Liberals both expected and hoped to achieve – the civilisation of the black man. Education, Christianity, employment was beginning to produce a new kind of African, an African who was thoroughly urbanised, literate, skilled, worthy of respect according to the established standards and as far from the stereotype of the dozy, rural drunk as it was possible to be. In many cases he had the vote, or would soon enough be eligible for it, and the only thing that marked him out as different from white people was the colour of his skin. And as this man rose up the scale of Social Darwinism, it was observed, as both Malan and Sarah Gertrude Millin so forcefully pointed out, that an awful lot of white people were heading in the opposite direction. Already there were black men, like the young Nelson Mandela, growing up in conditions that could hardly be described as lavish but who were, in the matter of educational opportunities, rather better off than many poorer white people. That there was a two-way process of social mobility had long been observed in India and several new castes – for that is effectively what they were – had evolved. The 'Brindians' were those, much like Gandhi, who were almost indistinguishable from upper class Britons in their tastes, education and culture yet remained very largely Indian by race and marriage; the Anglo-Indians were usually the offspring of lower, middle class British officials and soldiers and Indian girls and could often be found as teachers and railwaymen; the Eurasians came further down the scale and were often regarded as degraded, idle scoundrels. In the coloured people and the poor whites, whom Millin found to be increasingly inter-mingled, inter-married and, in her eyes, inter-mangled she found something that revolted her. For those white people who were neither poor nor yet assuredly comfortable, both these groups increasingly came to represent a threat and a warning; a threat because the respectable urban black person was competition for work and wages, a warning because the landless labourer - the *bywoner* - and the poor white scratching out a living on some Godforsaken patch of dry diggings along the Orange river served as a warning of what might happen to those whose elbows were not sharp enough for the Darwinian struggle. So for those whites at the bottom, or of the middling sort, the Colour bar became an attractive (if often uncomfortable) expedient for the protection of their status and standard of living, while for those whites at the top, it was something that could be lived with because it was not practical politics to oppose it; besides which, the people of colour that they came across were usually the educated, the cultured and the radical, who made agreeable dinner party guests but presented no threat to their status or wealth.

J.H. Hofmeyr, nephew of the founder of the *Bond* and a follower of Smuts, was one of those thinkers who saw the way the wind was blowing and didn't much care for it. This brilliant academic was a prodigy, as Smuts had been, and curiously enough shared Smuts' complete ignorance of art or music – Gertie Millin reckoned that he was smarter than Smuts by quite a chalk.[100] A Christian Evangelical, slovenly in appearance throughout his life, he was already in possession of three degrees before he left the Cape for Oxford, aged 18, with his possessive mother in tow (he never married and lived with her throughout his life). Coming back three years later with a Double First, he took up a professorship at the newly formed University of Witwatersrand and two years later, in 1919, he became its Principal. Initially flirting with Herzog's Afrikaaner Nationalism, and then decisively rejecting it, his opening address called for the university to be open to all regardless of class, wealth, race or creed. In 1920, Smuts invited him to visit (his mother came along too) and offered him a job as an organiser for the South Africa Party (which his mother made him refuse). Four years later, after Hofmeyr had dug himself into a hole over sacking a lecturer for being seen out with a young woman who was not his wife (which his mother got him into and out of; they were both terrible gossips; during the war she put it about that Smuts was having it off with a Greek princess), he accepted the post of Administrator of the Transvaal from Smuts. This was supposed to be a non-party post (nothing in the government of South Africa was non-party, really), so when Herzog came in after the election of 1924, Hofmeyr decided to stay on and fought off several attempts to remove him because even though he was Cape Dutch, he was known to be a 'Smuts man' and so not thought sufficiently Afrikaaner; 'Smuts man' began to acquire a similar meaning to the term 'Coconut' used by Left wing racists to describe black and minority ethnic (BAME) Tories; though he gained a reputation as an after-dinner speaker, he was never invited to address any of the Afrikaaner cultural groups. Even so, his talent was recognised and approaches were made from both sides of the political divide for him to join up with one or other party. During the 1929 election, revolted by Herzog's naked racism, he flirted with Smuts but refused the chance of a seat until a by-election vacancy came his way and into parliament he went.

He was not an immediate success but he did immediately find himself on the Select Committee appointed to look into the Native Question; and shortly after he opened the Fort Hare Bantu-European Student Christian Conference with a speech on Unity in Diversity, which was outrageous enough given the times and then seen as even more outrageous when Divine services were held which featured black and white praying together! Even worse! There was to be a rugby match in which black and whites would play against each other! The match was cancelled after widespread protests. That Herzog, Malan and the Nationalist message of *Swartgevaar* – fear of the black man -was reaching a much wider audience than the alternative message of the liberals was obvious; even among intellectuals, the message was weak; an examination of liberal South African values in the book *Coming of Age,* to which Hofmeyr contributed, sold less than 2000 English copies and less than a hundred in Afrikaans. The judgement of one hopeful contributor to the *Spectator's* series of articles on the issue was that opposition to the colour bar had captured the imagination of the youth of South Africa; but that judgement would need to be heavily qualified for it to retain any meaning at all.[101]

Hofmeyr hated the general prejudice against black people and was firmly against the colour bar, that 'outstanding rock of offence in inter-racial relations,'[102] but held the depressed and despairing opinion that 'in South Africa it would seem that white man and coloured man are destined to live side by side in relative separateness, and it is the task of its statesmen to determine how best they shall do so.'[103] And he hated it.

In 1931, he produced a potted History of the Native Question in *South Africa*, a contribution to a series on the problems of the modern world organised by the respected historian H.A.L. Fisher which traced the attempts to deal with what was effectively a clash of civilisations. There had been attempts to re-make black people in the image of Europeans, he argued, attempts to reinforce their tribal structures and identities, attempts to ignore the problem and hope it would go away, attempts to hand the problem to the imperial authorities in London and attempts to wrest control of it back to South Africa, attempts to settle the problem by locations and attempts to settle it by segregation and none of it had worked. What had emerged towards the end of the 19th Century through 'constructive idealism'[104] was the concept of 'differentiation' whereby facilities would be provided for the tribal people to progress and modernise but necessarily at a different pace to that of the European. He

[100] 'Hofmeyr and Havenga.' *The Spectator* 10th December 1948.
[101] C.F Andrews, 'South Africa Today', *The Spectator* 6th June 1931.
[102] J.H. Hofmeyr *South Africa* (London, 1931) p. 171
[103] J.H. Hofmeyr *South Africa* (London, 1931) p.34
[104] J.H. Hofmeyr *South Africa* (London, 1931) p.159

pointed to the Cape Colony's Glen Grey Act of 1894 which encouraged individual, rather than communal, forms of land ownership in the hope of starting the evolution of individual, independent, yeomen farmers but which also set up a system of Native Councils which allowed a wide measure of self-government to the Transkei. This, he thought, was the way forward and contrasted the Cape's ideas with those of the Free State and the Transvaal which were based entirely on subjugation, subordination and dispossession slovenly applied, but to be successful it would need more land to be allocated to the tribal people and though this was supposed to have happened with the 1913 Land Act, lots of people were still waiting. He saw no real hope that this situation would change; trouble was brewing; Malan was hovering; and unless more land could be freed up and 'differentiation' put into practice across the Union then the future could only be 'repression and subjection' rather than 'identity and equality'.[105]   For him, 'differentiation', which today we might associate with multiculturalism, was the only practical solution to the Native Question as it applied to rural areas. Looking at it today, it's hard not to see this idea as just as a softer form of segregation. 'This is the tragedy of Afrikaaner politics,' declared Alan Paton. 'That the most able men devote their lives drawing up blueprints for the impossible.'[106]

Hofmeyr's warnings about the danger posed by Native labour were also stark. The white 'aristocracy of labour' could only justify the high level of their wages by ensuring that the black people were kept to a correspondingly low level and the alternative of raising Native wages to a better level would bankrupt the mining industry on which the whole economy, black, white, coloured or Asian, depended. Here was a terrible dilemma that admitted of no easy solution.

> '…the native has become the essential prop of the white man's industry. Remove that prop by precipitate action, and the whole structure, constructed as it has been in the assumption of its presence, will crash to ruin.'[107]

Hofmeyr, however, was inclined to the view that only by gradually raising native wages could the wider problems of South Africa's economic ills be addressed. Only by raising the level of demand in the home market could over-dependence on mining be avoided, only by breaking down the colour bar would increased competition make *all* richer – including the poor whites who were such a feature of the Union landscape. In this, he was clear that socialist protection was the handmaid of segregation and denying the chance of advancement to two thirds of the population of South Africa was simply iniquitous. It was also iniquitous that educated natives should labour under political and social disadvantage too but, still, Hofmeyr reckoned that segregation in the social and marriage spheres was really the only practical way to approach the problem under the circumstances of the times. In adopting the image of black and white living in harmony as keys on a piano (*pace* Wacko Jacko and Paul McCartney), Hofmeyr rejected repression as the way forward, but accepted that 'constructive segregation' was the road on which South Africa was travelling.

And he hated it. In 1936, when Herzog sought to solve the Native Question by pushing for greater segregation by abolishing the colour-blind Cape Franchise, (an act supported by Smuts who feared that unless Herzog was given his head, his followers would not support Britain against the rising threat of Hitler), Hofmeyr, now a minister in the Herzog-Smuts Fusion government, went out on a limb to oppose it. In this he was supported by a growing body of white opinion who were increasingly coming to the realisation that if there was anything to Social Darwinism then it had to be admitted that the emergence of the civilised native entitled him to civilised rights. The Bill, Hofmeyr argued, was based on a profound fear of black people, a fear that was misplaced and retreating into laager was no way to address that fear of the future; putting black people onto a separate electoral roll and allowing only indirect representation through the Secretary for Native Affairs got rid of ancient rights, was not fair play, deprived good people of the right of a say in what went on and was, at bottom, an abuse of the power that white people were in possession of. Hofmeyr the Afrikaner seemed to have imbibed more than a love of cricket from his contact with the English. It was no use; the Bill passed, exceeding the two-thirds majority needed to make the constitutional changes needed by a comfortable margin.

---

[105] J.H. Hofmeyr *South Africa* (London, 1931) p. 172
[106] Paton, *South African Tragedy* p.120
[107] J.H. Hofmeyr *South Africa* (London, 1931) p. 242

Curiously enough, the passage of the Bill and Hofmeyr's opposition to it appeared to galvanise white liberal opinion in a way that no-one before had thought possible. The *Rand Daily Mail* supported him and said that he represented the future, rather than the old men who filled up the benches in parliament. He was 'painfully inching his way towards emancipation, with fear and caution, but not without courage.'[108] In 1937, he made public his opposition to a ban on mixed marriages, not because he approved of them but because he thought that the government should stay out of such personal affairs, and further opposed more restrictions on both Indian traders and Jewish immigration. And then, at Fort Hare, he leaped straight into the unknown by rejecting the idea of separate development altogether and opposing in parliament Herzog's Native Law Amendment Act which would turn the towns into a hostile environment for any black person, make it impossible to settle with a family there and make him utterly subservient to his employer through a more severe application of the Pass Laws than anything yet seen.

Yet he was wriggling by now, achieving nothing by staying inside the government and justifying himself only by saying that things would be much worse without him being there; he was kept on by Herzog because he outclassed everyone else at running his departments (Social Welfare, Mines, Labour, Interior and Education, all at once in 1937). The wriggling came to an end after the election of 1938, when he could take no more of Herzog's policy towards non-whites and he resigned and instantly became the darling of the 100,000 (according to Alan Paton) white liberals who had had enough of Herzog's policies towards non-white people too. There was talk of him leading a new Liberal Party. It might have been. It might have worked. Apartheid might have been avoided. But it was not and another ideological monster was midwifed into the world, this time by Hitler and Malan.

*

The background to the rise of segregation, the colour bar, the Purified National Party and ultimately Apartheid cannot be understood without looking at what was happening to black people. This was recognised at the time in the *Report of the Native Economic Commission* 1930-32, a quite remarkable in depth look into the conditions of rural poverty faced by black people that was, despite its title, part sociological, part anthropological, part *faux-* historical and part political that owed a lot to the 1905 Report. An admirable piece of research, it was part and parcel of that sympathetic, paternal and realistic Conservatism that lay at the heart of the *Pax Britannica*. In its openness to fair-minded debate on a very complicated issue, very many dissenting opinions on the situation were given a fair hearing and a hard-hitting 57 page protesting Addendum included. The influence of Social Darwinism in its thinking is still unmistakeable, but there is much that could come out of any development economists' handbook and very much that the modern multiculturalist would find difficult to disagree with. What makes it different from the 1905 Report is that there is a very strong sense that black people are on the cusp of breaking through into that civilisation which was for so long the desire of missionaries, colonial authorities and liberals, but the form of that civilisation will be different in important respects from that of the European; and that difference was, indeed, seen to be a good thing because it represented an African contribution. There are also strong indications that segregation was *not* a settled and accepted part of South African life and that very strong sections of opinion were very definitely against it; non-segregated neighbourhoods like Martindale, Sophiatown, Vrededorp and Doornfontein in Joburg were reasonably common. Perhaps indicative of this attitude was the fact that the appellation 'Kaffir', a term that was now beginning to acquire the unpleasant connotations that it retains today, was replaced throughout by 'Native'. This *was* the *Pax Britannica* in operation.

Before diving in, we need some context. Firstly, going by its own figures, the NEC estimated that the economy of South Africa was worth £186m while Britain's was worth £4bn. This is just to remind us that South Africa was still a poor country. Next, although the condition of the African peasant left much to be desired, it was still better by a country mile than that of the contemporary Russian peasant who was undergoing collectivisation, several purges, mass murder and deliberate starvation. Third, the population of South Africa doubled from roughly five million people to ten million between 1904 -1936 with blacks making up roughly 70%, whites roughly 20%, Asians 2% and coloureds 8% of the population. In 1912 alone, in Natal and Zululand, the birth

---

[108] *South African Tragedy*, p.193

rate exceeded the death rate by 984,320 souls bringing the population there to nearly a million.[109] It was moving too; in the same period, the urban populations increased by a third, with the number of Africans moving to the towns doubling; Joburg grew fastest, doubling to one million souls between 1921-36. It is important to keep these things in mind because otherwise it's all too easy to slip into the mind-set of rich whites running a capitalist system designed to oppress poor blacks. As I've already hinted, it wasn't the capitalist system causing the problems but the Nationalists and socialists' attempts to hamper its natural tendency to solve those problems most efficiently.

Cattle and Environmental Degradation.

The Commission began by recognising that the root of African poverty lay in the Reserves and that the task before them was how best to lead the vast majority of Africans who lived in them onwards into civilisation and participation in a prosperous capitalist economy, without so alienating the white population as to rule out any sort of progress from the realms of practical politics. Recognising that there were several cultural factors which impeded the creation of wealth by raising barriers to innovation and trade, they pointed first of all to the question of cattle. For the Africans, cattle were more than meat on the hoof, a store of wealth, a commodity to be traded or the necessary wherewithal for *lobola*, they were an end in themselves, all of which meant, in economic terms, that they were a complete waste of resources. On top of this, agriculture was hindered by the lack of modern equipment and ignorance of farming methods that had been adopted in European agriculture since medieval times (and a whole world away from the mass production that Smuts witnessed in America in 1929; maize yields per acre were only half those of the USA and Argentina); crop rotation was unknown, manure was used for fuel not fertiliser and ploughing was done with hoes rather than proper ploughshares pulled by oxen. Fences to preserve pasture were rare and so, as the herds grew, due largely to the successes of European veterinary science, over-stocking became critical; in the past, this had been solved by trekking or conquest of a neighbouring tribe but a mixture of quarantine regulations, the strictures of the 1913 Land Act and the *Pax Britannica* ruled out these options. By 1930, an environmental disaster was in the making as over-grazing reduced and loosened the top soil so that it washed away with the rains, the grass then being replaced by weeds. Unless Africans could be induced to see their cattle – and for the most part they were inferior breeds known as 'scrub cattle' – as slaughter animals, then the desertification that was well advanced in the Cis- and Transkei would produce famine in the very near future. Already, there was a problem with malnutrition in rural areas and it was often found necessary for an industrial employer to feed up a newly arrived worker before he could be employed at heavy labour for fear of scurvy. What was more, those Africans who could see the writing on the wall were often deserting the Reserves because the traditional authority of the chiefs and the communal nature of *uBuntu* – what the Commissioners called 'social communism' – effectively prevented them from innovating or becoming independent farmers and this then brought them into competition with poor whites, who resented them (Smuts himself had a problem with white *bywoners* squatting on his farm). 'The magnitude of the problem,' the Commissioners insisted. 'Was appalling'[110] and unless the problem was dealt with as a matter of urgency, 'outraged nature will exact her penalty and drive us off the land.'[111]

The answer, argued the Commissioners, lay in developing the Reserves into agricultural powerhouses by deploying specially trained agricultural 'demonstrators' who were to gain the sympathy, encouragement and support of the chiefs, without whom there could be no hope of change, for agricultural reform; 'doctoring' the fields, would be replaced by manuring them, better cattle breeds would produce more milk and more of them should be eaten or sold; afforestation and irrigation programmes should be started; communal landholding should be waived for those farmers who wanted to be independent; arable farming should be encouraged; scattered huts should be consolidated into villages; Co-ops and Credit Unions should be encouraged; home industries should be started. Addressing the problem of over-stocking was a priority; there were nearly two million goats, three million sheep, one and a half million cattle, and a hundred and twenty five thousand horses munching through the pasturage of the Transkei Reserves – and these figures were rapidly increasing. Roughly speaking, there were twice as many animals as the available grazing would bear and what was left was being

---

[109] CO 633/32 Native Affairs Department Report 1912
[110] *Report of the Native Economic Commission 1930-32* para.116
[111] *Report of the Native Economic Commission 1930-32* para. 278

destroyed by too many goats. If anything, the donkeys would have to go; in the Transkei Reserves alone there were nearly 9000 of them (it tastes awful and as a pack animal it leaves much to be desired, being so small. Mules are much better but I don't know what they taste like).

As would the Native Land Act 1913. The Commission came out against segregation of land because it violated the principle of free competition and that areas like the Transkei would benefit from being farmed by Europeans using European methods. They did, however, admit that segregation did prevent land being ripped off from Natives through sharp practice by European land speculators. However, preventing black people from buying land was a major cause of discontent and there was a well-founded suspicion that the Act was indeed just legal cover for a rip-off – a suspicion that was given a major boost by the fact that it was *not* applied in the Cape Colony and that promises of more land for Native occupation had gone unfulfilled. The only way that the Land Act could really be justified, said the Commission, was if proper agricultural education had been introduced in order to make better use of the land.

Adaptation or Assimilation?

There was also a strong recognition that no development or civilisation could take place without the active co-operation of the chiefs and that building on established custom and practice was the most reasonable and economical way to achieve it. This conclusion was fundamental because it contained within it the ideological choice of '*Adaptation – not Assimilation*'[112] as the policy by which the Natives could be drawn into the higher standard of living represented by modern capitalism, individual liberty and parliamentary democracy. The thinking on how this could be done, according to the Commission, had developed into the *repressionist* approach (keeping the Native in his present state), *assimilation* (turning him into a black European) and *adaptation*; 'taking out of the Bantu past what is good, and even what is merely neutral, and together with what is good of European culture for the *Abantu*, building up a Bantu future.'[113] This is a question that is still debated by development economists and multiculturalists today and the answer as to who is right depends entirely upon your political point of view; while it is observable that the more Leftwards one travels, the more *adaptationist* is the view, *assimilation* often seems to be the preferred option taken by those being adapted, especially when it comes to the material, educational and medical aspects of Western civilisation; 'You should value your own culture,' says the Western Aid worker: 'We want what you have and don't seem to value,' comes the all too frequent reply. The Commission came down firmly on the more gradual and consensual approach involved in *adaptation* and argued that major mistakes had been made in dealing with the Natives because Bantu culture had not been taken sufficiently into account and, indeed, much opposition to what were sensible agricultural measures (quarantine and culling of infected herds) had been engendered by working against the grain of Bantu institutions rather than along it. The influence of the Chiefs ought to be noted, respected and utilised, according to the Commission, and in this way mutual trust could be built up.

Here again the good sense of the conservative outlook was in evidence in that while the Commission recognised the theory and recognised that the theory was desirable, what they refused to do was inflict any grand theory of *Assimilation/Adaptation* onto local conditions where it did not apply. In the Transkei, the chiefs and institutions of the Bantu had survived intact but in the Ciskei they had disintegrated and there was no good reason why they should be re-imposed against the wishes of the inhabitants. Nor should greater powers be accorded to the uneducated or the more ignorant of the chiefs but, where they were men of intelligence and education, they should be encouraged; Native Courts, recognised as being more effective in administering tribal law by the 1927 Native Administration Act, should be strengthened; more use should be made of local languages – especially by European officials; chiefs should take over administrative functions such as recording Births, Marriages and Deaths; be responsible for medical and veterinary regulations; perhaps they ought also to be allowed to collect some local taxes? The grounds for optimism should be recognised and built on; Agricultural colleges, magazines and demonstration farms were having an effect; the Transkei was now exporting grain and tools; machinery, manuring, fallowing and fertilizers were becoming more common. Under no circumstances, though, should the seriousness of the problem be discounted: 'It is now a race between the enlightenment of the Native and the complete destruction of his land.'[114]

---

[112] *Report of the Native Economic Commission* para.199
[113] *Report of the Native Economic Commission* para. 200

Urban Life.

In considering the situation of those black people who had decided that urban life represented a better future than the one on offer in the countryside, the Commissioners began by considering the workings of the Urban Areas Acts of 1923 and 1930. These Acts had attempted to improve conditions in the towns by clearing away the slums and introducing better housing in segregated areas, a process that had thrown up a whole range of related and largely unforeseen problems. Conditions in the slums had long been a source of concern; ramshackle building, overcrowding, rack-renting, lack of clean water, air, light and decent sanitation were all features of rapid urbanisation and the 'squalor, misery and vice'[115] of Cape Town, Joburg, Durban or Port Elizabeth were no different from London, Birmingham or Paris in this respect. Then, as now; 'informal settlements' are a feature of many parts of South Africa and are mainly the product of an exploding population. Various reports had looked into the issue, but it was the regular and routine outbreaks of TB (1914), influenza (1918) and the spread of malaria down the Durban coast that made local authorities embark on slum clearance programmes. Some of the programmes, such as those at East London and Bloemfontein, were marked successes complete with hospitals, sports, church and educational facilities but in other places, strenuous objections were raised about labourers being moved considerable distances away from their habitual places of work. What was quite striking was the scale of the segregation; in the Transvaal, twenty three towns, including Pretoria and most of the Rand barred the residence of Natives entirely and Joburg admitted them only in parts; in the Cape, there were sixteen, including Cape Town, Kimberley, King William's Town; in the Free State, nine, including Bloemfontein; only in Natal was there any reluctance to embrace segregation where just three towns were segregated completely.

Many of the problems of the new locations arose with the question of cost. The terms of the Urban Areas Act effectively precluded private capital being employed in building better dwellings because the trade unions used the colour bar to prevent black people from doing the skilled work necessary. This meant that the cost of construction forced rents up to an unfeasibly high level and so made any private scheme unprofitable unless tenants were piled up and stacked three high. In order to prevent the problems of overcrowding replicating themselves, therefore, the municipal authorities were forced to subsidise the rent and thus did they begin to object, like Canute, to the growing tide of new arrivals from the countryside; Joburg spent £600,000, Cape Town £264,000 and across the country another £300,000 was taken out in loans for improved housing. Often, resentment at these costs resulted in opposition to segregation, or in new housing being built without street lighting, without proper sanitation and a reliance on standpipes; and too often, not enough of them. There were also complaints about the 'drab, sometimes hideous, uniformity of many municipally built locations'[116] (something that the architects of Britain's 1960s Council Estates drew great inspiration from; no doubt the crony contractors and slap-dash unionised workers were involved too) which led the Commission to the view that the only way to end this expensive and wasteful socialist perversion of good intentions into bad solutions was to make the colour bar illegal inside the segregated areas.

If this was challenging to the National Party, then the Commission's musings on the urban labour problem were explosive. Firstly, because white workers, who were presumed to be skilled or semi-skilled, were paid anything up to six times more than black workers, the majority of whom were presumed to be unskilled, the pressure was always on businesses to replace white workers with black ones. What was more, because there was a steady stream of unskilled black workers coming into the towns, the urban black could not increase his earning capacity because he was in turn undercut; in the early 1930s, a monthly wage of £6 was reckoned to be necessary for a black family on the Witwatersrand but the average wage was about half that and malnutrition was an observable fact as a result. It also meant there was no money for school fees, a situation that contributed to the appearance of *amalayta* gangs of petty criminal youths, prostitution and the illegal brewing and sale of liquor. This implied that poverty and all the degradation, crime and vice that went with it was actually being created by the colour bar; it also implied that the lack of demand for more and better products that comes with rising wages was actively holding back business in general. The report's Addendum reinforced this view of the

---

[114] *Report of the Native Economic Commission* para.349
[115] *Report of the Native Economic Commission* Annex.15
[116] *Report of the Native Economic Commission* para.497

colour bar. A process of legal chicanery had managed to prevent black people from being classed as 'employees' and so debarred them from joining trade unions (though not in the Cape Colony: racism is always ragged). The provisions of the Master and Servant Act and the Native Labour Regulation Act also made it virtually impossible for a black man or group of workers to go on strike, union or no union, while the 1924 Industrial Conciliation Act gave the powers to set the wages and hours of black people to employers and trade unions. This meant that coloured, white or Indian trade unions were able to protect their interests by selling out those of the blacks, an occurrence that was not infrequent. In the matter of apprenticeships, the colour bar was enforced by setting the educational standards at a level that few black teenagers could reasonably be expected to reach given the available opportunities. All of this was iniquitous in the eyes of the Commission and it recommended that the Cape Colony's example, where black people were being allowed into trade unions, should be followed if there was to be any hope at all of getting wages up.

This was good, solid, capitalist thinking at its best; whereas there might be a case for segregation on cultural or social grounds, there was absolutely none on economic grounds; 'economic principles are not affected by differences of race or colour'[117] thundered the Commission. Indeed, there were very great objections to the colour bar on Social Darwinist grounds too for if the Native could not get on in life, he could not achieve the improved level of civilisation that was so desired and the friendly association of the different races would never be achieved. The only way to solve this problem, considered the Commission, was to develop the Reserves to reduce the flow of cheap rural labour and so allow the free market to force up the wages of urban black people. *That said*, the Commission decided that it was not practical politics to end the Colour bar at the present time because it would lead to a collapse in white living standards. This was a conclusion that brought forth two very strong dissenting opinions, first from Dr. Roberts and then from Mr. Lucas:

> Dr. Roberts wishes to state that there are two cardinal principles which should govern the movement and employment of all citizens of the Union, namely freedom of movement, and freedom of occupation; and that to endeavour to limit the occupation or the movement of Natives is therefore an infringement of their rights as citizens of the land.[118]

> The colour bar is looked upon by the Natives as depriving them of a fundamental right to develop their own powers and to employ them lawfully as they please. It affords plentiful ammunition for Natives who speak and write against Europeans, and in this way does harm which far outweighs any possible advantage which it could secure for the European workman.[119]

Education.

By 1930, education was beginning to have an effect on black lives in a way that had been all but absent before. There was a growing recognition of the importance of literacy and a desire for more education; in the towns especially, adults were getting together to teach each other and parents were making great sacrifices to get some sort of education for their children. Business was recognising that an educated Native was of much more value than an illiterate one and that the increased competition that they represented provided a spur for white people to make more of an effort. It was also recognised that educated people were better for the economy because they produced more wealth and that the colour bar was hampering the creation of wealth by restricting labour competition.

The existing schools were run by a bewildering array of missionaries – Trappists, Moravians, Church of England, Baptist, Presbyterian, Germans, Americans, Swedes to name but a few - but the demand was rapidly outstripping the supply and by 1925 the government was beginning to be more and more involved. The aim was to provide basic and vocational education for the masses, enough literacy to provide for the brighter chaps as clerks, teacher training for a few more and higher education for those at the very top to prepare them for entry to Fort Hare college, established in 1916 to provide a university level education. This was in keeping with

---

[117] *Report of the Native Economic Commission* para.1054
[118] *Report of the Native Economic Commission* para.847
[119] *Report of the Native Economic Commission* para. 850

educational thinking in many other parts of the world at that time and not particularly indicative of any racial motives; the Commission found that the educational content was deemed to be satisfactory by the Natives, the main grievance being concerned with the inadequate scale of the provision. The Commission, however, took a very different view of what 'satisfactory' constituted; there were 300,000 pupils in school, but less than a third of these ever progressed beyond the most basic level, largely because the students were not taught in their own language and class sizes were in the higher nineties. This was a problem because black Africans insisted on being taught in English and regarded any attempt to differentiate the education given to their children from that given to white children as foisting a second-rate product on them. They wanted to learn English because that was the way to get a job; the Commission believed in education as development of the intellectual faculties; again the debate as to whether education should be about preparing people for the workplace or for personal development is still live today.

An even greater problem was the fact that only 20% of children were actually in school and of these only 0.5% were reaching the highest levels. What was more, the cost of providing for the missing 80% was reckoned to be beyond the capacity of the government to pay so the Commission came to the conclusion that in the circumstances the best that could be done was to press for education in the vernacular, expand the output of well-educated teachers and college level graduates 'to lead their people on the upward march'[120] and provide greater economic opportunities so that in the future, black people would have enough money to pay for more education. That this was an unsatisfactory solution the Commission recognised by foregrounding the dissenting opinions of its members who stated that the costs to the economy of not educating the Native were higher in the long run; there were unfilled posts in the civil service for want of educated candidates; there were shortages of doctors yet no medical college places for black students; and that white people had more to fear from a growling, illiterate, discontented mob than from an industrious, educated class of working people.

Taxation.

This brought the Commission to the question of taxation. For historical reasons, two distinct systems of taxation were operating; the Europeans paid income tax, while the Natives paid a poll or hut tax; both paid sales taxes. This had worked well up until urbanisation, capitalism and industrialisation had produced a steady population of urbanised black people who were now complaining that they were paying a poll tax that was, in effect, much higher than their European neighbours' income taxes. The main report of the Commission recognised that attempting to change the tax system was way beyond their competence but in the Addendum, plenty of evidence was included to indicate just how unjust the system was; in the Transkei, a virtually self-sufficient European farmer with 6,000 acres paid no income tax at all, but the Native with two acres was paying 30 shillings a year in Hut Tax; Europeans, Asiatics, coloureds and blacks might all live in cheek by jowl poverty on the diggings but only the black man had to pay taxes; an urban black would be paying taxes in his old Reserve area from which he gained no benefit. What was worse, the need to pay the hut tax in notes and coins meant that rural blacks were forced off the land and into the towns where they could obtain work – thus driving down wages and preventing the wider creation of wealth.

Pass Laws, Booze Laws and Trading Licences.

The Commission next considered the state of race relations; the main report put on a pair of rose-coloured spectacles and saw much to be pleased about in the way that black and white were co-operating in difficult economic circumstances and tended to dismiss the criticisms raised by black people as being the idle noise of a discontented few spending too much time reading idiotic statements in the newspapers. That said, there was a recognition that there was a rising black nationalism which needed to be acknowledged and as far as segregation was concerned, the Commission was generally for separating urban residential areas and against much in the way of inter-marriage or social mixing. As far as the Pass Laws were concerned, the Commission divided into those who thought that some sort of identity card was a useful thing and necessary to prevent a flood of rural blacks into the slums and those who thought they should be abolished immediately as being an outrageous infringement of civil liberties. The Pass Laws were unwieldy, irritating, vexatious and complex, frequently abused by the police, a standing insult to respectable men and women who were thereby forced to endure the

---

[120] *Report of the Native Economic Commission* para. 638.

petty attentions of every little local official Hitler with a clipboard and an inflated idea of his own importance, and criminalising large numbers of people who could in no other sense be regarded as criminals; getting a job meant first applying for a Pass; very often, a curfew was in force and an additional Pass was required to go out in it; there were 43,000 convictions for violations in 1930. The Cape Colony Pass Laws had been abolished years ago, they argued, and no deleterious effects had been felt that were not also present in areas like the Transvaal where the Pass Laws were strictly enforced (9000 convictions alone in 1912)[121] and as they were bitterly resented by black people, they should not be tolerated. At the very least, wide exemptions should be made for educated people and women should not have to carry them at all as it gave the police too many excuses for importuning them.

Much the same view was taken of the liquor laws; prohibition had failed and the fact that brewing the favoured low alcohol Native beer could not be done in secret meant that the bootleggers had turned to more potent forms of hooch that could be and respect for the law had suffered accordingly; 41% of European convictions were for selling liquor to Natives; there were 52,000 booze related convictions of Natives in 1930 alone. In Natal, a policy of providing beer in government monopoly beer halls had been instituted but these had proved unpopular because home-brewing was much preferred. The Commission recommended that pretty much all restrictions on brewing the preferred, weak *utywala* should be lifted as impractical, onerous and counter-productive.

This would no doubt have come as a welcome boon to a whole new class of black Africans – the small traders and entrepreneurs vital to a prosperous society. In rural areas, for historical reasons, most shops were in the hands of European traders who were granted a monopoly in a particular area (usually five miles diameter) and, as the money economy was so small, a great deal of the business was based on barter. With the coming of the motor lorry and the mail order catalogue, this was beginning to change and the Commission came out very much in favour of allowing more and more Natives to obtain trading licences; free trade would enrich all. It was in the urban areas that this new class were more commonly to be seen and it was the opinion of the Commission that these should be encouraged by the reduction in the cost of the trading licences and also by ending the colour bar which operated against them; not a single general traders licence had been issued to a black person in the Orange Free State.

The Condition of the People.

Here then is the condition that the black African found himself in twenty years after the establishment of the Union. If he lived in the countryside, he was staring at an environmental disaster in the making, the reasons for which he ascribed to white rule and the end of the 'good old days', even though in terms of peace and material well-being, things were better than at any other time in his History. Living in poverty, he had to make periodical trips to the towns to look for work in order to pay his taxes or afford such other items as the expanding market enticed him with. Such trips necessitated being away from home for anything up to ten months of the year, living in conditions that might vary from the utterly squalid, to the segregated and expensive, to the compound system where he ran the dual risks of catching TB from his fellow workers or VD from the rampant homosexual activity that grew up in the absence of women. He would know hardship and hunger, face harassment from the police for his pass and his beer, be refused employment opportunities by the trade unions and know no job security at all. If he chose not to return home, the bright lights of the city might give him freedom from tribal and family authority, but it would not free him from the other impositions he laboured under and, being increasingly literate and increasingly aware that his state was neither natural nor necessarily permanent, he was beginning to perceive that the white man's world was rigged against him; and that he had no real means of redress because his own unions were weak, divided and too often corrupt. His spiritual leaders were much the same, too often giving in to millenarian insanity which manifested itself in pig killing sprees (don't ask) or, worse, confrontations with the police such as the one at Bullhoek which ended in gunfire. Those who would be his political leaders were paralysed too, unsure of whether they should represent black people as a whole or just specific tribes, challenge the headmen and rural Native Councils for power or join with like-minded white people in pushing for socialism, communism or democracy.

---

[121] CO 633/32 Native Affairs Department Report 1912. Report of the Director of Native Labour.

*

Anyone who is familiar with some of the larger parts of our country will also know the sight that so often can be met on our dusty roads – the dilapidated half tent-wagon with the tatters fluttering in the wind, and harnessed to it a team of six or eight emaciated, tottering donkeys. After a few years' experience, one does not need to enquire anymore to know that the white driver with his listless posture and the neglected woman with her dull eyes are probably not members of a church, and are either completely unable to read and write, or can only do so poorly, and that the half-a-dozen uncombed and unwashed children have never seen a church from the inside – let alone a school ... They are the nomadic wandering type. Of every industry they know something. They do not have a firm understanding of anything. They are willing to do all kinds of work. None of which they can do well. Thus, they move from farm to farm, complaining bitterly about anyone who gave them work and accommodation on his farm, while the employer, in turn, complains bitterly about their unreliability, dishonesty and rudeness, and assures you emphatically that he would rather work with coloured people a hundred times over.

D.F. Malan, 1916.[122]

In the midst of all this there was a socio-economic, socio-political problem...the houtkappers. Over many generations from the time of the original woodcutters' posts there developed a breed of White people in the Outeniqualand forests isolated from the outside world and having their own way of life. They formed a reclusive society...inbred and decadent in the extreme...they developed a fear of the civilisation crowding around their retreat.

Arthur Nimmo, remembering contact during the 1930s.[123]

The poverty, distress, malnutrition, and housing, overcrowding, illiteracy, immorality, drink, lack of medical and dental facilities among the Coloureds and Poor Whites must be seen to be believed.

Chairman of the Divisional Council for Knysna, 1943.[124]

That there were pockets of prosperity in South Africa after the end of the South African War - mainly on the Rand, Cape Town and in those areas producing agricultural goods for export - could not mask the fact that most people, both black and white, lived in conditions of poverty or hardship. The *Pax Britannica* had removed the threat of starvation and had improved the condition of the people from one of extreme precariousness to one where the possibility of future improvement was more than a reasonable hope for those with good jobs in the mines, railways and farms but life was still hard and drought still feared. Spain, Italy and Ireland were still ahead of South Africa in terms of GDP and Argentina, Australia, New Zealand and Canada were far, far in advance and for the country's poor white population life seemed bleak. The ever decreasing size of their inherited smallholdings could not sustain life, their lack of education and skills meant that they were not much use in the skilled labour market of the mines and thus forced to compete for work on unfavourable terms with blacks and coloured people. On top of this, the expectation that they should live a 'civilised' lifestyle that they could not afford ate at their sense of self-respect. During the hard times of the 1920s, very many of them were dependent on public work schemes, existing as a steady pool of discontented voters, with the 'no better than a Kaffir' label hung around their necks.

For much of the 19th Century in Britain, the alleviation of poverty had centred around the concept of caring for the 'deserving' poor – those who were in straightened circumstance through sickness, old age or circumstances that were no fault of their own – and compelling the feckless, idle or drunk 'undeserving' poor to work for such benefits as were doled out to them. This eminently sensible system had been strengthened around the turn of the century by the introduction of social insurance schemes, the introduction of old age pensions and other such measures but increasingly the idea that the state should bear the primary responsibility for the welfare of its citizens was gaining credence. This was in part driven by genuine concern and philanthropy and in part by fear

---

[122] Quoted in Lindie Korf, *D.F. Malan: a political biography*. University of Stellenbosh Ph.D Thesis, 2010.
[123] A. Nimmo, *The Knysna Story* (Wynberg, 1976) p.96
[124] A. Nimmo, *The Knysna Story* (Wynberg, 1976) p. 117

of rising trade union radicalism and in 1909, Lloyd George's 'People's Budget' elevated and entrenched the principle that the state should tax and spend for the purpose of alleviating poverty. Hand in hand with this development was the equally radical idea that it was the state's responsibility to manage the economy rather than merely mitigate the distortions and dislocations inevitably produced by the free play of economic forces. This was the beginning of European Social Democracy; that this would ultimately be ruinous concerned those who set out on this path not at all because they rejected Edmund Burke's idea of a compact between the dead, the living and the unborn in favour of 'jam today and kick the empty jar down the road'. What few of them foresaw, excepting the revolutionaries, was that the expansion of the state into ever more areas of life laid the foundations for those in command of the state to pervert it to their own ends either by the simple expedient of bribing the electorate with their own (or other people's) money, or seizing control of it by *coup*.

This is essentially the road that Herzog set out on during the 1920s - with the important proviso that his version of the Burkian compact excluded those parts of South African society that weren't white. He intended to use the full machinery of government to succour the poor whites, give social security and well paid settled jobs to white workers in the towns and tax the Jewish and English capitalists of the mining industry to achieve this. A slew of reports followed (including the 1932 Native Economic Commission) but perhaps the most important innovation was the establishment of a Department of Labour whose brief was to make sure white workers were protected and give the state control over the capitalists. Old Age Pensions, Disability Pensions, Unemployment and Child benefits, rent-controlled housing followed while nationalised industries like ISCOR (steel) and ESCOM (electricity) were added to the existing government portfolio of railways, ports and harbours which, along with tariff barriers, were all aimed at expanding an economy that would provide more benefits and better paid jobs for white workers. By the late 1930s, roughly 20% of government expenditure went on welfare.[125]

The dangers of this essentially anti-capitalist approach were laid out in the 1925 Mills Report. While white workers were being paid far in excess of what their counterparts in London, California or Australia were earning, according to the mine owners, many of those white workers were less skilled than their international counterparts, did less work and were often employed in uneconomic supervisory roles. At the same time, although African wages were admittedly not particularly low in global terms - they were roughly the same as Italian and five times higher than Indian - the Commission argued that in South Africa, African wages were being kept low because white wages were being kept high. A similar situation existed on the railways but because they were a government monopoly the true cost of inflated wages for white workers was disguised because they were passed on to the travelling public or the taxpayer. The answer, according to the Mills Report was to get rid of the colour bar and reduce the enormous wage differentials between skilled and unskilled work.[126]

This was, of course, sound economic sense. Subsidising jobs goes against economic reality and sooner or later, that reality would bite. All that would be needed to collapse such a house of cards would be greater efficiency from Californian gold miners producing cheaper gold and the Joburg mining houses, which already operated on the wafer thin profit margin of 4%, would go under or require major subsidies themselves. However, the other members of the Mills Commission gave the view that white workers needed higher wages so that they could maintain a 'civilised' standard of living and that everyone should get higher wages paid for by cutting the dividends paid to foreigners. Mozambican labourers should also be excluded from the mines so that the wages of South African labourers would be forced up and more white workers would be encouraged to come to South Africa and so prevent white society from being 'swamped'. This, of course, was not sound economic sense.

But it did look like sound economic sense to many people at the time because, as a result of government planning and control of the economy and the massive expansion of industry consonant on WWII, between 1933-1945 South Africa enjoyed a boom that saw GDP double, wages for all sections of the population increase, a doubling of industrial employment, an expansion of the welfare state, the repayment of government debt, the accumulation of reserves and the running of budget surpluses; it was noted that even black people were beginning to redefine poverty as being *relative* to what other people had, rather than what they had had before.

[125] Jeremy Seekings, *The Carnegie Commission and the backlash against Welfare-State building in South Africa 1931-37,* Centre for Social Science Research UCT May 2006.
[126] Nicoli Nattrass and Jeremy Seekings, *The Economy and Poverty in Twentieth Century South Africa,* Centre for Social Science Research UCT July 2010.

It also saw a massive expansion of the government to manage all these things; by 1945, the government controlled steel, electricity, rail and maritime transport; welfare and pensions; a variety of Commissions controlled industrial development, agriculture, labour supply, wages and prices; also, arbitration of industrial disputes. Much of this growth in government power was driven by rather liberal idealists who saw the key to poverty alleviation, racial harmony, material welfare and a just society in the efficient utilisation of resources by the planning power of the state and in this they resembled the mild socialists of Attlee's Labour Party in Britain and, to a lesser extent, Roosevelt's New Dealers. The resolutely reformist Social and Economic Planning Council declared that;

> Rising social and economic standards and increasing opportunities need not threaten the economic security of the European groups; on the contrary, the ill-health, ignorance and poverty of the non-Europeans constitute a drag of immense proportions on the whole economy of the country, to the detriment of all races. Poor social conditions produce inefficiency, disease and crime, which affect the whole community.[127]

The flaw in their thinking was that they could not imagine state power as anything but benign.

*

---

[127] Quoted in Nicoli Nattrass and Jeremy Seekings, *The Economy and Poverty in Twentieth Century South Africa*, Centre for Social Science Research UCT July 2010.

When the African-American athletes went to the Berlin Olympics in Hitler's Germany in 1936, they were surprised to find that they were treated rather well and sometimes with more consideration that they received at home. It might be tempting to dismiss this as a function of the huge PR stunt that those games were, but their conclusions were echoed by WEB Du Bois, the first African-American to get a Ph.D from Harvard, who stayed on after the games on a study tour and reported that Germans were not naturally colour prejudiced.[128] This pretty much goes to prove that racism is not some naturally occurring feature in the DNA of white people. Nor, I might add, is it an inevitable concomitant of capitalism and even less is it some form of Original Sin. It has to be taught and it was D.F. Malan and the Nationalist Party who understood this and went about teaching it properly and systematically.

When Herzog came to power in 1924, his principal object was to regain full independence for the Boer Republics but having seen the Union formed, his vision morphed into full independence for a united South Africa under Afrikaaner control: Africa for the Afrikanders, no less. ('Africander' and 'Afrikander' fell out of use in the early 20th Century in favour of plain, old 'Afrikaaner; they share the same meaning to all intents and purposes). The 1914 rebels were released from jail, Afrikaans given equal status with Dutch and English and bilingualism in the public services was pushed and the South African flag – a symbolic mixture of the republican and British - was raised to equal status with the Union Jack. What surprised him was that in all these respects he was pushing at an open door; Britain had no more interest in directing the development of South Africa in 1925 than she had in 1899 - as long as the routes to India were secure. Herzog had, of course, been among those Bitter-enders who had not been able to see beyond their own noses in this respect but when the 1926 Balfour Declaration and the 1931 Statute of Westminster effectively accorded independence to Australia, New Zealand, Canada and South Africa by declaring that the British Empire was now the British Commonwealth, a free association of nations, Herzog reckoned that his job was done. Indeed, when he looked at the terms he understood that South Africa stood more to gain inside the Commonwealth – access to markets, capital, the still vital Bills of Lading and Exchange and the protection of the Royal Navy – than outside it and had the clause in the National Party constitution which committed them to independence removed. This was not met with complete joy, it has to be said, by D.F. Malan.

Instead, Herzog and the Labour Party focussed on pushing ahead with the colour bar, with the added spice of a bit of 'Blood and Soil' nationalism thrown in, united in their distrust of the free market and what was coming to be known as 'cosmopolitan capitalism'. This is really quite interesting because we have come to associate the National Party with being 'right-wing' and socialism with the 'left-wing' yet these are very poor terms to use because in many cases the policies and ideas they espoused were common to both. The National Socialist German Workers Party was transformed in the public mind shortly before the outbreak of WWII, from being the socialist organisation it actually was (the clue is in the name and they made no secret of it;[129]) into the 'Nazis', which was everything the Left claimed to stand against. According to WEB Du Bois, and many other contemporary observers, the Nazi takeover meant that Germany had 'lapsed into Bolshevism'[130] and indeed, there is probably less difference between the two ideologies than there was between Lenin's Bolshevism and Trotsky's Menshevism. George Bernard Shaw, poet, dramatist and socialist was a famous apologist for the Soviet Union, advocate of labour camps and secret police; he also called for the gassing of political opponents[131] and in 1941 objected to the bombing of Nazi Germany.[132] Richard Crossman, the famous socialist cabinet minister and diarist was convinced that Hitler was a fellow socialist.[133] They even used the same language; in the Nazi anthem the *Horst Wessel*, the enemy are their communist rivals, the Red Front, *and* the 'reactionaries'. This went for the British Union of Fascists too, led by an ex-Labour MP, Oswald Moseley and for the Italian Fascists, led by the socialist Benito Mussolini. It went for the collaborator political parties of Nazi occupied France, the Parti Populaire Français led by the communist Jacques Doriot and the Rassemblement National

[128] Julia Boyd, *Travellers in the Third Reich* (London, 2018).
[129] Julia Boyd, *Travellers in the Third Reich* (London, 2018).
[130] Julia Boyd, *Travellers in the Third Reich* (London, 2018).
[131] New Culture Forum, *Corbyn, Labour and the Communists* https://www.youtube.com/watch?v=NdqEg1OUM6M
[132] Richard Overy, *The Bombing War: Europe 1939-45* (London, 2014).
[133] https://www.telegraph.co.uk/books/what-to-read/appeasing-hitler-tim-bouverie-review-uncovering-unexpected-guilty/

Populaire led by the socialist Marcel Déat.[134]   It also went for the Communist Party of the Soviet Union, whose adoption of 'Socialism in One Country' was only distinguishable from 'National Socialism' in its relative economic inefficiency and more thorough brutality. Perhaps the only tangible difference between the Nazis and the communists lay in the Nazi view that capitalists ought to be mulcted to pay for socialism while the communist thought that capitalists should simply be exterminated.   In each case, a Utopian vision was established and dissent ruthlessly crushed; capitalism was decried to a greater or lesser extent as the tool of shady cosmopolitan monopoly capitalists plotting unsavoury deals in smoke filled rooms, or just plain old Jews. So too did the attitudes of Hertzog and the National Party resemble some of the more mystic aspects of Nordic Rune Nazism and Socialist Mother Russia's devotion to the simple peasant life alongside the more Modernist ideas of a planned future of industry, community and progress. There was also a similarity in the approach to women; the *Nine Commandments of the Workers' Struggle*, penned not by Trotsky or Lenin but by Hermann Goering, espoused motherhood and domesticity in a way that was instantly recognised by the traditional Afrikaaner - the strong, peasant woman in traditional dress which was such a feature of both Nazi and Soviet ideology - and set in stone in the monuments erected by the National Party during the 1930s.

This is probably the reason why in 1930 white women were given the vote; Herzog also intended it to entrench the position of white people in the constitution by effectively doubling the strength of their vote but in doing so, he also sought to extend the possibility of civilised people of other races being brought into the system rather than excluded from it. He had the coloured people in mind principally because very many of them regarded themselves as being a cut above black people by virtue of their white blood but also the Cape Malays, who were generally East Asian Muslims. This was a major consideration because, between 1926-38, many of the Bills needed for segregation foundered on the constitution as English-speaking people in the Cape defended their liberal franchise and Herzog hoped that by currying favour with the coloureds, (who generally spoke Afrikaans) he could undermine the English-speakers.

Still, Herzog won the election in 1929 and even when the Wall St. Crash set off economic ructions around the world, forcing South Africa to drop the Gold Standard, he was still able to form a coalition with Smuts to retain power in 1933. Smuts was desperate to be back in office, desperate to work and though he regarded Herzog as a dull, dim dog (he was) he was prepared to swallow the ordure that had been heaped on him by the hogshead in order to get his hands back on the tiller and guide the path of what he saw as a new South African nation. In 1934, however, when Herzog and Smuts, to all intents and purposes agreed now on the *fusion* of the English and Afrikaaner elements into one white dominated Union and one single United National South Africa Party, Malan had had enough (even though the United Party, as it became known, was still riven from top to bottom between Herzog and Smuts). For Malan, it really was 'Africa for the Afrikanders' and the English Jingoes of Natal, Joburg and Cape Town could go hang along with their King and Empire; he wanted to secede from the Commonwealth; retreat from a sympathy with the plight of the civilised coloureds, harden up segregation into Apartheid and lead a 'Purified' National Party. A rump of 19 MPs followed him onto the opposition benches where they would stay until 1948.

*

That should have been it for Malan and the extreme Afrikaaner nationalists. In theory, South Africa would now move in the direction of a Union dominated by Afrikaaners and English speakers but with increasing assimilationist tendencies as more and more black and mixed race people attained civilised status. The lower status of the majority of black people would remain for the foreseeable future, of course, but the acceptance of a gradual convergence would gradually, gradually, gradually be accepted much in the way that the Rhodesian neighbours to the North gradually accepted that black people would come to play a more prominent part in government over time; this was the basis of Rhodesia's commitment to a good standard of education for black people. Instead, Malan got hold of the levers of power and sent South Africa off on a road that was to lead to disaster. This needs to be explained.

One of the roots of the National Party's success lay in the memories of the Boer war. Despite the fact that the Boers were comprehensively beaten by the British, many of them could not bring themselves to accept this and

---

[134] Ian Ousby, *Occupation: The Ordeal of France* 1940-44 (London, 2017).

from this feeling emerged a 'stab in the back' myth like the one created by the Nazis to explain the equally comprehensive defeat of the German army by the British and French in 1918. (The same thing happened after the Second World War as German veterans of their comprehensive defeat in Normandy complained that they only lost because the British and Americans unfairly deployed better artillery and ground attack aircraft in bigger numbers. N.B. It's a General's job to work out how to defeat an enemy).[135] De Wet claimed in his memoirs that the Boers were only beaten when the National Scouts – Boers in British service – were employed, which was palpable nonsense; others railed against the unfairness of the 'overwhelming force' brought against them, as though war was really only to be conducted on jousting or duelling lines. Indeed, the myth making began before the war was half way over, with Afrikaaner newspapers regularly making things up; in January 1900, *Ons Land*, the Cape Dutch newspaper reported that the Battle of Modder River had been a Boer victory that left 3000 Tommies dead on the field and that at Colenso, 5000 more had been slain – the reality was that Modder River was a British victory with 72 killed and at Colenso, which was indeed a Boer victory, 147 had been killed.[136] (In 1901, the editor of *Ons Land* was jailed for libel after accusing Sir John French of war crimes).[137] This was all helped along by Leo Amery's *Times History* and Maurice's *History of the War in South Africa 1899-1902* both of which provided plenty of material, if selectively read, to 'prove' that the Boers might have actually lost the war but really won it by showing themselves better at everything than the British. Conan-Doyle and Kipling did their bit too when they displayed the traditional British regard for the underdog. The generosity displayed by the British establishment towards Botha and Smuts in paying tribute to a defeated enemy and deliberately playing down their own successes in pursuit of reconciliation, plus allowing full military honours for Kruger's posthumous return to South Africa, all contributed to the salving of Boer military pride. During the 1920s, commemorative medals were handed out to veterans of the war and in 1930 a War Museum at Bloemfontein was begun.

How quickly seized upon and how deeply ingrained these ideas of Boer military prowess became can be ascertained by the lengths that H.C. Bosman, whose father had fought against the Boers, went to satirise them. In *Mafeking Road*, the Boers who 'know the land' get lost. When the British Army arrives this changes; 'If we had difficulty finding the road to Mafeking, we had no difficulty in finding the road away from Mafeking.' *Peaches ripening in the Sun* attacks the notion that Boer women were all resistance minded viragos while in *The Affair at Ysterspruit* the story of the heroic Boer that now began to grace just about every Afrikaaner homestead is turned on its head to reveal (spoiler alert) the hero to be a National Scout. Yet even so, Bosman could not have achieved the popularity he later acquired without portraying the Boers as plucky fighters standing up against the Imperial colossus in defence of hearth and home – all mention of 'Africa for the Africanders' aggression now expunged – and it was the National Party who seized upon this heady brew of nostalgia, wounded pride and the desire to preserve a specifically Afrikaaner heritage in the face of Smuts' new South African identity; in the Afrikaans language, there wasn't actually a word which conveyed the meaning of 'South African' as a nationality – that concept was wrapped up in '*volk*', which was a very different thing indeed as it excluded everyone who wasn't, well, Afrikaans. That bastard pamphlet *A Century of Wrong* became the text from which a new generation of Afrikaaners were taught their pseudo-History. It was during the First World War that Malan put that little obelisk up commemorating Slachters Nek outside Cookhouse, just after his attempts to persuade Smuts to pardon the 1914 rebels failed and from that point on other obelisks began to pop up all over the Free State; the one in Memel that I came across actually celebrated the 1914 rising. This culminated in the 1938 reconstruction of the Great Trek, when ox wagon convoys from the Cape to the Transvaal packed with people in period clothing like some monstrous re-enactors event converged on Pretoria for torchlight ceremonies and the laying of the foundation stone of the Voortrekker Monument in front of 100,000 people; 'pure Nuremburg,' reckoned Allister Sparks.[138] There was a corresponding gathering at Blood River when an Ox wagon and friezes carved out of stone depicting the events of the trek were unveiled and Malan gave the key note speech. Among the recitation of the Boer War atrocity stories, the assertion of a

---

[135] See Richard Hargreaves, *The Germans in Normandy* (Pen & Sword, 2006) and Ben Kite *Stout Hearts: The British and Canadians in Normandy 1944* (Helion, 2014).
[136] Ash. *Kruger's War* p.472.
[137] Lindie Korf, *D.F. Malan: a political biography*. University of Stellenbosh Ph.D Thesis, 2010.
[138] Allister Sparks, *The Mind of South Africa*, (London, 1990) p.171.

simultaneous victim and superman status and outpourings of anti-English venom, Malan laced his call to action with images of the Great Trek and laments for the future of the poor white Afrikaaner.

The question of the concentration camps was also seized on by the Nationalists and exploited for their own ends. This was, of course, a traumatic issue. The British had established the camps initially as places of refuge for families made destitute by the usual depredations and destruction of war and had then developed them as part of the scorched earth policy aimed at removing the Boer intelligence and logistic network. Many of the inmates went to the camps voluntarily or, in the case of the many black people, because they needed protection from predatory Bitter-enders and by and large, the inmates enjoyed good, if sometimes Spartan, conditions, adequate rations, decent medical care, employment opportunities, education and humane treatment. Unfortunately what could not be catered for with the resources immediately to hand were the outbreaks of disease brought on by the primitive sanitary practices of the mainly poor *bywoners*, their sometimes bizarre folk remedies, the generally poor state of contemporary medical knowledge in the face of common diseases and the Boer preference for what Sol Plaatje called 'native bonethrowers' and 'Malay charmers' rather than actual doctors.[139] The big killers were measles and typhoid and though the numbers are shocking to 21st Century eyes, the death rates were in line with peace time mortality rates; European and mixed-race infant mortality in the Cape at the turn of the century meant that 30-40% of children would not see their first birthday; even as late as 1930, infant mortality rates for black children were in the 10-20% range.[140] Much the same can be said of the troops; roughly 14,000 British soldiers died of disease – twice as many as were killed – and another 66,000 were invalided home. In the event, it is thought that there were around 12,000 non-white deaths in the camps but the question of just *exactly* how many whites died was to give the Nationalists their opening - not least because there were more than a few guilty consciences among those Bitter-enders who had consigned their families into British care so as not to be encumbered by them in the field.

In 1906, Louis Botha gave his private secretary P.L.A. Goldman the task of finding out just how many people had died during the war including those who died in the camps and for the next eight years he toiled away at what was a mammoth task. What resulted was a mountainous dog's breakfast of bad research: and I just can't resist quoting the following conclusion from an article written by sociologists in 2009, just so you can thank your lucky stars that you never became one.

> ...the originating aim of producing 'the facts' in a statistical sense, concerning Boer deaths during the South African War. The Inventory also describes the collection as having four clearly distinguished sections. These are of *incoming* items, followed by *outgoing* items, followed by *provisional* data, eventuating in *final* data, implying a linear development from the first through to the fourth section. Within this classificatory framework, the collection is populated by 34 main Volumes (*Bands*), with clear summary descriptions of the contents of each Volume provided in the listing part of the Inventory. The Inventory states that this was the actual organisational order of the composing documents as these were received by the Transvaal State Archive component of the National Archives Repository in 1959. There is a hint of greater complexity, with an in-passing comment that additional organisational documents were interleaved at appropriate points within the order of this domain (T1: vii), although the tenor of this comment implies that order simply prevailed, with these extras not so much assimilated as finally put into their proper places.
> When the actual contents of the Volumes are examined, however, this shows something rather different from the tidy and carefully delineated archival domain as set out in the T1 Inventory. Beneath this collection framework is a complex, messier more fragmentary set of documents, inscribing aspects of a very complicated array of working practices which did not always result in full organisational records of an 'everything to hand and everything in its proper place' kind. There are always, drawing on Garfinkel (1967: 186-207), good organisational reasons for bad organisational records, and the organisational structure presided over by Goldman is no exception to this general sociological observation about the character of organisational structures and practices. Each Volume has a clear title or summary description of its contents in the Inventory (T1: 1-4), but actually the contents are very

---

[139] Sol Plaatje, *Native Life in South Africa*.
[140] Report of the Native Economic Commission 1930-32, para 792. Other figures are from Ash, *Kruger's War*.

mixed. The descriptions of the Volumes invoke documents, or a letter-book, or registers, or summaries and lists; but within is a greater complexity that always exceeds the descriptor: letters in and letter-copies out are, for instance, annotated and amended, while memos jostle with lists of places jostle with single words or names on scraps of paper jostle with memos and a writer's (name not attributed) notes to self. The stated content is then just one kind of document, not necessarily the dominant one, among the array.[141]

Like I said, it was a dog's breakfast. And Liz Stanley and Helen Dampier both deserve a medal for going through it all. What was happening across the country already was the bringing in of bodies that had been buried where they had fallen and re-interring them in cemeteries with suitable memorials along with the establishment of women's committees to do the same for the children who had died in the camps. It was on this that ex-President Steyn pounced, seeing the political potential inherent in the building of a big monument which would effectively accuse the British of being the murderers of women and children and from that point on he mobilised the resources of the Free State – particularly the Veldtcornets and the Predikants - to achieve just that end. What was more, the proto-political party *Het Volk* got involved in a deliberate attempt to skew the findings to show that the whole manhood of the two republics had been mobilised against the British and bury the notion that rather a lot of them were either fighting on the British side or skulking in the camps. To this end, Steyn, himself, made sure that the number of men who died in the camps was going to be kept off the monument which was due to be unveiled in 1913 at Bloemfontein as the *Women's* Monument; and an indication of how much he gave a fig for those who did actually die can be ascertained by understanding that had the men been included, the total number of those who died in the camps would have been substantially *higher*. By just having women and children counted, the impression would be created that Britain had deliberately tried to kill women and children, which was simply not true. Steyn was interested in secession from the British Empire and both History and the dead were to be sacrificed to this aim; and here's one for the conspiracy theorists – Steyn's own records of the Women's Monument Committee went missing and have never since been found. How successful he was in his aim can be judged by the continuing belief among many South Africans today that the deaths in the camp had been deliberate British policy.

Het Volk and other nationalist organisations were also instrumental in promoting and publishing women's accounts of their time in the camps and it was from these stories that they began to weave a collection of atrocity stories that were nothing less than baseless lies. Sarah Gertrude Millin noted that the myth of the British hiding fish hooks in tins of bully beef was getting applause at Stellenbosch University during the 1920s and from then on stories of ground glass in the mealies, poison in the sugar etc etc entered the lexicon; they were being taught as *fact* in Afrikaner school textbooks in the 1940s and on into the Apartheid era with such dismal works as Dr. J.C. Otto's *Die Konsentrasue Kampe* among very many others.[142] Taken together, the Nationalist narrative of the war became, pretty much, *Manly Men, Murdered Women and Innocents Slaughtered*. Louis Botha knew this; the Town Council of English-speaking Bloemfontein knew this too when they both opposed the erection of the *Vrouemonument* as blatant anti-British propaganda. Emily Hobhouse, the pro-Boer (and in 1914, pro-German) British woman who had campaigned against the camps knew this too; the sketch that she provided for the sculptors to turn into a bronze indictment of British inhumanity depicted a tragic scene of a woman mourning a child who had died in one of the camps – but that child had never been in a camp; de Wet and Steyn both knew this too; each of them chose to be buried there. Thus was a terrible tragedy turned into a *revanchiste* shrine (and the root of all those later vile Nazi propaganda claims that as Britain had invented concentration camps, so the Nazis were justified in putting the Jews in them too). 'Politicians in South Africa make the past die hard,' said Smuts' son in 1952.[143] The Nationalists were determined to keep the corpse on life-support, long after it had been declared brain dead in order to elevate a sense of victimhood. As Malan (who had *never* fought) put it;

---

[141] Liz Stanley and Helen Dampier, *The Number of the South African War (1899-1902) Concentration Camp Dead: Standard Stories, Superior Stories and a Forgotten Proto-Nationalist Research Investigation*. http://www.socresonline.org.uk/14/5/13.html>

[142] Fransjohan Pretorius, *The White Concentration Camps of the Anglo-Boer War; a debate without End*. Historia 55,2 Nov 2010.
[143] J.C. Smuts, *Jan Christian Smuts, by his son*. (London, 1952) p.89.

'As Afrikaners we have sprung from a generation that has, more than any other in the History of the world, fought and suffered for eternal principles. Therefore, among all the nations of the world, we have to be known as the nation with the most elevated, purest ideals, with the most steel in our blood.'[144]

The issue has not gone away either. Any questioning of the veracity of this carefully constructed myth is apt to provoke an outpouring of venom from diehard nationalists and academic attack from the chief candleholder of the sputtering flame of the Afrikaaner myth, Professor Fransjohan Pretorius; *Fools Rush In* was the comment of one of the better writers on the camps, Elizabeth van Heyningen, who has indeed questioned the myth.[145]

Who is right? The first bone of contention is whether the British were justified in establishing the concentration/refugee camps in the first place. Professor Pretorius and the Afrikaaner nationalists (not the same thing entirely, we should note) declare that the guerrilla war was entirely justified, that the women who helped by providing safe haven and logistics for the guerrillas were nothing short of heroic, that the scorched earth policy was entirely unjustified and the British were absolute bastards because they shut all these helpless victims in the camps. You've spotted the flaw in that logic already; if you provide heroic help and support to guerrillas, you can't claim victimhood when you get caught by the enemy. The British point of view was that as far as they were concerned, the war was over after the Boer armies were defeated and that most of those guerrillas had taken an oath to lay down their arms and go home peacefully. When the Bitter-enders insisted that those who had taken that oath go back to war, often with threats and menaces – what Professor Pretorius slyly called 're-mobilising' – and made their womenfolk provide logistics and intelligence then all the accepted, if uncodified, rules of war had just been ripped up and the British were perfectly justified in burning the farms and incarcerating the destitute families. Think about it; if you can't trust a surrendered man's word given under oath then the only sensible military alternative is to shoot him quick before he busts a cap in your ass the moment your back is turned. So, the scorched earth policy was effectively forced on the British by the Bitter-enders.

The second bone of contention is whether the men, women and children sent into the camps were treated well. The loony end of Afrikaaner nationalism contends that the camps were designed to either anglicise the Boers or kill them off in a genocide, while the milder end claims that indignities, cruelties and deliberate neglect were inflicted upon the camp inhabitants before the campaigner Emily Hobhouse shamed the British government into making some rather pathetic attempts at amelioration. Such efforts, they claim, did little to stop a holocaust among Boer women and children thus proving that the British were/are absolute bastards as charged. This argument falls apart on several levels; firstly, if the British wanted to kill off the Afrikaaners then there were several much easier ways of doing this, of which two spring immediately to mind – they could leave the poor devils on the veldt to starve or, even better, call in the Zulus, Tswana, Basuto, Swazi and all the other black peoples who the Boers had dispossessed or mistreated over the preceding century and invite them to avenge themselves.

As to the conditions in the camps, there can be no question that they were initially inadequate but this was rapidly and effectively addressed pretty much as soon as it was brought to the attention of parliament. Pretorius isn't having any of this and claims that the evidence of improvement given in the Parliamentary Blue Books was horribly and fatally tainted because the people who compiled them were those bastard Brits. Now, it is true that the Blue Books need to be handled with a certain amount of caution because they only contain a selection of the information available to the minister who is responsible for producing them and a certain amount of concealment and obfuscation can be smuggled into them. They are the bottom rung of the British government's recording system, the next being the Departmental files and the top being the Cabinet Office papers. However, these Blue Books are compiled for the information of parliament and that means the audience is a couple of thousand of extremely sharp, ambitious, educated, competitive, experienced people who keep their wits about them and their knives very sharp indeed, so a minister who intends to play fast and loose with these Blue Books takes a very great risk indeed. Politicians mess with parliament at their peril. So the selection is indeed a selection, but it is usually a fair and representative selection. Furthermore, the people who produced the reports were very often distinguished medical reformers not politicians and in several cases, Boers themselves.[146] That

[144] Quoted in Lindie Korf, *D.F. Malan: a political biography*. University of Stellenbosh Ph.D Thesis, 2010.
[145] Elizabeth van Heyningen, '*Fools Rush In': Writing a History of the Concentration Camps of the South African War* Historia 55,2 November 2010.

there were many deaths in the camps is undeniable but whether those deaths were directly attributable to the British is questionable. The mere suggestion that one of the reasons for the high death rates was due to the insanitary practices of poor, ignorant Boer *bywoners* sent Professor Pretorius into orbit and resulted in him calling one author, Liz Stanley, 'ignorant' and her book 'a mixture of subjective, faulty and ignorant viewpoints and remarks that reveal her prejudice against the Afrikaaner' alongside 'blatantly subjective and incorrect conclusions'.[147] Nevertheless, despite the paranoid tantrums, the statistical and medical evidence is on the side of the British; the single biggest cause of death – 43% - was measles, a disease for which there was no cure then. In short, the camps were a disaster but one for which the primary responsibility lies with the decision of the Bitter-enders to continue a war which they had already lost and which very many of their troops had already agreed was lost by surrendering. That the issue became of such enduring significance was entirely due to Afrikaaner Nationalist intent of building a *revanchist* myth.

As to fish hooks in the bully beef tins, well, what can one say? Just think of the logistics. Someone would have to go to Argentina (presumably in secret) and place an order with the beef processors that specified a certain number of fish hooks per ton be placed in the machinery which canned and cooked the beef. There would then have to be a record kept of the batch numbers for the adulterated tins, along with paperwork that prevented the bully beef being sold to the general public or issued to the troops. This paperwork would have to be readily available to the manufacturers, shipping agents, commercial suppliers, wholesalers, retailers, commissariat etc etc and all kept secret in case a journalist or other snoop found out and alerted their friendly neighbourhood pro-Boer MP. And I'm going to stop there because the whole thing is so completely absurd that only an idiot could believe it.

*

The issue of poor whites was also brought to the foreground by Malan's National Party. It had been an issue – perhaps the key issue – that had driven his views on race, religion and nationalism since the trip to Rhodesia. It was to save these people from themselves that Malan pushed his ever more extreme views on race. If the Afrikaaner people were to survive, he argued, then they would have to be protected from miscegenation, from competition from black workers with communist tendencies, from Jewish capitalists and English mine owners. During the 1920s, he was prepared to admit the coloureds into partnership and, in some cases, English-speakers, but by the later 1930s his views became increasingly narrow as he made the classic mistake of confusing patriotism with nationalism; patriotism is the love of one's country, one's culture, History, values and though it presupposes a willingness to defend it, patriotism is not essentially violent; nationalism is rather different in that it presupposes a superiority and a willingness to assert power and control over others and its first tools are usually virulence and violence.

After the break with Herzog, all restraint was abandoned as he climbed aboard the train of nationalism rolling through central and eastern Europe, hollowed out any concepts of 'trusteeship' of those further down the Social Darwinist ladder, and replaced them with the maintenance of white Afrikaaner domination. In 1938 at a National Party conference, Malan declared that 'We have gathered here with one great aim in mind, and it is to safeguard South Africa for the white race and to preserve the white race, pure and conscious of its calling, for South Africa.'[148] What was more, he declared, the Afrikaaner must be prepared to swim against the tide to achieve this; the threat of an educated black majority was something to be feared, something that was increasingly in evidence and increasingly advocated by British liberals with no other reason than to do the Afrikaaner down. With the anniversary of Blood River on his mind, Malan argued that the Afrikaaners were facing a similar existential threat to those who had fought in 1838: 'Our Blood River lies in the city and our Voortrekkers are our poor who, in the most difficult of circumstances, have to take up the cudgels for our nation against the swelling dark tidal wave.'[149] All this gradually established the National Party as the party of the

---

[146] Elizabeth van Heyningen, *'Fools Rush In': Writing a History of the Concentration Camps of the South African War* Historia 55,2 November 2010.
[147] Fransjohan Pretorius, *The White Concentration Camps of the Anglo-Boer War; a debate without End.* Historia 55,2 Nov 2010.
[148] Lindie Korf, *D.F. Malan: a political biography.* University of Stellenbosh Ph.D Thesis, 2010.
[149] Lindie Korf, *D.F. Malan: a political biography.* University of Stellenbosh Ph.D Thesis, 2010.

poor white Afrikaaner, especially in the rural districts but Malan's support came from a much broader base than just the *bywoners*.

Like many stupid ideas, Apartheid also had its roots in the Sociology departments of universities. Men like Professor Hendrik Verwoerd did much to promote the idea during his time at the University of Stellenbosch, but he was far from being alone. Geoff Cronje, Professor of Sociology at Pretoria had been busily pushing the idea of racial purity for years; his work on mixed-race ghettos had convinced him that Afrikaanerdom would be bastardised unless 'the germs of blood-mixing'[150] were bleached out. Quite a few of the PhDs held by Afrikaaners in these years were gained in Nazi Germany (including Cronjie and Verwoerd) and like many Utopians, they held fast to their beliefs regardless of the evidence of their eyes. What went for Afrikaaner academia went for the theological seminaries too, where the ideas of Christian Nationalism picked up in Holland reinforced the idea that the Afrikaaners were a Chosen People who must necessarily keep apart from the kaffirs and the English if they were not to be contaminated or 'bastardised' as Professor Stoker of Potchestroom University had it.[151] Apartheid was not just white supremacy – *basskap* - but a sacred mission; by 1948, the graduates whose heads had been filled with this sorry nonsense were rising to positions of authority and influence and, like the 1970s Marxists, were disinclined to employ people who did not share their views. None of these clever dicks seemed to have drawn the conclusion from their long contact with Britain that perhaps the British were onto something with their understated philosophy of parliamentary democracy, individual liberty, the rule of law and capitalism as a formula for success. Instead, they insisted doggedly and dimwittedly that their totalitarian world view was better, expounded it from lectern and pulpit, and would brook no dissent; when, indeed, some Afrikaaner churchmen challenged the religious basis for Apartheid in 1961, they were tried for *heresy*.[152]

As the 1930s went on, the Nationalist network of women's groups, predikants, and Bitter-enders coalesced into an interlocking grass roots network engaged in social, church, educational, welfare and sporting activities in a way that made it difficult not to join for any small town dweller who wanted to get on with his or her neighbours – and South Africa was and is a country of small towns. Behind much of this was an organisation called the *Broederbond*, a secret society dedicated to the advance of Afrikaaner Nationalism and the protection of Afrikaaner interests. Formed in 1918, it chose secrecy in 1924 and from that point on collected a socially and professionally elite group of predikants, lawyers, teachers, farmers and, crucially, a significant number of MPs. By the mid-1930s, what had begun as the sort of organisation that was fondly imagined to be like a Masonic lodge began to morph into something much more sinister. It was reorganised into a cadre or cell system familiar to conspirators everywhere but then moved decidedly upmarket to take in professors, senior professionals and businessmen all under Malan's control, with the avowed aim of taking over the state and running it in the interests of a self-declared white Afrikaaner destiny. This was part of a *Lewensbeskouing*, a 'total outlook on life', a governing ideology similar in its totalitarianism and refusal of dissent to Nazism, Fascism and Communism that the National Party had been developing for years. The net result was that the likes of neither Smuts nor Herzog were wanted in its ranks because, as Herzog put it, the aim of both the *Broederbond* and the National Party was to get 'their foot on the neck of English-speaking South Africa.'[153]

In 1944, in response to Smuts' decision to ban public servants from joining it, *Die Transvaaler* published what might be called Malan's *Broederbond's* manifesto; Apartheid, the end of the British connection, keeping foreign capitalists out, keeping white farmers in, keeping domestic capitalists in check (no more sinful usury, in theory), jobs for the (white) boys, promoting a Christian-National education and putting the Afrikaaner firmly in charge of everything (including those *bladdy Engelse*). In response to Herzog's opposition to the *Broederbond*, Malan could rest easy in the smug knowledge that Herzog's own son was on the books. But none of this was really a secret by this time.

During the 1930s, there was also a growing connection between the Nationalists and the National Socialists in Germany, largely based on a revival of the hopes that Germany might do rather better in a re-run of the Great

---

[150] Quoted in Allister Sparks, *The Mind of South Africa* (London, 1990) p.148.
[151] Quoted in Allister Sparks, *The Mind of South Africa* (London, 1990) p.158.
[152] Molly Cooper, *The Heretics* The Spectator, 3rd November 1961.
[153] B. Bunting, *The Rise of the South African Reich* p.45

War and so enable South Africa to liberate itself from the heinous yoke of the British Empire (which had already removed the yoke by granting virtual independence under the Statute of Westminster, remember). 'Blood and Soil' nationalism was also there, as noted, along with the ordering of society along racial lines with a good dash of community activism and solidarity thrown in. It was almost inevitable therefore that South Africa should get its own 'shirt' movement, although in this case the image conjured up by the name was probably more comically grubby than was intended – the Greyshirts – but there was also the *Boernasie* and the New Order. Oswald Pirow, Herzog's Minister of Defence, was a noted Germanophile who went off to Europe in 1938 to consult with Hitler, Goering, Mussolini and Franco and sent his daughter off to train with the League of German Maidens. In 1938, in response to the Ox wagon trek to Pretoria and the laying of the foundation stone of the Voortrekker Monument – which Herzog was emphatically invited *not* to lay – the *Ossewabrandwag* was formed. This was a para-military force, organised on Commando lines, that was supposed to be a cultural organisation to celebrate and promote all things Afrikaaner but as the Commando was central to Afrikaaner culture, the totalitarian nature of the National Party *Lewensbeskouing* ideal could no longer be concealed. Civil society was gradually being infiltrated and taken over in the same way that their fellow totalitarians in the Nazi and Communist Parties had achieved their political dominance; Bosman's third wife was a member of the *Ossewabrandwag*. By 1939, being an Afrikaaner meant being a supporter of the National Party and, as the English-speakers of South Africa were increasingly excluded, being a supporter of the National Party meant being an Afrikaaner.

Perhaps the most influential change in Nationalist philosophy emanating from the Nazis was the upsurge in anti-Semitism (although the Soviets weren't too keen on Jews either). Previously there had been a willingness to see poorer Jews as natural partners to the Afrikaaner because they too were a Chosen People Wandering in the Wilderness. This came to an end in 1930, when Malan introduced the Immigration Quota Act which put strict limits on Jewish immigration from Eastern and Southern Europe on the grounds that people from these countries were not able to assimilate; 'Jews' were not specifically mentioned, but everyone knew that a Polish Countess would not be refused a visa. What it did not do, however, was prevent the immigration of *German* Jews; it was the Greyshirts who did their best to prevent that, even when the figures, at around three thousand between 1933-36, were piddlingly small. It was also the excellent academics of the University of Stellenbosch, five of them led by Hendrick Verwoerd, Professor of Psychology, Sociology and Social Work[154] (and sometime editor of Malan's mouthpiece *Die Transvaaler*), who organised the demonstrations against the arrival of a passenger ship full of Jewish refugees chartered to beat new restrictions due to come into force in 1937 and from that point on the National Party began to absorb more and more of the Greyshirt membership. All this Malan encouraged; the Greyshirts began to call Smuts the Jew-King and when old Gertie Millin's Jewish husband was elevated to the bench, their journal *Die Waarheid* asked whether Aryans should have to stand trial before an Asiatic Jew; Judge Millin got his own back by ruling against Verwoerd in a libel case in 1943.[155] By 1940, the debate was pretty much over when the Transvaal branch of the National Party banned Jews from membership and Malan attacked Smuts for turning South Africa into a 'Jewish-Imperialist war machine.'[156]

Herzog and Smuts viewed these developments with more than a little dismay. For Herzog and Smuts, bringing the English-speakers into partnership with Afrikaaners to ensure a white South Africa was key, but Malan's National Party wanted something much more exclusive than just white supremacy. Similarly, Smuts was out of favour with them because he saw the British connection as vital; Malan dismissed him entirely as having forsaken his Afrikaaner heritage. The tensions came to a head in 1939 when the outbreak of the Second World War brought up the question of whether South Africa should declare war on Germany. Herzog favoured neutrality, a stance that led him into an inevitable split with Smuts who carried the vote for war in the Union Parliament by 80 votes to 67 on 4th September 1939. As far as Herzog was concerned, the war was all the fault of the Treaty of Versailles and poor old Adolf had been sorely put upon. Malan and the Nationalists voted with Herzog and Herzog, feeling that the United Party had gone against him - as indeed it had – resigned as Prime Minister leaving Smuts to take over, with J.H. Hofmeyr at his right hand. From that point on, it was only a matter of time before Malan held out a tempting olive branch to Herzog.

---

[154] Ronald Segal, *Dr Verwoerd*, The Spectator 31th March 1961.
[155] Ronald Segal, *Dr Verwoerd*, The Spectator 31th March 1961.
[156] Quoted in B. Bunting, *The Rise of the South African Reich* p.66

On 8ᵗʰ September 1939, an enormous meeting was called at the, as yet unfinished, Voortrekker Monument which was aimed at convincing Herzog to drop his English connections and bring him back into the fold of the *Volk*. Negotiations continued throughout the spring until in January 1940, it was announced that Herzog and Malan were joining forces in a reunited party, with Herzog as Leader of the Opposition and Malan as his deputy. But Herzog was already toast; Malan controlled the newspapers and the party machinery and had no intention of allowing any sort of English-inclusive compromise. In November 1940, at the Orange Free State National Party Congress a resolution was passed denying equal rights to English-speaking South Africans and Herzog stood up, put his hat on and walked out amidst a stunned silence. 'Instinctively,' wrote Brian Bunting. 'Everyone realised that this was the parting of the ways, that the old general was being driven out of politics after a life-time of service to the nation.'[157] He died two years later, no doubt as bad tempered, dictatorial and foul-mouthed as ever.

Only Smuts stood between South Africa and complete disaster now. And Smuts was 70 years old.

*

South Africa at War 1939-45

God! In spite of all our prayers we keep losing our battles. Tomorrow we are fighting a really big battle. We need help very badly, God, and there is something that I must say to You. Tomorrow's battle will be a serious affair. It will be no place for children. I ask You therefore not to send Your son to help us. Come Yourself.

Smuts in 1940, quoting Adam Kok.[158]

It's a surprising fact that the biggest volunteer army in History, two and a half million strong no less, was raised during the Second World War in India for the defence of the British Empire. On top of this, something like half a million sub-Saharan Africans served in the British armed forces during WWII and most of them were volunteers. Attempts have been made to dismiss these people's efforts as motivated by the merely mercenary incentive of higher pay but this is not borne out by contemporary accounts, such as Biyi Bandele's *Burma Boy,* or supported by Ashley Jackson, the leading authority on the British Empire during WWII.[159] Certainly military service offered a way out of poverty, a chance for adventure, travel and to play a man's part, but the fact that very many Africans fought with commitment and bravery when they could have occupied less strenuous rear-echelon labour positions indicates that notions of loyalty, *esprit de corps* and patriotism were also present.

As far as South Africa was concerned, the British were absolutely adamant that they would retain their control of this vital strategic position on the route to India, especially since the Italian position on the Horn of Africa had been strengthened by the occupation of Abyssinia – and in the course of the war 6,000,000 allied personnel would go around the Cape. They were also aware of the growing influence of the National Party and feared that this would result in the Union declaring neutrality and thus putting a knife to the imperial jugular alongside the expected and inevitable Irish stab in the back (Ireland put its hatred of England before right, justice, honour, liberty and decency and refused to fight the Nazis, refused the Royal Navy basing rights on the West Coast of Ireland and so consigned thousands of men with honour and backbones to their deaths at the hands of the U-boats. The Leprechaun fiddled shamelessly while the world burned).

The sigh of relief that went down Whitehall when Smuts brought South Africa into the war could be heard all the way to Cornwall therefore and it was decided on pretty quickly that in order to prevent trouble, South Africa would need to be treated with kid gloves. There would be no conscription and great efforts would be made to prevent any sort of economic privation touching white society. That did not mean that South Africa would not contribute to the war effort. Indeed, like Bechuanaland, Swaziland and Basutoland, Smuts saw very many

---

[157] Bunting, p.88.
[158] B. Williams, *Botha, Smuts and South Africa* (London, 1946) p.159.
[159] Ashley Jackson, *The British Empire and the Second World War* (London, 2006) p.187

opportunities for South Africa arising out of close co-operation with Britain and in the event 345,000 South Africans would serve in the Union Defence Force, 44,500 in the Air Force while the South African Navy, non-existent apart from a training ship without an engine in 1939, would have seventy eight vessels at sea by 1945; it was originally known as the Seaward Defence Force – inevitably, the *Seaweed* Defence Force (my, what wags those fellows were; Arthur Askey, eat your heart out). National Party attempts to sabotage recruiting failed miserably; Denys Reitz reckoned that only 25% of Afrikaaners supported the National Party's position; 190,000 white South Africans joined up out of an eligible 570,000 which, at about 30%, was pretty good; 65,000 women also served. Non-whites provided the Cape Corps, the Indian and Malay Corps and the Native Military Corps with 120,000 volunteers; they were only supposed to be armed with 'traditional weapons' and there are some truly remarkable contemporary photos of men exercising in gas masks and charging with spears;[160] no doubt the Polish Lancers would have been proud of them. In theory they would be employed in non-combat roles and were therefore denied modern weapons training but this was a stricture that was dropped once South Africa's sunny shores were left behind; it went the same way as the colour bar at the University of Witwatersrand medical school.[161] Under the stress of war, mixed race units became pretty much normal and from the beginning, South African units that were supposed to be segregated were brigaded with black regiments from across the empire, serving with distinction in North Africa and Italy. On top of this, many South Africans could be found serving in British units or on British ships.

The effect on the economy was explosive. Driven by Hofmeyr, industrial output doubled, coal exports increased from 1-4 million tons, and for the first time industrial output became more important than either mining or agriculture. Six million blankets and twelve million pairs of boots were among the articles produced, as well as 6000 armoured cars – the Marmon-Herrington being an example of military engineering that South Africa ought to be ashamed of; in 2014, I went to Normandy in a clapped out WWII American 6x6 that never did more than 11mph the whole bloody way from Yorkshire to the beaches and back and the Marmon-Herrington armoured car was the only thing we ever overtook, including bicycles. The industrial workforce quadrupled too bringing more and more black workers into industry and enabling them to get more and better training; Pass laws were relaxed and a blind eye was turned towards the expansion of the informal settlements around the towns that sprang up to house them. The food packing industry sent 53,000 tons of tinned fruit and jam to Britain and went a long way towards keeping the armies in the Middle East fed, the meat industry went haywire and small firms produced 34,250,000 pieces of personal kit for soldiers on every front including the Russian Front. The paper industry turned to local forestry in order to replace Norwegian timber imports and the nascent steel industry, *Iscor*, was given a boost it could never have expected. According to Bosman, the arrival of the RAF was also explosive, but mainly in the form of constant full scale raids on the Immorality Laws. All this was achieved without sweating the economy or forcing great sacrifices onto South African workers or consumers – although the Kimberley Club was forced, reluctantly, to engage a *female* chef and to face the real hardship in 1943 of not serving meat on a Wednesday. Indeed, by the end of the war, South Africa was more prosperous than it had ever been before.

Trouble with the *Ossewabrandwag* was expected though and Smuts took pains to prepare for it with emergency regulations on internment, confiscation of arms, importing help from MI5 and MI6 but there was no rising as there had been in 1914 because there was no unity among those who were opposed to the war. General Conroy, who took over from Herzog, pointed out that as the Union parliament had voted for war, that vote had to be respected and if South Africans need not be enthusiastic about war with Germany, they must not do anything material to interfere with the war effort. This did not stop the OB from playing at being urban guerrillas and anticipating the Glorious Dawn of a German Victory by cutting telegraph wires, blowing up power lines and pretending to be secret agents; under their leader J. van Rensburg (not the prophet of 1914 fame) – who had begun political life as Malan's secretary - they had formed the *Stormjaers*. The aim was to relegate the English-speakers to second class status, get rid of the Jews and the capitalists and bring in an Afrikaaner totalitarianism, and just how serious he was about this was shown in January 1941 when a meeting he was due to speak at in Joburg ended up in two days of pitched battles between the OB - supported by the police - and off-duty soldiers who, being for the most part unarmed, came off worse; 140 of them were hospitalised. Smuts responded by an

---

[160] https://samilhistory.com/2017/05/28/armed-sa-native-military-corps-in-ww2-this-corps-screams-out-for-a-definitive-work/
[161] Williams, *Smuts, Botha and South Africa* p.181.

intelligent use of internment, picking off the activists, removing OB members from the police forces and applying the law in cases of sabotage. In June 1941, the Germans got involved by landing Robbey Liebbrandt, an ex-boxer, on the Namaqualand coast with $10,000 and orders to overthrow the British Imperium in Africa. I can't decide whether to think of him as Jack Pulman's *Private Schultz* tasked by the SS to parachute into England and ruin the economy by inconspicuously spending several million pounds' worth of forged Fivers, or Captain van der Poel, the German spy posing as a South African, in *Ice Cold in Alex* – the movie that provided probably the best booze advert in the world and almost got censored for the needless tightness of Slyvia Syms' blouse. Needless to say, his mission was not the complete success he had hoped for and from then on interest in the OB understandably waned in proportion to the progress of the mongrel races of the world in providing practical proof of the flaws in Nazi racial theory in places as diverse as Stalingrad, El Alamein and Normandy.

None of this deterred Malan though. Throughout the war he trod a careful path, keeping just this side of the law but always building up his support and always looking for ways to discredit Smuts. If the OB was subversive, he stated provocatively during the dark days of early 1941, then let it be arrested (and thus spark a rebellion). In June 1941, he endorsed a *Broederbond* call for a new republican, Christian-National constitution which would establish the basis for a new Afrikaaner dominated state with all the trappings of the old *Vierkleur* flag, *Die Stem* as the National Anthem and with a President rather than a King as Head of State. This draft constitution was revealing in many ways; a constitution is supposed to set out the rules of government and the limits to its power regarding its ability to interfere in the lives of its citizens. Then as now, the model constitution was widely recognised as that codification of English Common Law and constitutional practice known as the US Constitution but although much head wagging and nodding in the direction of individual liberty, the separation of powers between the judiciary, executive and legislative branches of government and the need for the rule of law went on, everyone knew that there would be an Enabling Law or some other feature that would allow any so-minded person to ride roughshod over all these things. In this case, no-one, free speech notwithstanding, would be allowed to undermine 'public order or good morale,'[162] the President would not be responsible to parliament and opposition parties or any other organisation could be banned at will. What was more, the government would 'take the control and co-ordination of economic and social life under its supervision'; if this looked like National Socialism (or Socialist Nationalism), it did so because it was – and Malan's protestations that he believed in western democracy may be discounted.

Malan was fully convinced that Germany was going to win the war and for that reason was happy to absorb ever more National Socialist elements into the National Party but he was also determined that it was *he* who would be doing the negotiating with Hitler when the British threw in the towel (ha!). To this end, he outmanoeuvred Pirow's New Order and engaged in a long running feud with van Rensburg's OB until, with the turning of the tide and the discrediting of the Nazis, they became so weakened that Malan was able to absorb them; in 1944, he banned OB members from joining the National Party but welcomed the 20% of those who left its ranks. More shrewdly still, he advised those left to join a sister party, the rump Afrikaaner Party, which he could rely on to follow his lead but which he could disown if they started up with too much of the Nazi garbage. He was also astute enough to realise that all those soldiers at present fighting the Nazis had votes and that an awful lot of them were actually Afrikaaners and that if he was to get a parliamentary majority he would have to appeal to them too. It took a while for him to realise this though; the manifesto for the 1943 election foregrounded segregation – it was at this time that the word *Apartheid* entered the political lexicon - and the protection of Afrikaaner *and* English-speaking interests, buried the provisions of the draft Constitution for the moment and came out for a Nazi victory on the grounds that otherwise the Communists would take over the world. It wasn't a vote winner.

On the face of it, Smuts' victory in the 1943 election was overwhelming. His United Party increased from 70 to 85 seats and with his coalition allies, he controlled 110 seats; Malan's support – counting all those who had voted against the war – dropped from 67 to 43 seats. This, however, was not the whole story. Malan had absorbed pretty much all of the other Afrikaaner based parties and as the OB, being Nazis, did not believe in elections the number of his directly controlled seats had jumped from 27 in 1938 to 43 in 1943. Not only this, but whereas the UP had polled pretty much two thirds of the vote, the third that Malan had got was solidly

---

[162] Quoted in B. Bunting, *The Rise of the South African Reich* p.108.

Afrikaaner; it was hard; it would not diminish; it could only go up if he could somehow appeal to the English-speaking vote.

His first attempts were a dismal failure. In February 1945, an English newspaper was started but it went nowhere. When the war was over, the Nationalist Party decided to hold their congress in the centre of English-speaking Joburg but this turned into a riot when the Springbok Legion, a thoroughly liberal minded veterans organisation, many of whom had first-hand experience of Nazi atrocities and who had learned through hard practice that the colour of a man's skin was not particularly relevant when it came down to it, objected; (Job Maseka was decorated for sinking a German freighter with a home-made bomb and then escaping captivity in Tobruk; 'We were one, We fought as one; black and white soldiers,' said Sergeant Petrus Dlamini, of his time at El Alamein). The Congress was called off. Unfortunately, this multi-racial solidarity began to melt when the Afrikaaner soldiers were demobbed and went back to their small towns to be absorbed back into the *braai*, rugby, tennis and church network of National Party social and cultural organisations.

Pushing in the direction opposite to segregation came some new attitudes consequent to the changed situation in the cities that many soldiers found on their return to South Africa. Urban segregation had been introduced in 1923 in the wake of the Stallard Commission which assumed that African labour was almost entirely migratory and should be treated as such; the African would come to the city to work and when his contract was up, he would return home. This was assumed to be a reasonable assumption at the time but as more and more black people decided that city life was more attractive than life in the Reserves, that assumption began to fall apart; between 1921-51, the black urban population increased almost four times over (587,200 to 2,329,000) so that roughly 30% of black people were now permanent residents.[163] Many black people also rejected the notion that they should live in hostels or compounds and moved into the rapidly growing slums and informal settlements, especially when women and children began to join their menfolk. As already noted, the associated squalor and overcrowding (roughly half of the black population were lodgers of one sort or another) prompted many Town Councils to begin the process of slum clearance, relocation and segregation but with the coming of the war, such schemes as were in operation were rapidly overwhelmed. Joburg's population grew by half in the years 1936-46 and the number of black people living outside municipal locations, i.e., in slums and squatter camps, doubled from 86,000 to 176,000. The expansion of the wartime manufacturing economy promised an escape from rural poverty and hoovered up anyone who wanted a job but it also produced a housing crisis that no one had ever envisaged.[164] The 'Western Areas' – what would become Soweto – were notoriously dangerous, overcrowded and insanitary. At the same time, black workers were becoming more prosperous and moving into semi-skilled work. Even more significant was the emergence of a black middle-class of teachers, business people, lawyers and doctors who wanted better housing and security from the endless evictions that resulted from temporary unemployment.

They were pushing at an open door in English-speaking areas. The Johannesburg City Council were all in favour of secure property rights for respectable working people emerging from tribal, uncivilised roots and began to look for ways that this could be achieved. In 1946, they began to offer 99-year leases for new housing on generously sized plots (5,000 sq.ft as opposed to 400 sq.ft in the locations) which effectively threw the Stallard Commission's assumptions that black people were merely migrant labour into the bin. The fact that there was a permanent black residential population of Joburg was recognised and, crucially, *welcomed* and the JCC proposed to bring in a self-financing programme of urban development which would provide decent housing in decent neighbourhoods for these residents. Local businesses were in favour because it meant their workers were close by and much happier while ratepayers were looking forward to a time when they would not have to subsidise slum housing. The main opposition came from the Labour Party who refused to compromise on training black people to do the necessary work. When these developments ran into legal trouble because they conflicted with the Urban Areas Act, Smuts ordered the Fagan Commission to look into the whole matter. Judge Fagan reported that these housing developments should be encouraged and supported by central government funding and that home-ownership was a legitimate aspiration for black urban residents. The British ex-Servicemen's League, the South African version of the British Legion, also got involved and funded housing

---

[163] Paul Maylam. *The Rise and Decline of Urban Apartheid in South Africa*. African Affairs, Vol. 89, No. 354 (Jan., 1990).
[164] S.M. Parnell, *The Ideology of African home-ownership: the establishment of Dube, Soweto 1946-1955* (Wits, 1990).

for returning black and coloured soldiers, complete with a chapel and social centre in Dube, Johannesburg; Smuts was the founder of this organisation.

Smuts. Again, Smuts. It always comes back to Smuts. For half a century, what he thought mattered and since the Union was formed in 1910, pretty much what Smuts said went. And here, at the end of the Second World War, when Herzog and Reitz and Hitler were in their graves, when the British Empire had spent itself to save the world and had been replaced as arbiter by the Soviets and the Americans, when everything was different from 1939... what Smuts said and thought still mattered and what Smuts said and thought about the one, great question of South Africa's future was changing. Absurdly for a Historian, reading through the events of these years, I keep hoping that Apartheid might be avoided. I can't help an irrational and utterly illogical feeling that Malan is going to be defeated by Smuts, the bloke who grew up on a farm only a stones' throw away from that bloody reptile; that the story is just going through a dark moment before the *deus ex machina*, clothed in khaki and peaked cap, wearing his sharp, cold, Boer face complete with white beard and moustache, descends from the clouds and produces the happy ending that we are all half expecting. And I'm disappointed every time.

Smuts' early views on race and the Native Question were an intellectualised version of the contemporary Social Darwinism mixed in with an unhealthy dose of *Svartgevaar* – the fear of the black man. In his mind, the white races of South Africa needed to stand shoulder to shoulder against the threatening black tide and that the rights and responsibilities of citizenship could not safely be extended to black people in their present uncivilised state; it just wasn't practical politics to even think about allowing them a share in a democracy at that time. Nor, in the period after the Boer War did he think much of adding to the racial problems of South Africa by encouraging more Indian immigration (ended 1911) or Chinese labourers. During the First World War, however, there was a shift – not much of one – but his service in East Africa made him realise (with something of a start) that black and Indian soldiers were very often just as good as white ones; he had commanded troops from South Africa, Ghana, Nigeria, the West Indies, Kashmir, Jhind, Bhurtpur, Kaparthalu, Rhodesia, Kenya, Uganda, Tanganyika, Belgium and Portugal; his opponents, mainly black Askaris led by German officers, also demanded respect. He had also started to reject the growing view that 'race' depended exclusively on biology or that the 'ruling' races were composed of thoroughbred or 'pure' blood types – the coming Nazi ideal; for him 'race' meant the older definition based on nationality, language and culture as well as blood. What he feared was that miscegenation would lead to the overwhelming of white civilisation by black cultural barbarism or that white Christian civilisation would be submerged under an armed black tide before black people could be civilised properly. It was for this reason that he had pushed for South Africa to take over Africa as far north as the Congo after the First World War, so that any such developments might be managed or forestalled. This was not one of his better ideas. Nor was his idea for a federation of African states, which seemed to have grown out of his philosophy of Holism, received well; in the 1929 election, his Nationalist opponents claimed that he wanted South Africa to be a 'Kaffir state', which is emphatically not what he wanted.

The contradictions in his attitude to race continued to pile up during the 1930s when he opposed the Quota Bill restricting Jewish immigration and made several statements to the effect that the world owed the Jews an awful lot and that the least that could be done in payment of that debt was to allow the establishment of a Jewish state in Palestine. This went hand-in-hand with the frankly unconvincing picture he gave in his Rhodes Lectures at Oxford, of the happy, simple, carefree black man grateful for whatever the white man was prepared to hand down to him – the black man's discontent was just a result of him being led astray by clever, unscrupulous agitators apparently – and the rather more convincing picture he gave of the implications for segregation and political rights inherent in the arrival of the entirely new class of urban blacks. Furthermore, the development of his philosophy of Holism began to lead him (kicking and screaming) to the logical conclusion that black people would have to be admitted to a greater measure of rights than he had previously contemplated. This was, of course, fully in line with Social Darwinist principles; he had negotiated with Gandhi as an equal; it was the complicating factor in the South African racial question that Indians represented which he found irritating rather than the fact that they were Indians *per se*; he regarded the Bushmen as living fossils, 'ten thousand years behind the times'[165] and actually going backwards – degenerating - in the evolutionary process. On top of that, his great interest in science was increasingly clashing with his views on race: 'In this holistic universe man is in

---

[165] *Smuts by his son*, p.543, 548

75

very truth the offspring of the stars,'[166] he declared to the British Association for the Advancement of Science in 1931. Just how he was able to exclude black people from that description revealed either a narrowness of mind that he did not possess or a deep contradiction that he just did not want to address; his son gave the impression that he thought of black children as a rather pleasant species of fauna; one biographer, H.C. Armstrong, reckoned that he had a streak of intellectual vanity that could not admit that he was wrong while Alan Paton reckoned that no-one ever knew what he was thinking because he concealed his thoughts behind a 'barrier of optimism'[167]. The same can be said of his declaration at St. Andrews university in 1934.

> 'Individual freedom, individual independence of mind, individual participation in the difficult work of government seems to me essential to all true progress…. The fight for human freedom is indeed the supreme issue of the future, as it has always been in the past…. "Happiness is freedom, and freedom is courage." That is the fundamental equation of all politics and all human government, and any system which ignores it is built on sand...'[168]

A little while later, speaking to the Royal Institute of International Affairs, he made the point that 'more and more we are recognising that, in spite of racial and political barriers, humanity is really a whole'[169] and what the class of 1937 at the University of Cape Town made of the following is anyone's guess;

> 'Whatever may be the ultimate outcome of the rival Fascist and Communist systems now contending for mastery in Europe, I would ask you to believe that their hostility to the principle of toleration, of racial, religious and political toleration, must surely be a passing phase, a symptom of the confusion and unrest of the times. The human spirit having once broken its primeval shackles and emerged from its bondage will never again submit to them for good. Evolution never reverts back to discarded forms or organs.'[170]

When Malan defended Japanese expansionism, Smuts declared that if they tried to expand into South Africa he would arm every black and coloured person fit enough to carry a gun. This was followed in 1942 by a speech at the Institute of Race Relations when Smuts argued that segregation as a policy was effectively dead and would have to be replaced by something approaching Trusteeship, a restatement of his paternalism and aimed at protecting those non-urban un-educated natives who probably were not ready for the full blast of capitalism and democracy. 'The native,' he declared, 'is carrying this country on his back.'[171] His old chum Denys Reitz followed this up by proposing to legalise black trade unions while Hofmeyr delivered himself of the view that white and black should start to regard themselves as 'common citizens of a common country'.[172] A few more eyebrows went up when it was revealed that Smuts had had a major hand in drawing up the UN Charter at the San Francisco Conference in 1945, effectively committing South Africa to fundamental human rights…and then in 1946, he introduced a Bill to further disadvantage the Indians of Natal in the matter of property deals in return for granting a limited franchise. India protested, even though Gandhi's own disastrous inability to reconcile communal and racial divisions had resulted in bloodshed on a scale unimaginable in South Africa when India and Pakistan became independent in 1947. Smuts gave this acid response;

> 'It is to prevent such conditions of social clash arising in South Africa, where so many races, cultures and colours come together, that the Union is doing its best on fair, decent and wise lines to keep the different elements, as much as convenient and possible, apart and away from unnecessary intermixture, and so prevent bloody affrays like those in India or pogroms such as we read of in other countries. We are honestly trying to find a human way of life for a racially, socially and culturally mixed community such as South Africa, where different sections may dwell alongside each other in peace and with comparative goodwill...'[173]

---

[166] *Smuts by his son*, p.522
[167] Alan Paton, *South African Tragedy* p.96
[168] *Smuts by his son*, p.573
[169] *Smuts by his son*, p.587
[170] *Smuts by his son*, p.595
[171] Bunting, p.126
[172] Bunting, p.126
[173] *Smuts by his son*, p.801.

The truth was, it seems, that Smuts was wavering. The world had changed and he knew it. One of the first acts of the United Nations was to condemn South African segregation and as this handed Malan a huge stick to beat him with, it seems inescapable that Smuts knew that the segregation road that he had so far taken was looking increasingly like it was running into a *cul-de-sac*. Hofmeyr himself came out in 1946 and said to rapturous applause at Wits University that the Nationalist idea that the Afrikaaners were the *herrenvolk* or master race had to be challenged and that racial prejudice had to go; a little later in parliament, he said that the colour bar had to go too. The question now was whether Smuts had the prestige, the status and the energy left to start South Africa on a new course, whether he could raise the Highest Common Factor a little higher and avoid sinking the Lowest Common Denominator even deeper.

He did not and he could not. He had left it too late. He had made too many enemies over the years. The socialists remembered his strike breaking and the Labour Party was determined to maintain the colour bar in the trade unions; many Afrikaaners distrusted his attitude towards the English and his gadding about on the world stage, very many more distrusted his attitude to the Native question; the *predikants* had never loved him and suspected him of atheism – Holism, if ever they came close to understanding it, smacked of 'intelligent design' without the need for a God; the virulence of Herzog's attacks on him was maintained by Malan's mob; as ever, Smuts was dismissive and distant and unapproachable and out of sync with the rough egalitarianism of the small town Boer. Abroad, he was well regarded in Britain, but the rising generation of Americans had little time for him, the Russians hated him and India and the other emerging nations of the Third World had distrusted him ever since his spats with Gandhi. He looked like yesterday's man; he *was* yesterday's man.

*

Fagan and Sauer: A Tale of Two Commissions.

The record of the Native Affairs Department between the wars had been mixed, to say the least. Although they had produced a lot of good reports and had been able to influence policy in the Reserves and in the urban areas, the fact was that it had always been divided between those who looked forward to the end of segregation and equal rights and those who maintained a more ambivalent attitude to such a development. It was also hamstrung in many ways by the refusal of local authorities to allow themselves to be dictated to by central government, by a general reluctance to accept 'big' government intervention at all and by its lowly status in the bureaucratic hierarchy; action on many of the big questions was actually undertaken by the Ministry of Justice. They had no say at all in the big questions of labour recruitment beyond those concerned with general welfare and although they argued long and hard for the abolition of labour tenancy in agriculture, they achieved little beyond getting the backs of white farmers up for their near constant criticism of the treatment of farm workers. In the urban areas, the department came to view itself as a Cinderella service having been given the task of administering the locations and segregated areas but not allocated the necessary resources. Many of those involved in this thankless task believed that the municipal authorities had taken the convenient opportunity to off-load their responsibilities to the NAD.[174] What this meant was that as the cities exploded with the relaxation on influx control, the NAD was unable to meet very many of its obligations, which in turn led to an increasing exasperation with it on the part of both black and white and a realisation that, as the war was ending, something had to be done. Step forward Judge Fagan and his 1946 Native Laws Commission.

As we have seen, the basis of the Nationalists' approach to urbanisation was the Native (Urban Areas) Act of 1923 which had been the bastard child of the Stallard Commission's appalling *diktat* that;

> It should be a recognised principle of Government that Natives – men, women and children – should only be permitted within municipal areas in so far and for so long as their presence is demanded by the wants of the white population and should depart from therefrom when they cease to minister to the needs of the white man.[175]

---

[174] Ivan Evans, *Bureaucracy and Race: Native Administration in South Africa* (Berkeley, 1997).
[175] Quoted in Helen Suzman, *Digest of the Fagan Report* (Joburg, 1948).

Under this Act, Herzog and his pals in the Labour party hardened up a pretty ragged segregation into a legally binding one and passed over to municipalities the responsibility of housing black Africans (who handed them off to the NAD) while at the same time removing those who had ceased 'to minister to the needs of the white man.' As we have also seen, the attempt to enforce this policy had had Canute's success, economic forces being in almost every case, stronger than legislation, and the corollary to this 'success' was the failure of the municipalities, even those with the best intentions, to provide decent living conditions for the numbers arriving. As Helen Suzman noted in her *Digest of the Fagan Report*, the existence of a shanty town did not indicate unemployment – far from it as unemployment rates were down below 5% - but rather the inability of the builders to keep up with demand.

Judge Fagan considered the situation and reviewed the three most talked about solutions to the problem; Apartheid or total segregation; the removal of all racial discrimination; the co-existence of racial communities side by side with due consideration for separate legislation for specific circumstances. The first he dismissed as an economic impossibility; the second he dismissed as impractical because black Africans existed along a continuum of 'civilised, educated, urban' all the way to 'tribal, uneducated and rural' and the latter were not ready to exercise their rights in a responsible manner. He therefore went for the third option, co-existence, as being consistent with a gradual, evolutionary approach which respected the different institutions and outlooks present in the different racial groups. As far as the Pass Laws were concerned, he considered the mish-mash of legislation entirely unwieldy and that passes should be replaced by identity cards as a first step towards their complete abolition; at any rate, the power to exclude a man's wife and children while he retained the right of residence in an urban area should be rescinded forthwith as was the stricture that unemployment meant eviction. What this all meant in practice was that Stallard was dead and that the continued urbanisation of South Africa would require different racial communities to find practical ways to co-exist and co-operate; they were bound together by economic ties and those economic ties would inevitably develop into social ties too. Smuts' vision had been laid out. It was a practical way to harmonious relations and the development of a fellow feeling that would, with time, erode the instinct for segregation, an instinct that was already wavering in South Africa.

Verwoerd (and the *sixteen* Stellenbosch University professors who rejected Fagan's conclusions)[176] understood this too; he called the report 'the political Bible of the United Party'[177] and hit back with the National Party's own Sauer Commission.

> The entire migration into and from the cities should be controlled by the state which will enlist the cooperation of municipal bodies. Migration into and from the Reserves shall likewise be strictly controlled. Surplus Natives in the urban areas should be returned to their original habitat in the country areas or to the reserves. Natives from the country areas shall be admitted to the urban areas or towns only as temporary employees obliged to return to their homes after the expiration of their employment.[178]

Stallard, it seemed was not dead after all. What was worse was that Malan was planning to employ the full weight of the state to enforce not just segregation, but the much deeper separation of Apartheid.

*

The National Party Coup d'Etat and The Vision of Utopia 1948-58

You remark upon the absence of a Native franchise in the Transvaal and the Free State. Let me point out that the establishment by the British government in 1906 of what is virtually manhood suffrage of whites would necessarily subject any scheme of native franchise which fell short of manhood suffrage to criticism on grounds of Colour bar. The removal of the bar in this connection might in the present

---

[176] CO 537/3643

[177] Ivan Evans, *Bureaucracy and Race: Native Administration in South Africa* (Berkeley, 1997).

[178] Quoted in Ivan Evans, *Bureaucracy and Race: Native Administration in South Africa* (Berkeley, 1997).

stage of Native development mean that annihilation of the white man by the vote, which he has escaped by the assegai; and you can appreciate how delicate a matter it is in South African politics.

Smuts to Lloyd George, 12th May 1920.[179]

*

'Are youse Union Party going to give the niggers a vote?' he asked.

'Only the civilised nigg- that is to say, civilised Natives,' Robert E. Constable replied.

The young men in the back row laughed derisively. 'There isn't no such thing,' Faded Blazer shouted.

The next question was put by one of Faded Blazer's colleagues, a fat young man in a soiled shirt.

'Is youse Union Party going to give coolies the vote?' Soiled Shirt enquired.

'Only,' Robert E. Constable replied. 'Civilised coo- that is to say civilised Indians.'

More derisive laughter from the back row. Above the laughter Soiled Shirt called out: 'There isn't no such thing as a civilised coolie.'

It was Faded Blazer's turn again to put a question. And it was clear that Faded Blazer's bent did not lie in the direction of originality. 'Is youse Union Party,' he demanded, 'going to give the vote to Bushmen?'

At this question pandemonium broke loose in the back row. Robert E. Constable's reply was inaudible.[180]

H.C. Bosman, *Willemsdorp.*

*

...some South Africans talk about the native question without giving themselves the trouble of thinking at all....

Address delivered by Lord Selbourne Before the Congregation of the University of the Cape of Good Hope, on Saturday, 27th February 1909.

*

...their cause was nothing less than the strengthening of the Afrikaner people, in preparation for the great struggle which lay ahead of a white people on a black continent. Anyone who did not identify himself with the struggle must be pushed aside, no matter how honourable, how efficient, how impartial, how punctilious in the use of both official languages.

Alan Paton, *South African Tragedy.*

*

It is doubtful whether Malan can do much positive harm, unless indeed he manages to increase his majority at the further election within the year which he is already foreshadowing.

Professor E. A Walker, 1948.[181]

*

At this stage, we should pause and consider the character of the guide I've chosen to lead us through what was, in effect, a *coup d'état* by the National Party as complete as anything pulled off by the Nazis in 1933 or the Communists in 1917 or in Eastern Europe after 1944. His name is Brian Bunting and it will probably come as a shock to you that I've chosen a committed Communist who was expelled from the Union parliament in 1953

---

[179] CO 537/1198
[180] H.C. Bosman, *Willemsdorp* (1951).
[181] 'Dr Malan's Minority,' *The Spectator* 18th June 1948.

only to be re-elected in 1994. Born in Joburg in 1920, his father was one of those communists who watched the show trials of Stalin's enemies during the 1930s with great dismay but still could not bring themselves to believe that there was anything fundamentally wrong with the Soviet system. He couldn't admit that there was anything wrong with the blasted system even after he himself had been expelled from the Communist Party as a 'Right-wing deviationist' for opposing Stalin's plan to create the Soviet equivalent of the Bantustans – the independent Native Republics. Young Brian was no brighter and followed in his father's footsteps. Shamefully, he allied himself with the Greyshirts and refused to fight the Nazis until the Soviet Union was invaded. After the war, he went to Cape Town to work for the communist newspaper, *The Guardian*, and from that point on was harassed mercilessly by the Apartheid state. In 1952, he was elected to parliament and in 1953, booted out of it and for the next ten years was harassed further until he could stand it no longer. In 1963, he decided that exile was his only option and so chose the obvious thing and following his principles, moved to the Soviet Union where he could live as a communist and continue the struggle....of course, he didn't. The old fraud moved to good old capitalist, imperialist, racist London where he worked for that well known bastion of journalistic integrity, TASS, the Soviet news agency, and ranted on to the band of raddled old communists who collected around him about the necessity of following the Moscow party line. Just like his old dad, Brian, now a hereditary Soviet stooge, was prepared to dismiss the repression of Hungary 1956, the building of the Berlin Wall 1961, the Prague Spring of 1968, the 1979 invasion of Afghanistan and the crackdown on the Polish Solidarity movement during the 1980s, as slightly unhelpful blips on the road to Utopia, but understandable under the circumstances. If you want a flavour of the dishonest Marxist gibberish and slavish quoting of Stalin's genius he was given to writing, you could also check out his 1975 book *Moses Kotane, South African Revolutionary, A Political Biography*. He tried to excuse the proletarian slogan 'Workers of the World Unite and Fight for a White South Africa' by claiming that Marxist thought was unknown in South Africa then – I suppose all those Red Flags were just bunting, eh, Mr. Bunting?[182] (In fact, there had been much talk of 'Class War' in 1914;[183] and the SACP was hopelessly split on the race issue and would remain so until after WWII).[184] Even when he was re-elected in 1994 – five years after the collapse of the Soviet Union into terrible poverty and criminality – he still thought that South Africa should become a socialist country. In short, he was a deeply unpleasant person who was prepared to accept the death of millions of people, as happened in the Soviet Union, China, Cambodia and other socialist Utopias, in order to establish a totalitarian state in South Africa and do it all over again there.

And it is this that makes him such a useful guide because his 1964 book *The Rise of the South African Reich* is absolutely dripping with understanding and admiration for the way in which Malan and the Nationalists took over South Africa and Bunting just cannot conceal his jealousy at how it was the Nationalists and not the Communists who got to be the dictators. And I would bet the farm on the proposition that Nelson Mandela would have been banged up in the same cell on Robben Island if Malan hadn't beaten Bunting and his murderous mates to the prize. Oh...er...and I got the biographical details from those well-known right-wing organs of British capitalist propaganda *The Guardian* and *The Independent*.[185] I should also add in a brief bibliographical and biographical detail of my own here. I first came across Bunting's book back in the 1970s when, as a member of the Bolton Socialist Workers Party, I borrowed it from a fellow traveller with an impressive collection of works political, philosophical and polemical. It was also a very *economical* collection because I found out some years later that he had stolen – 'liberated' – most of them from the local bookshops, a fact that seemed to me to illustrate something fundamental about communists; I have wondered ever since if Bunting lost his royalties as a result.

*

> ...*self-preservation is the first law of nature, that it applies to racial and national communities as much as it does to individuals, that it creates a right for each of them which they may exercise freely, in as far as it does not infringe on the equal right of the other; that the white community in South Africa*

[182] https://www.marxists.org/subject/africa/bunting-brian/kotane/ch02.htm
[183] CO 537/564 Governor-General to Colonial Office 1st October 1914.
[184] David Pallister, Sarah Stuart and Ian Lepper, *South Africa Inc: The Oppenheimer Empire* (Sandton, 1987) p.39
[185] https://www.theguardian.com/world/2008/jul/09/southafrica.pressandpublishing. https://www.independent.co.uk/news/obituaries/brian-bunting-political-activist-and-journalist-871771.html.

instinctually and traditionally, as well as for valid reasons, places great store on their self-preservation as such; and that their safety can, apparently, only be ensured by their unhindered development on their own terrain, coupled to the appropriate consideration of the non-whites' identical right, also to be practiced on their separate terrain.

D.F. Malan 12th December 1946.[186]

During the later war years, Malan had done much to bring the fissiparous Afrikaaner Nationalist organisations to his side and as the 1948 election loomed, he could look forward to leading an almost united Afrikaaner front. He had also done much to cut through the agonised debating of the Native Question by replacing it with a clear declaration of *Apartheid*; there could be no equality between the races on any level simply because the black man was incapable of achieving a sufficient level of civilisation; it was better that he was allowed to develop in his own way, in his own reserves and locations; the black urban classes were to be regarded as migratory; it was the job of white civilisation to act as guardians to those so obviously inferior and so vulnerable to exploitation by communist agitators. This was all rather clever and sounded reasonable and straightforward to all sorts of apparently reasonable and straightforward people; backveldt Boers understood instinctively that the sjambok would remain firmly in their hands and for those of them that revelled in unreason, the utterly vile J.G. Strydom assured them that the sjambok would be wielded liberally and with gusto – for him it was the threat of the black man *becoming* civilised that had to be thwarted. Trade unionists liked the thought of jobs for the (white) boys without the inconvenience of a little healthy competition; liberal multiculturalists could stroke their chins and see Apartheid in terms of 'constructive segregation' and 'trusteeship', as an extension of the paternalism that many of them practised on their own farms, and that many of Smuts' supporters openly embraced; the Dutch Reformed Church liked the religious basis of it – had not God decreed the diversity of peoples through his actions regarding the Tower of Babel?

The people who didn't like this new hardened definition of segregation were the mine owners, increasingly conscious of the needs of their workers and aware that the colour bar cost them in profits and profitability, and urban businesses that depended on the money spent by urban blacks. Or the Indians, who it was imagined would be deported *en masse* as soon as it became practical. Added to this was a strenuous and sustained marking down of the new Deputy Prime Minister Hofmeyr as a *kaffirboetie*, a 'nigger-lover', out for equality between the races, as a man with an African mistress (his mother would never allow any mistresses at all), a liking for young boys, a Jew (all lies) and that if (the Jew-loving) Smuts got in, it would be Hofmeyr pulling the strings; black men might chat up white girls in the street, for heaven's sake.

Malan was also able to play on the uncertainties caused by the rapid expansion of Joburg and the squalor and dislocation that went with it. His influence reached deep into the trade unions where the economic insecurities of the post-war world made job reservation an attractive proposition for socialist workers who were as suspicious of Jewish capitalist mine owners as they were of black competition. In 1946, 75,000 black miners came out on strike and troops were required to compel them back to work while at the same time Indians began another campaign of passive resistance against Smuts' anti-Asian measures. *If this is what they were like without the vote*, muttered the National Party, *what would they be like with it?* Actually, it wasn't just muttered; it was shouted out loud: the National Party stood for Apartheid, which was just the posh name for *Baasskap*, white supremacy, and Smuts and his United Party stood for future integration, racial equality and miscegenation. When the election results came in the vagaries of an election system that gave more weight to rural rather than urban constituencies, (an effect that cumulatively added 12 seats to the backveldt Boers) allowed the National Party and their allies to pile up votes in the marginal seats of the countryside to take 79 seats, while Smuts and the United Party piled up votes in safe urban areas to take only 65 seats; the NP representation in the Transvaal jumped from 11 to 32; Smuts himself lost his seat. Malan formed the government: 'Today,' he declared, 'for the first time since Union, South Africa is our own.'[187] By *our*, he meant those Afrikaaners who voted for him; only about 60%.

---

[186] Lindie Korf, *D.F. Malan: a political biography*. University of Stellenbosh Ph.D Thesis, 2010.
[187] Bunting p.130.

The only silver lining to an otherwise miserable defeat for decency was that the National Party had actually lost the popular vote by 140,000 votes; they only gained 40% of the vote in total. This is important because it tells us that most white people were not convinced by the idea of Apartheid; they were *not for* Apartheid; they were *not for* the extreme racism of this vile Utopian vision. Rather, it seems, they were moving in the direction that Smuts was moving, recognising that things could not go on as they were and that the challenges of change would have to be faced if the future was to be one of peace, security and prosperity. Alongside that silver lining was one of the great might-have-beens; in 1923, Smuts had campaigned for Rhodesia to join the Union of South Africa but the whites there were predominantly British and very suspicious of the Afrikaaners and so voted 2:1 to reject union. If that vote had gone the other way and Rhodesia had joined the Union of South Africa, the United Party would undoubtedly have won the election, Apartheid would have been stillborn and South Africa would very possibly have gone on a gradualist path to equal rights, opportunities and representation.

*

On 16th December 1949, the Voortrekker Monument was finally dedicated by D.F. Malan. This huge block of granite perched on a ridge overlooking Pretoria had been consciously designed as a celebration of Afrikaaner Nationalism, with marble friezes, rich tapestries and paintings depicting the events of the Great Trek, replica ox-wagons harking back to Blood River decorating the surrounding walls, statues of the Trek leaders buttressing the four corners while a bronze depicting a *boervrau* and her children consciously echoed the *Vroumonument* in Bloemfontein. Under its foundation stone copies of The Vow, Die Stem and Retief's treaty with Dingane had been placed, while around the walls hung the flags of all the various Boer Republics, but most impressive was the dome above, which was pierced to allow a ray of sunlight to fall on the cenotaph at mid-day on the 16th December, the anniversary of the Battle of Blood River. It was an exclusive monument, not to be sullied by the English of whom there is no trace, and if anyone was in any doubt about this then the inscription on the cenotaph made the message clear: *Ons vir jou, Suid-Afrika*. 'Our all for you, South Africa,' is how it translates, but the metaphorical translation was the old slogan of 'Afrika for the Afrikaaners.' It was meant to be an enduring symbol of simplicity, epic endeavour, endurance, struggle and sacrifice which would inspire the Afrikaaner nation to greater and greater efforts and there is no doubt of the impression created. I went there in 2006 when the place was very nearly deserted and I had the place pretty much to myself and can testify to the awe that it was designed to inspire. The tragedy of the monument comes through not so much in the sense of victimhood, of a wounded people triumphing against the odds that it was designed to peddle but that it was built during the Second World War, when the foundations of Blood and Soil racial nationalism were being bombed to rubble by the RAF and USAAF and that it was opened just as the United Nations began its long condemnation of race as a foundation for rule. The writing was on the wall for Apartheid before it was properly begun and though hindsight is one thing, it seems reasonably clear that this cathedral to Afrikaaner Nationalism was not so much a symbol of triumph but a tombstone waiting for its corpse.

When the Union parliament assembled, Malan found that he had only the slimmest of working majorities because the Labour and coloured seats had sided with the UP; five in the lower House of Assembly, none in the upper Senate; and it was to this fact that he turned his attention. A couple of by-elections went his way but the first big rigging of the system came in 1949 with the proposal to give direct representation to South West Africa, a UN mandate under international law, but part of the Union in reality. The average constituency size in the Union was 9-12,000 but Malan made sure that it was only 4,000 in SW Africa and so put six MPs and four Senators, all Nationalists of course, into parliament. (Breath taking? Tony Blair pulled off the same trick during his years in office 1997-2007, so that the average English constituency was around 74,000 while the average Welsh constituency was only 56,000; Wales traditionally votes Labour, England Tory). After this came the absorption of the allied Afrikaaner party, which put another nine seats into Malan's pocket; in the 1953 election, the sitting MPs of this party were all replaced by Malan's nominees.

There was also the question of non-white voters, the existence of which the National Party regarded as anathema; they had already prevented non-whites sitting in the Union parliament in 1910 and now decided it was time for the colour-blind Cape franchise and the Natal Indian franchise to get the chop. The latter was done by the 1948 Asiatic Laws Amendment Act which did away with the Indian vote before it had ever been exercised, the former by the Electoral Laws Amendment Act 1946 which brought back all the problems of registration that had been heaped on the Uitlanders but this time were applied to coloureds. There were roughly 120,000 potential coloured voters and roughly 50,000 were registered; by the time of the 1958 election, that number had been halved by the Act but even this reduction was not enough for Malan. The Separate Representation of Voters Bill was introduced in 1951 to reduce the influence of the coloured vote even further by taking them off the normal electoral register and placing them on a separate one, from which they would elect their own MPs. This would virtually eliminate them as an electoral force in all the marginal constituencies where the Nationalists would probably lose out to the United Party. The measure was fought tooth and nail through parliament and the courts by those white people who believed that the colour blind Cape franchise was a thing to be proud of, as well as those party managers who knew what the nitty gritty of electoral mathematics meant on the ground. To no avail; in 1958 the Nationalists finally succeeded, mainly by packing the benches of the Courts – 'there can seldom in History have been a body of men so apparently unqualified to give a judicial opinion on the matter before them' was the opinion of *The Spectator*.[188]

Next came the enlargement of the Senate, and rigging the elections to it, so that the number of Nationalist Senators went up from 30 to 77 from a total of 89 which allowed them not so much to change the constitution as to rape it. This was followed in 1958 by the equally shrewd move of reducing the voting age from 21 to 18; the Afrikaaner birth rate was 30% higher than that of the English speaking population and so it was reckoned, correctly, that the National Party would gain. In 1953, the National Party took 94 seats to the United Party's 57, (or roughly 65% of the seats on 45% of the vote), largely because of the weighting given to rural constituencies; there the National Party got in on often small majorities while the United Party piled up majorities in urban seats where they were often unopposed. Had the allocation of seats followed a more balanced system, the National Party would have lost the election.

And it worked; in the 1958 elections the National Party took 103 seats to 53 largely by absorbing the Labour vote and winning the popular vote by 642,000 to 503,000. It had taken Malan and his successors ten years, but their *coup* was complete. But why? Where had all these votes come from? Why had those 140,000 people changed sides?

For a start, Malan set out to collect up all those Afrikaaner votes that he had missed out on originally by handing out jobs in such a way that any Afrikaaner who didn't vote for the National Party was not acting in his own self-interest. In order to achieve a full and lasting dominance, Malan began to remove English-speakers – 'Smuts men' - from government service and replaced them with 'bilingual' Afrikaaners. From the beginning, there were no English-speakers in his cabinet. In a tactic familiar to the Leftists and Diversity campaigners of today, it was represented as a great injustice that whereas most of the employees of a particular service were Afrikaans speakers, most of the managers were English speakers and that in the interests of fairness and equality this should be rectified by firing the over-represented English-speakers and hiring people based on their racial, cultural and linguistic backgrounds, whether they were competent or not; this meant that anyone trained or brought up in England was out of a job, including 100 of 284 specially recruited Air Force technicians, and large numbers of nurses; the 1948 Citizenship Act also lengthened the qualification period for British immigrants to five years in an attempt to stem the tide of all those Brits fleeing the grey skies and grey government of the post-war period (and prevent the 40,000 new arrivals from voting in the next election in 1953).[189] It also meant that unless you were completely fluent in Afrikaans, rather than simply competent, you could not expect to get the job in the first place, hold on to it when redundancies beckoned or ever see promotion – so goodbye Durbanites and Capetownians. In pursuit of this noble aim, one of the first acts of this busy and determined government was to free all the *Ossewabrandwag* traitors who had been imprisoned or interned during the war and restore them to their former positions and seniority in government employ. In many cases, special Grievance Commissions paid compensation too; £124,000 alone to 3,000 railway officials, which was the rough equivalent of £13.5m in today's UK terms (2018). In the judiciary, junior lawyers and judges were appointed to posts way beyond their experience and over the heads of more senior and more qualified candidates who had not seen fit to join the *Broederbond*. As a result, the government was almost completely Afrikaanerised, with the added

---

[188] South African Whirlwind, *The Spectator* 29th August, 1952.
[189] South Africa Boiling Up, *The Spectator* 24th June 1949.

delights that membership of the *Broederbond* or National Party was seen as the key qualification for appointment to any post.

The one great fear that all totalitarian utopians have is that the people who command real force, the armed forces and police, will lose patience with their illiberal incompetence and remove them. This was the primary lesson of the French Revolution that every revolutionary learned at Day One of the Slippery Slope To Mass Murderer School, i.e., that the failure to completely overthrow the old order at the required speed resulted in chaos which usually ended in a military *coup*. It was the reason why the communists in Russia kept a suspicious eye on Trotsky, their own murderous Napoleon in command of the army, and so missed the rise of the bureaucrat Stalin, who they arrogantly dismissed as a peasant who dealt with the paperclips. It was perhaps the last thing that went through Trotsky's mind before the ice-pick which Stalin sent him (an act of revolutionary justice which we must deplore as illegal but can only applaud as richly deserved). Stalin made no such mistake and kept the Soviet Army in line through regular purges and by posting popular generals like Zhukov straight from the victory parade to the outer darkness.

Malan and the National Party learned this lesson well and the new Defence Minister F.C. Erasmus, who despite having lived through two world wars and the Five Shilling rebellion had never heard a shot fired in anger, quickly moved to make sure of the armed forces by firing the deputy Chief of the General Staff, Everard-Poole, ex-Commander of the 6th South African Armoured Division in the Italian campaign, and abolishing his post within three months of the new government being sworn in. A new Chief of the General Staff was appointed, this time with a proper Afrikaans name like Beyers, but who tendered his resignation almost immediately because Erasmus kept appointing officers without qualifications and generally politicising the armed forces. Further resignations followed as men who had seen service in the war were replaced by *Broederbond* and National Party cronies; Erasmus himself admitted that of 146 Citizen Force units – the old Commandos – 68 of them were commanded by men who had no military experience at all and 31 by men whose experience had been gained in the school cadet force. What went for the army, went for the police too, with English speakers displaced by Afrikaaners whose loyalty was not so much to the country but to Afrikaaner nationalism. The Military Intelligence Department (DMI), which Smuts had used to round up so many OB members, was also gutted and its files mined for useful dirt to throw at the United Party.[190] Take all this together, then wrap it up with the social life that revolved around all those National Party dominated cultural organisations and increasingly it just became easier for an Afrikaaner to slip into being a National Party supporter without really being much interested in politics. For those who were looking for a specifically South African, rather than English, identity too; Bosman had *Mafeking Road* published in 1947 and voted National Party in 1948, even though he was editing a Union Party newspaper.

There was also a raft of specifically protectionist legislation of the kind that trade union and petty socialists were enthusiastically in favour of. The 1951 Native Building Workers Act made it illegal for a black man to look for work in a white area and illegal for a white person to contract a black builder; the 1952 Native Law Amendment Act made it illegal for a black person to seek work without the permission of the local authority which, in a small town, meant that the blokes in the pub had a veto not just on economic development but on the black man too; the 1953 Native labour (Settlement of Disputes) Act made it illegal for black workers to strike, something that was connived at by the trade unions and repaid in full with the 1956 Industrial Conciliation Act which allowed separate unions for black and white and racial job reservation. All this meant that the National Party indulged the one great desire of organised labour in a capitalist economy – to be protected from free and fair competition at the expense of all and everyone not in the union. To be fair, several leaders of the Labour party were beginning to reject racial policy but in this they were well in advance of a membership that they had long schooled into thinking that black workers were a threat rather than an opportunity; the Labour party was wiped out in the 1958 election and the National Party picked up just about all of those 34,000 votes.

And to cap it all, the National Party was able to get away with this because the opposition was so weak. The United Party could take no real position on the issue of Apartheid when the Nationalists were able to portray it as just an extension of their own segregation policies. Neither had it worked out any solution of its own to the

---

[190] Kevin A. O'Brien, *The South African Intelligence Services From Apartheid to Democracy* (London, 2011) p.53.

Native Question. And then the people who might have done it went and kicked the bucket - Hofmeyr who came to reject Apartheid in all its forms as unworkable, impractical and immoral just before he died in 1948;[191] and then Smuts himself in 1950. They were easily blamed for the chaotic conditions created by the rapid expansion of the cities because they had been in charge during the war and the opportunities to embarrass them over the many contradictions in their approach to race relations would have presented no great challenge to men less malevolent than Malan. Those organisations that did come out in opposition, such as the ex-soldiers of the Torch Commando (financed by that –irony alert - horrible, top-hatted, capitalist, diamond mine owner, bastard, Harry Oppenheimer), a new Progressive Party and an equally weak Liberal Party, plus the Black Sash, formed from the respectable ladies of uptown Joburg society, had nowhere near the punch (literally in some cases) that the Nationalists could deploy in campaigning. And none of the Indian or black organisations had a vote in parliament or any answer to a machine gun. The National Party was free to re-order the world and usher in Utopia in the way it thought best – and there was not a lot anyone else could do about it.

*

...this is the country - to turn to the art of living - which grows fine fruit and good wine, but lives on beefsteaks, bottled sauces and bad brandy; and where not even the biggest town, with a European population of a third of a million, has a permanent professional theatre.... That town - Johannesburg, the golden city - has one of the loveliest climates in the world, and is dead after dark because the white man will not sit in cafes or stroll the streets for fear of the African denizens of the shanty towns that surround it - slums so vile that the city's own Chamber of Commerce estimates that it would cost twenty-two million pounds to make them habitable. Johannesburg is the centre, summit and glory of the white civilisation that South Africa struggles so cruelly to save: it can boast the physical profile and spiritual achievements of a small Middle -Western boom town, the amenities and amusements of Leeds on a wet Sunday night, and is haunted, like everywhere else in the Union, by the fears and hatreds and shames that once stalked Hitler's Germany.

The Spectator 14th July 1950.[192]

The Afrikaaner vision of Utopia was a perfect, rose-tinted little dorp of jacarandas and wide, dusty streets, red wriggly-tin roofs, long shaded *stoeps* and gingerbread iron work balconies; lush gardens or open veldt to taste, with perhaps some good, solid Victorian brickwork and a colonnaded shopping arcade mixed in among a few, large, old Dutch gables, all sheltered under a *Tafelkop* and marked by a tall spire of a Dutch Reformed church. There would be a hotel, perhaps the *Imperial* or the *Station*, where there was a palm court and a long bar where a man could get a *dop* or a *Klippie*, and a steak with a bottle of *Chateau Libertas* or, even worse, sweet 'Worcester Hock, rich Sauternes type'[193]. Outside that little dorp would be the farm; a great wide open range of grass or scrub, vines, wheat or fruit, sheep, cattle and mealies as far as the eye could see and over which his word was law. Here he would sit on his *stoep*, eating his own mutton, greeting his neighbours heartily, rubbing along with his black farm workers while the *platteland* kids, black and white, wrangled about the veldt with mud balls, airguns, catapults and dolls; only come teenage would they be separated. There would always be good jobs, jobs for life and for the boy when he had finished at school, and safe profits (and cheap black labour) so that his daughter could get a job as a typist or secretary until she was ready to marry, pack her job in and become a good *boervrou*. There would be tennis, cricket, rugby, bowls for the *krimpies* and braais at the weekend; Christmas at the beach; their own *boeremusik* (none of that nigger Jazz or degenerate Rock and Roll, *baie dankie*) and proper square dancing; always sunshine and good rains; good beef and full barns; the Kaffir in his place at the mine or in his square house under the bluegums tucked away out of sight on the farm, his wife in the laundry or the garden; and everything pickled in the myth of Blood and Soil and the Good Old Days and no thinking whatsoever about the future - beyond educating the children to believe in the Vision, which they did deliberately and with malice aforethought and with Smuts' own words in *A Century of Wrong*. *The Spectator* nailed the essence of it back in 1919:

---

[191] CO 537/ 3643
[192] 'Dr Malan's Mission', *The Spectator*, 14th July 1950.
[193] 'Drinking Imperially', *The Spectator*, 6th February 1932.

In the solitude of the veld they cherish the memories of the past when South Africa had no mines or railways, and the scattered Dutch farmers, ruling in patriarchal fashion over the natives, did very much as they pleased. They decline altogether to recognise the vast changes wrought in South Africa by British innovation and by modern industrial developments. It is useless to argue with them, as it is foolish to abuse them for being what they are. Time alone can modify the attitude of these remote farmers.[194]

Old Bunting broke into a fit of slavering that he could barely contain when he wrote the chapter 'Indoctrinating the Young'. Starting with a quote from *Mein Kampf*, he followed up with the assertion that 'for the Apartheid state to endure, the Nationalists must exercise complete control over the minds of the young'[195] and then found a gang of evil conspirators who went by the name of the Federation of Afrikaans Cultural Organisations (FAK (sic)) and who had developed a plan to exercise this mind-control in the shape of the *Christian National Education* curriculum. He then began to fulminate against the principles of this curriculum because it was 'fundamentalist and totalitarian…based on outmoded educational and scientific precepts and envisages rigid centralisation…'[196] all of which was completely true, yet none of which, as a Soviet True Believer, he really disapproved of.

Let me point out a little educational theory before we start, just to make the above point clearer – I know I'm on dangerous ground here because I was a teacher for twenty-five years. Roughly speaking, there are two main approaches to deciding what to teach children. The first is the idea that a body of knowledge, skills, attributes and morals need to be imparted through the school so that a child will be fit to take his or her place in the modern world. So, the three 'R's are in there, as are such concepts as 'Muscular Christianity', *mens sana in corpore sano* etc etc. The second is the idea that the natural and inherent attributes of a child should be led out (*educare*) in such a way as to complete them into a whole person ready to go out into the modern world with an open, enquiring mind and the confidence to deal with new knowledge and solve the many and varied problems that will be faced. In reality, a good education will embrace both these approaches. In reality, a *bad* education will involve both these approaches too, the difference being that a good education prepares a child for the future world, a bad one attempts to engineer the future by programming the child with a set of concepts that will produce the world of the future. Some knowledge that is provisional will be taught as fact – usually History; some facts that are emphatically *not* facts, will be taught as facts - usually in Social Science; and some subjects will be banned altogether – in the Soviet Union it was Genetics, in Nazi Germany anything to do with Jews and in Fascist Italy, anything which irritated the Catholic church. So, what Bunting was condemning in the Apartheid education system, was not the methodology of that education system but only the content. As a TASS correspondent, he knew exactly the sort of social-engineering education that Soviet kids were getting and it differed from the Apartheid system only in the ideas, attitudes and assumptions it was hoping to churn out. Fortunately for the world, the smarter kids pay little attention to what the dumber end of the teaching profession spout; it's often an unintended by-product of any education system that the more intelligent sort learn to do their own thinking despite all efforts to prevent such dangerous and subversive individuality. Unfortunately, if there is no alternative narrative presented or available then the effect tends to be corrosive and widespread acceptance of the given is the result.

The principles of Christian-National education were quite reasonable at first glance; mother-tongue medium, an emphasis on Christian morality, the encouragement of knowledge of and love for the country. Looking deeper, however, the references to 'the national task'[197] and the conception of History as 'the struggle between the Kingdom of God and the Empire of darkness',[198] the rejection of bilingualism, mixed schools and the insistence that teachers should all be Christian-Nationalists reveals something that is neither Christian nor Nationalist but actually rather exclusive; the Nation is Afrikaaner and the religion is Calvinism and everyone else - the 88% who aren't either of these things - aren't invited. And going a little deeper, the insistence that even at university

---

[194] 'South Africa and Secession' *The Spectator* 14th June 1919.
[195] Bunting p.244
[196] Bunting p.245
[197] Quoted in Bunting p.248
[198] Quoted in Bunting p.248

level science should be dictated from a narrow Christian perspective (no Darwin?) begins to reveal that this is *bad* education indeed. For the coloured people, a Christian-National education was meant to safeguard them from 'foreign ideologies' and for black people, the aim was to 'inculcate the White man's view of life, especially that of the Boer nation, which is the senior trustee;'[199] they would be educated just enough for semi-skilled manual labour, but they shouldn't bother thinking about a white collar job. A book list was introduced and any book that wasn't on that list was forbidden to be used in school. In 1949, the Transvaal made mother-tongue education compulsory up to Standard 8, (the school-leaving age, or 16) and this was extended to the Cape in 1953; the Free State needed no instruction here, but it wasn't until 1967 that control of education was wrested from Natal and the policy imposed there. Those schools that refused to sign up for Christian-National Education would no longer be funded by the government; many of them were, of course, run by missionaries, a species of creature that had long aroused Calvinist suspicion; the Catholics refused to have anything to do with the curriculum and struggled on without official funding; the Anglicans closed their schools rather than suffer it. Text books began to feature the sort of barking mad racial theory that the world thought had been buried in the rubble of Hitler's bunker; even Social Darwinism as a working concept was dropped as not going far enough. The old hokum of heroic, plucky Boer struggling against savage blacks, and the cowardly, cheating English stealing South Africa's gold and diamonds was pumped up beyond History and inflated into legend. Apartheid became a naturally occurring feature of the world rather than a bad choice. And keep one eye on the laager, kids! The enemies are massing, there are spies everywhere and one day you'll have to fight your own Blood River! This was the real end of Christian-National Education: preparing the Afrikaaner youth for the day when they would have to fight the whole world for the privilege of living in fortress with all the doors barricaded and the blinds firmly drawn and shuttered against the onrushing certainty that the world of the perfect dorp couldn't last long.

For that dorp to be perfect, the black people would have to go. Not just the drunks, bums and unemployed hanging out by the Caltex or the stoep of the liquor store, but all of them. They were welcome to come into town to work, but once they were finished or by the time it got dark, they had to be gone. This was really at the root of Apartheid and all the pseudo-science, sub-intellectual political theory, literary and religious ramblings was little more than a cover for this basic desire. The National Party saw society as a pyramid with whites at the top, coloureds and Indians in the middle and blacks at the bottom and that's the way they liked it and that's the way they intended to keep it. Apartheid, was supposed to mean 'separate' or 'parallel' development but really, it was just meant shovelling the blacks into areas where they couldn't ruin the view anymore. Segregation had long been a feature of South African life but it is possible to see it as a practical solution to the frictions of living in a multicultural society; it was a crap solution, but in many cases it was probably kindly meant and by 1948, there were plenty of people who were beginning to accept (with a sigh and a shrug, perhaps) that it would have to come to an end. Apartheid was no such thing; it was not an attempt to solve a problem but to get it out of sight; it was a huge exercise in kicking the can down the road. Black people would live in the reserves, would be allowed to come to town to work as and when required, and then would go home, just like they had always done before the English and Jewish capitalists had ruined everything by allowing them to settle on the Rand.

In order to achieve this, the first problem to solve was just how to work out what colour everyone was; there were some white people with suspiciously dark skins and a lot of black people with suspiciously light skins too; quite a few immigrants from Mauritius were so light skinned as to be referred to as 'near whites.'[200] In 1950, therefore, the Population Registration Act required everyone to have an ID card with their race and tribe stamped on it and the person who would decide just what race would be stamped on your card would go off general appearance and culture. *General appearance* and *culture*; what that meant in practice was the *whim* of the petty official; the definitions of white and coloured given to him to work with was;

> A person who in appearance is, or is generally accepted as, a White person but does not include a
> person who, though in appearance is obviously a White person, is generally accepted as a Coloured
> person.[201]

---

[199] Quoted in Bunting p.248-9
[200] G.H. Calpin, *Mixed Marriages*, The Spectator, 17th March 1950.
[201] Quoted in Gordon Winter, *Inside BOSS South Africa's Secret Police* (London, 1981).p.48

Could anything be more mangled? The result was that an awful lot of people who thought they were white turned out to be no such thing at all; fifteen years later there was still a backlog of 150,000 cases appealing against the decision to stop them being white waiting to be cleared (exactly as *The Spectator* had predicted back in 1906). Perhaps it was to prevent the situation getting worse that the 1950 Immorality Amendment Act was rushed through to extend the 1927 Act, which merely forbade sex between white and black, to forbid whites from nipping into the bushes with coloureds and/or Indians. It didn't work (how could it?) and 6,000 people were convicted in the next fifteen years - which, given the necessity to catch the perpetrators in *flagrante delicto*, was certainly an under-estimate of the true scale of the illicit shagging. In 1957, the authorities thought the problem so serious as to add two years to the five year imprisonment penalty, which gave a whole new meaning to the Seven Year Itch.

The next thing was to clear away the offending people from the towns and for this the 1950 Group Areas Act was passed. The aim of this was to shift out non-whites from the centre of towns into properly segregated locations on the outskirts and while the National Party could claim that this was no more than an enhanced slum clearance programme, nothing of the size and scale of it had ever been contemplated before. It was also a huge violation of the very essence of the Western civilisation that the National Party claimed to represent; property rights and the liberty to live where you chose within the limits of the depth of your pocket. In Cape Town, the number of people affected over the next fifteen years were roughly 8,000 whites, 95,000 coloureds and 4,500 Asians; and this was before the big clearances of the later 1960s. The Indians of Durban alone stood to lose £5.5 million worth of property when the zoning went through. The 1954 Natives Resettlement Act allowed for the forcible removal of 57,000 black people from the Western Areas of Joburg, the removal of their Freeholds (!) and their resettlement in areas segregated not just along racial lines but along tribal ones too; this was done at gunpoint and the area re-zoned for white use was given the new name of *Triumph*, which at least showed that the National Party had a sense of humour.

Once out, they would be kept out through the 1952 Native (Abolition of Passes and Coordination of Documents) Act which abolished the hated Passes and…brought in new Passes which recorded all sorts of personal data and which had to be carried at all times, rather than under the old system when they had simply to be produced within seven days. The Native Laws Amendment Act of that same year restricted a man from being in any area without a permit for more than 72 hours; this allowed the 'endorsing out' of anyone deemed undesirable. These laws didn't work either; between 1955-58 alone, 150,000 people were convicted under the Pass Laws and related offences.

Even the National Party recognised that black people would have to come into town at some stage, if only to work in the gardens of white people, but they felt that something ought to be done to avoid the necessity of mixing with them; the Separate Amenities Act was just the first of those petty Apartheid laws which divided up everything into 'Whites Only' or 'Blacks Only'. Segregation on the Joburg buses cost the Joburg municipal transport department £500,000 per year and ended any hope of profitability. Even churches were supposed to be segregated. And hospitals. And taxis. And beaches. And cinemas. Everything. Except supermarkets, where black money was the same colour as white money.

*

Like all idiocies that begin with 'let's all get together and build a perfect world', Apartheid quickly came up against the awkward reality of lots of people saying 'I don't want your version of a perfect world, thank you very much. And next time, it would be nice if you had the manners to ask me if I want my world changed before you go rampaging through it with your muddy boots, platitudinous slogans and boneheaded stupidity.' There is a method of argument common to all idiots and it almost invariably follows this pattern:

Me: I say, don't you think that White is White and Black is Black?

Utopian (making one quick attempt at refutation): Er, I think you'll find that Black is actually *White*.

Me: No, look. I can see it with my own eyes.

Utopian (making an appeal to his superior knowledge): Actually, research shows that Black is, in 97% of cases, *White.*

Me: No. Black is the absorption of the colours of the spectrum, while White is the reflection of them all.

Utopian (attacking the person not the argument): Are you some sort of racist/imperialist/communist/fascist?

Me: No. It's just that I can't believe that Black is White.

Utopian (imposing censorship): I don't have to listen to this. I'm no platforming you and I'm going to get you banned from Twitter.

Exit Utopian (slamming door and spraying epithets).

I've left out the last stage, of course, but it is absolutely central to the Utopian world view and the logic of it goes like this: *if you disagree with me, you are maliciously impeding the birth of the perfect world. The problems of implementation are not to do with the stupidity of the original concept but because of your opposition and you are therefore to blame if the plan isn't working. Therefore, it is perfectly reasonable to use violence against you; after all, you can't make an omelette without breaking eggs and we are making Utopia. Anyone who doesn't want Utopia is clearly mad or bad, so it's the noose, Robben Island or the Gulag for you, mate.*

It always happens like this. The first revolutionary to think this up was Jean-Paul Marat who reckoned that the simplest way to make sure the French Revolution succeeded was to kill everyone who expressed the slightest reservation about it. This was later refined into the concept of 'Terror' which meant the elimination of opposition before it arose; you killed people not for what they had done, but what they might do. Lenin and Trotsky were the real experts on this, though Stalin refined it by institutionalising it just to keep everyone on their toes. Hitler famously used it against his internal party opponents during the Night of the Long Knives and then, picking up a few tips from Stalin, deployed the Gestapo to make sure there was no backsliding on the road to Utopia. Che Guevara was no slouch when it came to a bit of 'revolutionary justice' either while, of course, you can still hear the virtues of censorship, lynching and imprisonment without trial espoused by the members of the modern British Labour Party under the euphemism of 'workers' justice' or 'hate speech'. This the 'omelette and eggs' argument and there's a long History to it. It has been applied in every communist or socialist or fascist regime ever and it was applied under Apartheid and it will be applied by every organisation that thinks it has found the solution to all the problems of the world, simply because anyone who is so stupid as to think that they have discovered the answer to all the world's problems is stupid enough to think they can save the world by shooting, silencing or imprisoning the people who are pointing out their stupidity. 'I've seen the broken eggs,' says the despairing Everyman on the way to the noose, Robben Island or the Gulag. 'So where's the fucking omelette gone then?'

And like all the utopian socialists, communists, fascists and Nazis, the National Party responded to opposition and criticism in exactly this same way. In 1948, J.G. Strydom declared that;

> 'Anyone who purposely tried to upset the government's plans to put into operation the Apartheid policy or failed in their duty towards the realisation of that aim would be guilty of treason.'[202]

The cast of that wide net included much of the United Party, the veterans of the Springbok Legion, the Torch Commando, the posh ladies of the Black Sash and pretty much anyone who wasn't white.

And, what's more, they would be COMMUNISTS! Like all totalitarian utopians, the National Party needed someone to blame for their own stupidity and they chose to label anyone they didn't like as *communists* in exactly the same way that the Soviets chose to label even the mildest critic as a *Fascist, Imperialist* or, my personal favourite, *Capitalist Lackey and Running Dog of the Bourgeoisie.* Now while it is an eminently

---

[202] Quoted in Bunting p.194.

sensible thing to oppose communism the Nationalists made the cardinal error of attacking anyone who disagreed with them as 'communistic' and so prevented any reasonable dialogue and drove everyone with the slightest reservation about Apartheid into the arms of the Communist Party. Nico Diederichs, the National Party economist, declared that 'the doctrine of liberalism…is almost the same as the ideal of communism.'[203] No it isn't, Nico! It's the exact opposite because it starts from the premise that people are free to go about their business as they see fit without being told what to do by the government; everything is allowed until the Law forbids it; under communism, everything that isn't forbidden by the government is compulsory and the Law is no check on the government. During the Treason Trial of the ANC in 1957, Professor Andrew Murray, of the University of Cape Town Department of Political Science, was put into the witness box and asked to interpret a series of statements as to whether they were 'communistic'. In a moment of high comedy he identified each one as being 'communistic', despite the fact that they had been made respectively by Malan, Abraham Lincoln, Woodrow Wilson and, finally, Murray himself.[204]

In 1950, the Communist Party was made illegal and anyone suspected of being a communist could be subjected to a series of restrictions, including Banning Orders on organisations and individuals and being required to resign from public service; these were the measures that got Bunting kicked out of parliament and harassed from pillar to post. The restrictions applied might involve internal exile, severe limits on movement or publication, on being quoted and the cessation of all political or even social activity (one Liberal was prosecuted for playing billiards);[205]; and in 1953, the Criminal Law Amendment Act upped the penalties for breaking the law in any protest to include three years in the *tronk* and ten lashes (corporal punishment was virtually compulsory for the first fifteen years of NP rule). The Public Safety Act of 1953 allowed the government to rule by decree in an emergency while in 1954 came the Riotous Assemblies and Suppression of Communism Act which made it unnecessary to grant a hearing to anyone the government proposed to ban. It also forbade communists from standing for election and gave the government the power to outlaw any sort of protest; it was updated into a catch-all in 1956. To this we owe Tom Sharpe's brilliant 1971 novel *Riotous Assembly,* which lampooned Apartheid South Africa in, well, riotous fashion, and introduced the monumentally stupid and bloodthirsty Konstabel Els as the epitome of the South African Police Service – to which organisation he dedicated the book for their efforts to preserve Western civilisation with an irony so thick it dripped like treacle off the page. In 1959, another amendment to the criminal law introduced the concept of weekend imprisonment while the Prisons Act made it nigh on illegal to report on prisons, prisoners or ex-prisoners, which is always an indication that the government really does have something to hide. This Act was the result of a series of allegations in 1956 about torture, unhygienic conditions and rampant homosexuality in the remarkably named Cinderella prison in Boksberg which were reported in the press. Of course, the government rounded up fifty-six (nineteen hundred more would have been just *too* many) warders to swear that nothing of the sort could ever happen in a South African jail; the warders who made the allegations were subsequently prosecuted under the Act and themselves sent to jail, which was unnecessarily serendipitous I feel. Conditions throughout the prison system remained violent, revolting and brutal. And, of course, while all this was going on, the National party used the Suppression of Communism legislation to close down newspapers and generally harass editors and journalists with something in the region of a hundred separate regulations laying down what might or might not be said.

But none of the seven hundred or so regulations (according to Allister Sparks)[206] introduced to make Apartheid function could make it work. It didn't work because the protestors were too many and the National Party really lacked the stomach for the Soviet-proportioned purge and repression that would really be necessary to keep their utopian vision on the rails; even Joe Slovo, SACP, said that before 1960, the police were inclined to be 'gentlemanly'[207] and though the state would get better and better at repression, more effective, more brutal and more successful as the years went by, the basic facts of too many protestors and not enough stomach remained. As Lord Selbourne had said, all those years ago back in 1909, before this nonsense had seized hold of so many backveldt Boers and racist trade unionists;

---

[203] Quoted in Bunting p.197.
[204] N. Mandela, *Long Walk to Freedom* (London 1994) p.245.
[205] Randolph Vigne, *On Being Banned*, The Spectator, 18th September 1964.
[206] Allister Sparks, *The Mind of South Africa* (London, 1990) p.xviii
[207] TRC Vol.2 Ch.3 para 121.

'Is the white man to rule a line and say to the black man: "Thus far and no farther. No matter what Providence may propose for you, or with what qualities Providence may have endowed you, I am going to stand on one side of this line, and you are going to stand on the other. You will never be allowed to cross this line by any exercise of intellect or by any strength of character?".... How, in that case, does the white man propose to proceed so as effectively to arrest the native's development? If he were to cast behind him all scruples, he could carry a policy of repression to great lengths. He could inflict an immeasurable amount of cruelty and injustice on the native, and he could indefinitely deteriorate his own character; but he would in the end quite inevitably fail in effecting his purpose. He would only be trying to do what the Inquisition and other self- appointed substitutes for Providence have attempted to do throughout the ages - chain the human mind and arrest its development - and he would as miserably fail as they did. The human mind is unchainable. Its development may be temporarily checked; it may be warped or it may be diverted into unnatural and noxious channels; but it can never be permanently arrested. Therefore, I say, that the attempt, at whatever sacrifice... or however protracted, must fail.'[208]

*

The Background moves to the Foreground.

I want to tell him things that he might not hear from others, the first being that a natives' policy can only succeed if a large portion of the natives accept and support it. You cannot govern nine million people against the will of the greater part. We have not reached such a point yet, but if we do not seek and obtain the natives' cooperation and good will, we are headed for trouble. Furthermore, we need to obtain some clarity about what is possible with apartheid. We say that economic integration is fatal, but under this administration, economic integration is assuming even larger proportions. If it continues like this, we will have to face the fact that you cannot make a distinction on the basis of a man's colour forever. You cannot give the natives education, good employment and a high standard of living, and then say that they cannot become citizens of this country due to the colour of their skin. If apartheid is our policy, we will have to do more than just trying to halt the stream to the cities.

P.A. Weber, editor of *Die Burger* trying to get a message to Malan, 3rd February 1951.[209]

*

Mobutu is screwing up Zaire pretty good, you know. He simply has no idea how to run a country.

Bill Avery, CIA, 1975.[210]

*

If three Black men deliver speeches at a public meeting in South Africa today [1981], the spy is not in the audience. He's one of the speakers.

Gordon Winter, BOSS defector.[211]

*

One thing the 'old' and the 'new' South Africa have in common is a passion for inventing History. History is not seen as a dispassionate inquiry into what happened, but rather as a part of political mobilisation promoting some form of collective self-interest.

[208] Address delivered by Lord Selbourne Before the Congregation of the University of the Cape of Good Hope, on Saturday, 27th Feb., 1909.
[209] Lindie Korf, *D.F. Malan: a political biography*. University of Stellenbosh Ph.D Thesis, 2010.
[210] Quoted in John Stockwell, *Looking for Enemies: A CIA Story* (New York, 1978) p.96.
[211] Gordon Winter, *Inside BOSS South Africa's Secret Police* (London, 1981), p.42.

Frederik van Zyl Slabbert, Progressive Liberal Party. Quoted in *'External Mission: The ANC in Exile 1960-1990'* 2013.

*

The ANC struggle narrative is disarmingly simple and it goes like this:

> As the leading voice of black resistance to Apartheid since its foundation in 1912, the ANC steadily built up its strength until it was able to organise mass protests in the Defiance Campaign and the Freedom Charter. Met with brutal police responses, the ANC reluctantly chose the path of armed resistance until its leadership was betrayed to the security forces and arrested at Rivonia farm. After the incarceration of Nelson Mandela on Robben Island, the ANC continued the struggle from abroad under the inspired leadership of Oliver Tambo. Inside South Africa, it retained its primacy as the main focus of resistance to Apartheid while its armed wing, known as MK, fought a guerrilla war against the South African Defence Force. Inspired by the ANC, there was a near continuous series of popular revolts after 1975 which were met by increasing police brutality but which actively and effectively challenged Apartheid. In 1987, the SADF was defeated at the Battle of Cuito Canavale by the forces of liberation and the Nationalist government was forced to release Nelson Mandela and come to the negotiating table. After a period of difficult negotiations, hampered by a 'Third Force' of Zulu nationalists and diehard Afrikaaners, elections were held in 1994 which confirmed Nelson Mandela as president and the ANC as the legitimate and long standing representative of a non-racial and democratic future for South Africa.

Very little of this is true. The problem is that any and every challenge to it has been countered by claques of ANC supporters yelling 'Racist! Imperialist! Fascist! Colonialist!' It's fair to say that there is a certain amount of truth in the claims made for the ANC before the arrests at Rivonia but everything else is contestable. The reality is that after Rivonia, perhaps the only successes the ANC enjoyed were in the field of strategic deception whereby opinion in the West was manipulated into accepting the ANC version of any and all events. In particular, they managed to convince large swathes of opinion that the South African Communist Party had no control over the ANC, they being merely fellow travellers, and that the ANC represented a united, competent, morally pure, non-racial democratic alternative to the Apartheid state. This was not a difficult task, it has to be admitted; most people in the West were revolted by Apartheid and refused to listen to nuance, reality, or anything that besmirched the image of the idolised ANC. Very many people *still* refuse to listen, despite twenty-five years of ANC misgovernment and all the evidence any reasonable, thinking person could ask for. Beyond that, the record is one of dismal failure right up until the release of Nelson Mandela. Thus was the ANC the luckiest opposition group in History. They were handed the keys to the kingdom without doing very much to earn them and thereafter embarked on a looting spree that has continued to this day (2019).

In order to understand what happened in these years, we also have to be aware of the terminology. So far, I have used the term 'conservative' in the sense that the British conservatives use it; a preference for free market economics, small government and gradual change. This is emphatically *not* what a 'conservative' is in South Africa. There a conservative is someone who is generally committed to a stricter application of Apartheid, accepts a strong state in charge of the commanding heights of the economy, and is committed to the preservation of the language, culture and dominance of the *volk*. They were often referred to as *verkrampte* (unyielding) while those 'conservatives' who were more open to change were known as *verligte* (enlightened).

The term 'liberal' is also confusing; indeed, it has acquired almost chameleon properties. The original British liberals were committed to free market capitalism, small government, meritocracy and international co-operation/anti-imperialism but they have morphed over time into something not very distinguishable from any other bland European social democrats in their desire for international co-operation, supra-national government, personal liberties and a strong interventionist state managing the economy in order to finance welfare programmes. Since the end of the Cold War, the term has morphed once again, especially in the USA where the term is almost indistinguishable from 'socialist'. In South Africa during this period, 'liberal' was almost synonymous with being white, anti-Apartheid and pro-free market; in this sense South African liberals were rather closer to British conservatism than actual liberalism.

'Left wing' and 'Right wing' are terms inherited from the French Revolution when those in favour of more and faster change sat on the benches to the left of the hall while those who were rather more resistant to change sat on the opposite side. Since the Russian Revolution, 'Left wing' has come to mean those who are more inclined to socialism, revolution and the achievement of a utopian society; very often they call themselves 'progressive' and claim their opponents are 'reactionaries' who want to return to some mythical time when they could exploit and oppress the workers and peasants to their hearts content. 'Right wing' has come to be associated with those who are more resistant to rapid change, big government and utopian schemes. In reality, the terms are not very useful beyond a certain short-hand; as we have seen Nazis, socialists and communists all believe in pretty much the same thing – big government, the restriction of free speech and individual liberty, utopian visions, control of the commanding heights of the economy, the militarisation of society and intolerance of dissent - and yet, absurdly, Nazis are commonly assumed to be 'Right wing' while Communists are supposedly 'Left wing'. In South Africa, the National Party was assumed to be 'Right wing' whereas the ANC was assumed to be 'Left wing'. Similarly, during this period, Britain and the USA were assumed to be 'Right wing' and the USSR 'Left wing'. It is a common assumption, therefore, that Britain and the USA supported the National Party and Apartheid while the USSR supported the ANC and opposed Apartheid. These are assumptions that cannot really be sustained beyond even a cursory glance. While the USSR did support the ANC and opposed Apartheid, Britain and the USA emphatically *did not* support the National Party or Apartheid.

Right. So that's the terms defined, let's get on with the stuff we're interested in.

When thinking about resistance to Apartheid, it has become routine to foreground the African National Congress and then look for its roots but it is important to keep in mind the reality that before the end of the Second World War, the ANC was barely worth a mention. Indeed, in the early years of the 20th Century, there were few Africans who were both educated enough to understand how the South African government functioned and capable enough to exercise leadership. (In 1906, the Zulus rose up in a hopeless rebellion against the imposition of a tax in a time of depression and were promptly defeated, just as they had been before and illustrating, once more, just how poor African leadership was). This was because illiteracy was widespread and the emergence of English as a unifying language was still a very long way away so it was virtually impossible for black people to organise effectively.

Exceptions to the rule such as Solomon Plaatje, J.T. Jabavu, John Dube and Walter Rubusana, elected to the Cape Provincial Council in 1910, were just that and although there were several organisations and newspapers representing a nascent political awakening, they were riven by fundamental questions of aim and methods, tribal and religious affiliation, and debates about whether new democratic forms of rule should be adopted or the rule of the chiefs revived. A good example of this was the reaction to the Native Land Act of 1913; although subsequently held up as an example of a white land grab, the newly formed African Native National Congress, was divided on whether the Act should be opposed or not and, indeed, were in favour of some aspects of segregation and land reservation.[212] Protests tended to be about practical issues, such as the Pass Laws, new regulations and restrictions regarding cattle dipping and land ownership. As we have seen, the main source of political opposition before the First World War came from the Indian community in Natal, while after it the Industrial and Commercial Union of South Africa (ICU) was instrumental in bringing about a series of strikes with greater or lesser success on bread and butter issues; but this organisation too was riven by personal rivalries, general incompetence and organisational chaos. Throughout the period before the great watershed of the Sharpeville massacre in 1961, local frustrations did produce disturbances from time to time, such as the booze riot in Newclare, Joburg, in February 1950 which ended up with 650 people in the *tronk* after the arrest of one hapless bootlegger, but without much result.[213]

As for the ANC, led by the remarkably named Dr James Sebebuijwasegokgoboontharile Moroka – meaning; *I have come at last, having been criminally enslaved, but will bring rain, peace and freedom to my people*[214] - it was almost quite literally, 'more talk than action.'[215] Riven by questions of whether the organisation should

[212] William Beinart, *Twentieth Century South Africa* (London, 2001) p.92
[213] 'South African Unrest.' *The Spectator* 17th February 1950.
[214] Pallister et al, *South Africa Inc* p.54
[215] N. Mandela, *Long Walk to Freedom* (London, 1994) p. 159.

accept non-blacks, the ANC took a long time to concede that the movement should *eventually* become non-racial. The decision to co-operate in the campaign against Apartheid with the South African Indian Congress, the Communist Party and coloured organisations also took a while. The young Nelson Mandela was for a long time opposed to non-racialism, i.e. that there should be no distinctions based on race, but accepted that he had lost his point when both the National Executive Committee and the National Conference voted him down in 1951. (Even so, it should be noted, the ANC did not allow non-blacks to join until 1969 and even then, refused them permission to take seats on the National Executive Commission).[216] Before the Defiance campaign of 1952, therefore, there was no particular reason to point to the ANC as being much different from or more significant than any one of a number of fractious black political organisations such as the Pan African Congress.

Much of the hesitation about non-racialism was based on the suspicion of Indians and its worth pausing to look at the devastating riots between Indians and Zulus that broke out in Durban in January 1949 for what they can tell us about the shortcomings of the ANC version of South African History.[217] Beinart barely gives them a passing mention while Allister Sparks ignored them entirely, yet both gave prominence to the much less bloody Sharpeville Massacre which was elevated into legend mainly because the violence was white on black rather than black on brown (or brown on black). At Sharpeville, 69 people died when police opened fire on a provocative demonstration; in Durban, the race riots resulted in 200 dead, a thousand injured, widespread rape, 25,000 refugees[218] conveyed to safety by (white) police and 2245 houses, shops and stores destroyed, looted or damaged.[219] There can be no ducking the accusation that the importance of these events was played down in order to further the fiction that the struggle was throughout one of black versus white.

The disturbances began after an altercation in a shop which resulted in a Zulu teenager being assaulted by an Indian shopkeeper, who shoved his head through a window. It was late afternoon and the streets were packed with commuters who, upon seeing the broken window and blood, reacted by choosing sides and throwing punches. The assault took place in a prominently Indian area and the Zulus were attacked by all sorts of bottles and brickbats from the windows and balconies above and the violence became sporadic but general and it took until 11pm before the city was quiet. Meanwhile, all sorts of rumours went round which resulted on the 14th January with a rather more organised mob of Zulus descending on the city threatening violence and demanding the police step aside so that the Indian population might be ethnically cleansed or simply tossed onto ships in the harbour ready for deportation. Weapons were produced. Troops and sailors were deployed but it wasn't until the 17th that order was restored. If this wasn't bad enough, when an inquiry was announced, the ANC, the South African Indian Congress, the Natal Indian Organisation, the SACP and a plethora of trade unions of one sort or another engaged in an unedifying orgy of perjury, forged documents and false witnesses all aimed at apportioning blame, compensation-seeking or making political capital. Among the accusations made were that the police had been tardy in stopping the violence (untrue), had used too much force (untrue), not enough force (true), that some white people thought the brawling was a great spectacle (true) and that some white women, described as 'degraded specimens of their race', encouraged Zulu attacks on Indians (true). The ANC and the SAIC blamed the government for the riots (predictable and untrue) while the Zulus complained that the police had stopped them getting their own back on Indian merchants (true) who, they claimed, ripped them off (possibly true or untrue); the Commission claimed that the Indians were always too quick to claim racial discrimination if their demands were not immediately met (probably true), especially in the case of compensation for loss (also probably true) and that the loose language of European politicians gave the impression to the Zulus that the Indians were fair game (again, probably true).

Beneath these accusations, and allowing for the general impression given by the Report that the Indians were pretty much responsible for their own misfortunes, was a more complex picture of the strained relations between Zulus and Indians in Durban. As far as the Zulus were concerned, Indians dominated the lucrative bus trade, mistreated Zulus who used those buses and used their kinship networks to prevent anyone else acquiring a bus operator's licence. This went for trading licences too. They also complained that whenever a Zulu turned up in front of a magistrate after a dispute with an Indian, the Indians flooded the court with false witnesses

---

[216] Stephen Ellis, *External Mission; the ANC in Exile 1960-1990* (Oxford, 2013) p.76.
[217] 'The Durban Riots'. *The Spectator* 21st January 1949.
[218] CO 537/4561 Report by the UK Trade Commissioner at Durban 14th Feb 1949.
[219] CO 537/4561 Report of the Commission of Enquiry into Riots in Durban 1949.

represented by lawyers of dubious honesty with the result that they always came off worse. Even more galling was the fact that the wealthier Indians were preying on poorer Zulu girls and then, whenever they got pregnant, abandoning them for caste or family reasons. Much of this evidence was apocryphal to say the least, but it seems more than coincidence that the riots kicked off amid the everyday frustrations of a bus station noted for its rapacious Indian operators. It's also probably fair to say that the better educated Indians were also the possessors of the money and business acumen that the Zulus tended to lack and were organised enough to impose cartel conditions on the struggling mass of Zulu workers. That this was Indian racism, pure and simple, and the response to it Zulu racism, pure and simple, was something that neither the ANC nor their supporters were particularly willing to face up to in the years to come. Neither was this racism peculiar to Durban; the British Commonwealth Relations Office were interested in what they correctly called the 'race riots' as part of the growth of a general anti-Indian feeling throughout East Africa and circulated requests for political intelligence on the issue in 1948-49.[220] At the centre of this interest was a desire to protect Africans from potentially unfair competition from Indian immigrants.[221] Malan was also concerned, seeing in the riots evidence of a new Asiatic peril across East Africa which, he believed, would 'hamper the natural evolution of the African native'.[222] It's hard not to think though, that his concern was to prevent any more immigration from India in case it spilled over into South Africa rather than any consideration for the Zulus.

By far the most significant development in post-1945 black life was the continuing emergence of the black urban working classes and the increase in the number of professional, educated and prosperous black people whose links to the old rural life and traditional chieftainship were increasingly tenuous and who were increasingly attracted by Marxist thought. By 1960, the labour brought in to fill the compounds and work the mines was only 40% South African, the bulk coming from southern Mozambique and Swaziland, while by 1950, black employment in manufacturing had outstripped employment in mining. The demand for domestic workers brought more and more women to the towns too. On top of this, many black people had benefitted from the educational opportunities provided by the British and Imperial armies during the Second World War – the largest educational programme conducted in Africa up until that point and for long after – to acquire not just literacy, but also mechanical, medical and administrative skills which in turn made them eminently more employable in the many small enterprises that made up the bulk of the manufacturing sector. By 1960, a third of the black population (3.4 million)[223] had moved to urban areas, overwhelming attempts at 'influx control' and aggravating race relations as the police struggled to separate those who were legally entitled to reside in the towns and those who weren't; convictions under the Pass Laws ran at roughly 300,000 per year, while the humiliations at the hands of clod-hopping coppers during raids, inspections and deportations were legion. All this provided fertile ground for the nascent opposition.

In the meantime, the experience of the cities was continuing to undermine the authority of the chiefs in the rural areas especially when Malan's government sought to harden up Apartheid by handing more power to them under a system of tribal 'homelands' or 'Bantustans'. More and better education meant that there were more and more people who had been exposed to British constitutional ideas of *noblesse oblige* and democracy who were simply not content to accept the limitations of African chieftainship, which too often involved power without responsibility or accountability. When combined with opposition to white government, this led to accusations that the chiefs were mere placemen or government stooges.

The early career of Nelson Mandela illustrates this transformation rather well.[224] Born in 1918 as a high status member of a minor Xhosa clan, the Thembu, Mandela grew up in the Transkei imbibing highly coloured accounts of the warrior prowess of his tribe and with almost no contact with white people. Identified as being a possible future counsellor to the chief, he was adequately educated by missionaries before heading off to the premier institution for black education, Fort Hare, where he proved to be no more than an adequate student. There was little, beyond a certain stubbornness, in his career at Fort Hare that marked him out as the great leader he would become but it was his decision to abscond to Johannesburg in 1939 to escape an arranged marriage

---

[220] CO 537/4561
[221] CO 537/4737 Brief Note for Lord Listowel on points raised by Dr Malan.
[222] CO 537/4737 Attlee to Foreign Secretary, 20th April 1949.
[223] Beinart p.159.
[224] N. Mandela, *Long Walk to Freedom* (London, 1994).

that truly marked him. This was a complete rejection of the chief's authority and his concurrent decision to find work in a law firm while he studied for a law degree, was a complete rejection of rural life too. He had chosen, consciously or not, to become part of the black, urban middle class.

Given the widespread presence of the Communist Party there, it was inevitable that he would end up mixing with Marxists in the Johannesburg legal milieu and though he remained suspicious of the Communist Party throughout his life, in these years, he was gradually seduced by the simplicity of Marxist thought. It's probably fair to say that at this point in his life, Mandela was not the sharpest tool in the box – he got his BA in 1943 but then failed his law degree – and so failed to spot the rotten kernel in that tempting fruit of *from each according to his ability; to each according to his needs*.[225] Any such system based on that tenet needs to answer the question of who decides on an individual's needs and ability; and the only practical answer to that question is 'The State', overwhelming and all-powerful, for if the matter is left up to the individual, a sizeable number of skulkers, scroungers, loafers, malingerers and opportunists will claim that their abilities are zero and their needs limitless. More problematical too was the fact that black people were already facing an over-mighty state and though the pigment might be different in the future, the potential for tyranny would remain. These were theoretical issues that Mandela and most of the ANC didn't really examine in detail until imprisonment gave them all the time they needed to consider the issues in depth. His talents lay elsewhere than theory though; gradually moving into the ANC around 1943, he proved himself to be an excellent organiser, a patient listener and an increasingly committed activist.

There had been many protests before the election of the National Party government in 1948 but it was the Defiance Campaign of 1952 that brought the previously marginal ANC to the fore. In an attempt to make protest effective against the Apartheid measures then being introduced by the Malan government, volunteers were trained in how to get arrested, how to act non-violently, how to dress – it was cold in jail – and how to behave in a polite and dignified manner when under arrest or under the scrutiny of the press. From then on, detailed planning began for a series of nationwide protest demonstrations beginning on Founders Day, 6th April, the anniversary of Van Riebeeck's arrival, and then a Day of Protest in June with the aim of getting large numbers of activists arrested and crammed into the jails. From that point on, a steady series of ANC provocations resulted in 8,500 people being arrested, jailed and fined for petty offences. The subsequent publicity produced a surge in support for the ANC that pushed membership from 20,000 to 100,000. The trial of the leadership of the campaign, which included such rising stars as Walter Sisulu, J.B. Marks, Ahmed Kathrada and Mandela himself, provoked massive multi-racial demonstrations against the government and showed, for the first time, that black people were no longer just part of the background of political life in South Africa but very much front and centre. The 'Native Question' was no longer just a conversation between different groups of white people.

The ANC did not have it all their own way though. The campaign fizzled out and failed and though much emphasis had been laid on non-violence, terrible riots broke out in Port Elizabeth which left forty people dead. One of these riots involved the murder of the local cinema manager, a white man, Rudolph Brandt, with many friends in the predominantly black neighbourhood, the stabbing of his son and two assistants and the brutal gang rape of his wife which did nothing whatsoever to dispel the image of blacks being rather more of the savage rapists, looters and arsonists type than respectable working people.[226] Similarly, despite attempts to raise the countryside, the ANC made little progress and there were continuing racist arguments within the ANC about the desirability of co-operating with the hated Indians. Perhaps the most dispiriting blow came when Dr. Moroka, the president-general of the ANC and leader of the campaign turned his coat at the leadership trial and denounced both communism and the idea of racial equality.[227] The underlying problem was one of organisation though. The ANC was still a part-time outfit with few paid officials and the need for its leaders to earn a living necessarily limited their effectiveness; part of Moroka's betrayal was due to his fear of losing his lucrative medical practice if he was convicted.

---

[225] N. Mandela, *Long Walk to Freedom* (London, 1994), p.137.
[226] http://thecasualobserver.co.za/port-elizabeth-yore-defiance-campaign-1952/
[227] N. Mandela, *Long Walk to Freedom* (London 1994) p.158.

Perhaps the most interesting aspect of this inconclusive contest between the ANC and the National Party government lies in the exchange of letters between Moroka and Malan which opened the campaign.[228] Both written in careful English and moderate tone, they reveal much about the assumptions and pretensions of either side. The ANC claimed to be the voice of all Africans and that economic conditions for the African people were steadily worsening, both of which were completely untrue statements; Mandela was driving an Oldsmobile, Moroka's medical practice had made him wealthy by any standards, Sisulu was a successful Estate Agent and for all the Marxist nonsense spouted in the letter, it was increasing prosperity and the emergence of a wealthier middle class that was driving demand for equal rights. The claim that the ANC was campaigning for the *restitution* of democracy would also mystify any reasonable person because outside the Cape Province, there had never been any democracy for non-whites. In there was also the tried and trusted Left wing tactic of asserting that responsibility for the consequences of any action that the ANC might initiate lay with the government rather than the ANC itself; the gang rape of Edith Brandt, went the logic, was the fault of the government because the government had not immediately caved in to the demands of the protestors, rather than being the responsibility of the ANC for creating the conditions for a violent riot. Whatever the rights and wrongs of the cause, accepting this assertion was absolutely *not* democracy in action, but mob rule, and would establish a precedent for any group of agitators to demand anything of any government and be justified in using violence to get it if the government refused. The probability of violence erupting from a non-violent protest was well known and the risks rather cynically accepted; this had, after all, been a central part of Gandhi's 'non-violent' independence campaigns in India - though he and the other Congress leaders made a point of deploring such riots, they rarely did anything effective to stop them. Mandela himself was convinced that non-violence should be used as a tactic simply because the ANC could not expect to win a violent confrontation with the government and he was already toying with the idea of a guerrilla war.

Malan's response was equally remarkable in its assertion that Apartheid was meant to *protect* Africans from competition from whites but also blunt in its rejection of any possibility of Europeans being ruled over by Africans; it was a matter of self-preservation, he argued. There was also the assertion that however irksome the law was, Africans in South Africa were far better off under white rule than were Africans in other parts of the continent which, at the time, was a debatable proposition, but when decolonisation swept through Africa in the 1960s became an increasingly common reality. After this came the bald statement that any attempt to subvert the state would be met with the full weight of the state's resources, which really required no elaboration. From that point on, the lines were drawn and neither side would reconsider their respective positions in any meaningful way for the next thirty years; the ANC would protest, usually ineffectually, while the State would repress, always inconclusively.

In 1955, the ANC went on the offensive once more with the publication of the Freedom Charter. This was a series of demands for equal political rights, equal employment and educational opportunities and the end of restrictive legislation, none of which could possibly be opposed on their own terms by any sane non-racist person, even when assessed from the standpoint of 1955. The problem was, however, that the influence of the Communist Party was written all over it and this provided plenty of grounds for rejection because it appeared that the ANC was tied to an economic programme of expropriation of land, nationalisation of the banks, the mines and big industries. Not only this, but they also demanded that 'all other industry and trade shall be controlled to assist the wellbeing of the people'.[229] The Charter also opposed measures for stock control in a display of unworthy opportunism; unpopular as they were, government plans to limit the number of animals in the African rural areas were aimed at preserving an increasingly fragile ecosystem and opposition to such measures was courting a future disaster. It was these clauses that made those who would willingly have supported the political demands of the ANC draw back because they feared an ANC government would very quickly destroy the fragile prosperity of the country. In 1955, it was possible to dismiss these fears as groundless or just the workings of vested self-interest but as soon as decolonisation began with the independence of Ghana in 1957, it rapidly became clear that these fears were real enough. The example of

---

[228] Exchange of Correspondence between the African National Congress, the South African Indian Congress, and the Prime Minister of the Union of South Africa between 21 January and 20 February 1952.
https://web.archive.org/web/20150501052049/http://anc.org.za/show.php?id=2590
[229] The Freedom Charter, 26th June 1955. http://www.anc.org.za/content/freedom-charter

'Africa to the north' was always a very great argument against letting the ANC get their hands on the levers of power and, indeed, at the time of writing (2018), remains one for removing them from government. Nevertheless, the popularity of the ANC soared to the point at which the government decided that it was time to lance the boil for what they believed would be once, and for all. In December 1956, the whole of the ANC leadership was arrested, 156 in total, and put on trial for High Treason for suggesting that the state should be violently overthrown.

The trial was farcical, muddled, and revealed the complete incompetence of the Apartheid state. Amid a litany of botched administration, ludicrous legal manoeuvrings, elastic band parole releases, the stupidity of the Special Branch was revealed; a Russian cook book was produced as evidence of a communist plot, hilariously unbelievable witnesses were hired (one of whom was a convicted fraudster, others who claimed to have taken notes while undercover were revealed to be illiterate) and one of the charged men escaped courtesy of a useless warder (of which, according to Bosman in *Cold Stone Jug*, there was no shortage). *The Spectator* commented that the Special Branch 'works harder and understands less than any security branch in the world'.[230] A picture therefore emerged of dignified, intelligent, respectable men and women in the dock running rings around a boorish bunch of prosecution yokels who couldn't organise a piss up in a brewery, never mind run a country.[231] At one stage, the conflation of prison regulations and Apartheid restrictions meant that a special cage had to be constructed which separated men from women, black men from white men, white women from black women and yet allowed them all to converse together at once. The prosecuting counsel, the ex-Nazi Oswald Pirow, found that he rather liked the defendants and they him[232] while one of the judges, Justice Kennedy, chatted happily away in Zulu with Dr Wilson Conco, whom he clearly regarded as being more civilised than the Transvaal Afrikaaners. 'The only satisfactory feature in this tragic farce,' declared one of the accused, 'is the scrupulous fairness of the bench'.[233] In March, 1961, more than *four* years after their arrest, the defendants were finally acquitted and the National Party government reminded that in South Africa, the law was still something to be respected (as indeed it would remain, even against the odds). The problem was though, that several members of the ANC, including Mandela, had actually been dishonest throughout the trial, for they *did* want to at least consider the possibility of using violence to overthrow the state. Oliver Tambo had already left the country with a view to forming an extra-territorial base for just this purpose and Mandela was making preparations to go underground completely and develop the idea of an armed struggle. It was this tendency towards disingenuousness, and the acceptance of that principle most honoured by the Left, that the end justifies the means, that fostered a widespread distrust of the ANC leadership.

We should also take note here of the very real fact that the ANC was neither the only nor the most effective opposition to the Apartheid state. With the virtual collapse of the United Party after the death of Smuts – it was still committed to segregation and easily painted as being just a pale, English-speaking version of the Nationalists – a new party emerged. This was the Progressive Party committed to desegregation and the end of racial policies which split off from the United Party and in doing so single-handedly changed the political conversation from being about whether English-speakers or Afrikaaners should manage the Native problem to being about how to end the dominance of either and move towards a non-racial democracy, i.e., black majority rule. Needless to say, this was an ambitious and contentious aim – Verwoerd called them 'the suicide squad'[234] – and though they made little impact on the parliamentary mathematics in the coming years, it was the fact of their backers that made them a potent voice to be heard. This is an aspect of South African historiography that has been almost completely airbrushed out by the Left because that very effective opposition was what the Left call 'white capital' and what sensible, normal people call 'employers' or 'businesses'.

The backbone of this opposition was the Oppenheimer dynasty, a family of impeccably patrician, English manners and tastes, who in taking over the De Beers diamond monopoly and adding it to a near monopoly of gold production, had built the Anglo-American Corporation into the behemoth of the South African economy. A multi-national conglomerate of approximately six hundred separate companies with extensive minority

[230] Guilty Men, *The Spectator* 7th April, 1961.
[231] Guilty Men, *The Spectator* 7th April, 1961.
[232] N. Mandela, *Long Walk to Freedom* (London 1994) p.274.
[233] 'Wind of Change', *The Spectator* 11th March 1960.
[234] 'Wind of Change', *The Spectator* 11th March 1960.

holdings in very many more, it was reckoned to be the twenty-fifth largest in the world during the 1980s, directly employing around 700,000 South Africans and perhaps the same number indirectly in mining, finance, banking, merchant banking, food processing, agriculture, property, brewing, manufacturing, machine tools, chemicals, newspapers and retail;[235] it made up half of the capital of the Joburg Stock Exchange.[236] Put quite simply, if you spent a pound or a rand on food, beer, housing, clothing, petrol or trinkets there was a very good chance that it would be going into the Oppenheimers' pockets. If they pulled out of South Africa, the economy would come to a standstill and starvation would result. So when the Oppenheimers ventured their consistent opinions from the 1950s through to the 1990s that segregation was old hat, that Apartheid wouldn't work, that the future was a multi-racial democracy and that unless moves were begun to accept that future, the result would be civil war, Marxism and ruin, the government was obliged to listen.

Up to a point, at any rate. The largest corporation in the country was the government which owned steel, electricity, rail and transport, banks, post, arms and the Industrial Development Corporation giving it a total worth of around Rs90 million as opposed to the Oppenheimer's Rs75 million and given that they had the legislative power to nationalise anything they wanted, the limits of power were apparent. The result was that the Oppenheimers were obliged to tread carefully and this they did, building up their businesses, adapting to the changing market place, prodding the government in the right direction where possible, (sometimes quietly, sometimes very publicly), improving the pay and conditions of their workers and promoting black trades unions, all in the hope that a constant steady pressure would pay off in the end. The more excitable opponents of Apartheid who rather enjoyed the drama of riots, economic collapse, strikes and revolution – viewed from afar, of course - accused them of propping up the system but the Oppenheimers were a perfect example of that quiet conservatism that gets results by avoiding such excitement and sees no triumph in unemployment, starvation, the destruction of property and personal rights, and the collapse of pension funds that revolutions inevitably entail. Their aim was always to promote gradual change at a pace that the Afrikaaner could digest but which still gave hope to the masses, all the while delivering tangible improvement and avoiding the disasters of Africa to the north.

*

The Point of No Return

One of the problems of writing History is that the nearer the date, the more provisional one has to be simply because we are robbed of the inestimable benefit of long hindsight. There are several reasons for this, the first being that archival material is often not available. In Britain, the general rule for the release of government documents is that less sensitive material should be made available after thirty or fifty years, with everything being made available after a hundred years. This means that only an incomplete picture can be gained from looking in them for insights into more recent events. US files are generally more open but often heavily censored while access to Russian archives since the end of the Cold war has been patchier still – and they are in Russian. Some archives remain sealed because they are considered to contain material that might possibly end political careers, lead to prosecutions or destroy the reputations of national figures, a practice which in itself has generated all sorts of rumour and speculation, while others contain only careful selections of materials. Secondly, the resources available are plentiful - far, far, in excess of what is available for earlier periods and from a much wider variety of sources – which makes it impossible to read anything more than a tiny fraction of them. Thirdly, it's a common saying that if you gave an infinite number of monkeys an infinite number of typewriters and an infinite amount of time, sooner or later, one of them would write the complete works of William Shakespeare; when it comes to History, we aren't quite at that point, but boy are there a lot of monkeys bashing the keyboards in the universities, media and politics. As many of them have axes to grind, whistles to blow, arses to cover or excuses to make, selecting what is truthful, useful and believable becomes a much more difficult task. In some respects, studying the period within living memory presents the opposite problem to studying earlier periods, because while there are things that we cannot know about the distant past for want of

---

[235] David Pallister, Sarah Stuart and Ian Lepper, *South Africa Inc: The Oppenheimer Empire* (Sandton, 1987) pp. 4-10.
[236] Allister Sparks, *The Mind of South Africa* (London, 1990) p.121

sources, for the later period there are so many sources that with the best will in the world only a partial picture can be presented because they can't all be covered.

A further problem is that more reliance has to be placed on contemporary accounts and these too are apt to be incomplete. Journalism is notoriously unreliable and it would be a brave person indeed who would accept the judgement of such gadflies; as the ever cheerful academic Steven Pinker put it, often 'journalists put their elbows on the scale in a quest for eyeballs' and suffer from a 'crushing negativity...entrenched in their professional culture.'[237] It's also the case that journalists are not only selective in what they report, they also only report the stories that it is possible to report on and so distort the picture further; while US atrocities in Vietnam were gleefully reported, for example, no journalist ever visited a real Soviet Gulag - thereby skewing the overall Cold War narrative. Much the same could be said of the National Party's atrocities; as one journalist put it, while reporting on Steve Biko's death, 'in most of the rest of Africa, horror goes unobserved and certainly unreported.'[238] An observable problem is that journalists tend to spend an awful lot of time interviewing other journalists or writing reports drawn up from other reports, a process in the trade known as 'log-rolling' and which might, in many cases, be regarded as the blind leading the blind. My general rule is 'Journalism is always wrong' and I consult it mainly as a guide to the prejudices of the journalist or for first-hand accounts of particular incidents. Weekly or monthly journals usually tend to be better than the daily diatribes simply because those contributing to them have had more time to think, but this isn't an iron rule. We should also note that journalists are often even worse when they start writing History: Allister Sparks' account of the demise of the Khoisan, his characterisation of van Riebeeck and his take on the Battle of Grahamstown in *The Mind of South Africa*, along with much else, is complete tosh.[239]

Even where journalists have made long-standing commitments to a particular subject – and here we must take note of Fred Bridgland and Al Venter, who worked in Angola and Portuguese Africa, as admirable examples - there are often fundamental disagreements between them which, when added to the observable fact that an objective journalist is a rare beast indeed, makes their claims to be 'the first draft of History' often risible; besides which, no first draft is ever worth the paper it is written on. This is especially the case in South Africa where a natural opposition to Apartheid very often robbed journalists of any objectivity at all, removed all nuance and relentlessly played down any legitimate objection to the ANC; Allister Sparks' treatment of Mandela in *Tomorrow is Another Country* wasn't far short of sick-bag level hagiography in some cases, while the commercial failure of his beloved *Rand Daily Mail* during the mid-1980s led him to voice a sour, bitter and inaccurate portrayal of English speaking South Africans in general and the Oppenheimers in particular;[240] in these years, journalists were not above telling outright lies.

As we saw in Vol I, academics also engaged in a vigorous opposition to Apartheid which muddied the picture further by pushing Marxist perspectives to the exclusion of all others and establishing a binary choice; you were either for Apartheid or for the ANC, with nothing in between. Even the ending of both Apartheid and Communism has had almost no effect on these perspectives and the party lines that were pushed in the bad old days are often parroted out without acknowledgement that Marxism was in every case a complete disaster or that the greatest success in the alleviation of poverty and the condition of the people was achieved in China, where the Communist Party gave up their religion and embraced capitalism. It's also the case that many of the actors from this period are still alive, still in power or hanging on its fringes and though often vocal or in print, are sometimes economical with the *actualité*. As one commentator put it; 'documents can lie just as much as people'[241] and no-one lied quite so much as the Soviet Union and their dependent Communist Parties in these years.

Memoirs from the period are useful, but again all too often they are self-justifying, incomplete, often less than candid and in some cases, border on the fictional. On the other hand, before the advent of self-publishing and social media networks, many participants in the events of these years simply despaired at ever getting their

---

[237] S. Pinker, *Enlightenment Wars: Some Reflections on 'Enlightenment Now' One Year Later*. Quillette, 14th Jan 2019.
[238] Richard West, *The Aristocrats of Africa*, The Spectator, 20th March 1982.
[239] Allister Sparks, *The Mind of South Africa* (London, 1990), pp.10-12, 29-30.
[240] Allister Sparks, *The Mind of South Africa* (London, 1990) pp.70-71.
[241] Sue Onslow and Anna-Mart van Wyk, *Southern Africa in the Cold War, Post 1974* (Wilson Center, 2013).

stories told but fortunately the gatekeepers have been removed and there are now very many accounts easily accessed and readily available. Again, we noted the dominance of Leftist perspectives in publishing in Volume I – and it's getting worse[242] - but the internet has done much to threaten this near monopoly; this book would never be taken on by a mainstream publishing house, but now you are reading it. So, for example, there are now very many accounts of the bush wars of these years told from the varying perspectives of those involved but accounts from the armed wing of the ANC are more difficult to access, partially because of the lower literacy levels that the rank and file possessed, partially because the record of the liberation armies was not particularly good in military terms and partially, one suspects, because their record in terms of human rights abuses would not stand up to very much scrutiny at all. The ANC have also been assiduous in the creation of a narrative which is only now being seriously challenged and at least one researcher found a marked reluctance among veterans to talk about their time in MK, largely because their experiences did not fit that narrative.[243] There are also problems with incomplete archival records from ANC sources.

The difficulties associated with near-contemporary sources can be illustrated quite neatly by perusing Carol B. Thompson's *Challenge to Imperialism: The Frontline States in the Liberation of Zimbabwe* (Zimbabwe, 1985) which I read while being pestered by ostriches in Franskraal in 2018. The first of these difficulties is journalistic in nature; the writer is too close to the subject in time and is operating without the benefit of enough hindsight. The second is that she was one of those writing on southern African issues who was also committed to the overthrow of white rule and the advance of socialism and thus apt to prophesy rather than analyse. Thus Associate Professor Thompson was able to write of 'the general decline of the hegemony of the capitalist powers' (p.10) and 'the crisis of capitalist production; declining profits, stagflation, soaring unemployment' (p.7) a mere five years before the hegemony of the capitalist powers was underlined in the most forceful way by the collapse of the Marxists themselves and at a time when the Thatcher-Reagan reforms were enabling free market economies to absolutely let rip. And this blindness was quite general among those on the Left; Stanley Uys, something of a hero among South African journalists, agreed with Associate Professor Thompson's analysis, declaring that in 1985 'Capitalism in South Africa has now entered the fight for its survival.'[244] Not just the Left; a finer class of bollocks you will not find than that displayed in the 1963 Spectator article *The Last Acts of Apartheid,* which confidently prophesised the collapse of Apartheid within two years.[245] During these years, I was doing my bit for NATO and paying attention to Cold War politics and I will say straight out that *no-one*, and I mean *no-one*, saw the collapse of Communism coming – although quite a few clever dicks claimed afterwards that they had expected it all along. This handicap is not confined to people as brilliant as me either; the truly excellent analyst of South Africa's transition from Apartheid to Kleptocracy, R.W. Johnson, argued in 2015 that Cyril Ramaphosa's chances of succeeding Zuma were slim at best and yet in 2018, the great moonfaced apostle of *Expropriation without Compensation*, did indeed get his well-padded backside onto the throne.[246] Predicting the future has never been anything but a fool's game. It's why poverty-stricken bookies are such rare objects.

Muddying the water even further is the fact that all sides attempted to 'manage the news' and create a dominant narrative from which to draw justification for their own side and damage that of the other. Agitation and Propaganda -'Agitprop' - was a long established tool of the Left which, in essence, involved the establishment of front organisations to carry out an aggressive pushing of the party line without regard to truth but assessed by its utility in undermining the morale of its opponents. Western cold war warriors tended to be more subtle, less aggressive and more hopeful that the truth would shine through of its own accord in the end but this did not preclude them from propagandising in their own way. South Africa too carried out a media operation, which was finally exposed by the Oppenheimers in what became known as the Muldergate Scandal, in which attempts were made, among other things, to buy US newspapers in order to push their version of events. So now, any source has to be assessed against the testing questions of: *who wrote it and when? Were they in a position to know what they are talking about? What is the motive for talking? What is their potential for bias or conscious prejudice? Have they any reason to lie?*

---

[242] Tara Nykyforiak, *How Ideologues Captured the Canadian Publishing Industry*, Quillette, 26th January 2019.
[243] Saeboe Maren, *A State of Exile: The ANC and Umkhonto we Sizwe in Angola 1976-89*. MA Dissertation, University of Natal, 2002.
[244] Quoted in David Pallister, Sarah Stuart and Ian Lepper, *South Africa Inc: The Oppenheimer Empire* (Sandton, 1987) p.197.
[245] *The Last Acts of Apartheid*, The Spectator, 22nd November 1963.
[246] RW Jonson, *How Long Will South Africa Survive? The Looming Crisis* (London 2015).

Navigating this evolving landscape requires an open mind, great scepticism and a determination to follow the evidence wherever it leads. It also demands a more provisional approach to the conclusions reached simply because the mass of material *not* looked at virtually guarantees that those conclusions are absolutely, completely and definitely provisional.

There is another adjustment that is needed to the approach taken hitherto because from 1960 the isolation that defined South Africa from Van Riebeeck onwards evaporates. It's possible to discuss South Africa before 1960 with only brief references to powers other than Britain and to ignore Africa to the north but after this date it becomes impossible. Apartheid does not become the most important issue in the world but it does get bundled up with the Cold War, with decolonisation and the subsequent collapse of African governance and the inter-play between these issues and those problems of a more domestic variety becomes both vital and visceral. In both 1914 and 1939, South Africa might have opted out of the World Wars without too much difficulty but the option to opt out of the world after 1960 just did not exist. For the first time since the British occupation of the Cape, the Afrikaaners had to face up to the fact that the world had caught up with them and intended to shake them out of their pre-Enlightenment attitudes. This was a reality that no trek could avoid.

*

In 1954, between the Defiance campaign and the Freedom Charter, D.F. Malan decided that his work was done and that he could now safely retire. He had achieved the unity of the Afrikaaner people, he believed, had seen off the threat of poor whites being overtaken by blacks or absorbed into a mixed-race population, and was only a step away from waving good-bye to the waning British connection. What came next would be up to his successors and recognising that he was really too tired to address the new challenges of a world in which the USSR was on the march, the United Nations was railing against him, the Jewish capitalists were still plotting and now the Africans were making trouble. It was easy to look at the rural black people and see backwardness, superstition, squalor and inefficiency but to see the leaders of the Defiance Campaign as anything but sophisticated, savvy and perfectly able to meet any criteria that didn't involve melanin was too much for this unpleasant old man and he shuffled off to Stellenbosch, where he died in 1959.

His successor was J.G. Strydom (PM 1954-58), but the driving intellect behind the government was Hendrick Verwoerd, Minister for Native Affairs. Strydom's main difference with Malan lay in his hurry to complete the rejection of the British connection and to restore the republic but on Apartheid, there was nothing to particularly differentiate them beyond the personal animosities that were always so prevalent among Afrikaaner leaders. Verwoerd, however, was a different kettle of fish. One of those noxious social engineers that universities produce on an appallingly regular basis, he believed fervently in Apartheid and had done much of the donkey work for Malan and Strydom in its establishment. As Minister for Native Affairs, 1950-58, the 'brilliant administrator', 'persuasive ideologue and martinet without peer'[247] had ramped up a rather torpid, liberal, ramshackle Native Affairs Department, with its ethos of British paternalism, gradualism and infatuation with the rural areas, into one of the main powerhouses of Apartheid. This was done by Afrikaanerising it with young, crusading Nationalists intent on centralising and managing the relationships between the urban African and the Native Reserves; now the full weight of state regulation was to be used to keep the black man in his state-allotted place. Verwoerd's main contribution on becoming PM in 1958 was to add a sociological gloss to the theological justification for the system, by attempting to hide a straightforward determination to maintain white Afrikaaner supremacy behind a thin veneer of 'betterment', 'development at different rates', 'ethnic nationalism' and not least of all, 'modern methods of town planning'[248] which meant, in effect slum clearance programmes that also cleared the slum dwellers out of mixed neighbourhoods and into segregated ones; rough, tough Sophiatown bulldozed to create white Triumph and black Soweto; louche District Six bulldozed onto Mitchells Plain. It was Verwoerd whom Patrick Duncan, a liberal and son of one of Milner's kindergarten protégés, called 'the demolition hammer in the Hand of God.'[249] Persuasive, he was, and many people who should have known better were drawn into an intellectual acceptance of Apartheid by the force of his personality and arguments while others, if not convinced, were prepared to give him the benefit of the doubt; among them

---

[247] Ivan Evans, *Bureaucracy and Race: Native Administration in South Africa* (Berkeley, 1997).
[248] Ivan Evans, *Bureaucracy and Race: Native Administration in South Africa* (Berkeley, 1997).
[249] Randolph Vigne, *Notes from a Refugee,* The Spectator, 21st August 1964.

was C.W. de Kiewiet, an Historian of impeccably liberal values, and Herman Giliomee, University of Cape Town Professor of Political Studies (1983-2002), Historian and President of the South African Institute of Race Relations (1995-97).[250] It was Verwoerd who had the ANC leadership arrested and put on trial for treason and, probably more importantly, it was Verwoerd who missed the opportunity to set South Africa on a path that would have avoided much of the terrible bloodletting that was to come.

The opportunity came during the aforementioned Treason Trial when Mandela sent a letter to Verwoerd offering to accept sixty seats for black Africans in the Union parliament in return for an end to strife. This was far below what the numerical dominance of black people might ordinarily expect, but the thinking was that once the National Party had actually experienced working with black parliamentarians and once the white electorate had got used to sharing power with black voters, then much of the antagonism would disappear. At the end of five years, the arrangement would necessarily be reviewed and, hopefully, with the connivance of the Progressives and the Union party, a few more strides towards a multi-racial democracy would be taken. Verwoerd did not reply largely, *probably*, because he feared what the response from the more rabid sections of the National Party would be; because the election of 1958 had completed the Nationalist party coup; because he fondly imagined that the courts would find the ANC guilty as charged but mainly because his sociological theorising convinced him that Apartheid was actually the way forward. The rejection of Mandela's eminently reasonable, sensible and gradualist offer was a big enough blow to the ANC hopes of achieving progress through non-violence but when in 1961, police opened fire on a demonstration at Sharpeville organised by the Pan African Congress killing 69 and injuring 180 more, the case for armed struggle seemed to have been made.

The problem was that this was an elephant trap. Whatever the rights and wrongs of the decision to engage in armed struggle, the decision to seek the help of the Soviet Union and China to pursue it was possibly the worst decision the ANC ever made and set its cause back by decades.

When he went underground in 1961, Mandela made a point of reading up on military History and the theory of revolutionary war and though he drew several correct conclusions about the need for war to be an extension of political policy (Clausewitz), the usefulness of cell structures and the need for guerrillas to gain the support of the people (Mao), he also failed to understand how the strategic situation of South Africa negated the worth of much of his reading. This was because South Africa lay a long way away from the Soviet Union or China across wide oceans dominated by the navies of the West, which therefore ruled out the sort of large scale aid that had been provided to North Korea or North Vietnam. Secondly, the theory of revolutionary war demanded external bases from which the guerrillas would operate but there was nowhere that extra-territorial bases conveniently close to South Africa could be located. Angola and Mozambique were still under Portuguese control, Rhodesia was under white rule and thus highly unlikely to provide them while any base in Botswana would have to be located so close to the border that the South African Defence Force (SADF) would mop it up inside minutes. The nearest likely candidate was Zambia and this lay a thousand miles away across the Kalahari. Thirdly, the theory also demanded that guerrilla bases be set up inside the country but there were very few areas in South Africa remote enough to function as 'liberated areas' safe from the reach of the SADF. The options, therefore, for fighting a 'war of liberation' envisioned by his plan (codenamed Operation Mayibuye) on the classical grounds of internal insurgency, supported by external allies and secure extra-territorial base areas were severely limited from the start.

The decision for an organisation with democratic aims to seek aid primarily from Russia was also remarkable given that the ruling Communist Party of the Soviet Union was arguably the most barbarous, repressive, brutal and murderous regime ever to be visited on benighted humanity, with the main rival for the title being Mao's China. Setting aside the terrible purges and famines of the 1920s and 1930s, and setting aside the collaboration with Hitler in the Nazi-Soviet pact and even accepting Khruschev's weak excuse that although mistakes had been made – perhaps 15 million of them, excluding war deaths, but including one SACP General-Secretary who had been purged while training in Moscow – things would be better from now on, the record of the Soviet Union since 1953 could hardly be called exemplary. In 1953, tanks had suppressed a people's revolt in East Germany and another in Hungary, 1956, while in 1961, it had been found necessary to build the Berlin Wall to prevent the

---

[250] http://www.politicsweb.co.za/opinion/remembering-verwoerd

people of Eastern Europe from passing verdict on the relative merits of liberal, democratic capitalism and communism by voting with their feet; during the 1950s, every year the ANC celebrated Stalin's birthday.[251] In 1968, the ANC supported the crushing of the Prague Spring in Czechoslovakia under the tank tracks of the Red Army, took the Russian side in the Sino-Soviet dispute and, of course, were ever ready to swoon in the presence of Fidel Castro. Solzhenitsyn's *Gulag Archipelago* was still some years off publication, but he was three years into writing it by the time that the ANC took their fateful decision and there was already plenty of evidence of the malevolence of that system. And the Soviet system was self-evidently worse than Apartheid in the respect that Mandela and the ANC had just had their opposition to the government vindicated in a court of law after the collapse of the Treason Trial, something that would *never* be countenanced under the Soviet system. What this meant was that wide swathes of reasonable opinion in the West were paralysed by the prospect of overthrowing one dreadful system of oppression only to replace it with a worse one.

The reasons for the folly of the ANC in choosing to appeal to the Soviets are not difficult to discern. The first is that the influence of the Communist Party ran throughout the organisations opposed to Apartheid; indeed R.W. Johnson thought that the ANC had been hijacked by white, Jewish Communists from the 1950s onwards and that it was the SACP rather than the ANC that authored the Freedom Charter. Secondly, the SACP had access to funding and arms provided from Moscow and Beijing, had long experience in conspiratorial politics and underground organisation and could deploy the simple, seductive utopian creed of Marx to entrap the stupid and inspire the zealot. They could also supply the answers to the theoretical hoops that needed to be jumped through if the ANC was to be able to present itself as an 'anti-colonial' movement; the Afrikaaners could hardly be portrayed as 'colonisers' when they had been in the country for as long as the Xhosa and more than a hundred and fifty years before the Zulu nation had been invented. 'Colonialism of a special type' (i.e. not colonialism at all, but we'll call it that any way) was the verbiage of choice supplied by the SACP, along with 'Democratic Centralism' to describe the preferred method of leadership for the movement - a Central Committee dictatorship modelled on that of the Soviet Union (i.e. not democratic at all).

Stephen Ellis, the man who made the most extensive study of the ANC in exile, argued convincingly that the ANC was virtually a branch of the SACP in these years and that it was the SACP that pushed the ANC into the policy of armed struggle against its better instincts[252] - and without a formal declaration of armed struggle as an actual agreed upon and adopted policy. Walter Sisulu and Joe Slovo who, along with Mandela, founded MK - Umkhonto we Sizwe, *The Spear of the Nation* - were both SACP. (It was long rumoured that Mandela was secretly on the Central Committee of the SACP, a fact that was apparently confirmed by the SACP at his funeral and which meant, if it was true, that Mandela had lied at the Rivonia Trial. However, as the SACP had become as revoltingly corrupt as the ANC by that time, it would be a brave person indeed who would take their word for this. *That said*, Ellis piled up the evidence very convincingly that Mandela had indeed been SACP for at least a while and showed that his denials were often evasive).[253] Other leading ANC lights were also SACP; Govan Mbeki, Ahmed Kathrada, Rusty Bernstein and their lawyer Bram Fischer, while the Congress of Democrats, a white anti-Apartheid organisation, was shot through with communists too and, of course, we must not forget our old friend Mr. Bunting (who also said that Mandela was SACP). Ronnie Kasrils, a pal of Brian Bunting and an early recruit to MK was drawn into the anti-Apartheid movement through the bohemian circles of Durban and Cape Town, which were heavily influenced by Marxist thought; his autobiography is interesting in that he admitted that the SACP, of which he quickly became a member, already entertained the blindness to the behaviour of the Soviet Union so characteristic of the Left.[254] Yusuf Dadoo and Vella Pillay, also SACP, visited Mao during the famine of the Great Leap Forward (1958-61) without ever seeming to spot the myriad flaws in the theory. For the rank and file of the ANC, poor education made for widespread ignorance of the realities of Soviet life, an ignorance that was knowingly reinforced by the political commissars like Kasrils who carried out what can only be described as a structured indoctrination campaign in the full knowledge that there was no paradise behind the Iron Curtain, having been trained there and subsequently visited often, so while we may

[251] RW Johnson, *How Long Will South Africa Survive?* (London, 2015).
[252] Stephen Ellis, *External Mission; the ANC in Exile 1960-1990* (Oxford, 2013) p. 22.
[253] Stephen Ellis, *External Mission; the ANC in Exile 1960-1990* (Oxford, 2013) p. 22.
[254] Ronnie Kasrils, *Armed and Dangerous*, (Johannesburg, 2004) p.31.

perhaps excuse the rank and file for adopting Marxism, the same understanding cannot be extended to the leadership.

It was also the case that many African nationalist organisations were sympathetic to communism largely because of the contacts that their leaders had made with British and French communists during their various educational visits to Europe. Kwame Nkrumah, the first, disastrous president of Ghana, was a frequent visitor to the British Communist Party HQ in King Street, London, and though it is a matter of debate whether African nationalists believed in or just paid lip service to the tenets of Marxist-Leninism, they did find it useful to pose as sympathetic in order to get access to Soviet funding for their various movements.[255] It therefore became *de rigeur* to look to the USSR for help and thus a vicious circle was created; the more the Soviets were involved, the less inclined the West was to engage and the less the West were inclined to engage, the more African nationalism became dependent on the Soviets. And yet, as Mandela himself picked up, there were plenty of African nationalists who were *not* communists and who were extremely suspicious of the influence of the very *white* SACP, which prompted him (and others) to question whether the ANC should be so aligned with the very *white* SACP.[256] What might have come of this is anyone's guess because Mandela's arrest cut short the opportunity to pursue the issue; it's probably fair to say that Mandela dallied with the SACP willingly for a while for the useful things that it brought to the table but remained unconvinced of the theory.[257]

The conjunction of a particular brand of African nationalism with communism hindered the ANC in other ways too. Right from the outset, the practical record of decolonised African states weighed against a more vigorous support from the West. In Ghana, Kwame Nkrumah, a man whose only experience of practical economics had been a short stint as a fish seller in Haarlem, New York, and the passing of bad cheques in London nightclubs[258] took over a country with a thriving economy, an independent judiciary, an efficient civil service, a functioning democracy and a prosperous middle class and promptly wrecked it. Corrupt from the outset, he mulcted the cocoa farmers, handed out contracts to his party cronies, moved into a palace and started to prance about at international conferences dedicated to African socialism and 'Nkrumahism', declaring that 'Ghana inherited a colonial economy....We cannot rest until we have demolished this miserable structure.'[259] And demolish it he did, largely by attempting to turn it into a socialist paradise led by himself, without democratic opposition, with rigged elections, a personal army, surrounded by flatterers, press censorship, detention without trial, a new constitution, party officials on the take, and government funds squandered on useless projects – Job 600, an hotel and conference centre built on a grotesquely lavish scale established an entirely new low in the dire annals of African leadership. Overwhelmed by the responsibilities of the task and entirely unfitted for it, Nkrumah became increasingly withdrawn and paranoid, secretly married a woman who was *given* to him by President Nasser of Egypt and with whom he had no language in common and began to exhibit increasingly messianic tendencies. After a failed assassination attempt, he rigged the court so that the parties accused – and who were about to have the charges dropped – were executed. By 1961, the economy was already in free-fall, trade unionists were on strike or in jail, government procurement was a joke, cocoa production - upon which all else depended – was collapsing, debts were piling up on reckless borrowing and real incomes were down by 50%. Inviting in expertise from the Soviet Union to industrialise the country put the seal on it; by 1965, he had bankrupted the country and was duly removed by military coup.[260]

If this was only one example, then it would be possible to dismiss it as an aberration but it was not. Rather it became something of the model for Africa and as the idiocies piled upon idiocies – a low point among many others being the snow ploughs purchased by the government of Guinea – more and more people made the reasonable assumption that, however which way you cut it, black majority rule meant corruption, brutality, dictatorship, incompetence, economic collapse and impoverishment for all but a fantastically wealthy clique. Even the Russians found this out quite quickly when they made the remarkable decision to pay some Nigerian journalists *in advance* to set up a communist newspaper.[261] Whatever the legitimate desires for independence,

---

[255] C. Andrews, *The Defence of the Realm; The Authorised History of MI5* (London, 2009) p.451.
[256] Stephen Ellis, *External Mission; the ANC in Exile 1960-1990* (Oxford, 2013) p. 56.
[257] Stephen Ellis, *External Mission; the ANC in Exile 1960-1990* (Oxford, 2013) p. 33.
[258] Geoffrey Wheatcroft, *African Magnate*, The Spectator, 19th May 1984
[259] Quoted in Martin Meredith, *The State of Africa*, (London, 1997) p.144.
[260] Martin Meredith, *The State of Africa*, (London, 1997), p.179-86.
[261] Richard West, *Red Africa Stays Black*, The Spectator, 14th February 1976,

there were few places in Africa that were improved by the withdrawal of British rule and very many that were ruined. None of this did anything to make anyone think the ANC would be an improvement on the Apartheid regime. Only Botswana seemed able to buck this terrible trend.

If anything more was required for sensible thinking people to have second thoughts about the wisdom of replacing Apartheid with black majority rule, the concurrent example of the collapse of the Congo underlined the nervousness with which change was viewed. It is generally agreed that of all the European colonies in Africa, the Belgian Congo was the worst run. Originally a personal fiefdom of the Belgian king, it was removed from his control in 1908 after the brutal and scandalous way it was administered came to light, and thereon in run by a board of missionaries, bureaucrats and business interests. This vast sprawling territory contained huge mineral reserves – 10% of the world's copper, 50% of its cobalt and 70% of its industrial diamonds - rubber plantations and ivory and had the potential to produce much, much more under competent management, but on being handed over to the Congolese in 1960 it rapidly proved the worth of the adage that *nothing in Africa is so bad that it can't get worse*. There had been little preparation for independence, not much in the way of a literate population and little appetite in Belgium to remain. When, in 1959, it became clear that the Congo wanted its independence immediately and would not consent to the Belgian proposal to begin a gradual transition, the general view was that if the Congo wanted its independence, then it was welcome to it and that was that. Independence Day was set for 1st June 1960.

The man who emerged as President was Patrice Lumumba, a thirty-five year old rabble rousing beer salesman with little education, a capricious temperament and a conviction for embezzlement but his elevation was contested by many other groups; 'Congolese' was a nationality on paper only, and a least 120 groups based on tribal or regional identities emerged to begin a feeding frenzy on both public and private property. A mutiny in the Belgian officered army, driven by resentment and greed at seeing clerks and politicians suddenly snout deep in the trough, led to the Belgian officers being sacked and the *Force Publique* being handed over to Joseph Mobutu, who had once served in it as a clerk, and who possessed all the polecat, streetwise skills and charisma of a murderous gangster like Marlo Stansfield straight out of *The Wire*. What then followed was a series of indiscriminate rapes, murders and humiliations of white people – the *Italian* consul was burned alive in his car - made especially notable for the number of nuns singled out for brutal treatment. Within two weeks of independence the country had collapsed, sparking off a flight of white refugees, the secession of Katanga province and the despatch of Belgian paratroopers to prevent further outrages. Lumumba appealed to the UN and, with a speed not usually associated with that lumbering body, got immediate aid in both administrators and troops to restore order. When the UN turned up, he demanded that they use their troops to expel the Belgians and when this was refused, threatened to call in the Soviets – on a visit to Washington to discuss the crisis, he took the opportunity to demand a white, blonde hooker, which the CIA duly provided. Expressing himself in increasingly lunatic diatribes, the UN began to fear for the safety of its personnel and, when the Soviets provided him with military aid, Lumumba embarked on a genocide in the Kasai region. By December, the country was locked into a four-way civil war and by 1964, more than a million people had been killed, the country was in ruins, whatever passed for an educated class had been murdered and a massive rescue operation for whites trapped in the country had been mounted. Lumumba was assassinated by his opponents and the country came under the rule of Joseph Mobutu, perhaps the greatest kleptocrat on a continent that was dominated by them for decades to come. His subsequent misrule has been best documented by Michela Wrong's *In the Footsteps of Mr. Kurtz: Living on the Brink of Disaster*. You'll need a strong stomach. Even the Belgians could not do worse.

The fact that the African liberation movements were dominated by either – and in some cases, both - thoroughly corrupt men or men who were no better than badly educated students, marinated in Marxism and blind to reality meant that the obvious answer to the question of how to make independence a success was missed. In the case of the ex-British colonies, a hand was held out which offered membership of the Commonwealth, vital trade links and access to the financial system along with the continued work of competent administrators and soldiers until such time as 'Africanisation' could take place. In many cases, these links were rejected as 'colonialist', 'imperialist' or 'capitalist' by politicians who played to the gallery while helping themselves to the treasury or who had been so imprisoned by a Marxist mind-set that they really believed they could bring in a socialist paradise. (And I just can't resist adding Boris Johnson's *bon mot* about British imperialism in Africa: 'The continent may be a blot but it is not a blot on our consciences. The problem is not that we were once in charge, but that we are not in charge anymore.')[262]

Here the ANC was no different. Despite the obvious differences between English-speaking whites and Afrikaaners and despite the determination of the Afrikaaners to break the link with Britain, the leadership of the ANC could see no opening. In 1960, after a referendum of whites, South Africa became a republic, rejected the Crown, adopted a new flag and *Die Stem* as the national anthem, and replaced the Pound Sterling with the Rand all of which provided a golden opportunity for an opening to Britain. Despite the retreat from Empire, Britain was still a major power with a seat on the UN security council, the closest ally of the USA, had access to vast financial and diplomatic resources and though there could be no thought of Her Majesty's armed forces turning up for a Third Anglo-Boer War, the levers of economic power could certainly be used against Apartheid. Instead of turning to a liberal, increasingly tolerant, wealthy and successful country with a record of fighting racial prejudice and Nazis like Verwoerd, and a willingness to change and adapt to new circumstances – and no one could make this plainer than Harold Macmillan, the British Prime Minister himself, at the podium of the Union parliament in Cape Town in February 1960 when he condemned Apartheid and recognised the legitimacy of African nationalism – the ANC chose to align itself with a motley collection of African leaders who combined only the qualities of incompetence, brutality and corruption in varying mixes, backed up by the most repressive regimes in the world. It would keep them from power until the collapse of the Soviet Union at the end of the Cold War because the litany of African catastrophes that followed close on the heels of independence posed a real crisis for opinion in the West – support the ANC and see complete ruin or allow Apartheid to run its course and hope for the best.

And what was more, throughout these years, the greatest blows landed on the Apartheid regime from without came not from the Soviets or China, but from the West.

*

The armed struggle of the ANC was supposed to begin with acts of sabotage against government targets expressly selected to minimise the possibility of the loss of life and, if that didn't work, only then would they proceed to a guerrilla war. Utterly deluded about the realities of fighting such a war, their heads filled with Castro's triumph in Cuba and Marxist theories of History that declared that certain fundamental forces scientifically produced inevitable revolutionary outcomes – this bollocks is technically known as 'Historicism' – they thought that all they had to do was light the blue touch paper and stand well back. A few notable attacks on power supplies and the like resulted but the campaign was largely a flop simply because Mandela and the rest of MK were really quite hopeless as underground revolutionaries (and indeed, only about half the attacks were actually carried out by MK, the balance being the work of various other groups competing for influence). Necessarily amateurish, the organisation was penetrated, banning orders disrupted its operations, vigorous surveillance forced many members into exile and the security police quickly rounded up the greater part of the leadership – including Govan Mbeki, Raymond Mhlaba, Walter Sisulu and Ahmed Kathrada - and put it into the bag in 1963, after raiding their base at Rivonia farm while they were engaged in poring over the plans; just about everyone in the neighbourhood knew there was something odd going on at *that* farm.[263] Over the next few years, perhaps 10,000 political arrests were made and the police were given virtual *carte blanche* to interrogate, torture, kidnap, beat up and ultimately murder anyone they suspected of political opposition, so that the ANC as a significant force in South African politics was destroyed for more than a decade.

And it wasn't just black people who were intimidated; 'one feels the fear', as Robert Browne of *The Spectator* noted in 1961. [264]

The man responsible for the defeat of the ANC/MK was Hendrik van den Bergh. Previous to the establishment of the republic in 1961, it's fair to say that South Africa had no security services worth the name mainly because Britain did as much as it could to prevent the Nationalist government from acquiring them, being rightly fearful of the uses to which they might be put,[265] but after that date a capability was quickly built up. A close political

[262] https://www.spectator.co.uk/2018/09/is-it-possible-to-draw-serena-williams-without-being-racist/
[263] Stephen Ellis, *External Mission; the ANC in Exile 1960-1990* (Oxford, 2013) p. 33.
[264] Robert Browne, *Cape Town*, The Spectator, 22nd September 1961.

associate of Verwoerd's successor, B.J. Vorster, (they had both been interned as members of OB during the war) van den Bergh built up the police Security Branch and the more secretive Republican Intelligence and then, when Vorster succeeded Verwoerd after he was stabbed to death by a madman in parliament, drew them together into the Bureau of State Security in 1969. His first targets for recruitment were left wing journalists like Gordon Winter with good contacts in ANC circles and by liberally bribing those principled paragons, he managed to recruit a fair number who quickly infiltrated opposition groups. It was a tip off from a journalist that led to the Rivonia farm coup and the information supplied by journalists allowed RI to so harass the members of the anti-Apartheid Liberal Party that it ceased to function at all. It also allowed van den Bergh to plant useful stories in the press, to discredit others and generally keep tabs on journalists in general. There was also a dirty tricks department which was as effective as it was illegal and a team of assassins known as the Z-Squad. Against RI, the ANC were mere babes in arms.

Mandela was already serving a five year sentence for leaving the country to seek support from black Africa at this time and when the government put the leadership of the ANC on trial, it was confident that this time there would be no repeat of previous farces; the document haul, which included Mandela's diary, was enough on its own to convict. Already, the law had been extended to allow almost indefinite detention without charge or trial and both Verwoerd and his justice minister and fellow wartime internee, Vorster, were determined to wield the sjambok liberally and with gusto. What became known as the 1964 Rivonia Trial was meant to decapitate the ANC and bury its corpse on Robben Island and it very nearly achieved its aims. But it was here that the hapless Nelson Mandela, who so far had shown little talent or promise for anything other than sitting on committees and spouting nonsense about the coming liberation, finally found something worthwhile to say and the ability to act with grace and greatness.

The evidence presented by the prosecution was overwhelming, very largely credible and left little doubt that even on its own merits the defendants could expect conviction and the death sentence. However, it was this acceptance that the law had been broken that inspired Mandela to claim a moral justification for the use of violence on the grounds that non-violence had only produced an ever greater repressive response from the Apartheid state. He admitted that he had formed MK because he feared that a race war would break out which would sweep away any hope of the non-racial democracy he favoured and that black people had as much right to defend themselves as white. Admitting that he co-operated with the Communist Party, he also declared that the Freedom Charter represented the core of his beliefs and if he favoured any particular form of government, it was British parliamentary democracy. 'Africans want a just share in the whole of South Africa; they want security and a stake in society. Above all, we want equal political rights....'[266] It was the last paragraph of his statement from the witness box that marked him out as a different man to the mediocrity he had been in the past, and the implications of it made his lawyer beg him to leave it out. He refused and also declared that he would under no circumstances appeal against his sentence.

> 'During my lifetime I have dedicated myself to this struggle of the African people. I have fought against white domination, and I have fought against black domination. I have cherished the ideal of a democratic and free society in which all persons live together in harmony and with equal opportunities. It is an ideal which I hope to live for and to achieve. But if needs be, it is an ideal for which I am prepared to die.'[267]

Against this, there was no arguing and in making this statement he destroyed whatever intellectual, moral, sociological or religious foundations Apartheid could possibly stand on because they failed the test of basic decency and fairness. Calmly, he invited the death penalty, put his head in the noose and accepted that he would die for a cause that was so eminently reasonable that the justice of it could not be denied. South African newspapers printed his statement in full, defying the laws that prevented any reporting of his speech and so laid bare the awful reality that the utopian vision of Apartheid was, like all such visions, based on nothing but force and that it could not survive without hanging honest men. In making this statement of simple truth and hope though, he paid a terrible price; it would cost him the best part of three decades in jail.

---

[265] Kevin A O'Brien, *The South African Intelligence Services* (Abingdon, 2011) p.51.
[266] Mandela p.437.
[267] Mandela p.438.

Apartheid Triumphant 1964-76

The debate over the economic worth of Apartheid has been a particularly stale one with Leftist academics arguing that Apartheid was a particularly virulent form of rapacious capitalism which consigned black workers to the helot status of cheap labour for white, international monopoly capitalists to 'exploit' – a favourite word, indeed one almost inescapable in Marxist literature. What they failed to understand was that capital was, as the Oppenheimers repeatedly pointed out, colour-blind and therefore opposed to a colour bar that prevented a business from employing a black man if he was the best person for the job. After the Sharpeville Massacre of 1961, Anglo-American declared that;

> [The company] will seek ways of giving adequate recognition to higher skills and improving efficiencies among our native workers.... If we are to achieve higher levels of productivity, greater attention must be given to the abilities, personal needs, inclinations and aspirations of individual Africans.[268]

The business community was serious about this too; by 1964, it was starkly apparent that the colour bar would have to go if the demand for skilled and semi-skilled labour was to be met. Even the government was forced to fill positions in the Post Office and the railways with non-white workers because of a shortage of white labour and it was predicted that unless black people were allowed to take up jobs previously reserved for whites then by 1969 there would 47,000 unfilled vacancies. By 1970, 15,000 black people on the railways were working in formerly reserved jobs.[269] 'The more South Africa prospers,' noted Stanley Uys. 'The more the industrial colour bar bends';[270] what was more, he said, was that when the government 'has to choose between apartheid and affluence, it chooses the latter.'[271] (The cracks in the National Party's certainty about Apartheid were already appearing, but it would take another decade for them to admit, very quietly and only among the leadership, and only after Verwoerd's successor, B.J. Vorster had pushed it to the limit, that the whole policy was unworkable. Increasingly, Vorster looked like bloke who had been born wearing a brown shirt and clutching a sjambok in his hand, but giving the impression of someone who had realised that Apartheid wasn't working and couldn't work, but daren't say so. In a TV *Firing Line* interview given in 1974 to the American conservative intellectual, William F. Buckley Jr, his defensiveness in the face of suavely penetrative questioning was almost palpable). By 1965, Job Reservation was almost a thing of the past.[272] Elspeth Huxley, more famous for her book *The Flame Trees of Tikka* than for her political work, analysed the situation well;

> South Africa is like a pantomime donkey whose front legs, the government's policy, plod in one direction while its hind legs, economic realities, trot in the other. Sooner or later there must be either a split or an accommodation.[273]

To Helen Suzman, the sole Progressive party MP, it seemed obvious that when the drivel known as Apartheid conflicted with economic reality, the policy would be abandoned. She would wait a long time for this but, as Elspeth Huxley also pointed out, with more and more Afrikaaners going into business and learning something beyond the homespun economics of the farm, that time would come. In 1970 Harry Oppenheimer was even more explicit about the future of South Africa;

> ...where South Africa is virtually unique is that this shortage [of skilled labour] has been gravely aggravated by a racially based social policy which prevents the best use being made of African labour, with the result that African productivity and earnings, though they are rising, remain comparatively low and the home market is not enabled to expand as it should. Here is South Africa's major social and

---

[268] Pallister p.134.
[269] Nicholas Davenport, *Commentary*, The Spectator, 18th July 1870.
[270] Stanley Uys, *Jobs before Colour in South Africa*, The Spectator, 12th February 1965.
[271] Stanley Uys, *Jobs before Colour in South Africa*, The Spectator, 12th February 1965.
[272] Arnold Beichman, *Verwoerd and After*, The Spectator, 13th August 1965.
[273] Elspeth Huxley, *The Fourth Boer War*, The Spectator, 14th June 1968.

economic problem and, at the same time, here is South Africa's major opportunity. The facts of this situation are becoming clear to all South Africans and it is the incompatibility between these facts and the existing South African social and economic order, not any proliferation of protests and boycotts, that provides the best chance of a change for the better in race relations as a whole. The South African government is beginning cautiously to look outwards and is trying to counter, if possible, the increasing isolation into which South Africa has been drifting. Those in England who want to see change in South Africa brought about without violence should encourage closer links with South Africa in all fields and not, like the extreme South African protagonists of apartheid, seek to force South Africa back into a laager cut off from the rest of the world.[274]

Five years later, in 1975, Jan Marais of the Trust Bank called for the end of racial discrimination while Punch Barlow, Chairman of the Barlow Rand motor and mining conglomerate did likewise.[275]

Unfortunately, the main thing stopping business bringing about complete equality in the workplace was the opposition of the usual rabble of socialist racists in the trade unions who were determined to keep their privileges through the application of those standard tools of bone-headed Luddism known as 'maintaining pay differentials', restricting the necessary qualifications for promotion (the 'blasting certificate') to themselves and their cronies and threatening strike action.[276] It wasn't the Oppenheimers who referred to their workers as 'baboons' unable to think for themselves but rather the trades union leader, Arrie Paulus, who also declared to the *New York Times* in 1979 that 'All the Kaffirs can go and get stuffed.'[277] Without the co-operation of the trade unions, progress could only go so far.

The real problem for the Left to explain was that the Apartheid economy was demonstrably capable of generating wealth for both black and white in a way that had eluded the more 'scientific' and 'egalitarian' socialist economies of Africa, the Soviet Bloc and China. They responded to the challenge by, as Ronnie Kasrils acknowledged, ignoring it; despite the fact that between 1958-61, China's 'Great Leap Forward' killed around 60 million people – that's roughly three times the population of the *whole* of South Africa in 1960 - it was still common for many on the Left to describe themselves as Maoists without blushing. That the Apartheid economy did generate wealth was, of course, because the Afrikaaner Nationalists understood that only by improving the lot of black Africans could the well springs of opposition be removed, and that the best way to achieve this was to use economic management tools that looked very much like the ones used in European social democratic mixed economies. Arguably the most influential economist of these years was J.M. Keynes whose own views we might sum up as emphasising the importance of generating demand by increasing the purchasing power of the workers and so creating a virtuous circle of greater demand generating greater supply which in turn stimulated greater employment opportunities and thereby even greater demand. What this meant was that both the government and the Oppenheimers were agreed on improving the economic condition of black people because it paid both economic and political dividends to do so. 'If *they* don't eat,' went the saying. '*We* don't sleep.'[278]

The figures were impressive.[279] Between 1945-77, annual growth rates were 7%. Manufacturing became more important than mining and new industries exploded; textiles employed 10,000 people in 1945 and 90,000 by 1975. Government loans, tariffs and regulations fostered local industries so that, for example, car production went from 87,000 (with 20% locally made content) in 1960 to 195,000 (with 60% locally made content) in 1970. Steel, fertilizers, consumer durables and chemicals also boomed producing a demand for employment that grew at 4% per year. Foreign investment, with Britain at the forefront but with France, Germany, Japan and the USA close behind, rewarded the political stability that South Africa offered and Africa to the north was destroying. Gold production doubled at a time when the price went from $35 per ounce to a peak in 1980 of $200 per ounce, and uranium exports allowed the import of technology to set up a domestic nuclear industry which quickly produced nuclear weapons. (The export of uranium to Britain in return for that technology was

---

[274] Harry Oppenheimer, *Foreword to the Special Edition*, The Spectator, 18th July 1970.
[275] Roy McNab, *South African Mosaic*, The Spectator, 17th April 1976.
[276] Richard West, *The Gathering Storm*, The Spectator, 1st October 1977.
[277] Pallister, p. 143.
[278] Anthony Delius, *White Hopes*, The Spectator, 2nd May 1970.
[279] All the statistics are taken from Beinart.

negotiated by none other than Anthony Wedgewood-Benn, Left wing firebrand, anti-nuclear and anti-Apartheid campaigner, aspirant to the leadership of the Labour party, and committed socialist who left £5million in his will; Benn The Bomb, so to speak, 'did more than anybody since Cecil Rhodes for the cause of white supremacy in South Africa'. [280] Part of the resultant mine was known, entirely without irony, as 'the Benn Shaft'.[281] Ho hum).

Nationalised industry also forged ahead. The 'parastatals' covering electricity, water, rail, broadcasting, air transport and steel, plus SASOL, which produced oil from coal, all did their bit to power the economic miracle. Not least of these nationalised industries was ARMSCOR which quickly undermined the effectiveness of the UN arms embargo placed on South Africa in 1962; in fact, the embargo was probably a blessing because it allowed South Africa to produce a range of weapons which were far better than the ones it possessed. Perhaps the only area in which South Africa really lagged behind was in electronics and computing. There were also major hydro-electric projects, particularly the Hendrik Verwoerd dam on the Orange River which piped water down to the fruit farms of the Eastern Cape and the massive Cabora Bassa dam on the Zambezi. These huge achievements brought the usual cavilling about low productivity, dependence on cheap labour etc etc but there was no doubting that South Africa had performed better than any other country in sub-Saharan Africa.

For white South Africans, times were undoubtedly good. The government ran a low taxation policy which allowed for greater private investment, greater profits and rising standards of living. University education added social mobility and a strong, skilled managerial class developed with a 'can-do' attitude and an appetite for innovation and improvisation. Among Afrikaaners '*Maak 'n' plan*' became something of a motto and it remains a particular feature of South African life that when a problem is encountered, the last thing anyone thinks of is to ask the government for a solution. White blue-collar employment dropped from 40-27% while White white-collar employment increased from 29-65% and almost all public sector jobs went to Afrikaaners; this had the knock on effect of having the level of the colour bar rise so that more opportunities for skilled black men were created. Low density suburbs with swimming pools became the norm for English-speakers and the traditionally poorer Afrikaaners, with built in quarters for domestic servants and car ownership that doubled every decade, beach holidays on the Durban coast and camping in the game parks, with rugby, tennis, cricket, plenty of beer and the *braai* permanently lit and loaded with a pile of steaks and chops.

The greatest challenge for the Apartheid economy was one that the whole of Africa faces today; a population expanding at a faster rate than the economy could provide jobs. The demographic challenge was both known and daunting; in 1976, nature conservationists in the Cape were expecting the population to double from 25 million to 50 million.[282] In 1960, roughly 3.5 million Africans lived in urban areas; thirty years later it was *18 million*. The total black population in 1951 was roughly 8.5 million, 20 million in 1980 and 29 million in 1991 – and half of it was under thirty and necessarily volatile. In 1950, whites made up perhaps 20% of the population, in 1980 the figure was 16% and by 1990 only 14%; from being 3:1 outnumbered by black Africans (excluding Indians and coloureds), they went to being outnumbered 4:1. 'Demographic and economic factors are on the side of the blacks,' declared the British Ambassador in May 1984:

> 'Black skills are urgently needed to develop the economy and by the year 1990 there will be twice as many blacks living in urban areas as the combined total of whites, coloureds and Indians.'[283]

It is also possible to see these as good times for black people too, although the picture was necessarily more mixed. Employment opportunities expanded massively and real wages rose steadily with a doubling in manufacturing, commerce, transport and construction but also in white-collar and educational work. The 70,000 black professionals, 14,000 nurses and 25,000 teachers of 1960 had quadrupled by 1980 and if the most striking aspect of pre-1945 South Africa was the emergence of a black urban working class, perhaps that of post-1960 South Africa was the emergence of a black, urban professional class who clustered together in their own exclusive neighbourhoods. Consumerism produced a desire for much the same products and life style across the racial divide and it is possible to imagine this leading to an erosion of Apartheid if only the human contact

---

[280] Richard West, *Benn The Bomb*, The Spectator, 10th September 1977.
[281] Geoffrey Wheatcroft, *More a Way of Life*, The Spectator, 13th June 1981.
[282] Arthur Nimmo, *The Knysna Story* (Wynberg, 1976), p.vii
[283] UKE to FCO 30th May 1984. https://www.margaretthatcher.org/document/144544

between the black and European middle-class, common enough in many cases, had been increased rather than reduced.

It was in the Homelands and rural areas that the picture looked increasingly bleak. Although farming enjoyed a similar boom to that enjoyed by industry with new crops, rationalisation of farms into larger, more economic units and the spread of irrigation, the subsequent mechanisation – the number of tractors went from 22,000 in 1947 to 300,000 by 1980 - created both opportunities and threats. Demand for labour initially increased so that by 1970, there were roughly a million and a half people employed and large gangs were always needed at harvest time. Similarly, as white people sought better opportunities in the towns, so more managerial positions on the farms were made available for black people and wages went up. On the negative side, there were more than a few reports of appalling conditions for migrant workers and an increasing demand that squatters, African tenants who paid rent with labour, were now an inefficient anachronism; between 1967-1982, perhaps 1.6 million people were forced off the land and into agricultural slums in the Homelands or in one of the 74 new towns built in this period. Here services were limited, employment hard to come by and malnutrition, high childhood mortality rates and all the other diseases of poverty were rife. Those who did find gainful employ often faced grindingly long commutes on primitive buses.

Again, this all has to be kept in perspective because the situation in Africa to the north was infinitely worse. These were the years of the Biafran War where the last plane out of the starving enclave carried the erstwhile President Ojukwu's Rolls Royce, bought with aid money meant to relieve the famine; of the first Tutsi-Hutu Rwandan genocide in 1971; of the genocidal racist Milton Obote who expelled the Kenyans from Uganda and his rival, Idi Amin, the genocidal cannibal who claimed to be the King of Scotland and who, not to be beaten in the racism stakes, expelled the Asians from Uganda (the UN, of course, stayed silent on this because, of course, it was a dirty little secret that *everyone* in East Africa hated the Indians).[284] There was also the 1974 expulsion of the Portuguese and the destruction of the economies of both Mozambique and Angola in the subsequent civil wars; of Bokassa, 'the former sergeant, unblessed by intellect',[285] Emperor of Central Africa, who had a hundred school children executed for refusing to buy uniforms from his wife's shop; the dismal collapse of Julius Nyerere's African socialism, *Ujamaa*, in Tanzania; and the Ethiopian famine, caused by another socialist collectivisation programme enforced by Soviet and Cuban troops. These were agonies that South Africans, however miserable, were spared. And despite the fact that Apartheid propagandists, true-believers and apologists made much out of these events, the force of their argument was undiminished; South Africans of all colours *were* materially better off, enjoyed a greater security of life and limb, and could look forward to the future with at least a modicum of hope unlike almost any other Africans south of the Sahara.

*

Foreign Affairs

One of the remarkable things about studying South African History is that it is possible to study it as a stand-alone subject for virtually three hundred years. Apart from its importance as a British bastion on the route to India, the country had no significance at all to the rest of the world, pretty much. Whenever the outside world impinged upon it, as in the period 1878-1885 or the Second Anglo-Boer War 1899-1902, it was only because there was thought to be a threat to British control of the route to India and this the British were determined to control. After 1947 and the independence of India, that logic disappeared and with it, British interest in just about the whole of Africa – an expensive adventure that never returned on the capital outlay required to conquer and govern it. All that mattered now for the British was to get out of the bloody place as fast as possible, with the least possible damage to her reputation and with the least expense. The Union of South Africa itself had never had an independent foreign policy. Indeed, its foreign policy was, to all intents and purposes, to try to get an *independent* foreign policy and this was achieved progressively with the 1931 Statute of Westminster, followed by the declaration of the Republic in 1961 and the decision to leave the Commonwealth. What this

---

[284] *The Consequences of Amin for Britain*, The Spectator, 27th September 1972. See also V.S. Naipaul, *Zambia's Compromise with the West*, The Spectator, 11th June 1977.
[285] 'Napoleon in Africa', *The Spectator* 17th December 1977.

means is that from this point on, it isn't possible to study South Africa without studying the affairs of Africa to the north, and indeed the rest of the world. So here goes.

On gaining full independence in 1961, South African policy was based on Apartheid at home but in her relations with foreign states, her leaders were quite open to the idea of having multi-racial allies and, in turn, their black neighbours were quite willing to ignore Apartheid in order to get South African help, support and friendship. Indeed, the only real way to understand what was happening in these years is to accept that there were three separate but closely related conflicts occurring simultaneously across southern Africa. The first conflict was the struggle against Apartheid in South Africa and white supremacy in Rhodesia – which was complicated by the fact that many black African states depended on South Africa economically. Second came the desire of African nationalists to see the end of colonial rule – which was complicated by the fact that what replaced it was usually worse. Third was the Cold War conflict between the Communist bloc and the West – which was complicated by the Soviet use of Cuban proxies and the West's opposition to Apartheid.

As far as the Cold War issue went, before 1975, for the USA southern Africa was a place of very little interest while most of its attention was focused on the war in Vietnam, the running sore of the Arab-Israeli conflict and the heavily militarised confrontation on the North German plain and though there was a general condemnation of Apartheid, there was a reluctance to do much more. The importance of Portugal's colonial empire in Africa for the USA, was that it belonged to Portugal, a NATO member, and it was the bases provided in the Azores by that NATO member that outranked any concerns over her presence on Africa. This was pretty much the stance of the USSR up until the 1960s too; the KGB did not bother to set up an Africa department until then. After that date, however, they committed increased resources in the hope of gaining politically from the British and French retreat from empire but although they become the main supplier of arms and money to African liberation movements, they never really sent enough for them to win. This was because they understood that the West might allow a few Third World disasters to drop into the Soviet lap but South Africa would be a testing point and, being too far away from the Soviet Union across oceans that that the US navy controlled, there was no real point in contesting the issue. This was one of the many things that the ANC never understood.

If it isn't obvious now that the South African problem was never a question of black versus white it should be. Politics never is, on whatever issue or whatever crisis, simply because the world is too complicated to be reduced to Manichean terms. Foreign affairs, one might think, is the policy of a government towards its neighbours and so, when the government speaks, that is the policy. Yup. Right. In fact the different departments of government, and they are legion, conduct their own foreign policies as and how they see fit. So, there are roughly forty different agencies in the US – State, Trade, CIA, Defense etc etc – all vying for influence and fighting their bureaucratic wars. In Britain, the Department for International Development, that dreadful spavined offspring of Tony Blair's bid for international sainthood, often has more influence than the Foreign Office because it has more money and can thus hire more 4x4 vehicles and hire more 5* Hotels for receptions with corrupt Africans. In Afghanistan it virtually refused to co-operate with the British Army. In the Brexit negotiations of 2018, British PM Theresa May set up a whole new department to conduct the talks and then undermined it by carrying on her own policy behind its back. As in the rest of the world, so in South Africa where the Foreign Affairs department was undermined repeatedly by Defence and *vice versa*. So, when we talk about a government's foreign policy, we have to understand that the policy is often an amalgam of different interests, ideologies and personalities. It is never monolithic and very often chaotic.

Initially, South African foreign policy before 1974 had two main aims. The first was to convince the USA and Western Europe that it was, in some way, the southern arm of NATO which could be relied upon to resist the advance of communism and the Soviet Union and protect the Cape sea route around which 20% of US and 66% of European oil supplies came from the Middle East. In this, South Africa was only partially successful because of the growing revulsion at Apartheid. The National Party also knew from the beginning that this was a horse that wouldn't run in the long-term because of that revulsion and so gradually went into laager. This can be illustrated quite well by the South African response when, in 1975, the British PM Harold Wilson, in a fit of moralistic idiocy, cancelled the Simonstown Agreement which provided for British use of South African bases to defend that oil route, to which the South Africans responded by affirming that they would no longer defend western oil supplies.

The second aim was to convince black African states that South Africa was a stable, reliable partner – different certainly – but no threat and that therefore they should stop providing help to the ANC in exile. In this aim too, the Vorster government was successful up until the shock of the Carnation Revolution when the Portuguese Empire collapsed overnight. Between 1969-74, Vorster met with the leaders of Malawi, Lesotho, Madagascar, Ivory Coast, Senegal and Liberia in the search for a *modus vivendi*, despite the vigorous opposition of the Organisation of Africa Unity (OAU) which, in 1969, committed its members to support the armed struggle against Rhodesia, South Africa and Portugal. The lynch pin was Kenneth Kaunda's Zambia which wavered between accepting a co-operative relationship with South Africa regarding the Rhodesia issue and rejecting relations for pretty much the same reasons. Above all, Kaunda was conscious that he was dependent on Portugal, Rhodesia and South Africa for his transport links to the coast.

A little geography. Before 1974, South Africa lay at the tip of the continent with Namibia/SW Africa under its control to the north-west and Portuguese ruled Angola northwards of that. To the north lay Botswana then Rhodesia and then to the north-east lay Portuguese ruled Mozambique and then Swaziland to the east. There are no source-to-sea navigable rivers in Africa which means that anything exported from the Zambian copper mines must travel by rail. One of those railways, the Benguela railway, goes through Angola to the coast, another goes through Rhodesia to Beira on the Mozambican coast. Every other rail line or decent road goes through South Africa. Without access to this infrastructure, Zambia could neither import the food and fuel it needed to eat and keep the copper mines going, nor export the ore it needed to sell. These were hard realities and there was no escaping them because Zambia could not afford to build alternative routes and lacked the expertise to do so even if a windfall came its way. Zambia could therefore not afford to challenge Apartheid seriously, despite Kaunda's oft repeated assertions that it would. And if Zambia would offer no real challenge, then neither would the rest of black Africa; noise – yes. Action? No.

The most effective opposition to Apartheid in these years therefore came from Britain, a fact that went entirely over the heads of the ANC. This opposition came in a variety of forms and was aimed at the gradual undermining of the Apartheid state but without throwing the baby out with the bathwater and allowing a communist takeover to result. This was done in several ways, the first and most obvious being the provision of safe haven for those Apartheid activists who managed to flee the country. Brian Bunting, we have noted, took full advantage of this but Ronnie Kasrils was also given shelter, travel documents, police protection, free education and healthcare for his children, free rein to travel backwards and forwards between the UK, Africa and behind the Iron Curtain while his propaganda, recruitment and intelligence activities were allowed to go on unhindered. Not that he ever saw the irony of his position, or uttered a word of gratitude in his memoirs *Armed and Dangerous*, (which was an ambitious title by any stretch of the imagination; at least one credible commentator has accused him of a 'propensity for premeditated lying, in public'[286] and being a 'wanabee' without military experience[287]). This went too for the very many South African academics who were given coveted places at British universities and responded with a similar lack of grace. BOSS defector Gordon Winter estimated that by 1980, there were as many as 70,000 South Africans living in London, many of whom were active opponents of Apartheid.[288]

More obviously, and almost completely ignored by all and sundry, was Britain's policy towards the High Commission Territories of Swaziland, Bechuanaland and Basutoland. In 1910, it had been assumed that at some stage these three territories would be absorbed by the Union of South Africa but as Afrikaaner nationalism went from strength to strength during the 1930s, there was a growing ambivalence towards this idea in Britain, mainly because of reservations regarding Native legislation.[289] Once the Nationalists got into power in 1948, the possibility was squashed and Britain granted independence to the first two territories as Botswana and Lesotho in 1966, followed by Swaziland in 1968. These were small blows but pointed ones, especially at a time when Britain refused to recognise white ruled Rhodesia as an independent state.

---

[286] Stuart Sterzel, *The Angolan War* (2014) p.137.
[287] Stuart Sterzel, *The Angolan War* (2014) p. 303.
[288] Gordon Winter, *Inside BOSS* p.174.
[289] *The Claim of the Native*, The Spectator, 17th August 1934. Also, *The South African Protectorates*, The Spectator 17th May 1935.

More controversial was Britain's role in the United Nations campaign against Apartheid in which several resolutions and courses of action against South Africa were prevented.[290] This was largely because many of the calls for sanctions were made by countries that had nothing to lose by supporting them, by countries whose own record on human rights would bear no scrutiny and because they were so often motivated by Soviet Cold War aims; and also because many countries, including the Soviet Union, lied like, well, communists, about the fact that they were trading with South Africa in spite of sanctions.[291] It was also the case that sanctions were so very often impractical – a naval blockade, for heaven's sake, was proposed in 1964[292] – ineffective, provided incentives for smuggling and stimulated the growth of South Africa's home grown armaments industries; any number of items that were supposed to be embargoed were dual use, such as boots or radar, and the haggling over such details made a mockery of even the best intentions. There was also a moral question; how could the creation of unemployment among poor, black Africans produced by boycotting the import of South African oranges to a particular country do anything but make things worse for poor, black Africans? How would refusing to build power stations make the electrification of black townships possible? (In the 1970s and early 1980s, South Africa had the largest electrification programme in the world).[293] And just how would Basutoland/Lesotho, Swaziland, Botswana, Rhodesia and Zambia cope with being cut off by economic blockade? President Seretse Khama of Botswana took a whole different nuance on sanctions when he had a heart attack and was treated in a 'whites only' hospital in South Africa[294] but it's things like this that really sharpen up a ruler's understanding of an issue. The theoretical case needed to be answered too; did engagement with an erring state produce better results than sanctions? The answer to this question usually exposed the hypocrisy of those shouting loudest for sanctions against South Africa, for those same people so often resolutely advocated a policy of engagement for the Soviet Union. As the British Foreign Secretary, Geoffrey Howe, put it in 1983;

> 'You can only influence someone if you are willing to talk to him. That applies to the Western governments in their approach to relations with the Soviet bloc. And it applies with equal force to the Western governments and to the other states of Southern Africa in their relations with South Africa.'[295]

The UN did pass resolutions calling for an arms embargo in 1964, 1970 and 1977 but the reality was that they were shot full of howitzer sized loopholes and further extensions or tightening of the regulations were resisted tooth and nail by Britain, France and the US for commercial reasons and because the USSR continued to flood the continent with arms. Furthermore, sanctions or no sanctions, France was determined to maintain her lucrative position as South Africa's main overseas arms supplier and avid hoarder of her gold, while the Italians supplied Impala aircraft to be manufactured under licence in South Africa; all that was happening, complained many, was that British manufacturers were being put out of business in order to open up opportunities for the French, Germans and Italians.[296] And besides, just what would kicking South Africa out of the UN, as was vetoed by Britain, France and the US in 1974, actually achieve except to release her from whatever agreements she was in violation of?

Where the record was clearer was in the case of Namibia/SW Africa, where a series of Security Council resolutions resulted in the cancelling of South Africa's UN Mandate to rule in 1969 and in 1974 for South Africa's immediate withdrawal. The problem was that the UN undermined the effectiveness of these actions largely because the UN General Assembly went against the ruling of its own court and thus destroyed the legal foundations of its own case. It also, on no evidence and for no good reason at all, appointed the SWAPO guerrillas as the sole legal representative of the Namibia/SW Africa people, which guaranteed that they would be accepted as no such thing. In the event, UN policy towards Namibia/SW Africa was run by a 'Contact Group' of Britain, USA, West Germany, France and Canada from that point on. In reality, for most of the Cold War the UN was regarded by many in the West as being fatally compromised by the presence of the USSR on

---

[290] *Britain and South Africa*, The Spectator, 7th June 1963.
[291] Arnold Beichman, *Verwoerd and After*, The Spectator, 13th August 1965.
[292] *The Wrong Method*, The Spectator, 17th April, 1964.
[293] FCO Briefing for Margaret Thatcher 31st May 1984, p.43 https://www.margaretthatcher.org/document/144540
[294] V.S. Naipaul, *Zambia's Compromise with the West*, The Spectator 11th June 1977.
[295] G. Howe speech to The Royal Commonwealth Society, 14th Nov 1983. https://www.margaretthatcher.org/document/144501
[296] No.10 Record of Conversation *The UN Arms Embargo on South Africa* 19th Feb 1981.
https://www.margaretthatcher.org/document/126945

the Security Council, too often rottenly corrupt – UNESCO being the main, but not the only, culprit, – and resembling nothing more than a parliament of tyrants. Any organisation that allowed Idi Amin's Uganda to pontificate about racism and human rights in South Africa while remaining silent about the expulsion of the Ugandan Asians – succoured by Britain, of course - was an organisation that needed to take a good, long, hard look at itself; but mirrors are rare things at the UN and where they are present, they are usually of the fun house variety.

*

Rhodesia

British policy towards Rhodesia was another area full of potential for the ANC. In short, the aim of Britain in the period 1950-1980 was to get out of direct rule in black Africa while preserving the Commonwealth and preventing a Russian takeover. Much more problematic, and dreadfully painful for all involved, was the British decision to come out against white minority rule, against her own 'kith and kin', a decision which left a long legacy of bitterness and was mixed in its results. On a wider note, it was also recognised that what happened in Rhodesia was in some way a political dress rehearsal for what might happen in South Africa and indeed, lessons were drawn by many interested parties from the experience. Initially, British policy towards Rhodesia had been to create a strong, economically viable federation of Nyasaland, Northern and Southern Rhodesia (Malawi, Zambia, Zimbabwe) capable of withstanding any temptation to drift into South Africa's orbit. This foundered on the rocks of agitation led by Hastings Banda and Kenneth Kaunda who had their eyes firmly on the prize of black majority rule in Malawi and Zambia respectively which, in reality, meant one-party dictatorship with them at the helm. It wasn't helped either by the bungling British leadership provided by the fixer Sir Walter Monckton and the thoroughly disreputable Duncan Sandys.

Monckton was perhaps the epitome of the oily Whitehall insider who combined a forked tongue with a willingness to provide a taxi on the path of least resistance to anyone with the necessary connections. An accomplished barrister, he had managed the abdication of Edward VIII, had been a keen supporter of appeasement before the war, a keen socialist during the war and yet had deployed his charm so well that he was offered a seat in Parliament as a Conservative. Like very many socialists, he was also phenomenally wealthy and became Chairman of the Midland Bank. When he joined Churchill's government in 1950, he managed to combine his predilection for socialism and appeasement by caving in to virtually any and all demands made by the trade union movement. He also played his part in damping down any number of royal scandals, particularly those concerning the Duke of Windsor, which were legion, and which included a million francs of illegal currency dealings. Where Rhodesia was concerned, it was the Monckton Report that paved the way for Zambia to secede from the proposed federation, torpedoing its aim of a non-racial democracy in the process, and thus beginning the process of breaking the essential trust that the Rhodesian government had in the word of the British government.[297]

Sandys' record was not much better. As Minister of Defence in 1957 he had attempted to replace the RAF with missiles and had then virtually single-handedly destroyed the British aviation industry by forcing it through a series of mergers. Suave, handsome and married to Winston Churchill's daughter, he was also a *roué* who was implicated in a noted 1963 sex scandal as the 'headless man' on whom the Duchess of Argyle was performing a sex act during a foursome with a Hollywood film star. His particular contribution to the Rhodesian SNAFU was in bungling the 1961 constitutional conference. The background to this was the formation in 1957 of the Southern Rhodesian African National Congress under the leadership of Joshua Nkomo which had arisen out of dissatisfaction with land ownership, political rights and poverty in both town and country. The Rhodesian government read it as a precursor to riot and revolution and responded with vigour, banning the organisation in 1959, jailing 800 supporters and bringing in a raft of legislation which turned the country into potentially a police state. The overwhelming attitude of the white population to these actions was positive, believing as it did that poor, ignorant people were being preyed upon by communist agitators – which was a pretty accurate

---

[297] Andrew Roberts, *Eminent Churchillians*, (London, 1994).

analysis – and that it was necessary for change to happen gradually, if it was to be successful and not result in the idiocies that had so far attended black rule in Africa to the north. The problem with this idea was that their idea of gradual change was positively glacial, certainly generational and though the white Rhodesians were genuinely committed to non-racial democracy, they were not committed to the speed felt necessary by Nkomo, who formed the National Democratic Party in 1960 to replace the now banned Southern Rhodesian ANC. It should also be noted that Rhodesia was subject to all the strains of an exploding demographic that South Africa faced; the indigenous population in 1890 was thought to be something in the region of 300,000 but in 1960, that figure was 4-5 million, a number that rapidly outstripped the great and genuine efforts of the white government to provide sufficient education, healthcare and employment;[298] as in South Africa, over-stocking in the reserves was a major problem while labour unions were becoming ever more militant.[299]

At the 1961 Salisbury constitutional conference, Sandys negotiated a deal with Nkomo that he was, frankly, amazed to get away with, in which fifteen out of sixty-five seats were allocated to black voters under a complex franchise that would prevent black majority rule for the foreseeable future. His failure in not assessing whether Nkomo's supporters would accept such a deal was critical. When the terms got out, the reaction was of such outrage that Nkomo was forced to repudiate them ten days later whereupon the NDP split and faction fighting, looting, arson, murder and gang warfare erupted across the country. By December 1961, the NDP was banned, this time being replaced by the Zimbabwean African People's Union (ZAPU) and violence continued into 1962. Nkomo must also share much of the blame for this breakdown; like so many other African leaders, he had little formal education, not much experience of the outside world, an unsophisticated understanding of international politics, a very deep interest in his own financial affairs[300] and a belief that violence was the most effective means of solving a problem. He therefore allowed and encouraged the violence in the hope that things would get so bad that Britain would intervene directly and overthrow the white government. This was 1962 though, and all eyes were on the precedents being set in the Congo next door, on the concurrent violence led by Kenneth Kaunda in Zambia, and on the Berlin Wall, even further to the north.

For the British, this was becoming a difficult circle to square. Not only was there pressure coming from the Commonwealth, the UN and the OAU, there were also electoral pressures at home where the PM, Alec Douglas Home, was convinced that support for Rhodesian independence while still under white minority rule was a definite vote loser. The response was to prevaricate, hopefully until the 1964 election had secured a further Conservative term of office, which in turn produced a series of talks which convinced the Rhodesians that although they had been given cast iron guarantees of independence, these guarantees would not be honoured. The result was the coming to the fore of Ian Smith, committed to independence, anti-communism, paternal gradualism towards the black majority and seething with anger at what he regarded as British betrayal and duplicity; he had fought in the RAF during the Second World War and regarded Rhodesians as more British than the British. He also believed that politics and diplomacy was played according to the sportsmanlike ethos of cricket and rugby and was constantly amazed to find that the only sports it resembled were mud-wrestling and cage fighting. And this is not me writing a caricature; it's all in his appropriately named memoirs, *Bitter Harvest*.[301] Read them and you can hear the sound of his teeth cracking and crumbling as he grinds them to stumps in his frustration that nobody is playing by the rules of 'Lord's and the Oval, Twickenham and Murrayfield, Wimbledon, St. Andrew's, Epsom and Bisley'. In some ways admirable for his fortitude and constancy, he was also a rather narrow man who got his knowledge of imperial History from the *Boy's Own Annual* and, as Lord Blake, the brilliant historian said, understood little of the modern world and hated the little that he did.[302] There was no doubting his backbone, the depth of his convictions or his shrewdness but his main weakness was in not being able to appreciate either the position or motivations of the British government, who insisted that white minority rule could no longer be justified, and in too often mistaking the aspirations of black Rhodesians as being driven by Marxist agitators. That the Marxist agitators existed, and that their methods were almost unfailingly brutal, there is no doubt. Unfortunately, he was apt to confuse the symptom of violence with the cause of the discontent, which was frustrated black aspiration. Nor could he ever reconcile his defence of

---

[298] Ian Smith, *Bitter Harvest* (Johannesburg, 2001) p.57.
[299] Paul L. Moorcraft and Peter McLaughlin, *The Rhodesian War* (Barnsley 2008), p.28.
[300] Xan Smiley, *The Nkomo Factor*, The Spectator, 10th September 1977.
[301] Ian Smith, *Bitter Harvest* p. 314.
[302] Robert Blake, *War or Peace in Rhodesia?* The Spectator, 2nd October 1976.

Western civilisation, whose benefits he regarded quite rightly as self-evident, with the evidence of his own eyes that very many young, impressionable, black Rhodesians preferred the dreams and unicorn wonders of Marxism to the plough-horse of his paternal gradualism. What he was emphatically not, was a racist and the party he led, the Rhodesia Front, comprehensively trounced any and all attempts to bring in any form of Apartheid. Unfortunately, he had retained the habit of referring to black Rhodesians as 'our blacks' and gave the perfect quote for his enemies to use against him on his thoughts of black majority rule - when taken out of context: 'Never in a thousand years'.[303]

The issue came to a head after the 1964 General Election resulted in a Labour victory and the installation of Harold Wilson in 10 Downing Street. Wilson was a shabby, duplicitous man by nature, increasingly given to paranoid delusions about being spied upon by his own intelligence services, utterly dominated by his private secretary, the harridan Marcia Williams and unwise in his choice of friends, many of whom had unsavoury connections on the other side of the Iron Curtain – after his retirement as Prime Minister he became president of the GB-USSR Association.[304] According to one colleague, he had only scored so highly in his university exams because he had perfected the art of telling his examiners exactly what they wanted to hear, which when combined with his war service as a ministry statistician might lead one to draw the cynical conclusion that he had acquired the two most important qualifications for being a politician. The wit Auberon Waugh once claimed that he had been presented with a book entitled 'The Thoughts of Chairman Harold' which, on opening, turned out to consist of blank pages.[305] A leader, he was not. Lacking any sort of originality and capable of the sort of opportunism and hypocrisy that would shame Tony Blair (even Blair didn't send his kids to private school; Wilson did – after closing down the Grammars), he was distrusted by even his closest colleagues; in short, he came close to being the epitome of the nadir of post-war British leadership and his record reveals that there was hardly any situation that was not made worse by his intervention. The one thing that he had going for him was that he was an outstanding repudiation of the notion of white supremacy, for no-one who ever had dealings with this pudgy, pasty-faced man, who resembled nothing more than a swirl of dirty laundry churning in a washing machine, could ever come away thinking that he had any relationship whatsoever to a master race, however notional; most black African leaders treated him with the contempt he so richly earned. Milton Obote, the thoroughly debased, racist President of Uganda, so despised him that he called for Britain to be kicked out of the Commonwealth, which is an indication of just how low Wilson allowed Britain's standing to fall. It was no wonder then, that he would drive Ian Smith into a Unilateral Declaration of Independence for Rhodesia in 1965 and then the proclamation of a republic in 1970, through his routine and repeated dishonesty and mean-spirited treatment – on one occasion, Wilson had all the Commonwealth prime ministers up to Buckingham palace for lunch with the Queen and deliberately left him off the guest list. Fortunately the Queen noticed, she being a long way brighter than Wilson, and sent someone off to fetch him personally.

The breaking point came because Wilson would not accept the 1961 Rhodesian constitution which enshrined Smith's political gradualism. Smith's approach was justified on the thoroughly sensible grounds that parliamentary democracy was not widely understood by the *Indaba* of the traditional chiefs, who preferred a more traditional system, and that time would therefore be needed for education to produce a solid, responsible class of black voters and politicians; he was, in fact, against the allocation of seats on a racial basis and preferred an arrangement similar to the Cape Colony voting system. The second justification was that, on all the available evidence, handing over the government to African Nationalists would result in immediate disaster for everyone – Rhodesians had witnessed a steady stream of refugees from the Congo massacres – and that, therefore, transition needed to be managed. Wilson's answer to this was that immediate black majority rule was a moral imperative (and he was prepared to turn a blind eye to any and all of their tactics of intimidation) and that if the subsequent black government wished to bring down economic and political ruin on the country, then that was their democratic right. Smith, quite rightly, chose his path of the Unilateral Declaration of Independence as the more rational one – and everything that Smith said would happen did indeed come to pass when Mugabe got in in 1980[306] - but in doing so committed his country to a fifteen year war with all the odds stacked against it.

[303] Peter Godwin, 'If only Ian Smith had shown some imagination then more of his people might live at peace.' *The Guardian* 25th November 2007.
[304] C. Andrew and V. Mitrokhin, *The Sword and the Shield: Mitrokhin Archive and the Secret History of the KGB.* (New York, 1999) p.425.
[305] 'The Non-Politics of Harold Wilson', *The Spectator*, 27th September 1968.
[306] Richard Wood in Sue Onslow and Anna-Mart van Wyk, *Southern Africa in the Cold War, Post 1974* (Wilson Center, 2013), p. 193.

What was significant for the ANC was that the British government had sided with African nationalism, abandoned a 'white' colony to its fate and had even considered sending a British army to overthrow it.[307] Britain had also saved Nyerere, whose extraordinary charm was matched only by his extraordinary vacuity,[308] from being overthrown in 1964, through the intervention of the Royal Navy after his poorly paid troops mutinied.[309] Instead of interpreting this as a revolution in policy which opened up all sorts of possibilities for the struggle against Apartheid, they saw it as evidence of the decay of the Western world in the face of the advance of Marxist-Leninism and so stuck by their association with their brutal paymasters. As it turned out, a mixture of staggering incompetence, infighting and political bungling among the African nationalists meant that for the best part of the next ten years, the Rhodesian security forces were able to contain and defeat the forces of African liberation while the real blows landed on Ian Smith's UDI came from Britain, the USA and, quite remarkably, South Africa itself.

In Britain's case, the imposition of economic sanctions on Rhodesia was something of a curate's egg as far as effective blows went. As with many graduates of the Oxford University course in Politics, Philosophy and Economics, Wilson's grasp of economic realities was shaky at best with the result that the imposition of sanctions made less difference to the Rhodesian economy than the weather.[310] Actually, they made the economy stronger by stimulating home grown 'import substitution' in manufacturing, diversification in agriculture and a steady increase in mining; Rhodesians prided themselves on their pioneer heritage of improvisation, innovation and 'can-do' attitude.[311] Wilson also bungled the seizure of Rhodesian assets held at the Bank of England by prompting a retaliatory cancelling of debts which left Rhodesia £100m better off immediately with the prospect of gaining another £20m p.a. from unpaid obligations. And to compound his idiocy, he ceased paying the pensions of Britons resident in Rhodesia, which handed Smith an easy coup when he agreed to pay them instead.[312] An attempt to intimidate Smith by despatching an RAF squadron to Lusaka also backfired when it turned out that it was dependent on Salisbury Air Traffic Control. Auberon Waugh described him as a 'Colney Hatch Napoleon' who could not understand that in Rhodesia, Britain had 'responsibility without power.'[313] For sanctions to be effective, they need to be universal and this is always a pipe dream; Zambia was entirely dependent on Rhodesia for the export of her copper and the import of the coal needed to smelt it and in 1979, dependent on Rhodesian maize to prevent a famine;[314] South Africa, Mozambique (both pre- and post-independence), Gabon, Zaire and most other countries of the OAU continued to trade, Botswana allowed transit for Rhodesian goods on her railways while France, West Germany and Japan provided substitutes for British goods. The Soviets too joined in the bonanza buying chrome, tobacco and other agricultural produce through holding companies in Switzerland while Israel, Jordan and India were all willing to supply arms.[315] Added to this was Jack Malloch's sanctions busting air cargo routes while the Comoros provided the cover for the illegal import of arms. British oil companies also continued to supply Rhodesia with the full knowledge of the government.

Where the sanctions were effective was in restricting the supply of British arms. Much of the Rhodesian air force consisted of British made planes and the subsequent strain on them caused by lack of spares put them in great danger of wearing out. This went for all sorts of pieces of equipment, including rifles, which gradually wore out; there are all sorts of veteran's tales of barrels getting bent during para drops and being 'repaired' by sawing a few inches off the end; some of those para drops were done from a Dakota that had flown at Arnhem in 1944. Probably the greatest shortage was of helicopters and though the Rhodesian air force was able to keep a great many in the air, in the end it was dependent on South Africa for perhaps half of its effective lift capacity. That said, anything that the Rhodesians really needed was happily supplied by South Africa. In conclusion, we can probably say that the sanctions hurt Britain more than Rhodesia and that the main beneficiary of their

[307] Paul L. Moorcraft and Peter McLaughlin, *The Rhodesian War* (Barnsley 2008), p.28.
[308] See the interview with Jonathan Dimbleby, in which he blamed the lack of a World Government for the failure of his policies, *Thames TV This Week 1977*. https://www.youtube.com/watch?v=1t9gJd9p5ZM
[309] Tony Laurence, *The Dar Mutiny of 1964* (Brighton, 2007).
[310] Paul L. Moorcraft and Peter McLaughlin, *The Rhodesian War* (Barnsley 2008), p.119
[311] *End of Empire Ch.14 Rhodesia*. 1985. https://www.youtube.com/watch?v=0DuNhsLR9y0
[312] Ian Smith, *Bitter Harvest* (Johannesburg, 2001) p.112.
[313] Auberon Waugh, *Rhodesia down the Hatch*, The Spectator, 1st November 1968.
[314] Richard West, *Recognition for Rhodesia?* The Spectator, 12th May 1979.
[315] Paul L. Moorcraft and Peter McLaughlin, *The Rhodesian War* (Barnsley 2008), p.122

imposition was South Africa, who increased her influence over Ian Smith to the point where it constituted a stranglehold.

*

The Carnation Revolution

The strategic situation for the Apartheid government remained excellent right up until 1974. Rhodesian UDI removed the prospect of a hostile black nationalist state appearing on the Limpopo and flung it right back across the Zambezi where the Vorster government intended it to remain. Soft loans were extended to Rhodesia and substantial contingents of police and air force units were loaned in the counter-insurgency fight while much was done to circumvent the arms embargo through mutual co-operation. To the west and east, Portugal still controlled Angola and Mozambique and although there were substantial guerrilla movements operating there, the most important of which was FRELIMO in Mozambique, the co-operation between South African, Rhodesian and Portuguese forces did much to prevent the emergence of any real threat. The Zambian capital, Lusaka, became the home of African national liberation movements, whose squabbling and mutual antipathy – which included a significant amount of kidnapping, torture, mutiny, corruption and hanging out in the nightclubs of the capital with young women, but not much fighting - did much to make the Zambians regret playing host to them and caused Kenneth Kaunda to constantly urge peace talks on the Zimbabweans, if only to get them out of his country.[316] Botswana remained too small and too weak to be of any concern at all.

There was also much for the South African government to rejoice at in the state of the opposition. In August 1967, a combined force of ZAPU and ANC guerrillas attempted to establish a base in north-western Rhodesia but was quickly defeated and the two parties quickly fell out over who was to blame. A pair of similar operations in 1968 ended in much the same way while the routine intimidation practised by the insurgents kept up the flow of black Rhodesians into the *Rhodesian* armed forces. Similarly, the activities of Nkomo's ZAPU and the splinter organisation ZANU (Zimbabwean African National Union) in pressganging people into their own armed forces – which included the abduction of school children for military training – did much to discredit the insurgents.[317] Guerrilla camps were incompetently run and according to one ZAPU leader represented 'the depth and height of decay, corruption, nepotism, tribalism, selfishness and gross irresponsibility on the part of the military administration from top to bottom.'[318] Those ANC fighters who went off for military training in China, the Soviet Union or East Germany during the period 1965-74 found precious little use for it and, indeed, one can't help get the feeling that the main providers expected little return from their investment.[319] Much the same could be said, initially, for the SWAPO guerrillas of Namibia/SW Africa, also based in Zambia and also both staggeringly incompetent and divorced from their target area by hundreds of miles of desert and bush.[320] By 1974, Rhodesian security forces had so beaten both ZANU (its armed wing was ZANLA) and ZAPU (whose armed wing was ZIPRA) that their combined effective strength in the country was less than a hundred active guerrillas.[321] Soviet foreign policy was aggressive, but it was also realistic and although Moscow was willing to pay lip service to the ANC, they understood that the Cape was still a vital western interest and that the US navy could prevent anyone interfering there in decisive force. If they were not prepared to go to war for Cuba in 1961, they were certainly not prepared to go to war for South Africa in 1971.

What the Soviets were prepared to do, however, was support guerrilla movements in the Portuguese empire and African nationalists elsewhere as a first step in a very long game to gain control of the vital strategic minerals that South Africa possesses and which NATO needed for many of its advanced weapon systems,[322] and it was here that the first shifts in geopolitics happened. In 1974, the 'Carnation Revolution' in Portugal resulted in the

---

[316] Paul L. Moorcraft and Peter McLaughlin, *The Rhodesian War* (Barnsley 2008), p.41.
[317] Paul L. Moorcraft and Peter McLaughlin, *The Rhodesian War* (Barnsley 2008), p.38.
[318] Paul L. Moorcraft and Peter McLaughlin, *The Rhodesian War* (Barnsley 2008), p.34.
[319] Nerys John, *South African Intervention in the Angolan Civil War 1975-76: Motivations and Implications.* MA Thesis, University of Capetown, 2002 p.36.
[320] L. Scholtz, *The SADF and the Border War 1966-1989* (Capetown 2013).
[321] Paul L. Moorcraft and Peter McLaughlin, *The Rhodesian War* (Barnsley 2008), p.39.
[322] Stuart Sterzel, *The Angolan War* (2014) p.9.

declaration that the empire would be abandoned at the earliest possible moment and that interlocutors were now being actively sought to enable this to happen. In Mozambique, the interlocutor was the largest guerrilla group, FRELIMO, and power was handed over to its leader Samora Machel in 1975. Taking note of his threats and having some experience of what FRELIMO guerrillas were capable of, 200,000 Portuguese people immediately fled Machel's proposed socialist paradise. The rest were expelled with nothing more than a suitcase. At a stroke, the whole skilled managerial, entrepreneurial, artisan and technical wealth of Mozambique was cast to the four winds – or to South Africa and Europe, to be more precise. What was left was quickly destroyed by nationalisation, collectivisation, purge, prison camps and de-catholicisation. As if determined to plough salt into the earth, Machel then allowed ZANU to expand its operations along the Rhodesian border, which begged Rhodesian armed intervention, at the same time as starting a civil war with his rivals in the RENAMO movement. War would be a constant feature of the Mozambican experience for the next twenty years. When I drove up to Tete on the Zambezi in 2006, the scars were still evident, the mines were still being lifted and the port city of Beira, once the preferred holiday destination of a generation of Rhodesians, a rusting wreck. Outside Tete, people were living in holes in the ground.

*

Castro and his regime are not South Africans, and they are neither peace-makers nor liberators. They are war-mongers, and deserve no thanks for what transpired in South Africa. They did nothing for it except hinder and delay it.

Stuart Sterzel, ex-SADF Special Forces 2014.

In Angola, things were at least as bad. When independence came, the Chinese backed FNLA stood ready to seize power from their base along the Congo border, the Soviet backed MPLA held the capital and central Angola while UNITA occupied land in the south east. A coalition government was cobbled together but it had collapsed into civil war even before independence was declared. This time, 300,000 white managerial, technical, entrepreneurial, medical and artisanal people fled, again many to South Africa, leaving both the government and the economy in tatters. All this might have been contained as a purely local affair until the MPLA turned to Cuba/Russia for military assistance and the country dissolved into another murderous civil war and grand advertisement for why assisting the ANC to liberate South Africa was a bad idea. What that meant for ordinary Angolans, the new citizens of a state without anything resembling a decent health care or welfare system, was well described by Pedro Rosa Mendes in his remarkable (if surreal) travelogue *Bay of Tigers*: 'They fought for their land, hard and for a long time, until they made of it a land of guerrillas and no other crop.'[323]

For South Africa, the Carnation Revolution came as a very unwelcome surprise. At a stroke, the barrier separating them from black Africa was broken, bringing with it the reality of two Soviet backed states on her borders and exposing Rhodesia all along her eastern border. Adding a further layer of complexity to the problem was the fact that Zambia would now have, potentially, two Soviet-backed states on her borders too. Previously, Kenneth Kaunda had maintained friendly relations with South Africa in an attempt to restrain the strong communist influence among African nationalists, while South Africa had hoped that by demonstrating its willingness to coexist with black Africa – a form of détente - some of the international pressure might be relieved. The Carnation Revolution brought a new strand of thinking into Vorster's foreign policy; might it not be wise to accept a moderate black majority government in Rhodesia and so produce an anti-communist central African diplomatic bloc which would include Malawi and Zambia? Given that Mozambique would probably be too busy with its own affairs to be much of a threat for the foreseeable future and that concurrent South African efforts to bolster opposition to the MPLA in Angola might neutralise a threat from that direction, it seemed possible that this plan might work. To pressure the Rhodesians into beginning talks with Zambia and its own opposition groups, South Africa began to hold up arms shipments and petrol deliveries, then persuaded Ian Smith to free the jailed leaders, Nkomo and Sithole, as a precursor to talks at the Victoria Falls railway bridge aimed at bringing forward black majority rule. Ian Smith began to talk about Rhodesia being offered up as a

---

[323] Pedro Rosa Mendes, *Bay of Tigers*, (Joburg 2003), p.68.

sacrificial lamb by the Apartheid state – and he was not wrong to be so suspicious. In August 1974, South Africa pulled out its counter-insurgency police detachments, then co-operating against ZANU guerrillas on the Mozambique border, without informing Smith. Make no mistake; *this was the biggest blow struck so far against white supremacy in Rhodesia and it had been struck by the Apartheid state of South Africa.*

The conference was not a success. Indeed, negotiations didn't make it past lunch, according to Ian Smith, because opposition spokesman Bishop Abel Muzorewa (and never was a prelate more fraudulently named), under pressure from a fractured and mutually hostile collection of resistance movements on the verge of internecine war, could make no concessions and immediately broke the terms of reference for the talks in favour of presenting a list of demands that Smith could not concede. After lunch, talks failed because Smith thought he had been stitched up by Vorster and because the African delegation got pissed as penguins.[324] The only positive result of the conference was the establishment of good relations between Vorster and Kaunda, who was desperate to get rid of the resistance movements from Zambian soil and get back to trading with South Africa and Rhodesia. Smith was convinced, however, that he was now living on borrowed time and that his *idée fixe* of a British betrayal was now about to be supplemented by that of a South African betrayal.

The continuing meltdown in Angola caused Vorster to violate a major strand of his détente policy. He had initially opposed sanctions on Rhodesia on the principle of non-interference in the internal affairs of other countries and had held this carrot out to the states of black Africa as a way to tempt them away from the noisy but ineffectual protests of the OAU. Most of these states were vulnerable to disruption and internal opposition movements could be conjured up by South Africa without too much difficulty; few of the leaders of black Africa were sure of their crowns. In Angola though, the determination of SWAPO to exploit the collapse in Portuguese authority to move its base areas into Angola and the appearance of large numbers of Cuban troops backed up by Soviet advisors raised the spectacle of a serious military threat to the northern border of Namibia/SW Africa. It was this that led him to authorise military intervention in the Angolan civil war. It should be noted that the Cubans always claimed that they came to aid the MPLA *against* a South African invasion and there has been an academic debate about who did what first ever since, but frankly, the Cubans were masters of agitprop in these years and so it's probably best to discount most of what they said. The main mouthpiece for the pro-Cuban view was a chap called Piero Gleijeses (later backed up by Vladimir Shubin, ex-Soviet diplomat and generally unconvincing Soviet apologist) who was granted special and exclusive access to the Cuban archives for his thesis – which hardly makes for confidence in his sources since no-one else was allowed in (and the Soviet ones on this period were nailed completely shut as late as 2013). This goes too for the Cuban claims that they intervened without the permission of the Soviets – who were already giving military training to the MPLA in Russia[325] - a claim that really needs to be taken with a shovel full of salt; even if they did go without permission, they could not have sustained themselves there without Soviet acquiescence largely because they had no domestic arms manufacturing capability and depended entirely on the Soviets for everything from tanks to bullets.[326] Indeed, in a remarkably long and polemical document which was never intended to be published - and so, of course, immediately ended up on the internet - Stuart Sterzel made a very convincing case for the Cuban intervention being down to Castro's need for 'money, money, money, money and money'[327] to prop up his collapsed economy; the Cubans were first paid $6-12 billion per annum by the Soviets; then they *charged* the MPLA $1000 per month per soldier; then charged them *again* for the equipment that the Russians had given to Cuba *free* of charge. The Cubans served as Soviet proxies in Ethiopia and other places too on much the same terms.[328]

Vorster attempted to intervene in Angola secretly and from the middle of 1975 onwards training, weapons and troops were supplied to UNITA primarily but the presence of burly, sandy haired men with South African accents could not be concealed for long. This was done with the connivance of Zambia, Zaire and the US initially but as the presence of the South Africans became known, such public support began to waver. Again,

---

[324] *Bitter Harvest*, p.181.
[325] Vladimir Shubin. Sue Onslow and Anna-Mart van Wyk, *Southern Africa in the Cold War, Post 1974* (Wilson Center, 2013), p.19.
[326] Nerys John, *South African Intervention in the Angolan Civil War 1975-76: Motivations and Implications*. MA Thesis, University of Capetown, 2002 p.28. Also Stuart Sterzel, *The Angolan War* (2014) p.14.
[327] Stuart Sterzel, *The Angolan War* (2014) p.152.
[328] Stuart Sterzel, *The Angolan War* (2014) p.73.

the record is unclear as to just how much and how far and in what circumstances political, military and financial aid was provided to both South Africa and UNITA by the US but it is clear that the rug was pulled as soon as the South African presence became widely known. Henry Kissinger, the US Secretary of State, seems to have been unwilling to allow the Soviets to take over Angola without a token opposition and thus authorised an arm's length operation. The main whistleblower for the CIA's involvement was John Stockwell, who actually ran the CIA operation to supply arms to UNITA via the South Africans and another one to mount an FNLA invasion backed by Congolese forces but as soon as Congress found out about it, support was withdrawn. It was unlikely to have been successful anyway; the FNLA and Congolese forces were hopelessly incompetent and ran away at the first contact with Cuban artillery.

The immediate results for South Africa were twofold; first came the establishment of UNITA as an effective rebel state in the south east of Angola backed by South Africa, and the loss of Kaunda's friendship, who finally tore up his public involvement with South African détente. This came at the cost to him of the loss of the Benguela railway, now under the control of UNITA, which meant that his only outlet for Zambia's vital copper exports was through Mozambique at Beira. Kaunda also accepted the OAU position that armed struggle was the only way to deal with white minority rule in southern Africa. This was followed by the decision by the OAU to recognise the MPLA as the legitimate government of Angola, which was highly controversial to say the least as the motion only went through on the casting vote of Idi Amin, a murderous, incompetent, black racist, which did nothing to build confidence in the notion of black Africa being anything but racist, incompetent and murderous.

The fourth result was more complex. The Soviet advance in Angola happened at a time when the USA and the West had hit rock bottom. The defeat in Vietnam threatened to send America back into isolationism and when the Angolan issue came up, there was a widespread revulsion at the thought of committing to another foreign war. These were the years of détente in America too, when what was supposed to be a policy of peaceful coexistence with the Soviets was, in reality, very close to being a one-way street of appeasement down which Soviet President Leonid Brezhnev pushed every advantage that he could. In Western Europe, there was much the same malaise, as Britain's Edward Heath and much of its political establishment gave up on the thought of an independent future for Britain and entered the European Economic Community after a thoroughly fraudulent campaign; the British people thought they were joining a free trade area known as the 'Common Market' when in reality they were joining a project to create a United States of Europe. In Europe, the intellectual establishment lined up behind every Marxist revolutionary, however murderous, from the playboy revolutionaries of the Baader-Meinhof gang in Germany to the Red Brigades in Italy, to the Khmer Rouge in Cambodia, with that empty darling of student pseudo-intellectuals everywhere, Jean-Paul Sartre, with his raddled old procurer, Simone de Beauvoir, well to the fore. ('Charlie Brown,' wrote Brian Appleyard, arts critic and fellow Boltonian, 'is a bigger figure than Jean-Paul Sartre and Lucy van Pelt would have made mincemeat of Simone de Beauvoir'.[329] If French Existentialism is your thing, Albert Camus was miles better in my humble opinion – which is why Sartre and de Beauvoir hated him, of course[330]). Economies crumbled under the successive rises in the price of oil and everywhere, it seemed the Russians were on the march. The Campaign for Nuclear Disarmament was revived in Britain, its organisation infiltrated by Eastern Bloc intelligence agents and shot through with murky sources of funding while militant trade unions run by Left wing ideologues brought down the governments that resisted them and blackmailed the ones that didn't. It isn't too far to say that the collapse of the West looked imminent.

Fortunately, there were those who kept their heads when all about were losing theirs and one of these was Henry Kissinger, the American statesman who brought a much needed dose of *Realpolitik* to the management of US foreign affairs. Kissinger understood who the enemy was but thought much more in terms of geopolitics rather than ideological struggle. In effect, he looked for the people with the *power* rather than whether they were politically aligned with US free market democracy and then sought to do deals which brought about verifiable, tangible gains for America. It was Kissinger who rejected the idealism of the Kennedy years that had got America tied up in Vietnam and it was Kissinger who negotiated the exit from that war. It was he who outflanked Soviet power with the opening to China in 1969. It was Kissinger who initiated the overthrow of

---

[329] Brian Appleyard, *Comparing Peanuts to existentialism is an insult – to Peanuts*, The Spectator, 5th January 2019.
[330] Craig DeLancey, *Albert Camus: Unfashionable Anti-Totalitarian*, Quillette 26th March 2019.

Rhodesia and undermined South Africa in the belief that association with white minority rule was bad for long-term American interests. It was straightforward geopolitics; there were more black Africans than white ones and America needed them to be on her side rather than that of Russia – a fact that had been recognised by the Colonial Office back in 1948[331]. Indeed, Pik Botha, South African Foreign Minister 1977-1994, claimed that the Americans told him on several occasions that 'your problem is the policy of apartheid is attracting the Soviet Union. You are drawing the wasp.'[332] And the way Kissinger intended to bring down Rhodesia was to use the stranglehold that Vorster had established on Rhodesian arms and oil supplies. This was the fourth result of the Angolan debacle.

Desperate to keep his détente with Kaunda alive, desperate to keep SWAPO away from the Namibia/SW African border and hopeful of an easing of the US attitude to Apartheid represented by Kissinger, Vorster therefore decided that Rhodesia should be sacrificed in order for him to buy time so that he could start making changes to Apartheid. The necessity for this was made all the more clear to him when in 1976, Soweto went up and widespread revolt threatened to engulf South Africa itself. The blow was dealt in September 1976 when Kissinger and Vorster met with Ian Smith in Pretoria and delivered the blunt message that negotiations were to be opened up which would result in the achievement of black majority rule within two years; those whites who wished to leave would be compensated out of a $2bn fund and this was the best and last offer that he would get. If Smith had any thoughts about rejecting this offer then Vorster made it clear that the South African military and economic assistance on which Rhodesia was dependent would cease. Despite the attempts to dismiss this move as largely irrelevant – the Left tended to claim that it was international moral force and the military force of the guerrillas that drove the change[333] - this was decisive. 'Having a gun pointed at your head leaves no room for equivocation,'[334] was Smith's summing up of the position. On 24th September 1976, he went on Rhodesian TV to announce the transition to black majority rule.

And so, I'll say it again with a slight modification: make no mistake, *the second major blow struck against white supremacy in Rhodesia was struck by the Apartheid state of South Africa at the behest of the United States of America.*

That the subsequent conference at Geneva in late 1976 and early 1977 to implement this agreement failed was not Ian Smith's fault. Rather the responsibility lay with the opposition leaders Muzorewa, Nkomo and Mugabe, each of whom were now confident that the prize was theirs, and who therefore saw no reason to compromise either with Smith or each other. Indeed, knowing what did happen in Rhodesia after Mugabe took over makes it a real problem in trying to come to any sort of dispassionate judgment over this dismal situation; at the time of writing the disgusting, old reptile had reduced his country to the point where it does not even possess a currency. It was a state of affairs that Sellars and Yeatman's spoof History *1066 and All That* would no doubt describe as akin to the dispute between the Cavaliers and Roundheads; Smith was 'wrong but romantic' while the black opposition was 'right but revolting' or, paradoxically, the other way round.

*

The Rhodesian War 1965-79

'How was it possible? I mean... we won! Every time!'

I was in a bar off the Estrados Carlos Pereira in Beira back in 2006 when I heard the drunk slam his glass down in a fit of despair. He had clearly been there longer than I had, probably a lot longer, but his tight-mouthed, Rhodesian accent was easily discernible through the slurs and the sweat. I didn't answer his question because I knew the moment I did, my English accent would be noticed by him and I would be subject to at best a tirade about British treachery and betrayal and at worst, well, something worse. Now, while I was used to being upbraided by Afrikaaners for something that happened in a war that ended when my grandfather was two years old, this was Beira, Mozambique. It was rough and I suspected that the Rhodesian philosopher was not there

---

[331] CO 537/3643
[332] Pik Botha. Sue Onslow and Anna-Mart van Wyk, *Southern Africa in the Cold War, Post 1974* (Wilson Center, 2013), p.11.
[333] Carol B. Thompson, *Challenge to Imperialism* p.23
[334] *Bitter Harvest* p.208.

because it was his first choice of residence; he had all the hallmarks of a tough life in the bush and I guessed that neither the profession of mercenary nor the use of powerful narcotics were unknown to him. In those circumstances, it's always best to keep quiet, especially if you've already driven past the hospital and shuddered at what you've seen of the facilities.

It was a good question though and its one that many, many veterans of the Rhodesian forces have posed in a variety of excellent memoirs of the bush wars and one that South African veterans would come to ask in time too. How did the Rhodesians lose? Because it is a *fact* that the Rhodesian armed forces won just about every major battle or skirmish throughout the war, developed excellent new tactics and concepts, proved themselves to be skilled, dangerous, innovative, audacious and despite worn out kit and shortages, man for man, far superior to their opponents... and yet they still lost. It's also a *fact* - one that I first became aware of when I found it scrawled on a desk in the Brotherton library in Leeds, 1983, placed there by some disgruntled Rhodesian no doubt - that the Rhodesian armed forces contained very many black soldiers and had no difficulty recruiting more into both police and military units. This book is about South Africa but the Rhodesian war is important because, in many respects, it was regarded not just as a political, but also as a military dress rehearsal for what was expected to happen further south.

To begin with, the Rhodesian security forces placed emphasis on the police as the primary weapon against the guerrillas and those caught were tried and convicted before the courts. The army was used as a reserve or shock force to be deployed as and when necessary and consisted before 1974 mainly of the (white) Rhodesian Light Infantry and the (white officered) Rhodesian African Rifles. There was also a small SAS Squadron and, from 1973, a 'pseudo' regiment known as the Selous Scouts whose primary function was to infiltrate and turn guerrilla forces in the field. As has already been noted, these forces were perfectly capable of containing the situation, so that by 1974, Ian Smith's claims to have virtually won the war on the ground were perfectly defensible.

That the guerrillas were so easily defeated in this period can be ascribed to the lack of effective training, wild schemes for the formation of armoured brigades that could never hope to get across the Zambezi, the mutual tribal distrust of the predominantly Matabele ZAPU and the predominately Shona ZANU, the lack of suitable bases and the fact that more time was spent in political indoctrination than in gaining combat experience. It was also the case that the African nationalists really did not believe that they could possibly win a war under present circumstances and that, therefore, strength should be hoarded up for the future. This, in turn, led to the frustration among the guerrillas in the camps that led to the outbreak of widespread mutinies in 1974.

This situation changed radically in the period 1974-76. To begin with, the Carnation Revolution and the end of the Portuguese empire in Africa opened up the wide border of Mozambique for infiltration and permission was given for ZANU to establish more bases there. On top of that, the 1973 oil crisis and the subsequent ramping up of prices brought about a crucial change in the situation of the young, black, well educated people coming out of the Rhodesian educational system – without a doubt the best that Africa had ever known before or since. Previously, the economy had provided plenty of good jobs and opportunities but now unemployment beckoned. For the whites, the increasing military commitments of National Service did much to ruin businesses through the loss of skilled labour for considerable periods while the loss of promotion prospects and bonuses not covered by the government 'make up' pay became increasingly irritating to their employees. The third great change came when Ian Smith accepted the principle of black majority rule in 1976. This created a crisis of morale in the armed forces: why fight when the black nationalists were to be given power anyway? As far as the white population was concerned, this too was the signal to abandon ship; roughly 50% of the white population had only arrived in Rhodesia post-1945, 20% of it was of Afrikaaner stock and of those remaining, many had roots in the Cape and Natal. They saw no reason to send their sons to die for a Rhodesia which was about to become Zimbabwe and so sent them away to the UK, South Africa, Australia and New Zealand on what became known as 'taking the gap' or 'the chicken run'. Emigration quickly became a major factor, capital drained away, unemployment increased and new investment dried up as business looked at the complete SNAFU that black nationalists had wrought on the whole of the rest of the continent and decided to look elsewhere for opportunities. Irish passports were in particular demand, simply because the qualifications for getting one were virtually non-existent, and it became a standing joke that the only true Rhodesian patriot was one who couldn't sell his house, land or business to fund his escape. By the end of the war, emigration was running at 2000 whites per month, among them, yet again, the most skilled and entrepreneurial.

Nevertheless, military defeat still seemed a long way away. From 1974, the Rhodesians developed the concept of the Fire Force whereby a guerrilla force would be spotted by standing patrols, observed by helicopter and then a force of helicopter mounted 'sticks' of infantry dropped in front and on a 'stop line' behind them. At that point, the guerrillas would be attacked and driven towards the stop line, plastered by helicopter gunships and bombed by the air force. It was a tactic that rarely failed. These methods were supplemented by audacious cross border raids on guerrilla camps such as the attack on Nyadzonya, where the Selous Scouts drove right onto the parade ground after bluffing their way past the ZANLA guards and opened up a torrent of automatic fire which left a thousand guerrillas dead without loss to themselves. In 1977, the biggest cross border raid of the war took place when the huge ZANLA Headquarters at Chimoio in Mozambique was successfully attacked[335] but there were plenty more aimed at destroying the infrastructure which supported guerrilla infiltration.[336] In 1978, the Rhodesian Air Force took control of the whole of Zambian airspace preparatory to launching a raid on a ZIPRA base outside Lusaka. Deeper still, were the assassination attempts on the ZANU leadership; several attempts were made to kill Mugabe but each time he was tipped off, probably by British intelligence who had penetrated the Rhodesian Central Intelligence Organisation from top to bottom. For many years, it was suspected that its head, Ken Flower was on the payroll of Britain, Mugabe or perhaps someone else; it's a popular parlour game deciding who. Nevertheless, however spectacularly successful these operations were, the situation was ultimately hopeless because ZANU and ZIPRA simply had a greater supply of bodies than the Rhodesians could cope with; sufficient quantity will always outweigh superior quality in the long run. As Chris Cocks of the Rhodesian Light Infantry wrote of July, 1978;

> 'Because there were so few of us, we had little respite from the waves of daily callouts. Often after the conclusion of a contact, we would immediately be ferried to a new sighting, sometimes a hundred or so kilometres away from the first....The enemy had an inexhaustible supply of replacements, no matter how many we killed.'[337]

From 1976 onwards, the situation deteriorated steadily as ZANU expanded its operations from the Mozambique border into Rhodesia itself, with attacks on the vital road and rail links southwards, the murder of white farmers, the creation of base areas inside the country and, not least, massive and brutal intimidation of any black people inclined to oppose them. A major part of the guerrilla strategy was to collapse the civil administration of the country and so headmen were slaughtered, schools closed, mosquito and tsetse fly control stations destroyed, weapons given to teenage activists - *mujibas* - who thereby wielded authority over their elders and thus engaged in the predictable excesses. It's important to remember that Marxist notions of revolutionary war are focussed not so much on defeating the enemy as taking control of the population and as such the Maoist guerrilla is not so much a fish swimming in the sea of the people as a shark let loose in a shoal of sardines. The preferred choice of weapon for the guerrillas was also the landmine, with predictable and indiscriminate results; when I drove up the Chimoio corridor in 2006, mine clearance teams were still working there and the advice given was to camp on a track off the road and never step off it. It was much the same story in the rest of the country too as large numbers of people were either persuaded or intimidated into serving as informers, logistics providers and recruiters but in the cities, apart from one or two spectaculars, urban guerrillas fared rather badly. So too did the guerrillas themselves, who were usually badly led and badly trained and offered up as cannon fodder by Mugabe and Nkomo without much regard for their welfare or chances of survival.

It's impossible not to note that the violence employed by the guerrillas steadily assumed a quality all of its own. It's a phenomenon common to warfare that the longer the conflict goes on, the more it is waged with ever decreasing pity and there is little doubt that both sides were prone to excesses and a certain level of atrocity. That said, the guerrillas tended to have fewer ethical qualms regarding violence against civilians and held to a much colder interpretation of Clausewitz's dictum that *war is the continuation of politics by other means*; perhaps a better rendering of their view would be *violence is a useful method for the achievement of political*

[335] Ian Pringle, *Dingo Firestorm,* (Cape Town, 2012).
[336] Chris Cocks, *Fireforce,* (Pine Town, 2012).
[337] Chris Cocks, *Fireforce,* (Pine Town, 2012).

aims. Where white farmers proved stubborn enough to resist attempts to drive them off their land, black farm workers were deliberately targeted and murdered to remove the labour supply; the mutilation and killing of headmen and others suspected of supporting the government was often done publicly and grotesquely; when Nkomo's guerrillas shot down a Rhodesian civilian airliner in September 1978, a case could be made for it being a legitimate act of war – but neither the cold-blooded killing of the survivors nor his public chuckling over it really strengthened the case. The biggest terrorist bomb attack of the war came in August 1977, killing eleven people and wounding seventy more in the Salisbury Woolworth's store – all of them black - while perhaps the most egregious came in June 1978 when twelve missionaries, eight adults and four children were raped, mutilated and beaten to death by ZANLA guerrillas at the Elim Pentecostal Mission near Umtali. Through the many memoirs of those who fought in the Rhodesian forces runs a common theme of revulsion at the often obscene violence employed by the guerrillas and this cannot be dismissed as post-facto justification for Rhodesian atrocities, simply because many of these memoirs are distressingly frank about the shortcomings of the Rhodesians themselves. One ZANU veteran revealed that very often there was a level of deliberate brutalisation within the guerrilla camps while another spoke of a real lack of discipline among the guerrillas that raided and kidnapped schoolchildren from the St. Alberts Mission in 1974.[338] Many such atrocities continued after the war ended; one black Selous Scout was skinned alive.[339]

Although ZANU and ZAPU found it increasingly difficult to co-operate, they were certainly united in their aim of overthrowing the Smith regime and infinitely more skilful in their use of propaganda. ZAPU tended to concentrate on pushing their message through appeals to the historical 'wrong' of the original conquest and subsequent land appropriation while ZANU pushed more Marxist themes of inequality and discrimination but both churned out heaps of material that was questionable at best and downright fiction at worst; a basic principle of Marxist tactics is that the end justifies the means and very many guerrillas were extremely disappointed at the end of the war when they turned up at government offices to pick up their promised free house, car, and long awaited appointment at the pilot/doctor/engineer training centre; they were lucky to get a hectare and a hoe. This went for the international environment too, where Rhodesian attacks on guerrilla camps were almost always characterised as attacks on 'refugee' camps. Nevertheless, it is also the case that young, well-educated and privileged black people who might be assessed as being able to think for themselves could also be found heading for the guerrilla ranks. Peter Godwin, who made his name by reporting on the Matabeleland Massacres of 1982, recalled how one of his classmates at his elite Salisbury school went off to join ZANU just as he was heading for his National Service call up.

The decision to accept black majority rule in 1976 was to lead to the formation of an interim government and then the election of Abel Muzorewa as Rhodesia's first black prime minister but almost from the go, this was revealed as a horse that wouldn't run. Muzorewa was weak, incompetent and indecisive as were most of his colleagues and Smith was careful to keep security matters away from his control (and I simply cannot help but associate his rather feminine features in my mind with Mrs Atherton, a teacher at my Primary School; come to think of it, that fierce old battleaxe would almost certainly have made a better job of being Prime Minister than Muzorewa). It was also the case that without Nkomo and Mugabe's participation in the government, the war could not be brought to an end. Much effort was directed towards bringing Nkomo into the government but he too was weak, indecisive and incompetent and firmly believed that he only had to wait for his Soviet and Cuban backers to provide him with enough military hardware for him to sweep all before him sometime in 1980-1. At the same time, the war was intensified against Mugabe's ZANLA in the hope of breaking the back of his forces and so driving him to the negotiating table in a much weakened state. Mugabe, however, combined those essential characteristics of the sociopath - a ferocious intelligence, a lack of empathy and an uncanny ability to discern and appeal to the baser motives of his opponents - and, secure in the knowledge that his Chinese backers were supplying him with increased amounts of hardware, decided to weather the storm; his cadres were increasingly dominating the countryside even though his Mozambican bases were regularly hammered. What Smith had gambled on was the lifting of sanctions in return for his 'internal settlement' but when this did not materialise, his position was hopeless. Margaret Thatcher's Conservative Foreign Minister, Lord Carrington,

---

[338] Wilbert Sadomba and Wilfred Mhanda in Sue Onslow and Anna-Mart van Wyk, *Southern Africa in the Cold War, Post 1974* (Wilson Center, 2013), p.204.
[339] Paul L. Moorcraft and Peter McLaughlin, *The Rhodesian War* (Barnsley 2008), p.181.

was convinced that unless a settlement was achieved, the Soviets would become more active, the Commonwealth would break up, European allies would turn on Britain and there might be UN sanctions on Britain itself.[340] President Jimmy Carter refused absolutely to lift sanctions too. The result was that Smith was left with no choice but to accept the Lancaster House deal forced on him in 1979 for Commonwealth supervised elections in which ZANU and ZAPU would be recognised as legitimate candidates. The game was up.

The Lancaster House talks aimed to produce a power sharing arrangement that would bring the war to an end before the economies of Zambia, Botswana and Mozambique ground to a complete standstill. No-one particularly wanted Mugabe to win the subsequent election (and many believed that he would continue the war if he did not win),[341] but just about all the powers involved believed that any government would have its hands too full with reconstruction to contemplate a further war with South Africa. Britain wanted rid of an albatross round its neck, America wanted to remove the excuse for more Soviet intervention in Africa while South Africa wanted a pliant black government on the Limpopo, intimidated into refusing base areas for the ANC. When Mugabe did win, largely through widespread, brutal intimidation and voting along tribal lines, the news was greeted with some dismay but the fact that Rhodesian domestic politics were so fractured meant that indeed, Mugabe was too busy to contemplate anything more than entertaining harsh words for South Africa.

So, to return to our distressed mercenary pouring rotgut down his throat in a beat up bar in Beira, the answer to the question of how Rhodesia lost the war was quite simple. Ian Smith never developed a political vision that he could sell to the black majority and without this, military victories however skilful, daring and downright impressive, could achieve nothing. On top of this was the fact that Britain and America could not countenance white minority rule and then, when Muzorewa took over, they could not believe that this would be enough to stop a coming escalation of the Rhodesian war as Cuban, East German and Soviet advisors and equipment began to pour into the region. Chaps such as my disgruntled and very dangerous friend would no doubt have been among those who, as the election pointed towards a Mugabe victory, wanted to stage a coup but if the security chief who was actively considering one, General Peter Walls, had called it then the only result would have been a terrible bloodletting. It was to his credit that Walls decided against the move – and also to the man from the Foreign and Commonwealth Office, Robin Renwick, who faced him down. There were many soldiers who wanted to roll the dice one more time or go down in a blaze of glory or who thought Rhodesia could be held as some form of Rorke's Drift last stand – the recriminations were legion - but the reality is that back in 1879 the defenders of Rorke's Drift were down to their last box of ammunition when the Zulus retired and the difference in 1979 was that Mugabe's forces were tooled up with more kit than they had ever had before. The Rhodesians, like everyone else, would in the end always go down to overwhelming numbers.

That Rhodesia/Zimbabwe then entered a downward spiral after 1980 was entirely the responsibility of those Zimbabweans who voted for Mugabe and though we can only lament the destruction of the bread basket of Africa, the subsequent genocide, economic collapse and brutal dictatorship, this is not something for which fundamental responsibility can be laid at the door of Britain, America or South Africa. In a democracy, you get what you vote for and if you vote for a Marxist you will be voting your liberties away and you have to live with the consequences.

*

The Angolan War 1975-87

Operation Savannah, the 1975 South African intervention into Angola, was a remarkable success in purely military terms. Although failing in its political aim of preventing a Cuban/Soviet/MPLA government taking over and allowing SWAPO to establish bases across the Angolan border, it demonstrated the ability of the SADF, even in its undeveloped *ad hoc* state, to take on and defeat pretty much any conventionally handled army it faced. The rapid advance towards the Angolan capital of Luanda convinced many veterans that had they just pushed a little harder, they could have snapped it up but this was a non-starter as soon as large numbers of

---

[340] Carrington Memo circulated to the OD 11th May 1979. https://www.margaretthatcher.org/document/116695
[341] British Consulate-General to FCO 15/02/1980 https://www.margaretthatcher.org/document/121051

Cubans began to arrive in the country. Nevertheless, the display commemorating the operation at the Bloemfontein School of Armour still spoke of the professional pride involved when I visited it in 2013, even though it was getting a little tatty. The vast amounts of kit they captured also allowed them to arm UNITA, whose leader Jonas Savimbi had decided to drop his Maoism in favour of a straightforward anti-MPLA alliance with South Africa. The decision was also taken to absorb the armed forces of the FNLA directly into the SADF.

> ('I've seen some disgusting armies...but this lot were really bad... barefoot and sores all over them... staggering around with hunger,' said Jan Breytenbach, the commander who turned them into the very successful 32 Battalion).[342]

More concrete still was the fact that the SADF had given the Cubans such a bloody nose that, for all his empty noise, rhetoric and agitprop – and there were few men emptier, noisier or more rhetorical than he – Fidel Castro kept his forces well away from the SADF from then until 1987. What Castro and the MPLA did do was to provide training for SWAPO (armed wing: PLAN – People's Liberation Army of Namibia/SW Africa) in bases in southern Angola which meant an immediate escalation of the guerrilla war on the border for which the SADF was completely untrained and unprepared for. For two years, SWAPO was allowed to run amok pretty much unchecked.

Something had to be done about this because if Namibia/SW Africa fell to the uncompromisingly pro-Soviet SWAPO then the next thing that would happen would be Cuban/Angolan armoured brigades supplied through Walvis Bay and trained by the Russians lining up on the South African border on the Orange River. The border with Angola/Namibia/SW Africa could be defended because it was thick bush and bad tank country but the same could not be said of the border on the Orange. There, wide open spaces would allow air superiority to be established and full on armour clashes developed with all the advantages handed to the Soviet proxies. So a counter-insurgency campaign would have to be organised to keep SWAPO well north of the Angolan border as a matter of extreme urgency.

The SADF leadership was not made up of blinkered men and they quickly began to access the wide range of military theory that had grown up around counter-insurgency warfare. Previous to the British experience in Malaya, the French experience in Algeria and the US experience in Vietnam the standard model of warfare had remained virtually static since the days of Athens and Sparta. In short, when a dispute arose and diplomatic means of resolution had failed, a declaration of war would be made that effectively ushered in a different set of rules and expectations than those accepted in peacetime. The main differences were that murder would now become legal and that soldiers became different from civilians through the adoption of a uniform or other defining badge. The two armies would then form up, fight a decisive battle and the vanquished would then be required to submit and accept terms of a greater or lesser severity and then sign a treaty which ended the state of war. Revolutionary war turned all these principles on their heads. Where a dispute occurred, there was no aim at resolution beyond the complete defenestration of the existing legitimate government, which was denied any legitimate status at all, and no distinction was made between the soldier and the civilian. Murder was not made distinct from killing on the battlefield, no limits – cultural, legal or otherwise - on the use of force were respected, and the object of the war became the capture of the population preparatory to the seizure of total political power rather than the seizure of a capital or a province, the payment of an indemnity or the establishment of a new treaty. It was also accepted that revolutionary war was expected to be long, perhaps even generational in length, and that destruction of the economic infrastructure was perfectly acceptable regardless of the effect on the civilian population as long as it led to the eventual successful seizure of power. This 'people's war' or 'war among the people' was total war in that it accepted nothing but the unconditional surrender of the established government.

To counter this, many leading counter-insurgency thinkers believed that it was necessary to win over the people through what was variously called a 'hearts and minds' or 'total' strategy which aimed to convince the people that they had a better future with the existing government than with the revolutionaries. Crucially, to be successful, the strategy could only be partly military and had to include economic, political, diplomatic and psychological tools. The second strand of this theorising was that the government could not be passive in

---

[342] *32Bn Betrayed*. https://www.youtube.com/watch?v=HYMtvwT6XzM

fighting such a war, relying just on the police and criminal justice system to deliver a victory, but needed to be active, to be on the offensive against the revolutionaries across all fields of government so as to take the initiative away from the guerrillas. The third strand was that particular types of armed forces needed to be formed to fight the revolutionaries because guerrilla armies operated in a way that was explicit in its rejection of the 'decisive' battle, preferring to wear down the political will to resist through subversion, terror and agitprop before launching a crushing military blow. Above all else, the South African leaders realised that the political aspects of the war were more important than the military and in Rhodesia, they could see that lesson being drummed home every single day.

Faced with the collapse of the Portuguese empire, between 1977-80 the South African government undertook a series of fundamental reviews of its situation and came up with a 'Total National Strategy' which put counter-insurgency at the heart of its thinking. Defence was no longer the sole responsibility of the Department of Defence, argued the originator of the strategy P.W. Botha, but the responsibility of every department and they must all participate in it. The geopolitical desire of the Soviet Union to control the mineral resources of southern Africa on which the West depended was identified as the greatest threat and the Cubans and black nationalists identified as their proxies.[343] This was a profound statement because the defeat of Soviet communism was given a higher priority than the maintenance of Apartheid and indeed, as part of this strategy, Apartheid was to be extensively reformed in order to give black people a better stake in South Africa, even if white rule was going to remain.

Perhaps just as profound was the realisation that despite South Africa's claims to represent Western civilisation, after Angola, they could not rely on the USA coming to their aid against Soviet expansionism. In pursuing this geopolitical view, Botha divided up southern Africa into three categories; the heartland of SW Africa and the Republic; militarily important border areas which included southern Angola, Mozambique south of the Zambezi, Botswana, Swaziland, Lesotho, and Zimbabwe; anything further north was considered strategically important as far as politics went but unlikely to cause problems militarily. In particular, a clear aim was selected for the strategy in SW Africa and Angola: accepting the UN demand that Namibia/SW Africa become independent with an elected government at some time in the future, it was determined that SWAPO must never be allowed to win an election while Angola was to be destabilised in order to prevent SWAPO gaining the strength necessary to effect either military or political victory.

The SADF was extensively remodelled as a result of this new thinking on counter-insurgency (COIN) warfare. Under the tutelage of Constand Viljoen, Roland de Vries, Joup Joubert and very many other talented soldiers, the army sloughed off the memory of the Infantry and Armoured Divisions of WWII and adapted the writings of the British military theorist, Frank Kitson, to produce a completely different kind of army. In many parts of the world, for both historical, training and administrative reasons, different combat arms had tended to hive themselves off into almost separate entities but the new SADF would combine different types of soldiers into new units. These 'combat teams' would place a high reliance on individual initiative, high mobility and devastating firepower and would not attempt to occupy territory, protect supply routes or hold ground. Rather they would be used to destroy enemy forces and bases in order to cause maximum casualties, maximum destruction of logistics and so put the guerrillas on the defensive. In this they would be supported by paratroops and air forces well versed in the Rhodesian concept of the Fireforce.

The SADF was also re-equipped. The most startling innovation was the *Ratel*, a wheeled armoured cross-country vehicle that carried a squad of infantry plus a 20mm cannon or a 90mm gun. There was nothing else like it in the world and it gave the SADF a major advantage. New artillery, the G5 and G6, was produced which was matchless, while *Buffels* and *Casspir* mine-protected troop carriers were deployed; they were so good that they provided the models for the MPVs deployed to Iraq and Afghanistan by NATO forces. A multi-launch rocket system, the *Valkyrie*, was also introduced to counter the Soviet supplied BM-21 while the old British supplied Centurion tanks were upgraded to become *Olifants*. There were still gaps, noticeably in air defence equipment and the rather old air force Mirage fleet, but the threat from the MPLA in this respect was not very great. At sea, the navy's large warships were gradually replaced by fast, missile craft which were much more

---

[343] L. Scholz, *The SADF in the Border War 1966-89* (Capetown, 2013) p.36.

use for supporting Special Forces and operating on the coastlines. From January 1978, National Service was doubled to two years to facilitate a much more rigorous training regime and embed the system whereby the Permanent Force provided the experience for the National Service soldiers, while the Active Citizen Force provided a reserve to be called up when needed.

The changes didn't stop there. As far as the Namibia/SW Africa strategy was concerned, Vorster, consistent with his growing realisation that Apartheid as a policy was a blind alley, was already beginning to rein it back. He had already conceded that the UN had a say in what went on there and in 1973 had abandoned the idea of establishing 'Homelands' but in 1975, under pressure from business interests like the Oppenheimers, he began to repeal very many of the Apartheid laws that had been enacted in both South Africa and SW Africa; job reservation, the Pass Laws and sexual restrictions were abolished; while in 1978, the principle of equal pay for equal work was accepted.[344] Between 1975-79, in Namibia/SW Africa the whole structure of Apartheid was progressively repealed. What was more, the armed forces began accepting ever greater numbers of non-whites; to 32 Battalion was added 31 Battalion (Bushmen), 101 Battalion (Ovambos), 201 and 203 Battalions (Caprivians), 202 Battalion (Okavango) and 911 Battalion (ethnically mixed). The Special Forces were completely integrated by the late 1970s; 55% of them were indeed black, including the most highly decorated SF soldier.[345] The police counter-insurgency *Koevoet* units also recruited large numbers of blacks, while the navy depended on Asians for much of its staff at the Durban dockyards. The subsequent formation of the SW Africa Territorial Force (SWATF) meant that it was, by the 1980s, 30,000 strong and 90% non-white.

The assault on SWAPO in Angola began in May 1978 with an airborne assault on Cassinga, 260km beyond the border which, despite being incredibly high risk and at times touch and go, resulted in the destruction of a major base and was quickly followed up with a further attack on a second base at Chetequera. Operation Reindeer, as it was designated, established the pattern for Operation Sceptic (1979), Protea and Daisy (1981), Askari (1983) which put the highly mobile, highly aggressive and highly innovative SADF up against the poorly trained and often under-motivated PLAN forces and the Soviet trained Angolan army (FAPLA) under whose wings they increasingly sheltered with predictable results. Supported by a host of smaller cross border infiltrations and attacks, the SADF steadily degraded the ability of PLAN to operate in SW Africa by pushing them back ever further from the border until it became virtually impossible to reach their target areas and still be effective. Between 1980 and 1985, PLAN activity in SW Africa was virtually halved, the number of PLAN soldiers likewise virtually halved, while kill ratios in the same period were roughly 20 PLAN soldiers dead to every SADF soldier killed.[346] It also made the MPLA desperate to find some sort of peace.

There is little doubt that the SADF broke the back of SWAPO in these years, the only significant failure being in the area of propaganda. This, however, was an aspect of the war they were never likely to win in the first place; the international reporting of the war was almost a case study in why one should never believe anything one reads in a newspaper. Leopold Scholtz's analysis of the standard of reporting of the Border War provides a damning indictment of any claims to objectivity or truthfulness of much of the left wing press, even when mitigated by the routine ignorance of journalists regarding military matters. After the attack on Cassinga, SWAPO flew in Jane Bergerol of the BBC who reported that the mass grave she was taken to was full of pretty frocks and jeans worn by helpless victims and inferred that this was, therefore, the massacre of a refugee camp rather than an attack on a military base. Needless to say, the *actual* photographs show only one female victim amid a mass of men and so contributed to the establishment of those well-earned nicknames for the BBC – the *Bolshevik Broadcasting Corporation* and/or the *British Bullshit Corporation*. (In the interests of the famed BBC incorruptibility and 'balance', we should also note that the BBC journalist John Coker was on the South African payroll to the tune of Rs125,000 pa plus air fares – roughly £30,000pa - which was an enormous sum in the 1980s and testimony to the longstanding commitment of its employees to get their snouts so deep in the trough that only the ankles are visible).[347] Various left wing activists claimed that babies and pregnant women had been bayoneted, despite the fact that the SADF did not carry bayonets; that the SAAF had dropped poison gas, despite the fact that the SADF did not carry gas masks nor possessed suitable weapons;[348] while the usual

[344] L. Scholz, *The SADF in the Border War 1966-89* (Capetown, 2013), p.50.
[345] Stuart Sterzel, *The Angolan War* (2014) p.129.
[346] L. Scholz, *The SADF in the Border War 1966-89* (Capetown, 2013), p.202-3.
[347] TRC Vol.2. Ch.6 para. 22 p.528

collection of academics accepted all SWAPO claims without bothering to look at the evidence.[349] Much the same happened after Operation Protea when Marga Holness of the Angolan news agency made the wholly fictitious claim that '36 Centurion M-41 tanks' were used; even allowing for her confusion of the *Olifant* with the *Centurion*, she was incapable of recognising that the M-41 is an American Walker Bulldog tank and also ignorant of the fact that neither the Centurion, the Olifant or the Walker Bulldog were used.[350]

Cross border operations to keep SWAPO off balance and increase the distance that PLAN soldiers had to travel before they got to the border, or heavily mined 'Cut Line' as it was known, was only one part of the strategy. Inside SW Africa, a major development effort was made to pipe water in, dig wells, tar roads and build schools and clinics in an attempt to win hearts and minds. This had only patchy success and, generally speaking, only really worked in those areas that were disinclined to support the mainly Ovambo SWAPO on tribal grounds, but it did limit the room for SWAPO agitprop and increase the numbers of people prepared to inform on the insurgents. The information and intelligence gained allowed the unsegregated *Koevoet* – 'Crowbar' – units of the anti-terrorist police to run down and kill insurgents at a fearsome rate. Indeed, *Koevoet*, units consistently attained the highest kill rates of the war and though they were inclined towards rough justice and in some cases, atrocity, they were highly effective and really no worse than the PLAN units in this respect. The result was that SW Africa became an increasingly hostile environment for SWAPO; only able to travel across the arid wastes during the rainy season for want of water, they were instantly trackable once they crossed the Cut Line and lacked the mobility that the *Koevoet* Casspir vehicles enjoyed. Poorly trained, if often brave, these were virtual suicide missions for the guerrillas and though at first they had gone out aggressively looking for South African forces to engage, they were increasingly reduced to planting mines with the usual indiscriminate results.

It was also the case that SWAPO were a very poor advertisement for themselves too. Not only did they engage in the usual Maoist tactics of killing headmen and destroying infrastructure but they also behaved appallingly in exile. Apart from the abuses common to ragbag revolutionaries, of leaders living high on the hog's back in Lusaka or Luanda while the troops starved in the bush, of leaders selling foreign aid to line their own pockets or set up lucrative sidelines, SWAPO's Sam Nujoma was also murderous, dictatorial, apt to go 'berserk'[351] at diplomatic conferences and inclined to jail his critics rather than answer their grievances. In 1976, rank and file members complained too loudly for his tastes and so he had fifty shot, several others imprisoned in a Zambian jail and, when writs of *Habeus Corpus* were produced, had them flown to Tanzania where that paragon of socialist virtue, Julius Nyerere obligingly banged them up. No democrat, when Henry Kissinger offered him the chance to take part in South African sponsored elections (known as the Turnhalle process), Nujoma made it perfectly clear that he would have nothing to do with it and, election or no election, SWAPO was going to seize power and then push forward with a programme of full bloodied Marxism. In 1981, a Security Department was set up which imbibed all the lessons of the KGB, learned how to make people disappear, how to arrest, question and torture those who they felt were not sufficiently committed to Nujoma's leadership – even his wife and sisters were held and questioned. Confessions were beaten out of the accused, filmed and despatched to cadres abroad. When Nujoma was confronted by SWAPO protestors over this in Strasbourg 1987, his response was 'You will die!'[352] None of this made any difference to Nujoma's supporters in Europe or Canada, however; for them, human rights abuses committed by black nationalists and Marxists were excusable, where human rights abuses committed by the white defenders of Apartheid were not (and though the UN were vociferous in demanding elections in Namibia/SW Africa, they remained entirely silent about the possibility of elections in Angola).[353] Within SW Africa though, very large numbers of people who were not Ovambos realised that a government run by SWAPO would be infinitely worse than a government run by South Africa.

If this wasn't bad enough, SWAPO was also forced to devote resources to helping the MPLA (armed wing FAPLA) fight UNITA in the south east and central parts of Angola. Clandestinely armed, trained and supported by South African Special Forces, Jonas Savimbi was able to steadily drive back FAPLA until by the end of

[348] TRC Vol. 2. Ch.6 paras 40-45, p.520
[349] Scholtz, p.82
[350] Scholtz, p.146-7.
[351] No.10 Record of Conversation between Margaret Thatcher and PW Botha 2nd June 1984.
https://www.margaretthatcher.org/document/144533
[352] Scholtz, p.228
[353] Fred Bridgland, *The Angolan Quagmire*, The Spectator, 12th September, 1981.

Operation Askari in 1983, the MPLA were ready to seek terms. Peace talks failed to materialise mainly because Castro threatened Jose Eduardo Dos Santo, the MPLA leader, with the withdrawal of Cuban support if he even thought about it – and in doing so ensured that both the war would continue and, possibly more importantly, the vital subsidies from the USSR and Angola would continue to flow into his pockets. 'Fact of the matter is,' said Pik Botha in 2013, 'in 1978, the South African government accepted Resolution 435'[354] (that South Africa should withdraw from SW Africa) and it was the Cubans who kept the war going. This was a fair point; after Operation Askari in 1983, talks took place in Lusaka where the South Africans declared that they were prepared to disengage from Angola if the Cubans went too; 'It's as simple as that and the Americans agree,' PW Botha told the Portuguese in 1984,[355] (and the US did agree);[356] at that moment the Angolans agreed too and joint FAPLA/SADF patrols – incredibly – were engaging SWAPO patrols.[357] (The documentary evidence is in the footnote, but this was confirmed to me privately by veterans groups). This was doubly frustrating for both SWAPO and the MPLA because the Cubans simply would neither go home nor venture anywhere near the South Africans and when confronted by UNITA were simply withdrawn out of harm's way. As far as Castro was concerned, the Cuban intervention in Angola was meant to feed his desire to be taken seriously on the world stage and to serve his nebulous conviction that revolution was an end in itself. It was not meant to end in casualties that might feed the ever-present discontent of his ever further impoverished people back home. And, as already noted, he made a lot of money out of it.

Cuban tardiness was something that the Soviets had noticed and after Operation Askari, they made clear their dissatisfaction with Castro's excuses about not being able to fight South Africans superior weaponry by shipping out masses of new kit which was more than a match for much of what the SADF possessed. FAPLA still failed to make much headway in 1985-86, largely because the South African Air Force shot the lumbering FAPLA armoured columns to bits. It became even clearer that until UNITA was beaten, SWAPO would remain beaten too.

At the beginning of 1987, under Soviet pressure and supplied with a major airlift of weapons and supplies, FAPLA began to prepare for a major offensive against UNITA. The plan was to push east and south eastwards down a route known as the Old Portuguese Road from the base at Cuito Canavale – 'KK' to the Angolan troops[358] - to take the air strip at Mavinga and then move on to UNITA HQ at Jamba. This was an advance that UNITA could not stop and when Jonas Savimbi appealed for aid, the South Africans could hardly refuse because if FAPLA took control of the whole border the resulting overstretch would be too much for the SADF. During August a ponderous FAPLA force of some 6,000 men (supported by 24,000 support troops) kitted out with the new Soviet weaponry began its advance; the SADF assembled a force sufficient to stop it. In September, they launched Operation Modular which not only stopped the advance but routed it in a series of brilliant victories along the Lomba River forcing FAPLA to call off the operation. For the loss of three armoured vehicles, one spotter aircraft, 17 dead and 41 wounded, the SADF destroyed 61 tanks, 83 armoured vehicles, killed 1,059 men and wounded 2,118, captured a top secret Soviet SA-8 anti-aircraft missile system intact and severely cheesed off the accompanying Soviet advisors.[359]

So unexpectedly successful was this operation – achieved with only a quarter of the forces that FAPLA deployed, the South African government authorised a further operation aimed at destroying FAPLA's offensive capabilities well into 1988. This time the use of tanks was authorised after it was pointed out that a Ratel was no match for a T55, needing six shots to knock it out where one shot from a T55 would total a Ratel, and a Squadron of Olifants was sent north. In November, a combined force of 32 Battalion, 101 Battalion, 61 Mech, 4 SA Infantry and UNITA engaged what remained of FAPLA in what became known as the 'Chambinga Gallop',

[354] Pik Botha in Sue Onslow and Anna-Mart van Wyk, *Southern Africa in the Cold War, Post 1974* (Wilson Center, 2013), p.200.
[355] UKE Lisbon to FCO 1st June 1984. https://www.margaretthatcher.org/document/144539
[356] FCO Briefing for Margaret Thatcher, 31st May 1984 p.55. https://www.margaretthatcher.org/document/144540
[357] No.10 Record of Conversation between Margaret Thatcher and PW Botha 2nd June 1984.
https://www.margaretthatcher.org/document/144533
[358] Pedro Rosa Mendes, *Bay of Tigers*, (Joburg 2003) p.26.
[359] Igor Zhardkin, *We Did Not See it Even in Afghanistan: Memoirs of a Participant of the Angolan War, 1986–1988*, (Moscow, 2008). Quoted in Sue Onslow and Anna-Mart van Wyk, *Southern Africa in the Cold War, Post 1974* (Wilson Center, 2013).

driving it all the way back to Cuito Canavale where it dug in behind minefields, and where, finally, the Cubans turned up.

What followed has become known as the Battle of Cuito Canavale, a series of set-piece attacks made by the SADF in early 1988 during Operations Hooper and Packer aimed at grinding down FAPLA and pushing them back over the Cuito River.   In one respect, FAPLA as an effective fighting force was virtually finished by these attacks, allowing the SADF to claim a high degree of success but because the Cubans were able to prevent their final destruction through the deployment of substantial forces and deep minefields, the offensive ended in a stalemate.   At the very end of their supply lines and beyond really effective air cover, the 2,500 SADF soldiers could not make progress in the face of Cuban air superiority (even after the runway at Cuito Canavale had been made inoperable by artillery bombardment), 20,000+ FAPLA troops, overwhelming firepower and the lack of suitable bridging equipment - but nor could the Cubans do anything to dislodge the SADF.   In an attempt to force the SADF to retreat, Castro, true to form as the foolhardy gambler portrayed by the brilliant academic (but terrible musician) Greg Mills,[360] sent in new forces from Cuba and attempted to outflank them by heading south towards the SW Africa border only to be stopped by a combination of failed and incompetent logistics arrangements, further South African attacks and the rainy season.

'We are going to increase our troops by 15,000,' declared Jorge Riquet, one of the more bombastic Cuban negotiators.

'Well, I would ask our military to increase our troops by another thousand,' replied Pik Botha, cuttingly.[361]

Right out on a long limb, the Cubans were isolated and at the mercy of the SADF as soon as the rainy season ended and preparations were in hand for their complete destruction.   Castro and his adoring sidekick Ronnie Kasrils claimed that the Cubans did not advance further out of a sense of restraint but then Castro often said the first thing that came into his head and the several versions that he offered up about the whole campaign are, well, inconsistent to say the least.   Vladimir Shubin claimed that Castro had been ordered not to advance over the Namibia/SW African border by the Russians.[362]   My own judgement on this is that it was rather the South Africans that exercised restraint as there was a strong feeling that to destroy the Cuban columns would give Castro an excuse to pull out of the peace negotiations that had just begun and prolong the war just as he had done in 1984.

True to form though, Castro unleashed a propaganda offensive claiming that this was a massive victory for his enlightened leadership, the Cuban army and FAPLA, claims that are still accepted by many in Cuba and South Africa today despite being entirely unfounded.   Few people in the Soviet Union believe them; technically speaking, there was no 'Battle of Cuito Canavale' but rather a series of aborted attacks on the ground east of the river known as the Tumpo Triangle; Ronnie Kasrils parroted the nonsense too in order to gain some credit for the SACP[363] while Peter Polack, a Jamaican lawyer, brought out a whole book entitled *Black Stalingrad*, which one of its contributors described as 'superficial, shallow and seriously lacking in any form of serious military historical substance.'[364]

This noise was needed because Castro was in serious trouble at home.   When the Soviet subsidy was removed in 1989, whatever was left of the economy tanked, GDP dropping by 85%,[365] and famine forced the Havana zoo animals onto the plates of the people – the so called 'Special Period' - while discontent at the losses in Cuba (in both human and financial terms) was rife; troops who were repatriated after the war were disarmed by the Cuban secret police in Havana harbour before they were allowed to disembark while the commander, General Sanchez and his staff were shot on trumped up narcotics charges; those poor buggers who had contracted AIDS were packed away in out of the way camps to die.[366]   The only hope left to Cubans was that 'no evil is eternal.'[367]

---

[360] I went to a book launch of his. At the end of the presentations, he accompanied the singer Robin Auld on the bongo drums.

[361] Pik Botha in Sue Onslow and Anna-Mart van Wyk, *Southern Africa in the Cold War, Post 1974* (Wilson Center, 2013), p.353.

[362] Sue Onslow and Anna-Mart van Wyk, *Southern Africa in the Cold War, Post 1974* (Wilson Center, 2013), p.38.

[363] Ronnie Kasrils, *Cuito Canavale, Angola. 25th Anniversary of a Historic African Battle*, reproduced in Stuart Sterzel, *The Angolan War* (2014) p.202.

[364] Stuart Sterzel, *The Angolan War* (2014) p.194.

[365] Cuban Ambassador Villa in Sue Onslow and Anna-Mart van Wyk, *Southern Africa in the Cold War, Post 1974* (Wilson Center, 2013), p.486.

[366] Stuart Sterzel, *The Angolan War* (2014) p.19.

(And it is entirely noteworthy that when the Cubans went home and the 'Special Period' began, the MPLA government sent not a single dollar in aid to their erstwhile allies). Castro needed to convince Cubans that this tremendous balls-up really had been worth it and his preferred method was to claim a victory and prove it by repeated assertion rather than the deployment of evidence, a standard Left wing style of argument. In this fantasy, he was encouraged by Pik Botha in the belief that unless Castro's ego was massaged, he would never give up.[368] The reality was that the Cuban intervention had been a disastrous failure for the Cuban army and people, a disaster for Angola and a complete failure in terms of its own aims – which were to defeat UNITA and turn the MPLA into a vanguard for the advance on Apartheid South Africa. Indeed, it is rather ironic that Namibia/SW Africa was left in a much improved state, in terms of infrastructure, government, education, medicine and economy by the South African occupiers and ranked second only to South Africa itself in the Human Development Index – double the level of any other state in sub-Saharan Africa and certainly better than Cuba itself.[369]

In material terms, during the campaigns of 1987-88, Cuban/FAPLA forces lost 194 tanks and armoured vehicles, 80 guns, 389 trucks, 18 aircraft and helicopters and almost 5,000 men to the SADFs loss of 14 armoured vehicles, 3 aircraft and 42 killed (UNITA casualties were not recorded although rough figures were often announced to the press).[370] In strategic terms, the FAPLA offensive had been driven back to its point of origin, the credibility of its armed forces destroyed, its trust in its Cuban allies severely dented and any hope of resisting the next UNITA offensive had evaporated. It had also exhausted the patience of the Soviets, who had seen all their efforts wasted. In fact, for all his sound and fury, Castro was now desperate to get out of Angola simply because he feared that the new forces he had committed – by far and away, his best – were in danger of being decisively defeated should they advance further. It was also beginning to cost him money; the $300m p.a. that the MPLA paid for the privilege of hosting the Cuban army dried up in 1986 when the world price of oil collapsed. Furthermore, this was 1988 and the Soviets, now under Mikhail Gorbachev, were looking for a way out of, not just Angola, Afghanistan and the other Third World conflicts that it was sponsoring to the tune of $5bn p.a., but also the whole of the disaster of communism, and as they were the ones who bankrolled Castro's banana-less republic, when they insisted that peace negotiations be initiated, not even his monstrous ego could avoid the logic. In May, 1988, peace talks were opened in London and New York that would result in the withdrawal of all foreign forces and an independent, democratic Namibia/SW Africa within a very short time indeed. This was the basis on which Ronald Reagan had offered to mediate ever since 1981 and there was nothing substantially different in the final terms to those that had been offered then and subsequently at a series of secret talks between Angola and South Africa held in Cape Verde.[371] For the South Africans this was a major victory as it removed the Cuban/Communist threat to Southern Africa, booted the ANC and MK out of Angola, while allowing them at the same time to get out of Namibia/SW Africa and back into the good books of the UN. For the MPLA, it finally allowed them to get rid of the Cuban succubus and end a war that they could never win.

*

The Total Strategy.

Vorster's *détente* strategy had been based on the belief that support for the ANC among the black African states would come second to their economic needs and that therefore South Africa could trade economic support to those African states in return for the reining in of the ANC, SWAPO and FRELIMO. This fell apart with the Carnation Revolution and Operation Savannah and a new approach was adopted, headed up by the spectacularly undiplomatic, autocratic and bad tempered P.W. *'Piet Wapen* (Piet the Weapon)' Botha. This was the Total Strategy. In essence this was the creation of a new *cordon sanitaire* based on hard-headed military and

[367] Jorge C. Carrasco, *60 Years On. Reflections on the Revolution in Cuba.* Quillette, 7th January 2019.
[368] Pik Botha in Sue Onslow and Anna-Mart van Wyk, *Southern Africa in the Cold War, Post 1974* (Wilson Center, 2013), p.353.
[369] Stuart Sterzel, *The Angolan War* (2014) p.66.
[370] *Scholtz*, p.423. Also Stuart Sterzel, *The Angolan War* (2014) p.304.
[371] Christopher Saunders in Sue Onslow and Anna-Mart van Wyk, *Southern Africa in the Cold War, Post 1974* (Wilson Center, 2013), p.330.

economic measures designed to convince black Africa that South Africa was really too dangerous to tangle with. In SW Africa, as we have seen, this meant a forward strategy against SWAPO and support for UNITA. In Rhodesia, this meant the creation of a moderate black state dependent for its links to the outside world on South Africa which, although unsuccessful in its attempts to prevent Mugabe coming to power, was successful in persuading him to withhold support for the ANC. In Mozambique, the careful application of military power through support for the rebel group RENAMO and Special Forces operations against Beira, the port for Zambia, Zimbabwe and Malawi, piled pressure on the government of Samora Machel to restrict ANC operations and prevent the formation of guerrilla bases there.

The establishment of this strategy was accompanied by something of a coup in the ranks of the National Party. The growing realisation that Apartheid was not just unworkable at home but causing all sorts of unpleasant consequences internationally combined with the failure of détente and a weakening economy to fatally weaken Vorster. The man tipped to succeed him was Connie Mulder, a man with all the right attributes for a National party leader being genial, *Broederbond*, a minister of the church, leader of the National Party in the Transvaal and at the time, the Minister of Information and Interior, but here things went awry in almost comical fashion. Mulder and Hendrick van den Bergh, who headed up BOSS, had been attempting to stem the increasing flow of anti-Apartheid reporting in both the domestic and international press and in order to do this had attempted to buy newspapers in the US (*The Washington Star* and *The Sacramento Union*; why Sacramento, for Heaven's sake?), set up the entirely bogus *The Citizen* in Johannesburg and established the eccentric 75 year old, Gerald Sparrow in London as head of the 'Committee of Ten' to promote the Apartheid line; (eccentric, to say the least; an ex-legal adviser to the Thai Ministry of Justice, he had survived a Japanese internment camp, married a Thai and so hated the legal profession that he turned to writing pot-boilers and tourism guides for a living; he lived in Derbyshire, of all places). Unfortunately for Mulder, the Oppenheimer backed *Rand Daily Mail* got wind of a number of exquisitely large, highly unusual payments made to rather colourful intermediaries and in 1978 began to track down a story which included a villa in Miami, mistresses, executive jets, a fertiliser millionaire, a long-legged secretary called Trixie, a flop of a movie (*Golden Rendezvous*; no, don't bother; Richard Harris' glasses are truly alarming), a braai on the polar ice, two murders, Swiss bank accounts, and a high level whistleblower hiding out in Quito. No, really; read all about it. It's generally known as the 'Information Scandal' or 'Muldergate'.[372] Once it went to press, Connie Mulder was toast and PW Botha – who has since been widely suspected of being involved in the leaks - stepped into Vorster's shoes when he retired in 1978, with General Magnus Malan as Defence Minister.

P.W. Botha had been appointed Minister of Defence in 1966 and had spent the intervening years restructuring the rather moribund SADF and reducing its dependence on British kit and concepts. In particular, he had driven an approach towards counter-insurgency that differed somewhat from the ideas that Vorster had embraced. In short, this was the idea that Intelligence should lead any military strategy rather than it being primarily a police matter backed up by military force – 'Military Aid to the Civil Power' in British parlance – and he restructured the SADF into a trident of conventional forces (units like 61 Mechanised Battalion) to fight enemies like FAPLA, SWAPO and the Cubans; counter-insurgency units for 'area defence' against MK infiltration (generally the part-time Citizen Force units); and Special Forces (the Recce Commandos) tasked directly by the Department of Military Intelligence for secret missions against strategic targets. Botha distrusted the Americans completely and regarded much of their criticism as being of the pot-and-kettle variety largely because he was furious that they had failed to predict the 1974 Carnation Revolution and had first encouraged and then pulled the rug on the intervention in Angola.[373] On top of that, he thought that President Carter and the Americans were 'hostile witness'[374] and representative of a 'timorous Western world which is so captivated by the soft music of détente from Moscow,'[375] and thought, with some justification, that criticism of South Africa from communists especially was nothing more than the application of double standards on an industrial scale.[376] As a result, he was also unconvinced by Vorster's decision to abandon Rhodesia at Kissinger's behest and so did much to encourage the continued co-operation between the Rhodesian security forces and those of South Africa

[372] Mervyn Rees and Chris Day, *Muldergate* (Johannesburg, 1980).
[373] Ben Mabugane in Sue Onslow and Anna-Mart van Wyk, *Southern Africa in the Cold War, Post 1974* (Wilson Center, 2013), p.64.
[374] British Consulate-General to FCO15th April 1980. https://www.margaretthatcher.org/document/121065
[375] Quoted in Sue Onslow and Anna-Mart van Wyk, *Southern Africa in the Cold War, Post 1974* (Wilson Center, 2013), p.172.
[376] British Consulate-General to FCO, 1st April 1980. https://www.margaretthatcher.org/document/121061

in terms of training, and both formal and informal assistance. South African security forces were supposed to have been withdrawn but when Abel Muzorewa took over as head of the Rhodesia-Zimbabwe Government of National Unity, they went straight back in with his permission and were operating with a greater or lesser degree of secrecy almost right up until the end in 1980.[377] This marked Botha's determination that the SADF and the Department of Military Intelligence should take the lead over security strategy rather than the police and the Bureau of State Security – who had also failed to predict the Carnation Revolution.[378] In Namibia/SW Africa, after Operation Protea, it was the SADF who ran counter-insurgency operations rather than the police.

Botha and General Malan believed that South Africa was facing a 'Total Onslaught' from the international community, black Africa, internal dissent and above all, international communism whose final goal was the capture of South Africa (and that the Americans under the incompetent Carter were a worse threat than the Russians).[379] In order to survive this, South Africa would need a 'Total Strategy' which would rest on three pillars; vigorous military action, the maintenance of a strong economy and, not least, an internal reform programme aimed at removing the causes of discontent – which meant nothing less than *the progressive dismantling of Apartheid*. The corollary of this was of course, power sharing and then the eventual establishment of black majority rule but few people within the Afrikaaner Nationalist community dared to even whisper the thought, holding as they did to a much more Apocalyptic vision of the future under that particular circumstance. That this would have to be faced eventually was obvious to all, but Botha intended to dictate the terms of such a transition by killing off the leadership of the opposition, co-opting as many of the coloured, Indian and English-speaking communities as possible and holding up the mailed fist to everyone else. It was an effective strategy and it almost worked.

*

Mozambique Revisited

By the late 1970s, a combination of Samora Machel's socialism and the Rhodesian army's cross-border operations had reduced Mozambique to a basket case; the former being rather more destructive than the latter. Nevertheless, the damage wreaked on the infrastructure of Mozambique was huge – there is really only one north to south road in the country and as the rivers (apart from the Zambesi) tend to be wide, shallow and seasonal, bridges are difficult to construct and expensive to maintain – which of course meant that the Rhodesians kept blowing them up. By 1979, Machel could no longer afford the costs of the Rhodesian attacks on ZANU – said to be in the region of $500m - and was pressurising Mugabe into finding a settlement with Ian Smith. When Margaret Thatcher got involved, he was enthusiastic in backing her, simply to get Mugabe and the war out of his country.

He needed the war out of his country because his policies had been so ruinous as to create a plethora of resistance groups, the most famous of these being the National Resistance Movement better known as RENAMO. There have been very many attempts to portray this group (like UNITA) as mere pawns of South Africa and Rhodesia but this is not really tenable. The origins of these charges are twofold; Ken Flower of the Rhodesian CIO claimed to have been instrumental in setting up the organisation in 1975; the other root lies, of course, in the propaganda of FRELIMO and its fellow travellers.[380] That the Rhodesians were instrumental in training and equipping RENAMO for their own ends is indisputable, but it is also indisputable that RENAMO formed itself from substantial indigenous anti-FRELIMO elements and were supported by very many peasants. Led by Andre Matsangaissa, a graduate of one of Machel's gulags, RENAMO appeared in 1976-77 as a small force made up almost entirely of recently liberated inmates which, on entering Rhodesia, were picked up by Flower and linked with a radio station set up to annoy Machel and encourage other like-minded individuals. Small cross-border operations began almost immediately and by 1978, with its armed strength at around 900 and, supported by Rhodesian SAS teams, it was ready to move into bases inside Mozambique. By the end of

[377] Sue Onslow and Anna-Mart van Wyk, *Southern Africa in the Cold War, Post 1974* (Wilson Center, 2013), p.173.
[378] Kevin O'Brien, *The South African Intelligence Services*
[379] British Consulate-General to FCO, 10th April 1980. https://www.margaretthatcher.org/document/121063.
[380] Stephen A. Emerson, *The Battle for Mozambique* (Solihull, 2014).

1978, Matsangaissa was recruiting directly from the peasantry and by 1979, RENAMO was reckoned to be an efficient enough force to be accorded the credit for the South African attack on the Beira fuel depot in March. In April, the Tete-Mutarara railway was sabotaged and by the end of the year much of central Mozambique had been turned into a war zone. Not even the loss in battle of the charismatic Matsangaissa could stop its momentum.

The view from South Africa was also being revised by P.W. Botha. Aware that Rhodesia was unlikely to turn into a neutral black state of its own accord and observing that the Mozambican army was being reformed from a guerrilla organisation into a Soviet-trained conventional force whose aim could only be assessed as being prepared for an armoured invasion of South Africa at some convenient moment – the Cold War was heating up very nicely at this point and tensions in Europe were bringing the possibility of World War Three nearer and nearer - Botha began sending ever more aid to the Rhodesian army in its cross-border operations. Realising the potential of RENAMO, raids, such as the aforementioned attack on the Beira oil storage facilities, and the sinking of the dredgers in the harbour which caused the port to quickly silt up, were designed to both cripple the Mozambican economy and, by leaving behind RENAMO leaflets, promote their cause. By 1980, every bridge over the Zambezi had been damaged or destroyed, telecommunications and power had been severely damaged and the main road between Beira and Maputo was essentially out of commission. On top of this, RENAMO units were increasingly confident enough to mount operations without Rhodesian support; in December 1979, RENAMO assaulted and took a heavily defended ZANLA/Mozambican training camp at Toronga and another position in Gorongosa, capturing large quantities of supplies in the process. When Mugabe won the 1980 election in Rhodesia, P.W. Botha took over the role as main supporter, lock, stock and barrel.

'Commander Charlie' van Niekerk, a 'no nonsense officer committed to the defence of the apartheid regime'[381] took over the running of RENAMO's support and training for the next ten years. The aim was to use the organisation to pressure Machel into refusing the ANC base or residency rights, and to emphasise the dependence of the Mozambican economy on South Africa; throughout the Apartheid era, Mozambique supplied labour for the South African mines and Maputo/Lourenco Marques acted in the role of the port for Johannesburg. Ultimately, it was considered a possibility that RENAMO might just be able to overthrow Machel himself. In May 1980, the territory occupied north of Beira was abandoned and the main base of the movement came south under the command of Matsangaissa's deputy, Afonso Dhlakama, where it could more easily defend South African borders and threaten Maputo until the new South African trained and supplied guerrillas (many of whom were press-ganged Mozambican illegal immigrants into South Africa)[382] came on stream.

By 1981, RENAMO was causing a major headache for Machel, even after enduring several major setbacks at the hands of the Mozambican army. In November, the Beira-Umtali oil pipeline was sabotaged and the Cahora Bassa transmission lines were brought down while in December, a new base was established to threaten Beira not far from the original Gorongosa base. It became known as Casa Banana. From 1982 onwards, RENAMO guerrillas were increasingly penetrating FRELIMO's home turf and although Machel began to restructure the army back into guerrilla mode, his repeated application of socialist measures aimed to gain support from the peasants had, predictably, the opposite result. By 1984, the whole of the country was alight in a devastating war of attrition costing $500m p.a., with both sides committing repeated atrocities and neither able to strike a decisive blow. Thousands of schools, clinics and shops had closed, business was in ruins, transport infrastructure at a standstill, port traffic at Maputo was down by 75%, the government in debt to the tune of a billion dollars and, to cap it all, agriculture was collapsing under the impact of a three year drought and a cyclone.[383] Not a bad return on Pretoria's investment of a mere 'R250,000 a year and a few national servicemen' boasted Van Niekerk; he was exaggerating, but he wasn't too far from the truth.[384]

---

[381] Stephen A. Emerson, *The Battle for Mozambique* (Solihull, 2014).
[382] Stephen A. Emerson, *The Battle for Mozambique* (Solihull, 2014).
[383] Stephen A. Emerson, *The Battle for Mozambique* (Solihull, 2014). Also FCO Briefing for Margaret Thatcher, 31st May 1984 p.93 https://www.margaretthatcher.org/document/144540
[384] Stephen A. Emerson, *The Battle for Mozambique* (Solihull, 2014).

Frustrated beyond belief by the failure of his Marxist philosophy to produce Utopia and by the failure of his Soviet trained army to defeat RENAMO, Machel had visited Washington in 1983 in the hope of finding a way out of his entirely self-inflicted problems and in 1984 floated the idea of a joint US-USSR-Mozambican meeting to discuss demilitarisation. Feelers were also put out to South Africa and to Western nations who were in a position to provide the economic aid that the Soviets were unwilling to provide.[385] This in turn led to direct talks in March 1984 which produced the Nkomati Accords. Here a completely humiliated Machel (who arrived at the talks in a Rolls Royce)[386] agreed to expel the ANC from Mozambique in return for the ending of South African support for RENAMO. This was a major victory for the South African Total Strategy; South Africa's problems were solved but FRELIMO's remained largely because RENAMO was now big enough to stand on its own two feet. What was more, there were enough elements within the South African military who distrusted both Machel and South African diplomacy to ensure that RENAMO continued to receive covert support albeit at a reduced level; the shortfall was only partially made up by private donors, Kenya and Malawi. By 1985, Machel was begging the South Africans to broker secret peace talks between him and RENAMO while both Mugabe and Julius Nyerere offered help against RENAMO; the forces of black Marxist liberation were now engaged in a war against black nationalist liberation rather than fighting the war against South Africa that they were always mouthing off about. It would last until Mandela was out of jail.

*

Rhodesia/Zimbabwe

The election of Robert Mugabe as President of Zimbabwe in 1980 was greeted with horror by P.W. Botha and measures were immediately put in place to ensure that there would be no Zimbabwean Army lining up on the Limpopo ready to escort the ANC into Pretoria. The prevailing view in Pretoria was that the unwillingness of Mugabe and Nkomo to co-operate with either each other or Muzorewa would lead to a repeat of the Angolan debacle; at best there would be a Muzorewa government with Mugabe fuming from the sidelines. Instead, it looked like there was going to be another Mozambique. Fortunately for the Total Strategy, South Africa had a number of strong cards to play. The first was economic; 91% of Zimbabwean trade including 41% of her manufacturing exports went to South Africa and almost 75% of her debt was held by Pretoria. This dependence was almost immediately reinforced by ensuring that all attempts to open up new transport links through Mozambique were defeated; Special Forces and RENAMO repeatedly attacked road, rail, and pipeline links between Mutare and Beira between 1981-84 which cut capacity by almost 50%.[387] In December 1982, the fuel tanks at Beira were blown which wiped out ten weeks' worth of the Zimbabwean fuel supply and caused an acute shortage of fuel; my Missus had to park her car in the garage overnight in order to be first in the queue for petrol in the morning. Zimbabwe became completely dependent on South African supplies and Mugabe was forced to send the army into Mozambique to protect the Beira corridor rather than send it down to South Africa. Much the same happened to the main road northwards into Malawi and Zimbabwean troops ended up guarding the Tete Bridge over the Zambezi too. If this wasn't enough to persuade Mugabe to give up on any idea of leading the charge into South Africa, in August 1981 South African Special Forces blew up R45million worth of munitions at the Inkoma barracks and then, on 25th July 1982, broke into Thornhill Air Force base and blew up thirteen aircraft including eight Hawk jets newly supplied by Britain. Mugabe responded by arresting and torturing several senior Zimbabwe-Rhodesian Air Forces officers, putting them on trial for sabotage and, when they were acquitted, immediately re-arresting them. (One of the defence team was Peter Godwin who drew the appropriate conclusion about Mugabe's commitment to the Rule of Law and changed profession to that of the journalist).

*

By the end of the 1980s, there can be little doubt that South African policy in southern Africa had been a success. In Angola, the MPLA was locked in a disastrous civil war with UNITA, defeated in battle with the SADF, desperate to be rid of the Cubans and increasingly aware that socialism was a busted flush. This last

---

[385] April 1984, US Defense Intelligence Agency Report , "Soviet Military and Other Activities in Sub-Saharan Africa," DNSA-SA01629.
[386] Stephen Ellis, *External Mission; the ANC in Exile 1960-1990* (Oxford, 2013) p.208.
[387] UKE Harare to FCO 8th Jan 1985. https://www.margaretthatcher.org/document/145323

point, MPLA leader Agostino Neto had realised as early as 1980 but he had then been called to Moscow for medical treatment where he died on the table in distinctly murky circumstances; from then on the MPLA elite went to private clinics in London for their check-ups.[388] His replacement, Dos Santos was Moscow trained and more reliable, but even he could not ignore the evidence of his eyes; as soon as the Berlin Wall fell, he would abandon socialism altogether and take the road of the kleptocrat. Namibia/SW Africa was secure, SWAPO had been reduced to military irrelevance and with the assistance of the USA in the form of the brilliant diplomat Chester Crocker, the deal on the table was that South Africa would withdraw and allow the UN to conduct elections if the Cubans did likewise. Botswana maintained a cautious neutrality, Mugabe's Zimbabwe lay cowed while Mozambique had gone the same way as Angola. Beaten into submission, wracked by civil war, fully aware that socialism had failed and looking for a realignment with the West since his visit to London in 1983, in 1986 Samora Machel died in a plane crash in circumstances that were as murky as those surrounding Neto's death. Conspiracy theorists reckoned the South Africans deployed a false beacon in an area of poor radar cover to lure the Russian piloted aircraft into a mountain but even the Truth and Reconciliation Commission wouldn't endorse this. (There is a neat irony in this: the Anti-Apartheid Movement had long protested the sale of the decent radars to South Africa that might have avoided this).[389] The most likely explanation is probably just incompetence but it's also worth bearing in mind that the Soviets had most to gain from Machel's death; plus, they had form on this going back to the murder of UN Secretary-General Dag Hammarskjold in the Congo in 1961 when the KGB allegedly put a bomb in his aircraft. Take your pick. (And then for afters digest the fact that Pik Botha was due to fly to New York for Namibia/SW African negotiations on Pan Am 103 on the day it was blown up over Lockerbie). If the Soviets did kill him, it made no difference; by 1987, Mozambique was angling to join the British Commonwealth.[390] As for the ANC, the question of what they were doing during all this can be summed up very simply as …not very much.

*

The ANC in Exile 1960-84

Admittedly, not much was made widely known about the ANC when it was in exile and what was made known was sanitised beyond recognition. No doubt the ANC would have preferred to keep things this way after it swept to power on that wave of euphoria in 1994. Unfortunately for them, by this time the Berlin Wall had come down and the new unified German government opened up the archives of the East German Intelligence service, the notorious Stasi, into which Stephen Ellis plunged. An accomplished researcher on African affairs, from around 1991 he began to publish a series of works which cast new light on the ANC in exile and which cast very many less than flattering shadows across their pristine self-constructed image. This work culminated in *External Mission; the ANC in Exile 1960-1990* published in 2013 and which has a fair claim to be regarded as the definitive work to date on the subject. Ellis had early on become sick and tired of the endless propaganda, self-regarding platitudes of the ANC, and their frequent and frankly dishonest denials that they were not, as the Apartheid authorities branded them, mere Communist wolves in the sheep's clothing of racial harmony. As the ANC in government was progressively revealed to be ever more incompetent, ever more corrupt and ever more gloatingly self-satisfied, Ellis' ire seemed to grow and *External Mission* was the result; it is for this reason that I have chosen him to be the guide for this section of the book. The respected historian Christopher Saunders thought that Ellis had been rather too polemical.[391] For myself, I don't think he was polemical enough.

Like so many other virulent opponents of the unholy trinity of 'colonialism, imperialism and racism', when Oliver Tambo left South Africa in 1960 he headed not into the welcoming embrace of his ideological brethren in Moscow, but to London, the supposed home of that unholy trinity which also provided safe haven for the rest of that ragged band of third rate revolutionaries. Yusuf Dadoo, Vella Pillay, Joe Slovo, Ruth First and other SACP members were already there suffering for the cause; they ensured that they would not have to endure Iron Curtain hardship by declaring at their conference in Prague, 1965, that London would be the base where they

---

[388] Fred Bridgland, *Power Politics in Angola*, The Spectator, 13th March 1982.

[389] FCO Briefing for Margaret Thatcher 31st May 1984, p.22 https://www.margaretthatcher.org/document/144540

[390] Margaret Thatcher speech at Vancouver 1987. https://www.margaretthatcher.org/document/106943

[391] Chris Saunders, *The ANC's 100 Years. More recent work on its history* (Historia 58, 2, Nov 2013).

spent the Moscow subsidy on which they were completely dependent; the rank and file went mostly to Tanzania, where they were dumped. Inside South Africa, the ANC had virtually ceased to function and when, in 1965, Bram Fischer went into the *tronk* that was pretty much it for both it and the SACP.

Nor was the outlook bright. Although the Soviets provided them with their dole and some empty blather at the UN, they remained sceptical of the value of both the SACP and the ANC. Some military training was offered, but not much; 2,000 ANC members were trained in Soviet military institutions over the next 28 years – so, 70 a year on average;[392] no more than a couple of platoons and most of those who received their training in 1965 would be well past any meaningful use by 1980. You only have to look at the ludicrous pose of Ronnie Kasrils in his book *Armed and Dangerous* to get a sense of this; Dad's army ain't in it. Nor was the funding anywhere near adequate; £210,000 for the ANC and £56,000 for the SACP per year. What was more, London based Oliver Tambo had no authority to lead the ANC because he was merely a deputy; Albert Luthuli was leader, but he was under house arrest and as there was no effective means of communication between the external and internal wings, there was no way of transferring authority. Those ANC members in Tanzania were also adamant that leadership should be based in Africa rather than London and Tambo, never a forceful man, really did not have the nerve, wish or personality to force them into subordination. As to MK, its leadership was mostly in jail and what was left answered to the SACP rather than the ANC.

The main problem facing the ANC was that of its claim to non-racialism. Before 1960, the ANC had ducked this question for two main reasons; firstly, because it was felt that if white and Indian people were allowed to join, they would quickly dominate as they were better educated and black people would be relegated to a subordinate position; secondly, because there was a feeling of inferiority among black people, and a feeling that success had to be 'Black' if it was to mean anything – this was at the heart of 'Black Consciousness' (of which more later) – and, of course, black people were no more immune to racism than any other.[393] Up until this point, the ANC had backed a 'Congress Alliance' of Trades Unions, Indian, coloured and white organisations opposed to Apartheid, but times had now changed. Most of the SACP was white and Indian and as the SACP controlled the purse strings and was virtually running the organisation, the issue of race would have to be addressed.

For the SACP, the black nationalist 'anti-colonial' struggle in general and the struggle against 'colonialism of a special type' was to be supported and controlled as the precursor to the establishment of communist states. This 'two-stage' revolution presupposed the establishment of black nationalist governments which would then embark on socialist transformation once the capitalists, colonialists and imperialists had been shot, imprisoned, dispossessed or deported. The problem for the SACP was that they were well aware of the fact that many black nationalists had no intention of going down the socialist road and so, in order to prevent backsliding, the SACP was determined to ensure that they would be in a position to guide (i.e. 'dictate') the course taken by the ANC. In 1965, Joe Slovo began manoeuvres that would ultimately lead to the ANC becoming a junior partner of the SACP while creating a structure that made things appear to be the other way round.

'The revolution has a rule book,' is one of the firmly held tenets of the extreme Left and it is their attention to the minutiae of party constitutions, procedures, resolutions and committee memberships that allows them to wield an influence out of all proportion to their numbers. Positions are decided privately, well in advance, and then presented as a *fait accompli* in packed sub-committees and contrived votes produced by every procedural dirty trick in the book. Once these positions are arrived at 'democratically', they are then ruthlessly enforced by 'democratic centralism' (i.e. dictatorship), no dissent is tolerated and those who persist are simply purged. It was these qualities that allowed them to take over the British Labour Party in 2015 after the sub-optimal Ed Miliband, inadvertently changed the rules to allow in all the pocket revolutionaries and string-vested socialist loons that Tony Blair had spent most of the 1980s expelling from the party, and who then handed the leadership to a worthless collection of rag-bag revolutionaries led by Jeremy Corbyn.

This was exactly what Joe Slovo embarked upon, quickly running rings around Oliver Tambo in the process. It wasn't just the money that the SACP controlled (the ANC Treasurer was SACP) but also the patronage that sent

[392] Stephen Ellis, *External Mission; the ANC in Exile 1960-1990* (Oxford, 2013) p.45-46.
[393] See, for example, Remi Adekoya, *Anxiety about Immigration is a Global Issue* (2019) https://quillette.com/2019/01/01/anxiety-about-immigration-is-a-global-issue/ or,

ANC members for training in Moscow and as this meant bursaries, education and prestige, anyone who wanted to be anything in the ANC had to cultivate an SACP connection. So when Tambo decided to set up a committee to examine the whole membership issue, it came as no surprise that it was headed up by SACP members Slovo (who the British Foreign Office thought might well be a KGB officer),[394] Matthews and Dadoo. When ANC members objected to their proposal that the ANC should be open to all races, another committee was constituted – which was also staffed by the SACP.[395] This pleasant wrangling over tea and biscuits in London, or on the plane to a sunny conference venue in Tanzania, went on for years until in 1969 at the Morogoro conference (which the SACP organised) Slovo carried the day and ANC membership (excluding positions on the NEC) was opened to all races – whereupon the SACP entrenched itself on a new body, the Revolutionary Council, and so took over control of MK and thus the real power. At the same conference, they also set up NAT – the security department (no-one really knew what the acronym stood for) or, to give it a plainer name, the secret police. The ANC had been annexed by the SACP. Meanwhile the rank and file rotted.

Most of the volunteers who had left South Africa to join MK had been dumped in a completely inadequate camp at Kongwa near Dodoma in Tanzania and although some subsequently went off to a variety of training courses in sundry unsavoury countries, it was back to Kongwa for them when the courses were over. Four hundred strong, bored, frustrated, badly treated and wondering when they were ever going to be sent into battle, the troops got caught up in tribal rivalries and political faction fighting between two ambitious men, Ambrose Makiwane and Joe Modise. The first was a Fort Hare graduate and ANC royalty with a taste for the bottle, while the second was an ex-Joburg gangster who never managed to get past the 'ex'. Corruption was rife, discipline arbitrary, homosexual abuse – so common in prisons and mine compounds - unchecked and rivalry between Zulus and Xhosa out of control. Rumours of treachery abounded, often the result of accusations aimed at undermining a rival faction, private 'security' services abounded – one was actually called the 'James Bond section'[396] - and patronage became the order of the day. Desertion was common and disillusion rife to the point that even such royalty as Walter Sisulu's nephew threw in the towel. In October 1965, a Zulu mutiny broke out which was only quelled by Tanzanian troops; the protestors were jailed. It was to head off any more mutinies that the ANC decided to send MK into battle.

The (well named) Wankie campaign of 1967, run in conjunction with ZIPRA against Rhodesia was a complete disaster. Among the many shortcomings revealed by this short lived insurgency was that despite the supposed sophistication of their training, MK was hopelessly inadequate to take on even the scratch forces that Rhodesia deployed against them (and this was long before Fireforce tactics were developed). Joe Modise was revealed to be a liar and incompetent after claiming to have reconnoitred the ground personally; half the 80 MK soldiers were killed; their political commissar, Chris Hani, fled to Botswana where he was arrested and jailed; others were handed over to the South Africans; some survivors were convinced they had been sent on a suicide mission and sought asylum in Kenya while others joined the South African police out of sheer disgust. When Hani was finally released, he began a mutiny of his own.

The survivors who got back over the border to Lusaka were furious at the incompetence of the MK leadership but also incensed by the refusal of anyone in authority to take responsibility for or even reflect on the defeat. When they finally got to meet with the ANC Secretary-General, Duma Nokwe, all they got was the bird. When Hani and six others put their thoughts into a Memorandum, in which they named Modise and Nokwe as corrupt, self-satisfied careerists with opulent lifestyles who spent their time jet-setting around to conferences, running corrupt businesses with ANC funds, using security details to suppress dissent, carrying out brutal punishments on the troops and, not least, pissing it up with the generously provided for US Peace Corps staff (all of which was true) they were threatened with being shot. Arrested for treason, then released on Tambo's insistence, they were first suspended from MK and then, in 1969, booted out of the ANC altogether. Hani was fast becoming the ANC's very own Dreyfus.

The Morogoro Conference of 1969 (which, with Tambo's typical efficiency, took thirteen months of jawing to organise)[397] was important not just for the annexation of the ANC by the SACP but also because it was here that

---

[394] FCO Briefing for Margaret Thatcher 31st May 1984, p.26 https://www.margaretthatcher.org/document/144540
[395] Stephen Ellis, *External Mission; the ANC in Exile 1960-1990* (Oxford, 2013) p.49.
[396] Stephen Ellis, *External Mission; the ANC in Exile 1960-1990* (Oxford, 2013) p.56.

Oliver Tambo was confirmed as leader of the ANC after Chief Albert Luthuli was run over by a train and killed in 1967. As the conference assembled, it looked rather likely that Tambo's many critics were going to unseat him on the entirely reasonable grounds that he was weak, a ditherer and had allowed the ANC to become corrupt and ineffective. Many of these criticisms were justified. Tambo feared above all else that the ANC would split on his watch and as a result had developed the habit of leading from behind, always agreeing with the majority on whatever committee had been called to consider the decisions that a leader was supposed to take, always seeking a consensus and rarely taking action against malefactors. He was the sort of leader that the troops would follow only out of curiosity, only as long as he was paying and only in the absence of someone better. This, of course, was exactly the man the SACP had in mind for the leadership and so kept him in power when he offered to resign; there really was *no-one* else available; it was said that there were only two people in the ANC outside Robben Island who could actually write in English and they, a pair of lawyers, loathed each other. If this wasn't enough, when Nokwe was replaced as General-Secretary, the SACP made sure that the next three holders of that office were their own men. Joe Slovo, along with Duma Nokwe and Jeff Mathews (another member of the ANC royalty), was also responsible for defining the future direction of the ANC when his document 'Strategy and Tactics' was adopted. This was entirely driven by dreams of a worldwide Soviet-led revolution and committed the ANC to providing the leadership for the struggle of the urban working class against Apartheid. It was, of course, nothing more than wind while MK existed in its present useless state; the only thing that MK did of note at Morogoro was get Joe Modise co-opted onto a slimmed down NEC, where he could continue his rise.

For those not privileged to be invited to these conferences and who had less time for faction fighting and committees, the impression created by the SACP and ANC was less than appealing. This was inevitable; in a party committed to emulating Lenin and Stalin, everyone recognised that unless they became Lenin, they would go the way that Stalin sent Trotsky and so the constant manoeuvring across endless tedious resolutions and hair-splitting doctrinal debates became far more important than actually fighting the SADF. Party functionaries were appointed on patronage or for loyalty rather than competence; corruption and bureaucracy were rife, while MK continued to deteriorate beyond the point where it almost entirely abandoned what slim pretensions to being an army it had ever possessed. It can come as no surprise, therefore, that it was Thabo Mbeki (son of Govan Mbeki, ANC royalty, SACP) who was chosen to study first at Sussex University, then at the Lenin School and then, at the whim of Joe Slovo, propelled onto the NEC in 1970. The following year, he was appointed to the Revolutionary Council at the grand old age of 29, having never done a days' manual work or carried a gun into combat in his life; he had, however, managed to organise a twenty four hour vigil against Rhodesian UDI at the Brighton Clock Tower. This is not the stuff of which revolutions are made.

Morogoro also resulted in the reinstatement of Chris Hani and his fellow mutineers as a reward for providing the ammunition required for the SACP to gain control of MK. This was not met by universal acclaim by other MK factions and a spate of fighting broke out in Lusaka which, when added to a wave of rape, drunkenness and violence against local Zambians, resulted in the MK being pulled out just before the Zambian authorities booted them out. The Tanzanians had also come to the conclusion that MK was a complete waste of space and its disorderly behaviour intolerable; 'drunkenness was... a major feature of our office in Dar Es Salaam,' complained one ANC member. 'Some comrades were drunk for days on end....'[398] MK members had already been restricted from access to the capital[399] before, in July 1969, being ordered out of Kongwa camp and the country as a whole; a short while later, the 'troops' were flown to the USSR, the only place that would have them. It took two years of grovelling for them to be allowed back. By January 1972, even the OAU was losing patience with MK's inactivity.

It was at this point that Joe Slovo, whom Ellis described as the ANC's leading military thinker, aided by those other giants of military thought, Yousuf Dadoo and Ronnie Kasrils, brought forward 'Plan J'.[400] This vision, of truly Nelsonian brilliance, proposed that a ship ought to be chartered, filled up with men and weapons and then

[397] Saeboe Maren, *A State of Exile: The ANC and Umkhonto we Sizwe in Angola 1976-89*. MA Dissertation, University of Natal, 2002.
[398] Ben Turok quoted in Saeboe Maren, *A State of Exile: The ANC and Umkhonto we Sizwe in Angola 1976-89*. MA Dissertation, University of Natal, 2002.
[399] Saeboe Maren, *A State of Exile: The ANC and Umkhonto we Sizwe in Angola 1976-89*. MA Dissertation, University of Natal, 2002.
[400] Stephen Ellis, *External Mission; the ANC in Exile 1960-1990* (Oxford, 2013) p.87.

sailed down to the Transkei where a secret base would be established and the peasantry roused into rebellion. Chartered, the ship duly was, and in 1973 it picked up weapons in Somalia and headed south. Unfortunately, the old rustbucket never made it, the SAP were all over it from the beginning and the Soviet Union was so cheesed off at the bungling of Joe 'Napoleon' Slovo, Yusuf 'Montgomery' Dadoo and Ronnie 'The Great' Kasrils that they cut their subsidy.

From that point on, factionalism returned with a vengeance. Those who opposed the admittance of non-blacks into the ANC began to agitate once more while the SACP responded with an offensive against this 'Gang of Eight'. Allegations of tribalism resurfaced, as Zulu members complained at the dominance of the Xhosas, others complained about the dominance of the SACP, while in London one Robert Resha, ANC Ambassador to the UN, was raising eyebrows at the lavish lifestyle he enjoyed without visible means of support. Those MK members who had managed to infiltrate back into South Africa were known more for their drunken swaggering, terrorising the locals and generally acting like the *tsotsis* so many of them were than for their revolutionary zeal. None of this was helped by Tambo's habitual dithering and dislike of confrontation, or by the fact that of the nine members of the Morogoro re-structured NEC, two were dead, one had thrown in the towel and gone to Botswana, while a fourth was an invalid. When Mac Maharaj was released from Robben Island and was quickly appointed to head up the ANC's Department of Internal Reconstruction (the supposed underground organisation inside South Africa) in 1977, he found that its files were empty and quickly realised that the most important qualities required of an ANC official was never to make a mistake and never to criticise; the arse-covering creed of the timid mediocrity everywhere. The truth of the matter was that the ANC/SACP was hopelessly incompetent, thoroughly corrupt, its soldiers mutinous and its bureaucrats concerned mainly with lining their own pockets. It posed no threat whatsoever to the Apartheid state; and the depths to which it would sink had not yet been plumbed.

One would have thought that the Carnation Revolution, the defeat of America in Vietnam and the coming to power of Jimmy Carter and his craven embrace of détente would have provided sufficient opportunity for the SACP/ANC to open up some space for manoeuvre or even an opportunity to engage the SADF in Angola. Such a fortuitous series of events, when coupled with the 1975 Soweto Uprising (of which more later), would perhaps have led a reasonable person to reckon that they had been gifted the prize but as usual, they muffed it. For a start, they never saw any of it coming and being almost completely ignorant of the situation inside South Africa were taken by surprise when large numbers of young people started turning up in neighbouring countries determined to find refuge, then arms, then some way to get back into the fight. These brave, committed young people were looking for leaders; what they got was the SACP and the ANC (who had already revealed to the Russians in 1975 that they were not in a position to render any military support whatsoever).[401]

Shepherded into newly established ANC camps in Angola, the ranks of MK swelled to more than ten times their former number until there were perhaps 5000 trained guerrillas under command, 85% of whom were of school or university age, split 60:40 male and female. Few of them had any political views beyond a general determination to overthrow Apartheid, an insecure grasp of Black Consciousness and a complete ignorance of Marxism-Leninism or the ANC. This, of course, would never do; the ANC were utterly opposed to Black Consciousness because it wasn't Marxist so Steve Biko was quickly smeared as a CIA agent and a programme of political indoctrination introduced.[402] The camp at Novo Catengue on the Benguela railway was established in 1977 for precisely this purpose and quickly acquired the nickname of 'University of the South'; all the political commissars were, of course, SACP and many recruits were packed off on the Potemkin tours so beloved of Ronnie Kasrils in Cuba, North Vietnam and Holy Russia; the most talented were secretly inducted into their very own *Broederbond*, the SACP, and told to keep that fact secret from their ANC colleagues. Political indoctrination and the promotion of the Soviet Union was not spared; nor did the leadership spare themselves the relative luxury of the Villa Alice in Luanda[403] or the delights of Swedish state aid.[404] What was spared was the routine administration of the camps where bad food, sexual exploitation (of both South Africans and local Angolan women) and boredom became once again the trade mark of MK. 'The course on South

[401] Saeboe Maren, *A State of Exile: The ANC and Umkhonto we Sizwe in Angola 1976-89*. MA Dissertation, University of Natal, 2002.
[402] Stephen Ellis, *External Mission; the ANC in Exile 1960-1990* (Oxford, 2013) p.115.
[403] Saeboe Maren, *A State of Exile: The ANC and Umkhonto we Sizwe in Angola 1976-89*. MA Dissertation, University of Natal, 2002.
[404] Saeboe Maren, *A State of Exile: The ANC and Umkhonto we Sizwe in Angola 1976-89*. MA Dissertation, University of Natal, 2002.

African History developed by Jack Simons continued for years. Some cadres went through it several times,' noted one commentator drily.[405] So utterly incompetent and corrupt was the supply department that in 1982 Operation Clean Up was launched - and duly failed – while appeals were made to Oxfam for the wherewithal to set up a farm to produce food for the troops;[406] an art exhibition that was supposed to tour Cuba and Sweden was lost on the road; malnutrition was recorded while malaria and dengue fever went untreated; theft from Angolans and a black market in supplies resulted; accommodation was poor and in many cases the troops were under canvas for extended periods; visits from the leadership were rarer than a decent meal. The reality was that MK wasn't so much an army as a refugee camp run by incompetents. On 29th September 1977, a serious bout of food poisoning ran through the camp which required immediate intervention from a Cuban medical unit. This was quite obviously a result of poor hygiene and bad meat supplied from slovenly Soviet workers; this could not be admitted of course, so a confession was beaten out of one poor chap for being a South African agent – the ludicrousness of his confession was revealed by the fact that he admitted to being part of a ring of sixty-four conspirators – and he was duly executed. The vegetarians suffered no ill effects.

The influx of recruits also caused the SACP to upgrade the most important of its structures – the Security Police or NAT – and for the necessary training, the SACP/ANC turned to those paragons of international virtue, the East German STASI, an organisation that the great Nazi hunter, Simon Wiesenthal, regarded as being worse than the Gestapo.[407] Additional help was provided by that other beacon of liberty, Gaddafi's Libya.[408] Recruits were quickly trained to look out for ideological dissidents rather than South African spies, which gives a clear indication of the SACPs priorities, and very quickly acquired a reputation as being above the law; they also acquired the nicknames of *Mbokodo* – the grinding stone in Xhosa – or in English, 'BOSS'. Remarkably, the first operations of the NAT were directed at mutinous troops demanding to be sent to fight the SADF rather than sit rotting away in Angolan camps. In 1979, a similar protest took place at Fazenda camp but whereas previous protests had been dealt with indulgently, this time three of the most determined were despatched to Camp 32, more popularly known as Quatro – the ANCs very own torture gulag (despite Tambo having signed the Geneva Convention). Accompanying this hardening up was a wave of assassinations, disappearances, punishment beatings and a purge of Trotskyites; incredibly, Martin Legassick, one of those fellow-travelling Marxist historians, was suspended and later expelled from the ANC. Needless to say, the head of NAT from 1978 was Moses Mabhida, General-Secretary of the SACP, and probably also needless to say, those in the camps began to report how the camp administrators were according themselves privileges denied to the rank and file.

Things were no better at ANC HQ in Lusaka where a report in 1980 condemned the bureaucracy, idleness, corruption, excessive boozing and lack of leadership. The author of this report, Alan Brooks, resigned his SACP membership in disgust and went back to London to join the British Communist Party. One of his main criticisms also related to the corruption that ran through the ANC's veins like a drug – indeed, the drug was called Mandrax, a recreational drug of which the ANC became a leading supplier. Car theft, customs fraud, diamond smuggling were all sources of income for ANC officials while MK units were often deployed to protect such contraband consignments when they were moved from Lusaka to Luanda. Counterfeit currency provided by the Stasi was supposed to be used only by operatives inside South Africa, but much of it ended up being spent by officials wherever it could be tendered. Donations from Sweden and other places abroad (probably some of it mine) disappeared into private pockets, all with the connivance of the ANC Treasurer, Thomas Nkobi (another ex-Joburg gangster) – who was acquiring property in his native Zimbabwe throughout this period. In September, 1980, a commission was set up to investigate corruption and in the style to which the ANC would rapidly become accustomed once in power, appointed the biggest smuggler of them all, Nkobi's old mate, Joe Modise, to sit on it. Modise liked his clothes to be smart and his shoes to be finer and was known to send MK operatives down his networks to buy shoes for him at the exclusive Joburg firm of Johnston and Murphy. Tambo was, of course, unwilling to do anything about this because he was terrified of the *tsotsis* - even when there were reasonable grounds to suppose that both Modise and Nkobi were on the SAP payroll.[409]

---

[405] Saeboe Maren, *A State of Exile: The ANC and Umkhonto we Sizwe in Angola 1976-89*. MA Dissertation, University of Natal, 2002.
[406] Saeboe Maren, *A State of Exile: The ANC and Umkhonto we Sizwe in Angola 1976-89*. MA Dissertation, University of Natal, 2002.
[407] https://archive.nytimes.com/www.nytimes.com/books/first/k/koehler-stasi.html
[408] Kevin A. O'Brien, *The South African Intelligence Services From Apartheid to Democracy* (London, 2011) p.123
[409] Stephen Ellis, *External Mission; the ANC in Exile 1960-1990* (Oxford, 2013) p.169.

While the bulk of MK was kept in Angola, a presence was also established in Mozambique from where it was envisaged that small groups would infiltrate into the Transvaal and Zululand in order to commit acts of urban guerrilla warfare; for this the ANC took yet another step into the gutter and turned to the IRA for the necessary training. This marked a shift from the original strategy of trying to rouse the peasantry in the direction of trying to get control of the urban discontent before some other political organisation did so but it also provided the opportunity for the ANC to do what it did best – organise a conference for late 1978. For three years, they had done little or nothing effective to capitalise on the crisis that had hit South African foreign policy and now they were off to Vietnam where they hoped to tap into the wisdom of the victorious General Giap. Tambo, Slovo and Modise learned at great expense what they could have picked up by a brief reading of the briefest précis or summary of Clausewitz – that a successful military strategy requires a political strategy to direct it. Honestly! It is beyond belief how dim these people were! People - good people - were dying in South African prison cells for the anti-Apartheid cause while these intellectual pygmies were struggling to comprehend the basics of warfare. The conclusions that they drew from these extensive consultations and bottom-of-the-class discussion groups was that MK should start setting off bombs to attract attention to their cause; this was the policy of 'armed propaganda' and was as profound an observation as 'grass is green and trees grow upwards'. Indeed, in March 1979 the earth shattering conclusions of these military and political dunces were put into a document called the Green Book and, just so that the South Africans wouldn't guess what they were up to, then kept secret from the people who were supposed to apply them. The 'Four Pillars of the Revolution' would now be armed struggle, the establishment of underground structures inside South Africa, popular mobilisation and international isolation, (i.e. exactly what they had so signally failed to do so far) and it would all be over by Christmas 1982. But first, declared the ever dynamic Tambo, there would have to be (another) conference.

To this dismal record of constant failure was added Zimbabwe. Here again was a perfect opportunity to capitalise on the destruction of the Ian Smith regime and open up yet another front, yet once again the SACP bungled it. This was largely because they had gambled on an alliance with Joshua Nkomo's ZIPRA on the orders of Moscow. Unfortunately, Robert Mugabe's ZANU were rather more aligned with Beijing and incensed by the attacks of the SACP on him as being a stooge of 'international capital' quickly expelled MK from Zimbabwean territory. It was also the dismay at Mugabe's unexpected election victory that caused the SACP to declare publicly that 'one man one vote is wrong'.[410] Just how useless the SACP/ANC were was underlined when the South Africans quickly infiltrated the Zimbabwean CIO and assassinated Joe Gqabi, the ANC's representative in Harare and apparently one of their most experienced operatives, in July 1981.

Perhaps the only real success in this period was the attack on the Sasol plant in June 1980 in which millions of gallons of fuel went up in the smoke of armed propaganda. The response was swift; in January 1981, SADF Special Forces drove all the way into Maputo and attacked the ANC offices there and killed sixteen staff. In February 1982, taking note, the Swazis agreed to Pretoria's demands to keep the ANC out of its territory. In August 1982, Ruth First, Joe Slovo's wife and as hardline a Stalinist as anyone could wish for, was killed by a parcel bomb; she was hoist by her husband's own petard, the parcel bomb being a particular favourite of the IRA's; it was meant for him.[411] The following December, Maseru in Lesotho was hit too. And then in 1985, Gaborone got a visit. 'South African policy,' said the British Ambassador,

> 'is based on the assumption that South Africa must not be deterred by international criticism from hitting back hard…to take a softer line would only be to encourage the ANC and cause neighbouring countries to be more accommodating towards allowing the ANC to operate from their territories.'[412]

The attack on Maputo had other, more far reaching consequences than the death of handful of worthless ANC *nomenklatura*. From 1980 onwards, the troops in the camps in Angola had been growing ever more restive and issuing ever more strident demands to be sent into combat. Reeling from the accuracy and reliability of the intelligence that had facilitated the SADF attacks in Maputo, the ANC panicked and began seeing spies everywhere – and particularly in MK in Angola. Tambo had been planning a purge since 1979 in response to the growing dissent in the camps and in 1981, the go ahead was finally given for it to proceed. What became

[410] Stephen Ellis, *External Mission; the ANC in Exile 1960-1990* (Oxford, 2013) p.134
[411] Kevin A. O'Brien, *The South African Intelligence Services From Apartheid to Democracy* (London, 2011) p. 163.
[412] UKE Cape Town to FCO, 21st June 1985. https://www.margaretthatcher.org/document/145301

known as the *Shishita* – the sweeping – began with a speech made by Moses Mabhida which was taped and played throughout the camps; discipline would be enforced, dissent rooted out and dagga smoking banned on pain of death; had this last stricture been made known internationally, ANC funding and support would have collapsed overnight; as it was, several smokers were hung up in trees for days, according to Amnesty International, and at least one died from this mistreatment.[413] Tambo wandered around warning of spies everywhere while NAT went to work arresting anyone with a spliff or a bottle of beer (this, at a time when Central Committee member – and South African dupe[414] - Francis Meli was sent repeatedly to East Germany to dry out; Yusuf Dadoo was frequently pissed). Detainees were tied to trees and beaten senseless, a spectacle which Tambo appeared to enjoy, especially when special praise songs were sung to him on these wonderful occasions. Some hundreds were treated this way and as several senior ANC figures were also implicated, a climate of fear was created throughout the organisation – which was, of course, the intention; these people were Stasi trained, after all. Anyone questioning the leadership got the chop and as the purge went on and the victims at Quatro named names just to stop the torture, the number of victims continued to increase. By 1982, the ANC had virtually destroyed the morale of MK and had certainly killed more of its members than the SADF had; for most of the ANC, Angola was now seen as a place of exile rather than the spearhead of the fight.

But this was not the end. In September 1982, Tambo set up a huge sting operation in the form of a consultation with the troops at Viana camp outside Luanda. This was straight out of the middle-managers' playbook and had been used by Mao in his 'hundred flowers blossom' campaign of 1957 in which he invited criticism, ostensibly to strengthen the party's relationship with the masses but in reality to identify the troublemakers and then be rid of them. Shortly after the troops had submitted their thoughts, Hani and Modise turned up to root the dissidents out – this was sheer cowardice and hypocrisy on Hani's part. Tambo had learned one lesson from the Kongwa mutinies however, and that was to get MK into battle as soon as possible….So he sent MK to fight the black nationalists of UNITA. You could almost hear the clinking glasses and uproarious laughter in Pretoria.

Led by Chris Hani, the MK brigade sent into action against UNITA was badly beaten and became quickly demoralised by serious casualties, the usual incompetent logistics and disgust at being made to fight other black nationalists rather than the SADF (in this they were probably fortunate though; the SADF would have made mincemeat of them). On 16th December 1983, they mutinied and in January 1984, having got wind that Tambo and the NEC were about to arrive at Caculama camp, just 80 km away, decided they would make their grievances known personally. Tambo, showing his usual bravery, refused to meet them and ran off to Luanda, hoping that the Cubans and Angolans would put down the mutiny for him. The troops, now supported by 90% of MK, followed, all the way down to Viana camp. Again, Tambo, Thabo Mbeki, Hani and Modise, ably assisted by NAT (who murdered two soldiers before they could broadcast news of the revolt), conned the troops into electing a Committee of Ten to present their grievances in February…and then sent the Angolan army in to disarm them and arrest the Committee of Ten. The camp was broken up and the troops dispersed, many of them were imprisoned in Angolan jails where they went on hunger strike after the female troops were beaten up by NAT, several went off to Quatro, while still more were sent to Pango camp where they mutinied again. The camp was stormed and sixteen of the mutineers were killed. Others were executed by firing squad and still more tortured; the leader of the Committee of Ten, Ephraim Nkondo, was found hanged in his cell – testimony to the fact that NAT had learned many useful lessons from the SAPS. It wasn't until 1990 that all this came out because the ANC refused anyone access to the camps; the subsequent report makes unpleasant reading; ritualised abuse, deliberate humiliations, disgusting conditions and sexual abuse of women prisoners. But nothing that you wouldn't expect from an organisation trained by the Stasi.[415]

Let us pause here and consider. In 1974, a ragbag bunch of defeated revolutionaries called the FNLA had been brought under the wing of Jannie Geldenhuys and within a year, he had turned it into the elite 32 battalion. *Six years* – that's longer than the Second World War - after the 1976 influx, the ANC had still not managed to get MK into fighting shape. And these young people were the *best* of the ANC, eager to challenge the enemy in battle, people whom the utterly dishonest Tambo himself would later describe in 1987 as 'magnificent

[413] *SOUTH AFRICA: Torture, ill-treatment and executions in African National Congress camps* (Amnesty International, December 1990).
[414] Stephen Ellis, *External Mission; the ANC in Exile 1960-1990* (Oxford, 2013) p.245
[415] *SOUTH AFRICA: Torture, ill-treatment and executions in African National Congress camps* (Amnesty International, December 1990).

combatants for the liberation of our country'[416] not the lounge lizards of Lusaka, London and Luanda. When they objected to *not being employed in the firing line,* something that Tambo, Modise, Kasrils, Mbeki, Slovo and the rest of the lounge lizards avoided like the plague, they were arrested, imprisoned or executed. This was like Montgomery having the Desert Rats shot for wanting to fight Rommel. It was Orwell's pigs sending Boxer to the knacker's yard. FRELIMO's slogan was *La Luta Continua!* – The Struggle Continues! The ANC's slogan was: 'Where's the buffet and is the bar free? I can't believe this is a 5* Hotel.'

This then, was the ANC in exile. If you ever gave money to them like I did, now is a good time to wash your hands.

*

Apartheid at Home

The architects of Apartheid wanted to see not just a hardening up of segregation and an end to miscegenation through the control of contact between the races in what became known as 'petty apartheid' – Pass Laws, Job Reservation etc etc – but also a much broader separation in what became known as 'Grand Apartheid'. This was the idea that each particular community should have its own 'Homeland' where it could pursue its own separate development and which eventually resulted in the creation of what were supposed to be independent states, notably in the Transkei and, spread across the northern end of the Transvaal, Bophuthatswana. The problem with this idea was that in order to achieve this, a great deal of land (70% white owned) would have to be given up and agriculture severely disrupted. At a time when production, profitability, and the range of crops was increasing – sugar and maize production doubled between 1945-60 – mechanisation was racing ahead and employment of black people booming, to interrupt the process was clearly madness, especially when the population was growing. Nevertheless, the programme went ahead with the Transkei being granted self-government in 1963, followed between 1976-80 by independence alongside Bophuthatswana, Venda, Lebowa and Ciskei. None were successful experiments in self-government, becoming quickly corrupted by patronage networks but in terms of economic development, some progress was made. Money was poured in from Pretoria to buy out white farms, introduce irrigation and expand education while businesses were encouraged to set up in neighbouring regions to make use of the available labour and later to invest there directly. The most famous of these enterprises was Sun City, the casino and leisure resort where my Missus danced with George Benson, a tale that she takes great delight in regaling when she feels the need to keep me in my place. By the 1980s, however, even those who were in favour of the policy, on the grounds that it did provide opportunities for African advancement, were looking at the cost of the subsidies and the levels of corruption and wondering if the game was worth the candle. Perhaps the only successful homeland was KwaZulu under Chief Buthelezi, who revitalised Zulu culture and created an effective political party in Inkatha, while refusing an independence he regarded as bogus.

The years of Apartheid saw a shift in demographics very many saw coming but chose to ignore. The first noticeable change came with the shift to the cities so that although South Africa remained a country of small towns, most whites and Indians – over 90% - lived in the towns and cities rather than out on the farms. After 1960, the percentage of black Africans who lived in the towns changed from roughly 30% to roughly 60%, but more striking still is the change in the actual numbers – from 3.5 million urban dwellers to perhaps 20 million. In 1951, whites had made up 20% of the population but by 1990, this was down to 14% while the total black population went from 8.5 million in 1951 to 20 million in 1980 and then 29 million by 1990 which, in turn, meant that by 1990, almost half of black people were under twenty years old.[417] Demographics alone meant that the Apartheid dream of keeping Africans in reserves or Homelands and away from the towns would be swept away. Neither 'influx control' nor shovelling Africans into the slums of the wretchedly overcrowded Homelands could halt the process. Between 1962-67, convictions under the Pass Laws doubled to nearly 700,000 annually.

---

[416] Quoted in Sifiso Mxolisi Ndlovu, *The Road to Democracy in South Africa* (SADET, 2011), p.337.
[417] The figures are from Beinart unless otherwise stated.

There were many reasons for this population explosion; the most obvious reasons were better food and medical care which, in particular, reduced infant mortality without touching polygamy. Illegal immigration was also a constant problem under Apartheid as the citizens of the newly independent nations to the north passed judgement on the success of that process by voting with their feet. In terms of urbanisation, as many as two million Africans were forced off the land through the ending of tenancy practices in favour of large commercial farming projects. This was a tsunami of change that no government however organised could hope to manage; in 1975, Punt Janson, Deputy Minister for Bantu Administration and Education stated that for black education to be made compulsory, he would need 97,000 more teachers and another R450 million for that year alone.[418] Indeed, it may be said that it was demographics above all else that defeated Apartheid;

*

The ANC was banned, you wouldn't hear of the ANC then; there was just no ANC. Whatever happened, happened under the ambit of the Black Consciousness Movement.
Fikile Ngcobo, Sowetan teacher.[419]

The decapitation of the ANC at Rivonia and their complete incompetence as a revolutionary resistance movement opened up political space for alternative responses to Apartheid to appear. The most influential of these alternatives was the Black Consciousness Movement, a rather nebulous collection of thoughts and ideas that emerged from a variety of church and grass roots sources. Difficult to define, and even harder to refine into an actual programme, even its most famous exponent, Steve Biko, was unable to express its tenets in straight forward prose (however splendidly frenetic and full of spleen it was). 'The fact that we are not all white does not necessarily mean that we are all black'[420] and 'being black is not a matter of pigmentation – being black is a reflection of a mental attitude'[421] were two of his more gnomic pronouncements; he also thought that the desire for a coke and a burger was a recipe for chaos. He was also wrong in most of his analysis of how the 'colour question' arose, having swallowed the argument that capitalist economics produced the race issue, when the race issue was an issue long before the Afrikaaners had heard of capitalism; nor was Biko the Xhosa any more indigenous to South Africa than Jannie the Boer;[422] he was a bit hard on the missionaries too and his characterisation of white society as 'Anglo-Boer culture' would have had Malan, Vorster, P.W. Botha and the rest of the *broederbond* choking over their *pap en wors*. But roughly summarising, the thrust of the argument was that black people should stop trying to emulate white people, should be proud of being black and shun notions of inferiority and servitude to white people, should band together and push for political power and, probably most importantly, should create a different society based on black principles. This was problematic to say the least; 'Who is the Tolstoy of the Zulus?' asked the American novelist Saul Bellow; to which we might add Michelangelo, Mozart, Mansa Musa, John Stuart Mill, Sun Tzu, Buddha, Barnes Wallis, Nelson Rockerfeller, Ibn Battuta, Cabot, Drake, Nelson or Marie Curie. And just to make the point, the co-operative system that Biko so favoured was invented in Rochdale, Lancashire; nor was the concept of *uBuntu* that he pointed to as being distinctively 'black' particularly unique, for extended families and 'sharing, charitableness, co-operation'[423] are hardly unknown outside Africa. The southern African cattle cultures of the 19th Century had produced very little in the way of culture, material, scientific, artistic or philosophical, and had collapsed on contact with the Europeans. In terms of successes, they could produce very little beyond the odd transient military triumph and had variously succumbed to disease, war or, in the case of the Xhosa, national suicide in the cattle killings. What South African black people were faced with was finding a way forward from Ground Zero and a place in a society that was fundamentally different from that in which they had existed a century before, 'a transition more dramatic in its compression of human experience into a short space of time than any other community in History'[424]. When boiled down to its simple truth, however, its message was powerful: 'I

[418] Sifiso Mxolisi Ndlovu, *The Road to Democracy in South Africa* (SADET, 2011), p.318.
[419] Sifiso Mxolisi Ndlovu, *The Road to Democracy in South Africa* (SADET, 2011), p.329.
[420] https://www.sahistory.org.za/archive/definition-black-consciousness-bantu-stephen-biko-december-1971-south-africa
[421] https://www.sahistory.org.za/archive/definition-black-consciousness-bantu-stephen-biko-december-1971-south-africa
[422] Steve Biko, *Black Consciousness and the Quest for a True Humanity* (SASO Newsletter).
[423] Buntu Mfenyana quoted in Allister Sparks, *The Mind of South Africa* (London, 1990) p.14
[424] Allister Sparks. *The Mind of South Africa*, (London, 1990) p.21.

could understand the need for being proud of myself, being proud, being able to accept myself as I am and do things for myself and start being involved,' declared one teacher.[425] This is the beginning of real wisdom.

Indeed, there was much that was laudable about Black Consciousness. Biko and others really did have a valid point in rejecting large swathes of what white culture had brought to South Africa. There can be little objective doubt that South Africa, and indeed the world, would have been better off without Kruger, Marx, Lenin, Trotsky, Stalin, Hitler, Slovo and the rest of the European Utopian visionaries, and the realisation that for black people to have pride in themselves, they had to start doing things for themselves, was also a reasonable and sensible proposition. Where the theory fell down was in conflating capitalism with white culture; Adam Smith no more invented capitalism than Isaac Newton invented gravity; every culture that had adopted money as a medium of exchange, a store of value, a measure of value and means of deferred payment had realised that capitalism was the way to get rich; Renaissance Italian bankers, Chinese pottery merchants, West African traders in gold and slaves and the Jews in the Temple all knew this. The medieval Christian prohibitions on 'usury' - the earning of interest on loans – was perhaps the first anti-capitalist reaction and the practice remains forbidden in Islamic law. The Afrikaaners themselves were determinedly anti-capitalist for most of the 19th Century and the National Party English language newspaper, Citizen, went out of its way to bash Harry Oppenheimer and what it regarded as Anglo-Jewish capitalism.[426] Where both Biko and the ANC were wrong was in defining 'capitalism' as a man-made system when the reality is that it is the expression of a natural law every bit as uncompromising as gravity itself; it's why there is never a tie in the game of *Monopoly* and why the Pareto Distribution produces such extremes of ownership. This too has been known for centuries, as the King James Bible reminds us; 'For whosoever hath, to him shall be given, and he shall have more abundance: but whosoever hath not, from him shall be taken away even that he hath.'[427] The upside of this, however, was that capitalism created a rising tide of wealth that floated all boats and if 10% owned a disproportionate share of the wealth created, the other 80% were doing pretty well out of it and able to exert political pressure to ensure a reasonable redistribution to the 10% of society who would always fall behind. No other system produced this happy result.

What was particular about Black Consciousness was that it rejected Marxist notions as being quite clearly wrong when applied to South Africa; it was the poor whites in the trade unions who, in the Marxist orthodoxy ought to be allying with poor blacks, but who were the greatest obstacle to freedom. This was something that the Marxist ideologues of the ANC found particularly threatening. Black Consciousness was also deeply rooted in the Christian churches, whom the SACP hated on principle, hence the smearing of Biko in the camps in Angola and later claims that Biko was about to submit himself to Tambo's authority just before he was killed. 'Black Consciousness' was itself relabelled 'reactionary Black racism' by the SACP.[428]

The other problem with Black Consciousness was its rejection of any thoughts of alliance with similarly minded white people when it was an observable fact that it was the wealthy, middle class whites in big business and the media – not least of which was Donald Woods and the Rand Daily Mail who went a long way out of their way to champion him - who were the most effective opponents of Apartheid during the late 1960s and 1970s. Again, Biko was apt to be downright nonsensical; he could hardly argue for the rejection of white culture while speaking in English, at a university, while wearing a tweed jacket, collar and tie, before going for chicken and chips and a glass of whisky. Stripping everything back to black African culture was neither possible nor desirable and smacked of some of the wilder ideas of the Apartheid theorists themselves. Nor could his much desired understanding of black History be achieved without accessing the records which white and Arab people had collected over the years simply because black Africans had never developed a written culture. Even the proposed name for the new South Africa, Azania, came from the Evelyn Waugh's 1932 novel *Black Mischief* (the origins of the term are either Ancient Greek or Arabic).[429] In short, Black Consciousness was an intellectual dead end because the world in which black Africans existed had been so shaped by white culture that it was impossible to construct a political programme on its foundations that would not throw out the baby of

[425] Sifiso Mxolisi Ndlovu, *The Road to Democracy in South Africa* (SADET, 2011), p.321.
[426] Richard West, *South African Scandals*, The Spectator, 11th November 1978.
[427] Matthew 13:12
[428] Centre for Strategic and International Studies; Africa Notes No.89, Sept 1st 1988.
[429] Christopher Hitchens, *Mischievous Azania*, The Spectator, 21st December 1985.

capitalism, material well-being, the Rule of Law, personal liberty, personal responsibility, science and Reason with the soiled bathwater of Apartheid. Richard West, a correspondent with great sympathy for Biko, thought that the concept of Black Consciousness was 'a slogan plucked from some sociological rubbish dump';[430] harsh but fair, I'd say. It was also impossible to shrug off the accusation that Black Consciousness was first cousin to White Supremacy, however much that comparison was unfair; it would be the later race, class and gender obsessed 'Grievance Studies' academics and activists who would pollute that legacy and make the accusation gain force,[431] but even contemporary observers like the coloured academic Jacques Gerwel were suspicious: 'It's not so much a desire to be black,' he said. 'It's more a hatred for Whites.'[432] Still, Biko died a young man of thirty and it's fair to say that he was not given either a sufficient education or sufficient time to hone his undoubted intelligence into a maturity of judgement.

Black Consciousness grew up at a time when 'Afrikaaner Consciousness' was approaching its height (or *nadir*, depending on your point of view). As the Afrikaaners grew wealthier, ever more dominant over English speakers, ever more defiant of the outside world they also began to assert themselves culturally. During the 1930s, Afrikaaner cultural associations had concentrated on preserving Afrikaaner culture but under Malan and Vorster, there was a new push to oust what was left of the Smuts/English/British connection. The popularity of H.C. Bosman grew and grew in these years and the Christian National education curriculum, with its emphasis on Boer war heroes like de la Rey and de Wet and the myths of British brutality in the concentration camps, combined to produce a new, tough, confident concept of Afrikaanerdom; a white tribe every bit as African as the Zulu or Xhosa, just more efficient, better at warfare and better at government than anything Africa to the north could show.

The symbol of this assertiveness was the Taal Monument built high on the ridge above the Cape Dutch heartland of Paarl. This remarkable structure, opened in 1975, was supposed to show how the 'shining West' connected to 'magical Africa' to produce the language of Afrikaans and demonstrate its growing use as the language of the country but its construction of concrete and granite conveys no such impression. Indeed, I'm tempted to think that it was a huge practical joke played on gullible taxpayers by shyster architects – which is not anything unusual, admittedly. There is nothing remotely Dutch, Flemish, Cape Dutch, Huguenot, English or African, magical or otherwise, about the structure at all. It bears no relation whatsoever to either the Vrouemonument in Bloemfontein or the Voortrekker Monument in Pretoria. If anything, it owes its style to the vile brutalism of Le Corbusier that so disfigured the towns and cities of post-war Britain, mixed in with the sort of aggressive, triumphalist monumentalism so favoured by Stalin. Standing out like a bishop in a brothel – the 'phallic symbolism of the chauvinist ideal'[433] as Allister Sparks put it - it is without doubt one of the ugliest buildings in South Africa.

The construction of this monstrosity was, however, part of a policy worked out inside the *Broederbond* in 1968 which intended to make Afrikaans not just the undisputed national language but also the second language of black people, rather than the more commonly used English.[434] This was quickly transmitted into the official policy of the Bantu Education Department, and justified by the claim that almost four million whites and coloureds used Afrikaans, plus seven and half million blacks, as against only one and quarter million white people using English as a first language, and that as Afrikaans was the language of the farms, mines, railways, administration and hospitals, it was more useful than English to the Bantu. Added to this was the fact that many black people took Afrikaans as a High School subject to examination level and several subjects were already taught in Afrikaans, so it appeared quite reasonable to assert that Afrikaans should become the main medium of instruction for black people. In 1974, the policy was hardened up; from now on it would be compulsory to study maths, science, History and geography in Afrikaans in 'White areas'. And 'White areas' included one of the strongholds of Black Consciousness; Soweto.

---

[430] Richard West, *The Gathering Storm*, The Spectator, 1st October 1977.
[431] Coleman Hughes, *Tiers of Pride and Shame*, Quillette, 16th January 2019.
[432] Xan Smiley, *God's Stepchildren*, The Spectator, 3rd July 1976.
[433] Allister Sparks, *The Mind of South Africa* (London 1990) p.79
[434] Sifiso Mxolisi Ndlovu, *The Road to Democracy in South Africa* (SADET, 2011), p.324.

Soweto in the 1970s was overcrowded, without electricity, plagued by drugs, crime and gangs amid which very many ordinary, decent people struggled to make a life. Church groups proliferated in an attempt to provide an alternative to the shebeen, *tsotsis* and despair while those who could afford it invested whatever they could in an education for their children which would, hopefully, present the possibility of a better life. During the 1950s, more than 50,000 houses had been built in Soweto but once the Homelands policy kicked in, this number was drastically reduced until by 1965, no houses were being built at all. Between 1962-71, no new schools were built even though there was a baby boom and as class sizes reached 100 and teachers were coping with two shifts per day, the system was already grinding to a halt. This lack of investment in infrastructure was predicated on the provisions of the Bantu Homelands Citizen Act of 1970, which turned black people into citizens of the Homelands according to their ethnicity even when many of them had never been anywhere near them, and was intended to force them out of Joburg and back to the boonies.

Economic reality intervened to make a mockery of this policy. A brief recession in 1968-69, focussed the attention of business on the need for a properly educated black workforce situated close by their places of employment; no-one wanted illiterate employees who arrived at work exhausted by long commutes in rough buses, and pressure was put on the Apartheid authorities to roll back on many of their most cherished schemes. In 1971, Labour restrictions were widely lifted and in 1972, the government accepted the need for better black education and allocated funds to it that were not directly linked to black taxation. Soweto started to get new schools at last; 40 of them, built between 1972-74, with a 300% increase in enrolment. In the following two years, enrolment rose again until the 12,655 pupils of 1972 had become the 389,000 pupils of 1976. This would be a challenge to any school system but when the price of gold dropped in 1975, the government tried to save money by abandoning the last year of primary school. This meant that *two* year groups had to be accommodated simultaneously as the new school year began; 257,000 pupils turned up, but there was space for only 38,000. It was against this background that Afrikaans as the main medium of instruction was introduced.

The first protests came from the teachers, many of whom were not capable of teaching in Afrikaans, while others objected on pedagogical grounds; generally speaking, primary school children were taught in the vernacular initially with more and more English being introduced as they went up through the grades. English was the most common medium in secondary school but when in 1975, Afrikaans was introduced, many children simply couldn't cope with being taught mathematics in three different languages in three consecutive years. The 1953 Bantu Education Act had pretty much ruined the provision available already but this was another step on the downward slope; in 1948 the Matric pass rate had been just over 50% but by 1961 it was down at 18%.[435] Moreover, entry to university was getting harder and harder; in 1960, Fort Hare had been 'tribalised', which meant only Xhosas could attend, leaving a grand total of 627 university places for all other black people; in theory Cape Town, Natal and Wits were open to them but only four out of 190 applications were successful – the say so of the Minister of Education was required for them to be admitted.[436] Parents, unions, journalists and Homeland leaders all began to complain that while Afrikaans was indeed useful, English was far *more* useful as it was rapidly becoming the international language. To these quite reasonable complaints, a deaf ear was turned; at the beginning of 1976, School Board members who opposed to the policy were being dismissed, while others resigned *en masse*. By March 1976, a significant number of pupils, wound up by parents, teachers, Black Consciousness activists and journalists, were themselves beginning to protest. In May, one group of pupils (aged 12-14) threatened to beat up the Headmaster, threw their Afrikaans textbooks out of the window and went on strike.

This was the point at which those parents, teachers, journalists and other activists should have administered six of the best and brought proceedings to a close. These were *children*, not adults, and any notions that they had about education could hardly be considered in the category of measured judgement by dint of their age, but nothing effective was done and the strike spread to several more schools; the majority of strikers were aged just 10-14. Further attempts to get the children back into school were frustrated by older children, who began to bring a degree of organisation to the protest through the Soweto Students Representative Council (SSRC), an influence that was entirely baleful. Nor was the presence of those few ANC members who were not in jail or

[435] Marion Freedmen, *The Hungry Sheep Look Up*, The Spectator, 23rd February 1962.
[436] Marion Freedmen, *The Hungry Sheep Look Up*, The Spectator, 23rd February 1962.

skulking in Lusaka helpful at all – in 1977, the SACP would be boasting about the part *they* played in stirring up trouble, when the reality was they did, as usual, nothing effective – while the roles of the Pan African Congress and the South African Student Movement were characterised by a cynicism bordering on pure evil; children were being wound up deliberately to provoke a response from a SAPS known for its brutality. A particularly low form of life by the name of T.W. Kambule, principal of the Orlando High School (who had once taught Desmond Tutu), then abandoned his duty of care to his pupils by backing the strikes and thus paved the way, on June 13th 1976, for a motley collection of SSRC, ANC, SASM, Black Consciousness and PAC representatives alongside teenagers and *primary age school children* to call a demonstration for June 16th. The organisers of this accident waiting to happen later claimed that they never expected things to turn out the way they did, but this is questionable to say the least; it was utterly unforgivable in the first place and cowardice of the first order to send school children into a situation which they knew would be volatile. They were also fully aware of the capacity for violence that the pupils presented; already there had been incidents of stone throwing and in May, 1976, a hundred pupils had beaten two *tsotsis* to death who had tried to rob their teacher; another teacher had been stabbed by a pupil with a screwdriver, while still others had been accused of being police informers; the police too had been attacked and police cars torched; and it was openly stated that if the pupils were attacked by the police they were to fight back.[437] And it is certainly the case that many parents were kept in the dark about what was being planned.[438]

What became known as the Soweto Uprising has entered mythology in the same way that the Storming of the Bastille or the Winter Palace have. The ANC claimed it as part of their struggle History, even though they had very little to do with organising it, and of course the dimwits of the SACP decided that a desire to learn mathematics in English was evidence of the advance of Marxist-Leninist thought in revolutionary Soweto.[439] If there was any real political thought behind the events of that day, it was probably some rather vague notion of Black Consciousness, but mostly there was just a combination of rage at the crap associated with Apartheid restrictions which combined with the feral destructiveness that children are surprisingly capable of (have a look at Mao's Red Guards during the Cultural Revolution if you doubt this; *Wild Swans* by Jung Chang, is a good start) and the opportunity for looting and the settling of scores. The events of the day were investigated thoroughly by the government in the Report of the Cillie Commission in 1980 which, despite being boycotted by many of the participants, drew evidence from a wide range of sources, not all of whom were police stooges; Sifiso Ndlovu, Professor of History at the University of South Africa and firmly in the 'glorious revolution' camp reckoned it was a reliable enough record to use, so I reckon its good enough for a sceptic like me. A close reading of it reveals that, just like the Storming of the Bastille and of the Winter Palace, the facts would not bear the weight of the claims that were later made for it.

The day began with a rabble-rousing speech by the student leader, Tebello Motapanyane, at the Naledi High School; clearly disturbed at what was happening, the vice-principal attempted to intervene but was chased away. Shortly afterwards the march began, the intention being to join up with pupils from other schools, proceed to the Orlando stadium and from there to the Education Department offices. From the outset, there were incidents of unruly behavior which the organisers of the march did nothing to restrain; schools that had decided not to join the demonstration were flooded with pupils who intimidated teachers, caused principals to run for it and dragooned the remaining pupils into participation. Cars were stopped and occupants were forced to give the Black Power salute (a raised fist, clenched, said to symbolize the crushing of whites) or have their cars burned; other cars were stoned or burned while one school inspector was assaulted and only managed to get away by waving his pistol at the children. This was the first of several racist attacks on whites; and all this was before 8 a.m.

By 9 a.m., trains had been attacked, the first stones had been thrown at the police and the first tear gas canister fired. Taken by surprise, the police deployed to protect the railway stations and ordered all whites and government officials out of the area; a white female reporter was warned to leave one school by the terrified staff and was threatened on her way out by the pupils. Outside the Orlando West High School, a crowd of 6,000

---

[437] Report of the Commission of Inquiry into the Riots at Soweto and Elsewhere from the 16th of June 1976 to the 28th of February 1977, Volume 1(1980). Known as the Cillie Commission.
[438] Sifiso Mxolisi Ndlovu, *The Road to Democracy in South Africa* (SADET, 2011), p.341.
[439] Sifiso Mxolisi Ndlovu, *The Road to Democracy in South Africa* (SADET, 2011), p. 336.

pupils – which subsequently grew much larger – confronted a force of eight white and forty black police officers led by Colonel Kleingold, who had already used tear gas and fired warning shots to disperse a smaller force of demonstrators. Calling on this much larger group of pupils to disperse produced no effect and though – inevitably – it was much disputed who threw what first, stones came from one direction and tear gas from the other; but the tear gas grenades were old, faulty and 90% of them did not go off. Feeling increasingly nervous and being increasingly surrounded, Kleingold then decided that he would have to fight his way out of the situation by going straight at the crowd because there was no room in the narrow street to turn his vehicles around. Dogs and batons were deployed, but this only produced a temporary effect; two of the dogs were beaten to death and attempts were made to set the carcasses alight; his calls for reinforcements went unanswered. Kleingold fired warning shots over the heads of the crowd only to be answered with a hail of stones; by now all the police had sustained injuries; and then, as the crowd charged, the police firing became general. Sergeant M.J. Hattingh drew a bead on 17 year old Hastings Ndlovu who was coming towards him armed with a rock and a club and shot him in the head; his father, a teacher, was unaware that his son was intending to be at the demonstration. Hector Pietersen, 12 years old, was killed by a stray bullet at around the same time. After that, the police climbed into their vehicles, drove through the rioting crowd and out of immediate danger.

At this point, the demonstration began to disperse as some pupils, no doubt shocked and frightened, went back to school or went home while others milled around or began looking for trouble. Four white women delivering vegetables were seriously assaulted by a gang of pupils; J.H.B. Esterhuizen, a white official, was dragged from his car, beaten senseless and left for dead; a young, white, female social worker in the company of her black mentor was dragged from the car, beaten, robbed and then made to beg for her life. She was only saved by the intervention of her colleague and the timely arrival of the church minister whose house she had then sheltered in; a four hour ordeal in which the house was repeatedly stoned before the police rescued her; welfare officer Dr. Edelstein was not so lucky, being beaten to death in his own Youth Centre, which was subsequently burned down. By noon, rioting had become general, with no fewer than nineteen liquor stores broken into, shops looted and cars – cars and shops belonging to the hard working, industrious and respectable section of Soweto society – burned out. Buses went up too and more trains were attacked – things that the *actual* working class depended on to get to work – and every *scollie, schelm, tsotsi*, loafer and bum in the area had joined in and was helping himself to the stolen booze and the contents of respectable storekeepers' shops; four clinics, two libraries, two banks, one post office, three garages and four shops plus most of the local government offices were burned out and two schools seriously damaged. During the following afternoon and evening, another eleven people were shot by the police, four of whom were under 18.[440]

Fifteen people dead. In Africa, every carcass attracts a vulture and as the riots continued into the evening and the following day, the biggest vulture of them all descended; Winnie Mandela. Her response to the tragic deaths, the destruction of hard-earned property and the destruction of the Soweto education system was to propose that mass funerals should be held for the dead in four days' time, certain in the knowledge that more riots, more deaths and more destruction would happen. And it should be noted here that Winnie Mandela had nothing to lose by the destruction of the Soweto education system; like many others of her ilk her own children were educated at an eye-wateringly expensive fee-paying school. In this case, it was Waterford School in Swaziland, whose other alumni included Samora Machel's children (spared the indignity of attending the Mozambican schools that their father had destroyed), the children of Desmond Tutu, Walter Sisulu, and Nadine Gordimer and whose laboratories had been paid for by the hated, white, capitalist oppressor, Harry Oppenheimer.[441] Nor were her children likely to suffer any consequences from any of other proposed acts of destruction; Zenani had met and married a Swazi prince while studying at Boston University; Zindzi was sixteen at the time of the riots but does not seem to have been allowed anywhere near the trouble and would go into internal exile with her mother in 1977, before also heading off for Waterford. Somewhat dimmer than her big sister, university would elude her as the path of the gangster's moll proved more appealing. She would be implicated by the TRC in several murders committed at her mother's behest.[442]

---

[440] Report of the Commission of Inquiry into the Riots at Soweto and Elsewhere from the 16th of June 1976 to the 28th of February 1977, Volume 1(1980). Known as the Cillie Commission.
[441] https://waterford.sz/index.php
[442] TRC Final Report Vol. Ch.6 para. 23

Though denied the funerals by the government, Winnie got her way. On the following day, 65 more black people, of whom 14 were under 18, were killed by police; seven others died in a fire as they looted the vegetable market. As rioting continued, 19 year old Tsietsi Mashinini ordered school children not to go back to school and demanded that their parents should come out on strike. The next day, Friday, the police killed a further 31 black people but the disturbances died down as the responsible people of Soweto kept their children at home but even then, when the schools re-opened on 22nd July, either out of intimidation or fear of the police, few pupils turned up. Not content with the body count, the activists kept up the pressure with a series of attacks on railways and buses in the hope of enforcing a strike that few workers were interested in joining. Mashinini, now utterly drunk with revolutionary hubris, demanded that pupils use violence to prevent workers going to their jobs; signaling equipment on the railway was damaged. In the early hours of 4th August, Mashini then encouraged a mob of (by now) feral children to assault workers and demand the release of those pupils who had been arrested for the murder of Dr. Edelstein. The Black Parents Association, watching their children being offered up, not so much as martyrs to the cause but as sacrificial lambs, tried to get the crowd to disperse; Mashini responded by attacking the homes of black policemen. Sometime during all this, someone attempted to burn down Winnie Mandela's house by mistake; unfortunately, they did not succeed; happily though, it was burgled at a later date by *tsotsis*.

On 23rd August, activists demanded once more that the workers must come out on strike and when the workers decided that going to work was actually more important than running around mouthing off empty slogans, another wave of intimidation began; the police shot three more people dead. The next day, the workers went to work, many of them, no doubt to try to earn enough money to replace the cars that the pupils and activists had burned out. Thereafter, a Zulu migrant workers' hostel was attacked by pupils and burned out in reprisal for not striking – so much for this being a *workers'* revolution; in a taste of what was to come, one worker was doused in petrol and threatened with a match. When the Zulus responded with likewise violence, more respectable black workers were treated to a beating, arson and rape; eight hundred Soweto inhabitants sought refuge at one police station; thirteen more people died, of which the police were responsible for seven. As the violence continued over the next two days, another 39 black people were killed by the police while countless others were beaten by demonstrators and Zulu migrant workers. Sporadic violence continued into September when the activists demanded that students go to Joburg to protest against the visit of Henry Kissinger. This incident alone is indicative of the idiocy and ignorance of the activists; Kissinger, as we have seen, was just about to 'put the gun' to Ian Smith's head and force him to accept black majority rule in Rhodesia but the thought that white 'imperialist' USA might actually be willing and, more importantly, capable of achieving more than a dimwit bunch of rioters and the 'progressive' forces of international socialism was beyond the comprehension of both Black Consciousness and the ANC. Even worse, children and activists began a reign of terror by demanding that shebeens be closed on their say so alone and several acts of sabotage were committed. Around 845 people were arrested. It wasn't really until February 1977 that some sort of peace returned to Soweto, the schools were functioning again and the workers allowed to go back to work, replace their property and get on with their lives without riot, arson and intimidation. All in all, 262 people were killed in the riots, of whom only four were white; 208 were killed by the police and 59 were under the age of 18.

This is the reality of revolution; organized minorities, intimidated workers, accidental deaths of innocents, destruction of hard earned property, the collapse of trust between police (who as well as being 'instruments of oppression' are the people who catch the burglars emptying your house of your possessions), state and people, the collapse of education, the emergence of a spirit of *Lord of the Flies* among children who were often better educated (and thus more arrogant) than their parents and, as ever, complete failure to make life better rather than worse. Amid the banners of defiance, the unspoken cry of the respectable, church-going, working people went up: 'We oppose Apartheid just as much as you do but how does burning down my local shop, destroying my kids' school, torching my car and sending children up against bullets help bring it to an end?'

As for Mashini, well, he fled the country in August 1976 where he was feted by various African leaders, lodging in the presidential guest house in Nigeria before moving to Liberia where he married no less a person than Miss Liberia herself. Two children later, he left her to progress around the campuses of Britain and the USA, hanging out in the Student Union bars and impressing the impressionable with his great wisdom; not for such a 'fearless fighter'[443] as him were the dungeons of Apartheid or the fetid MK camps of Angola. The ANC naturally claimed him as one of their own, despite the fact that he never joined any liberation organization; perhaps he feared being drafted and made to *actually* fight instead of inciting children to do it. He died in Guinea in 1990, after apparently being mugged. Kambule was offered a position at the University of Witwatersrand in 1977 for his part in the uprising but Tebello Motapanyane was not so fortunate; joining the ANC and MK in exile, he was arrested and tortured at the 'Iran' prison outside Luanda by the ANC then, after 1994, they forgot about him. He died in poverty in Joburg in 2006, with his wife denied citizenship and his children denied hardship grants by the Nelson Mandela Children's Fund after he had been critical of the government's refusal to support him in 2004.[444] *Sic Transit Gloria Mundi.*

The riots were not confined to Soweto and activists from Black Consciousness, the Pan African Congress and other organisations made sustained efforts to spread the disturbances. They met with mixed results; in Alexandra, East London, Mossel Bay, Beaufort West, Graaff-Reinet, Bredesdorp, Ceres and at Marikana near Rustenburg (a mine made famous when the ANC government opened fire on striking miners in 2012 killing 34 of them), parents intervened quickly to keep their children out of trouble and there was at least one incident of police handing arrested children over to them 'for a hiding'.[445] In other places, the police were met with 'cold neutrality'.[446] Racist attacks on Indians, coloureds and Chinese were also recorded while, as might be expected, the white students of the University of Witwatersrand, marched about waving placards; 43 more people on the Rand died, of whom 37 were killed by the police. In the East Rand, strikes were called, pupils and workers intimidated, bottle stores looted, workers went to work under police protection, rioters were shot and parents and teachers tried to call for peace. Further south, in Sharpeville, parents went to the schools to guard them from the agitators while in more remote places, Black Consciousness ideals took on an overtly anti-white racism, notably at the University of the North. In Port Elizabeth, an 18 month old child died when her house was torched. In some places, policing was sensitive, in others, completely hopeless, as in Bothaville where a film show was halted just before the end because the proper permits were not in place; no refund was offered and the public, quite reasonably, kicked up a fuss. Generally speaking, the Cillie Commission was critical of the police for being unprepared, heavy-handed and poorly trained while conceding that it was their job to suppress the riotous behavior; as the Truth and Reconciliation Commission later noted 'lack of capacity was reflected in their tendency to use maximum force.'[447] In general, the intensity of the rioting, found the Commission, was in direct proportion to the state of community relations more generally; in much of the Orange Free State, there were few disturbances at all. In the Cape, disturbances were small scale, with only the white students of the university making any impression, although in September and October, things were considerably worse with the bottle stores being the favoured targets. 137 people died in the Cape riots between August 1976 and February 1977 of whom 108 were killed by the police, including poor little Sandra Peters, 12 years old, who was sent to the shop by her mum, arrived as looters were attacking it and was killed by a stray police bullet. Much of this fighting was instigated by militant youth groups called the 'Comrades' who closed down the shebeens, enforced a ban on booze by searching for and punishing anyone they suspected to be in possession of it – in some cases making them vomit it up - and attempted to ban Christmas. Migrant workers, who refused to be ordered about by such youths, fought back; five more schools were burned down; on Boxing Day alone, 77 houses were burned down and 15 cars torched; the 5 year old girl under the care of Deborah Luvuno was killed with an axe and thrown into a burning building; for much of this time the police were employed in keeping the two groups apart and arranging peace talks. Natal stayed generally quiet, largely because community relations were better and the ruling over Afrikaans did not apply because most schools were administered by the KwaZulu Homeland authorities.[448]

Again, in Africa every carcass attracts a vulture, in this case one by the name of the Reverend D.P.H. Russell, a collaborator of the South African Students Organisation who had not been present at any of the events, but who concocted a number of documents of questionable veracity which blamed the police for all the trouble; they

[443] https://www.sahistory.org.za/people/teboho-tsietsi-mashinini
[444] Paul Trewhela, *Inside Quatro: Uncovering the Exile History of the ANC and SWAPO* (Joburg, 2010) p.136.
[445] Report of the Commission of Inquiry into the Riots at Soweto and Elsewhere from the 16th of June 1976 to the 28th of February 1977, Volume 1(1980). Known as the Cillie Commission.
[446] Report of the Commission of Inquiry into the Riots at Soweto and Elsewhere from the 16th of June 1976 to the 28th of February 1977, Volume 1(1980). Known as the Cillie Commission.
[447] TRC. Quoted in *The Cambridge History of Africa*, (Cambridge, 2011) Vol. 2 p. 420.
[448] *The Cambridge History of Africa*, (Cambridge, 2011) Vol. 2 p.422.

were smuggled out and presented to the UN in the interests of 'truth and peace'[449] which was stretching the first of those terms beyond what any reasonable person would regard as breaking point and which had no interest in achieving the second. Indeed, the Cillie Commission – which was no whitewash by any means – went to great lengths to refute Russell's claims individually and in detail ('devoid of all truth' was the judgment on one allegation); it even offered to hear his testimony, an offer which was declined, and only just stopped short of calling him an out and out liar.

The rebellion could not succeed without clear aims, effective leadership and effective force, none of which were in evidence and it soon began to resemble a movement whose only aim was to keep the rebellion going *ad infinitum*. By early 1977, it was petering out even though by September 200,000 pupils were nominally boycotting classes; how many had simply dropped out or were too afraid or intimidated to return is a moot point as attendance was not compulsory. The cost of failure was high too; 587 people dead, 2,389 wounded, 6,000 suspects arrested, 7,000 going into exile; parental authority among large swathes of young people had been eroded to the point where arrogant, under-educated brats felt empowered to call their elders cowards and liars.[450] Black Consciousness was closed down by banning the whole (fractious and endlessly bickering) network of organisations inspired by it and Steve Biko was arrested, detained and beaten to death. Even as a philosophy it lost purchase as the older commitment to a non-racial future gradually seeped back into the discourse.[451] As a political challenge to Apartheid, Black Consciousness had gone the way of the ANC.

*

Build a bonfire! Build a bonfire!

Put the teachers on the top,

Put the prefects in the middle

And burn the rotten lot!

A popular English primary school ditty c.1973.

What, then, are we to say about the causes and consequences of the Soweto Uprising? According to ANC orthodoxy and mythology, the uprising was the result of politically aware students motivated by Black Consciousness spontaneously mobilizing against the Apartheid regime on the issue of Afrikaans education and being met by police brutality. The problem with this explanation is that, despite the tenacity of the assertion, the evidence seems to me to point to something both more banal and complex of which there were several competing and complimentary strands. The first strand is undoubtedly the overcrowding that occurred in the schools which led, in several cases, to the staff and principals losing control of what went on in them. Is this possible? Having had experience of working in a particularly dismal British state school where the pupils were quite definitely in charge, where little learning took place under an incompetent management despite lavish – and I mean *lavish* – funding, I will tell you that it is. A teacher can only keep control over so many pupils; my rule of thumb (and I was the bastard who you got sent to when your own teacher was sick of you) was that I could *control* twenty-eight or so teenagers, but that number would have to come down to around twenty-two if any meaningful teaching was to take place. In Soweto, class sizes were regularly in excess of 50. On top of this, education was not compulsory for black children and though, in theory, they would start school aged 7 and take the final exams, or 'Matric', at 17, many pupils started later, drifted in and out of school as funds, the need to work or the inclination varied. In many cases, there were pupils aged 20 still in class – indeed William Beinart reckoned that 20 was the *average* age of a matriculating pupil[452] - and such grown people could not and would not be expected to respect the rules and discipline necessary to keep younger pupils on the straight and narrow. Inevitably, they found the situation frustrating, to put it mildly.

---

[449] Ministers' Fraternal of Langa, Guguletu and Nygana, *Role of the South African Riot Police in Burnings and Killings in Nyanga*, (Cape Town, Christmas 1976). United Nations Centre against Apartheid.
[450] *The Cambridge History of Africa*, (Cambridge, 2011) Vol. 2 p. 423.
[451] *The Cambridge History of Africa*, (Cambridge, 2011) Vol. 2 p. 426.
[452] Beinart, p.236

The second strand is that very many of the brighter pupils understood the need to pass Matric if they were to stand a chance in the job market and make their parents proud. This was a real challenge because as many as 90% of their teachers had never passed Matric themselves. It was going to be difficult enough to pass their exams in English without now having to do so in Afrikaans, a language that neither they nor their teachers were familiar with. What the introduction of Afrikaans also did was to give an entirely reasonable excuse for those less committed and less able pupils who stood only a marginal hope of passing in the first place to stop working altogether and – and this is a commonly observed feature of the behaviour of less able or motivated pupils - to stop the brighter ones studying too. It seems to me to be no coincidence at all that demonstrations were called for examination days and widespread intimidation deployed to prevent more committed pupils sitting those exams.

The third strand was the socio-economic condition of Soweto at the time; rampant crime, no electricity, overcrowding, under-employment, the prevalence of gangs and the fact that large numbers of school age children – perhaps as many as 80% of those eligible for secondary education – were not in school at all. All this provided an underlying dissatisfaction that was largely apolitical but still the stuff of paraffin and matches; when a 'Committee of Ten' was formed to demand reform of the Soweto local government, one of its first demands was that property rights be affirmed through the granting of Freeholds; hardly radical Marxism at work.[453] Only then can we point to Apartheid, largely because for children growing up in Soweto, it is quite possible that they had little or no personal experience of the system and though newspapers did exist and were widely read, they were heavily censored; TV did not get to South Africa until 1976. The root cause of the Soweto Uprising, it seems to me, was the mismanagement of the school system during a period of rapid expansion which presented the brightest with the distinct possibility of failure and the less able with an excuse to avoid it. When the able are denied opportunities for advancement and the less able handed an alibi for not taking up the available opportunities ('It's the *system*, mate, innit?') then the proper operation of capitalism begins to break down. *This is how revolutions begin.*

*

P.W. Botha: Brutality and Reform

We did not regard ourselves as being a minority as the Rhodesians did in Rhodesia.... We believed that we were a nation coalescing around the Afrikaners, with a right to self-determination. That was our point of departure. The central theme in Afrikaner History since 1652 was the wish to rule themselves and to maintain their right to self-determination. Twice during the 19th century, the Afrikaners took on the greatest imperial power of the time, Britain, in defense of that goal. The whole of the History of the 20th century for the Afrikaners was the reestablishment of this right to self-determination. So, for the great majority of white South Africans at that time, it wasn't a question of defending "Whites Only" signs and lifts, as Mr. Botha pointed out. It was a question of whether this national group would survive as an entity in South Africa. That was the core of our underlying strategic concern. And also, this nation was broadly Western; it was broadly democratic too at that time. We didn't see any future in a society that would come under the rule of a communist party in South Africa.

David Steward, F.W. de Klerk Foundation, 2013.

*

...nothing, absolutely nothing, which has occurred in African countries since independence suggests that South Africans of any race would benefit from Black rule here. Furthermore the White man's everyday contact with Blacks at their present state of development inspires no confidence whatsoever in their ability to run the country. The White South African is very aware that he and his forebears have built a modern and, even in these hard times, prosperous country from nothing and that every development from the railway system to the humblest shade tree is the result of his initiative, and that

---

[453] *The Cambridge History of Africa*, (Cambridge, 2011) Vol. 2 p.424.

to allow the country to fall into the hands of a people who had achieved so little before his advent would be fatal to all future development.

A white man from Natal's letter to The Spectator 22nd October 1977.

*

How can one ever explain what is at once a tyranny and a free country?

Richard West, *The Spectator* 8th October 1977.

*

For this is the Great Truth about South Africa today: traditional apartheid no longer suits the interests of capitalism. And it is capitalism, not socialism or even black nationalism, which will end traditional apartheid.[454]

Geoffrey Wheatcroft, *The Spectator* 1981.

*

A hard, dour, belligerent professional Afrikaaner politician. (In the Second World War he only just avoided being detained for being a Nazi sympathiser). He has a reputation for a quick temper, and intolerance of criticism. He is not an intellectual....He relies heavily on military advice...is critical of the general weakness of the West in the face of what he regards as the world-wide Marxist threat and instinctively favours a tough go-it-alone policy for South Africa....a hard man who can be disagreeably rude if he chooses.

British Foreign Office assessment of PW Botha, 1984.[455]

*

Pik Botha is one of the few South African politicians with charisma. He is good on television combining robust defence of South African interests with sincerity and occasional wit. He adopts at times an aggressive manner in order to avoid damaging criticism of being 'soft'. His influence is probably on the side of reason and realism....He has a disconcerting tendency to conduct a private conversation as if it were a public meeting and is not a good listener. At times – perhaps deliberately – he allows himself to get carried away by his own performance and emotions. But just as you think he is going over the edge he switches, equally disconcerting, to sweet reason.

British Foreign Office assessment of Pik Botha, 1984.[456]

*

The Carnation Revolution, the intervention in Angola and the looming loss of Rhodesia to black nationalism had torn South African foreign policy to shreds and, it appeared to many in the government, that the Soweto riots presaged an internal crisis which could only result in disaster. As we have seen, P.W. Botha's reaction to this 'total onslaught' was the development of the 'Total Strategy' in foreign policy which succeeded in beating the so-called Frontline States into abject submission by 1984 and underlining that submission at Cuito Canavale. The assumptions on which this counter-insurgency driven strategy was based would also be applied to the situation inside South Africa and what followed was a policy to ameliorate and gradually abandon Apartheid, coupled with a ruthless repression of organised political opposition. What Botha intended to do was to defeat black opposition so that when the inevitable time for a settlement arrived, Afrikaaners would be negotiating from a position of strength.

---

[454] Geoffrey Wheatcroft, *More a Way of Life*, The Spectator, 13th June 1981.
[455] FCO briefing for Margaret Thatcher, 31st May 1984. https://www.margaretthatcher.org/document/144540
[456] FCO briefing for Margaret Thatcher, 31st May 1984. https://www.margaretthatcher.org/document/144540

In order to ensure that there would be a complete focus on the 'Total Strategy' at home, Botha re-wrote the constitution so as to entrench the security forces – or 'securocrats' as they became known – at the apex of the government. From 1983 onwards, the State President (Botha) ceased to be a figurehead and took over the executive, reducing parliament to effectively a consultative role while the Cabinet, though still powerful, was in reality subordinated to the State Security Council. At the heart of government policy was the National Security Management System whose trident aimed to maintain efficient government – the twenty Cabinet Committees were slimmed down to just four - to 'command, coerce and eliminate'[457] the enemy, and win the support of the population. Although centrally controlled, there were twelve regional Joint Management Committees to ensure that the policy aims were applied with reasonable conformity but adapted to local conditions.

There was also a root and branch reform of the intelligence apparatus which resulted in the end of BOSS and the foregrounding of the Department of Military Intelligence to run a counter-insurgency strategy to replace the police-led approach of BOSS. This was an important ideological shift as it abandoned the old 'British' notion that the ANC and its supporters should be treated essentially as criminals and dealt with under the law (in theory at least) and took up the view that the ANC opposition were essentially enemies of the state in the same sense that a foreign invader would be. The effect would be the sanctioning of heavy-handed responses, draconian measures and not least, covert operations of the type associated with war rather than civil unrest. What the DMI, as the lead organisation of a plethora of different intelligence and security agencies, hoped to deliver with the NSMS was a military victory rather than a political solution. And they were told they could take the gloves off to achieve this; whatever the legality or morality of a particular tactic, be it murder, torture, detention without trial or targeted assassination, if it worked, it was acceptable.[458] Botha had taken a page from the communist's book; the end *would* justify the means. This was the stick.

The carrot came in the shape of a reform programme which accepted that there would have to be a genuine attempt to provide better socio-economic conditions for black people and for power sharing as a first step towards drawing in all South Africans into government; coloureds and Indians would be admitted to a measure of power at the national level, while blacks would be encouraged to participate at the level of local government. There would be a National Welfare Management System, electrification of the townships, the easing of black Trade Union restrictions and a more liberal approach to influx management; there would also be a commitment to the eventual equalisation of educational opportunities. Petty Apartheid restrictions would either be repealed or allowed to lapse while an extension of free market economics would be promoted in order to create and maintain the prosperity that would underpin a peaceful transition to a more equitable political order – which would, of course be guided by a strong state able to guarantee stability and the destruction of violent political opposition. And if this caused unease in white Afrikaaner circles, so be it; 'Adapt or die' was Botha's advice in 1978[459] while Piet Koornhof, *Broederbond* and National Party, announced in Washington in 1979 that 'Apartheid is dead.'[460]

Making the transition would clearly be difficult and somewhat akin to removing the fastening from a heavily pressurised container. To begin with, even to embark on change was to admit the injustice of the present situation and to remove whatever historical or other justifications existed for it. What would inevitably follow would be vocal and justified demands for the process not simply to speed up but to become immediate and then, right on the heels of those calls, would come demands for restitution, reparation and perhaps revenge. Demands for political rights would inevitably raise the question of property rights and a proper level of economic redistribution, all of which would appear to permit of simple solutions; democracy, redistributive taxation and the restitution of land rights. The dangers buried in such simple solutions would not be readily apparent, or perhaps would be seen as irrelevant in a febrile situation but would, if ignored, provide the material for a terrible conflagration that would be infinitely worse than the existing unjust situation.

These dangers were legion. An attack on property rights would drive away the foreign investment that produced the vitally needed new jobs and prosperity (Allister Sparks reckoned that Soweto was already probably the

[457] Kevin A. O'Brien, *The South African Intelligence Services From Apartheid to Democracy* (London, 2011) p.128.
[458] Kevin A. O'Brien, *The South African Intelligence Services From Apartheid to Democracy* (London, 2011) p.119.
[459] Beinart p.245.
[460] Beinart p.245.

wealthiest black city in Africa),[461] encourage those who owned property and capital to send it outside the country before an incoming democratic government could get its hands on it and thus destroy existing employment and prosperity; (during the Rhodesian transition in 1979, farmers stopped planting and the price of maize rose 25%, just at the moment when the whole of central Africa was facing a drought induced famine);[462] furthermore, any threat to property rights would provoke those who could not liquidate and emigrate into violent resistance in defence of their property. Given the strong possibility that a popular government would include a correspondingly strong dose of SACP influence, there might well be a socialist drive to 'smash capitalism' and thus collapse the economy entirely. To resist demands for reform would surely provoke those making them into even greater frustration and marginalise moderate leaders in favour of extremists, rabble-rousers and socialists. To this disaster in the making might well be added the possibility of race war as blacks turned on whites, Indians and coloureds, tribal war as Zulu turned on Xhosa, and gang warfare as *tsotsis* and organised criminals took advantage of a demoralised and de-legitimised police force. Mass emigration of whites, as had happened in Angola, Mozambique, and perhaps the expulsion of Asians, as had happened in Kenya and Uganda, would result in the disappearance of the skilled, educated and entrepreneurial capital on which the country's health, education, industry and commerce depended. Should any of these developments look likely, then there was also the possibility of a praetorian spirit emerging in the armed forces or a reappearance of the Boer laager mentality. Any and all of these things were possible and the results might well be Hobbesian to say the least. It was for this reason that Botha put internal security and the defeat of the Frontline states right at the heart of his strategy; reform had to be slow, piecemeal, the opposition contained and the safety valve released gradually if an explosion was not to occur, however agonisingly tedious the process. 'The need for change,' thought the British Ambassador in 1980,

'seems to have comes through his head rather than his heart. He wants change not for his own sake, but to ward off revolution. For this purpose the minimum necessary becomes the optimum desirable and the speed of change must not get out of control.'[463]

Apocalyptic the future might appear, but Botha was able to point to a number of things that might provide some optimism. The first was that wide swathes of the business community had long been sceptical not just of apartheid but also of the socialism espoused by the ANC/SACP and might thus be relied upon for support. Harry Oppenheimer, as usual, made the relevant point in 1984;

'Although I have spent a lifetime fighting against policies of racial discrimination in South Africa, I certainly would not willingly accept a political settlement which involved any serious risk of South Africa's developing into a Marxist-orientated, one party state.'[464]

The economic argument was a powerful one, not only because there was an increasing recognition throughout the world – including the socialist world - during the 1980s that socialism of whatever variety simply could not produce anything like the prosperity that capitalism could. Also because in Britain and the USA, there was a new assertiveness in that belief that had long been missing from the Western world. On top of this was a settled determination led by the Oppenheimers to open up cracks in the façade of Apartheid wherever possible and advance the prosperity of black workers as a deliberate long-term policy to undermine it completely and create a more socially homogenous society – what the British Foreign Office called 'the Oppenheimer thesis'.[465] Citing the need for places to meet black entrepreneurs, the Johannesburg Carlton centre, a shopping and hotel complex run by them was given the special designation of 'international' which meant, in effect, that its bars and restaurants were desegregated. The first Miss South Africa contest was sponsored by the Rand Daily Mail/Sunday Times; the winner was still white, but her colleague and runner up was black.[466] Over 90% of British companies (and plenty of Canadian[467] and European ones[468]) operating in South Africa signed up to a

[461] Geoffrey Wheatcroft, *African Magnate*, The Spectator, 19th May 1984.
[462] Charles Douglas-Home, *Zimbabwe; the Threat to Africa*, The Spectator, 13th October 1979.
[463] UK Ambassador Cape Town to Carrington, South Africa: Annual Review 1980. 15th January 1981.
https://www.margaretthatcher.org/document/142372
[464] David Pallister, Sarah Stuart and Ian Lepper, *South Africa Inc: The Oppenheimer Empire* (Sandton, 1987) p.163.
[465] Fergusson Minute for Reeve 8th July 1985. https://www.margaretthatcher.org/document/145274
[466] Richard West, *Racial Art in South Africa*, The Spectator, 8th October 1977.
[467] UKE Ottawa to FCO 9th July 1985. https://www.margaretthatcher.org/document/145345
[468] FCO Minute for Powell 8th July 1985. https://www.margaretthatcher.org/document/145273

Brussels code too which insisted that the interests of black employees should be advanced.[469] The USA took a similar approach with the Sullivan Code. Both Barclays and Standard bank enjoyed good reputations for advancing black employees,[470] as did RTZ's mining operations in Namibia/SW Africa[471] – whatever the student rabble in Britain believed - and, of course, a prosperous black population meant more potential customers. Ranged against these positive developments were, of course, the trade unions who, in common with their British counterparts in their fiefdoms at the docks and British Leyland, were determined to keep black and Asian hands off 'their' jobs.[472]

The second was that there had always been a core of white voters who were opposed to Apartheid. Assessing the actual size of that core from voting patterns is, of course, problematical because the main opposition party, the United Party under the leadership of De Villiers Graaff, was itself split over the issue of segregation, but when combined with the Progressive Party vote it is not beyond the pale to suggest that roughly and variously 20-30% (sometimes as high as 40%) of white voters embraced the idea (whether more or less willingly) that Apartheid would have to go; the leader of the opposition, van Zyl Slabbert told Margret Thatcher in 1980 that Botha could count on 70% of the white electorate being in favour of reform;[473] the 1983 whites only referendum on introducing coloureds and Indians into parliament produced a 66% majority approval on a 76% turnout. This gave Botha room to abandon the more deranged of his own supporters – several of whom had already split off to form the Herstigte Nasional Party in protest at what they regarded as Botha's appalling liberalism - on the reasonable assumption that he would make up the shortfall from this constituency. By 1989, that calculation resulted in Botha's successor picking up around 66% of white voters in the whites only referendum paving the way for black majority rule.

The third reason for optimism was that although the black opposition was spectacular in that it provided excellent TV pictures for activist journalists, its reach was a lot more limited than those journalists would have the world believe. Outside the townships of the Transvaal and Port Elizabeth and one or two other urban areas, those who accepted even the notional leadership of the ANC were few. In Natal, Buthelezi's Inkatha remained unconvinced by the ANC, while in the Cape they had very little purchase and even less in the rural areas excepting the Transkei. Large parts of both the Indian and coloured communities also harboured suspicions of the ANC based on the fear of socialism, race war and the possibility of a spreading violent insurrection.

It was also the case that very many people remained in virtual ignorance of what was happening in the townships because censorship was so effective. It seems incredible, but I have heard this point made time and time again from those who lived through this period; 'it wasn't like that in this area', 'the media did not tell anything like the truth', 'I never noticed because I was not interested in politics', 'there was a bit of trouble sometimes, but it was never very serious' are all such common remarks that I cannot just dismiss them as being simply selective memory or wilful blindness. No doubt there was a general understanding that things were not all rosy in the garden but it is a cardinal error of both journalists and historians to ascribe more significance to a particular event than it merits simply because it is of interest, or to misinterpret it completely; the Cambridge History of Africa described the 1973 Durban strikes as 'The Workers' Rebellion' when the reality is that it was just a series of strikes for higher wages.[474] Similarly, an art exhibition held at the Johannesburg Market theatre in 1977 to expose the death of Steve Biko and the torture of political detainees no doubt attracted the attention of artists, journalists and activists but how much impression it made on the general public out in the Marico boonies is anyone's guess.[475] Allister Sparks of the Rand Daily Mail made the point at the time of the Soweto disturbances that censorship restrictions made it impossible for him to even begin to explain what the main principles of Black Consciousness were;[476] declining circulation also put his paper out of business during the 1980s, which clearly indicates that fewer and fewer people were interested in what it had to say, possibly because what he had to say was becoming more and more detached from any sort of objectivity. Long standing

---

[469] FCO Briefing for Margaret Thatcher 31st May 1984, p.41. https://www.margaretthatcher.org/document/144540
[470] Richard West, Recognition for Rhodesia? The Spectator, 12th May 1979.
[471] Geoffrey Wheatcroft, More a Way of Life, The Spectator, 13th June 1981.
[472] Richard West, A Lynching Mood, The Spectator, 12th November 1977.
[473] No.10 Record of Conversation 17th September 1980. https://www.margaretthatcher.org/document/121042
[474] The Cambridge History of South Africa, (CUP, 2011) p.410.
[475] Richard West, Racial Art in South Africa, The Spectator, 8th October 1977.
[476] Allister Sparks, Fear and Trembling in South Africa, The Spectator, 27th October 1977.

correspondent Richard West was convinced that although Biko was well known in the Eastern Cape, he was hardly known at all in Soweto until Donald Woods blasted the government over his death.[477] He also observed that the death in custody of Neil Agget in 1983, a white doctor and anti-Apartheid activist, provoked less interest than a particularly lurid murder trial.[478] Even such events as the death of Biko, widely reported both in South Africa and abroad, and producing reactions ranging from utter disbelief (especially at the gross comments of Jimmy Kruger, the Justice minister, and back bench National Party MP Frikkie 'I would have killed him myself' Le Roux) to aghast outrage, tended to be of transient effect. Relentless government propaganda cocooned the white population, according to the British Ambassador, John Leahy, in 1980,[479] while even when the state of emergency was declared in 1985, one Cape Town resident journalist said that 'If South Africa is to go bang, it certainly doesn't feel that way to those of us who live here.'[480] At a time when Nelson Mandela's image was on the lapel badge of virtually every hip student in Britain, it was possible for the police to take him out and about on day trips in South Africa without anyone recognising him. My Missus used to hitchhike from Harare to Cape Town in the mid-1980s with never a thought that she might end up choking on tear gas or stopping a stray bullet from the riot squad. Indeed, for a while in 1985, the ANC adopted the slogan of 'Take the Fight to the White Areas' simply because so many of them were undisturbed. This would change from the mid-1980s, but it really wasn't until the end of that decade that most white people were forced to confront the changes about to take place. As Spark's himself put it;

> 'The black South African world is as distant from the white world as Outer Mongolia….probably no more than five percent of white Johannesburg has ever been to Soweto….Most could not even tell you how to get there.'[481]

Botha's first steps at constitutional reform were of limited success and backfired rather badly. Ruling out 'one man, one vote' - his preferred option was a 'constellation' of more or less self-governing ethnic states[482] - he began in 1980 by attempting to associate coloureds and Indians on a new 'President's Council' and then in 1984 with elections to a new tri-cameral parliament. This produced some co-operation, but in general, the new arrangements were met with a great deal of scepticism. Among black people, the reaction was of exasperation at the assumption inherent in these arrangements that they were represented through the Bantustans; privately, Botha simply did not believe that black people were capable of government; 'it would be like giving a pistol to a child,' he informed a British envoy in 1980.[483] The loathing was mutual. The 1976 rebels were now in their twenties, with police records, without employment or the qualifications to get them, seething with frustration and with each passing year another year group joined them. Forced removals, such as the eviction of the residents of Mogopa in the Transvaal, were achieved by destroying the schools and water pumps; the residents had bought the land in 1906, had been served notice to shift in 1964 but it wasn't until 1980 that action began to be taken;[484] according to the Surplus People's Project Report, 3.5 million people had been shunted around like this since the 1960s while another 2 million were awaiting removal.[485] The heartless way in which slum clearance operations were carried out – sometimes in mid-winter as in the case of Nyanga outside Cape Town in 1981[486] – piled up resentment on hardship; when the government relented, promising jobs and allowing relief organisations to help those evicted, things got worse because the promises attracted even more desperate people to the slums and squatter camps; at Nyanga, the original camp mushroomed from 400 people to 2,300 over a weekend;[487] to resentment and hardship was added disappointment. Crossroads, another shanty near Cape Town, was subjected to 'frequent and brutal raids'.[488] Each person arrested and beaten by the police came with

[477] Richard West, *Fighting over Biko*, The Spectator, 19th November 1977.
[478] Richard West, *The Murder of Mr Smith*, The Spectator, 29th January 1983.
[479] UK Ambassador Cape Town to Carrington, South Africa: Annual Review 1980. 15th January 1981. https://www.margaretthatcher.org/document/142372
[480] Stephen Robinson, *A Job for the Army*, The Spectator, 27th July 1985.
[481] Allister Sparks, *The Mind of South Africa* (London, 1990), p.xvii
[482] British Consulate-General to FCO, 11th April 1980. https://www.margaretthatcher.org/document/121064
[483] British Consulate-General to FCO, 11th April 1980. https://www.margaretthatcher.org/document/121064
[484] FCO Briefing for Margaret Thatcher, 31st May 1984 p.77 https://www.margaretthatcher.org/document/144540
[485] Bryan Rostron, *South Africa Plays Bop*, The Spectator, 13th August 1983.
[486] UKE Cape Town to FCO, *Police Action against Illegal Black Residents*, 12th August 1981. https://www.margaretthatcher.org/document/143551
[487] UKE Cape Town to FCO, *Squatters* 17th August 1981. https://www.margaretthatcher.org/document/143549
[488] FCO Briefing for Margaret Thatcher, 31st May 1984 p.77 https://www.margaretthatcher.org/document/144540

a family and friendship network who might well have been content to get on with life undisturbed by politics otherwise; BOSS agent Gordon Winter defected in 1980 when his maid's daughter, Cynthia Montwedi, whom he knew to have no political interests at all, was arrested, tortured, beaten senseless and detained for three weeks because a friend of her husband brought a bomb into her house which went off prematurely.[489] There was a new sense of assertiveness among the trade unions too and although too much should not be read into the increase in strike activity as being evidence of political motivation, it was certainly the case that union leaders were increasingly inclined towards militancy and the articulation of demands that went beyond the merely pecuniary – also, only around 10% of the black workforce was unionised. A trickle of MK and ANC operatives did manage to evade the police and begin to organise opposition in the townships, but by and large they were ineffective, unable to communicate with different parts of the country or with the leadership in Lusaka, London or Luanda.

What was effective was the upsurge in 'civics', church groups, youth groups and community associations of one type or another dedicated to opposition, which organised boycotts and protests, closed down schools, published underground newspapers and pamphlets and generally made a nuisance of themselves and in doing so exploded the widely held view within the police that disturbances were solely due to the presence of troublemakers and student radicals. In 1983, these came together in the United Democratic Front, an umbrella organisation led by Archbishop Desmond Tutu, Albertina Sisulu and the rather less appealing Winnie Mandela, which generally endorsed what they knew of the ANC's policies – the policies themselves were unclear due to censorship and because the third rate leaders of the ANC could barely articulate them themselves. The UDF adopted demands for the release of Nelson Mandela but refused to endorse the armed struggle while maintaining a deeply cynical ambivalence about the use of violence.

They also put paid to Botha's hopes of associating the black middle class with the reform programme by handing over power to them in the form of local councils. A UDF campaign to boycott the elections drove turnout down below 12%. The fact was that these reforms were all too little and too late. Rather more cynical was the assessment that with power comes responsibility and the most unpleasant responsibility was the one that involved raising taxes. In 1979, rents had gone up in Soweto to pay for improvements and in 1983, they went up again, a fact that the UDF made the most of; the councils were also instantly corrupted as bribery, the manipulation of licences and the disappearance of revenues into private pockets became widespread.[490] As the townships and squatter camps continued to grow, councils also attempted to conduct slum clearance operations which provided more ammunition for the UDF; councillors were attacked as 'sell-outs' and in 1984, the mayor of Sharpeville was killed on his own doorstep after shooting two demonstrators.[491] By 1985, widespread calls from the ANC and the UDF to 'Render South Africa Ungovernable' were beginning to be realised, with terrifying and terrible results.

Make the country ungovernable. This is the sort of slogan that revolutionaries provide as a vaccination against clear thinking about consequences but it is essential to actually think through those consequences if we are to understand what those slogans actually mean for ordinary people. First of all, it means that taxes are not collected and if taxes are not collected then civil servants, teachers, bin men and nurses don't get paid and their families go hungry, basic services collapse to the inconvenience of all and progress towards a better municipal future grinds to a halt. Secondly, it means that the authority of the police is refused which gives free rein to revolutionaries to substitute their own 'police' and 'people's justice' but also opens up space for burglars, gangsters, rapists and the criminal fraternity in general to go about their business unhindered. Thirdly, without law and property rights, shops get looted, businesses collapse and unemployment results. This, of course, is all very exciting for those revolutionaries who are on a secure payroll (such as Desmond Tutu, Winnie Mandela and Albertina Sisulu) but rather less exciting for the mass of people trying to make the most of their circumstances, get their kids into school and put food on the table. Fourthly, 'ungoverned spaces' are seldom ungoverned; rather they become the personal fiefdoms of gangsters, militias, self-defence organisations, vigilantes and self-proclaimed revolutionaries which in every case are worse than anything the police could ever

[489] Gordon Winter, *Inside BOSS*, (London, 1981) p.613.
[490] Beinart p.256.
[491] Beinart p.257.

think up. And, of course, the areas that did become 'ungovernable' or *liberated* during the mid-1980s were not the pleasant white suburbs but the townships. Fifthly, while there can be little doubt that most township dwellers were in favour of change, the organisers of the many protests took little care to ensure that demonstrations were not taken over by the murderous, the thrill-seekers or the irresponsible and turned into rampaging mobs; indeed, in deliberately confronting the police, many activists hoped for exactly this in order to provoke the police into over-reaction whereupon the resultant funerals of those killed could become the basis for another demonstration in a cycle of protest and violence that became almost self-sustaining. The results were, as one contemporary observer described them, horrific.

> It has produced these young 'comrades', who now fight side by side with the tsotsis, the young thugs, the most dehumanised victims of apartheid. Black workers returning to the townships are made to give the clenched-fist Black Power salute, and while their arms are raised their watches are stripped from their wrists and the money snaked from their pockets. The jittery police, who will now shoot anything, even a child, if it moves the wrong way are bad enough; workers also have to reach home through a tight cordon of youths with dead eyes and long spikes cobbled up from bicycle spokes. An old friend, an elderly black woman, weeps because her son is a policeman and she thinks her house will be burned down and she murdered inside it. The townships are hell-holes because everyone is afraid. Transport drivers are afraid. Garbage collectors are afraid. Rent collectors won't go near the townships. Repairmen are afraid. Residents are afraid. God knows, maybe even the tsotsis are afraid.[492]

The symbol of this 'ungovernability' was the *necklace* which, before going any further, I would recommend you witness by pulling up any of a number of videos on the subject from your favourite video-sharing website. Once you have seen how 'revolutionary justice' is applied and enforced by means of a tyre filled with petrol, hung around a person's neck and then ignited then perhaps your enthusiasm for 'liberation' and 'the struggle' as envisaged by the ANC, SACP and UDF will be somewhat tempered. I experienced this crisis personally in 1989, just before the Berlin Wall came down, when during my course in Multicultural Education a fellow student rattled a tin at me and asked me for a donation to the ANC. I was utterly opposed to Apartheid and had no time whatsoever for racial discrimination and had previously put my spare coins in such tins but then, at that time, the media was awash with images of Winnie Mandela's supporters putting necklaces on black people who they felt were insufficiently dedicated to the cause. This was Conrad's *Heart of Darkness* writ large and when I thought that my donation might be used to buy a gallon of petrol and a box of matches for such a purpose, I baulked. No amount of 'what about the police brutality?' could excuse this barbarism. Similarly, when I raised the objection that Winnie Mandela herself appeared to be quite deranged and an Imelda Marcos in the making, I was met with this less than reassuring counter-argument: 'Well, Walter Sisulu has had a word with her and she's going to calm down a bit from now on.' The result was that I could not bring myself to donate, because I could not reconcile the desired end to these appallingly undesirable means. However bad things were under Apartheid, I felt that things could only be worse with Winnie Mandela in charge – she had already been responsible for the murder of 14 year old Stompie Moeketsi[493] – and that I would only make things worse by committing to a side.

It is true that these organisations did make some attempts to dissociate themselves from the practice, but this was nothing more than the 'shameful shuffling of feet';[494] with Winnie Mandela repeatedly declaring that 'with our boxes of matches and necklaces, we will liberate this country,'[495] and ANC spokesman Alosi Moloi asserting that 'we want to make the death of a collaborator so grotesque that people will never consider it,'[496] they could do nothing else. Still, their attempts to classify this as 'defensive violence' because the security forces committed violence too, are nothing more than contemptible sophistry. Mealy-mouthed and leading from

---

[492] Marq de Villiers, *White Tribe Dreaming* (Canada, 1987) p.361
[493] https://www.nytimes.com/1997/12/04/world/winnie-mandela-s-ex-bodyguard-tells-of-killings-she-ordered.html
[494] Quoted in Reidwaan Moosage, *A prose of Ambivalence; Liberation Struggle Discourse on Necklacing* (University of Western Cape, 2010).
[495] Quoted in Reidwaan Moosage, *A prose of Ambivalence; Liberation Struggle Discourse on Necklacing* (University of Western Cape, 2010).
[496] Quoted in Reidwaan Moosage, *A prose of Ambivalence; Liberation Struggle Discourse on Necklacing* (University of Western Cape, 2010).

the rear as usual, Oliver Tambo condemned the practice but felt 'unable to condemn'[497] those who used it. As one commentator put it:

> They could not explicitly condemn the practice [of necklacing] and risk losing their mass support base, nor explicitly condone the practice and risk losing the support of important internal and international constituencies.[498]

The TRC named Councillor Benjamin Kinikini as the first victim of necklacing when, on 23 March 1985, he and four of his sons and nephews were 'stoned, stabbed and necklaced.' His widow testified before the TRC that;

> 'I was told that he was stabbed by a spade on his head, then they stabbed him several times. He was made to drink petrol, they put a tyre over him and then they ignited him. During this time my younger son was hiding under the car, some of the petrol got to him and when he was trying to escape somebody saw him.

> Silumko was hiding in one of the shops at Mboya. He asked one of the businessmen to hide him under the counter. They took him and they ignited him alive in front on the shop. I am telling you as it is. They cut his testicles while he was still alive....at that time I had not seen [the bodies] yet ... I will not be able to tell you about the head of my husband.'[499]

Ms Fulani's ordeal of April 1985 was worse, if that can be imagined. After shooting her policeman husband;

> 'They took him out of the house. They had black plastics and five litres of petrol and some tyres ... Then I was made to watch him. I was made to look at him for the last time. During all this time I had only a night-dress on. I was told to stand outside and look as this dog was dying. Then I asked them to burn him with me because I could not endure to listen to his cries. They said the petrol that they had was only for him. They were going to burn me up tomorrow. They made him drink petrol and he was also crying that he must be burnt with me ... They burnt him right in front of me until he died.'[500]

She was only spared because she was pregnant and because the mob had run out of petrol; eight hundred people died in circumstances such as this and just about all of them were black. These were tactics indistinguishable from those of the Ku Klux Klan.

Benjamin Kinikini and Aubrey Fulani were killed because they were state employees and it can therefore be argued that the murders (if not the method) were justifiable acts of violent political resistance but 'ungovernability' let other demons out of their cages - quite literally in the case of the youths who killed 32 elderly ladies in Lebowa after denouncing them as witches[501] and in the case of the three poor women who were tortured to death in January 1986 with red hot iron bars for the same offence.[502] Phinda Baartman survived a necklacing – he was actually a UDF supporter but 'ungovernability' meant that an accusation was as good as a conviction to the 'comrades', gangs, 'street committees', and kangaroo courts of feral youth. Nor were Councillors willing to simply stand back and be massacred but instead formed self-protection/vigilante groups such as the Peacemakers in the Port Elizabeth area while other groups, such as AmaAfrika were formed to prevent the UDF completely disrupting life with boycotts and school strikes; in each case, fighting with pro-UDF groups of greater or lesser discipline resulted.[503] In Natal, the fighting took on a further dimension with bloody clashes between Inkatha and the UDF. Indeed, reading through the TRC reports, you can't help but be struck by the sheer formlessness – 'anarchic'[504] even - and variety of the violence before you have even begun to deal with the political violence or the security force responses. The UDF certainly succeeded in rendering

---

[497] Quoted in Reidwaan Moosage, *A prose of Ambivalence; Liberation Struggle Discourse on Necklacing* (University of Western Cape, 2010).
[498] Reidwaan Moosage, *A prose of Ambivalence; Liberation Struggle Discourse on Necklacing* (University of Western Cape, 2010).
[499] TRC Vol.3. Ch.2 para.269
[500] TRC Vol.3. Ch.2 para.270
[501] Beinart p.261.
[502] TRC Vol.3. Ch.2 para.270
[503] TRC Vol.3 Ch.2 para.240
[504] No.10 Record of Conversation, Chequers Seminar 13th September 1985. https://www.margaretthatcher.org/document/145419

many – but my no means all - of the townships of South Africa ungovernable in 1985 but in creating a political vacuum that they had neither the skill not the ability to fill, they brought misery to many thousands of mainly black, urban South Africans and advanced the cause of liberation not one jot. Indeed, mind-boggling incompetence was one of their hallmarks; in 1984, several UDF activists decided to occupy the British Consulate in Durban but in choosing their target they neglected to note either the actual size of the Consulate or the absence of toilets, which meant that they were confined to a 7ft x 10ft room on the seventh floor of an office block for an extended period of time, most of it cross-legged (a chemical toilet was eventually squeezed in for them), with no direct access to the media.   Elsewhere, across most of the country, the government remained firmly in control.

While all this was going on, the ANC was busy putting down the mutinies in MK and continuing to do nothing very effective against Apartheid. Indeed, unable to establish proper channels of communication between its activists inside the country and those outside it, it was forced to allow the UDF and other organisations to operate as a sort of franchise whereby they could claim inspiration and the general direction of the ANC without actually being directly linked to it. When the government tried to prosecute on the grounds that it was just a front organisation for the ANC, all such prosecutions failed simply because the UDF was *not* such an animal. This in turn led Tambo and the Lusaka lounge lizards to fear that they might be displaced and side-lined as the main opponents of apartheid and frequent criticisms were made of the UDF's efforts to bring about change by legal methods rather than the violent ones that the ANC promoted but couldn't actually organise. Early on, Indians were singled out for suspicion, including Pravin Gordhan[505] who would do so much to prevent President Zuma's ANC from stealing whatever was left of the national wealth during his disgusting tenure of office. Much the same went for the ANC's view of Inkatha whose leader Buthelezi was attempting to carve out a non-racial, non-communist, Africanist future and who dominated Natal. His habit of pointing out that Tambo & Co had no mandate, had never put the concept of armed struggle to the vote and had abandoned black Africans for a life of comfort in exile did little to endear him to the ANC who were showing the same dictatorial tendencies which made them demand that as Black Consciousness should recognise their primacy, so should Inkatha. By the mid-1980s, the rancour of the ANC resulted in a number of death threats being made against Buthelezi to which he responded by forging links with the government to create what would later become known as the Third Force.[506] Thus did the bungling Tambo drive the leader of the largest ethnic group in the country into opposition to the ANC.

Nor was the ANC able to do very much to intervene directly in the township revolts, mainly because they had more important things to do such as moving out of Mozambique after the 1984 Nkomati Accords saw their expulsion. There were several hundreds of members there, all eating and soaking up the donations in payroll, none doing anything very effective and all now needing to be relocated first to Swaziland and then, after being expelled from there too, to Lusaka. Yet another report into the ANC reported drunkenness, incompetence, racism, weak leadership, a brutal security department and interminable gossip to be its main characteristics and like all such previous reports, it was roundly ignored.[507] With non-military donations rolling in from the UN and Scandinavia running at around $50 million p.a., plus the lucrative drugs and smuggling sidelines, there was little incentive to change. Indeed, with the townships going up and a revolutionary situation developing, the ANC did what they were best at; they organised another conference.

The Kabwe conference of June 1985 in Zambia finally committed the ANC to non-racialism and opened up the NEC to white people – whereupon the SACP put its whole politburo including Joe Slovo and Ronnie Kasrils onto it, which meant that two thirds of the NEC were now SACP. Tambo was retained as their tame leader mainly because he made an acceptably mild frontman for them and because he 'could generally be relied upon to deliver whatever speech was put in front of him'.[508] Billed as council of war, the conference was dominated by further blather about tactics and whether the distinction between civilian and military targets should be blurred. It was a nice distinction but rather academic considering the incompetence of MK to attack any targets at all or even to identify who their enemies were; was it all whites, or just those who worked or voted for the

[505] Stephen Ellis, *External Mission; the ANC in Exile 1960-1990* (Oxford, 2013) p.212.
[506] TRCVol.3 Ch.3 para. 96
[507] Stephen Ellis, *External Mission; the ANC in Exile 1960-1990* (Oxford, 2013) p.214.
[508] Stephen Ellis, *External Mission; the ANC in Exile 1960-1990* (Oxford, 2013) p. 219.

National Party? Were black people who worked for the government targets too? When the more rabid functionaries such as Chris Hani favoured killing all whites, it had to be pointed out that there were several whites on the NEC itself. As usual, nothing much of use got past the hotel buffet, largely because of internal jealousies and rivalries, an inability to communicate with or organise sufficient forces inside South Africa, the interception and defeat of most of those MK groups that did attempt to cross the border and, of course, the fact that the organisation was riddled with spies and informers; and because NAT spent most of its time trying to root out such spies from the flood of recruits coming over the border from the townships. Not that the recruits were in for anything more serious than being warehoused in Angola against the glorious day when the leadership might actually put down its knives and forks and actually decide to fight the SADF.

Perhaps the only other thing of note achieved here was the burying of the report into the abuses of NAT power in Angola as rivalries between Hani and Mbeki and between MK and NAT, began to assume ever greater proportions. The persistent rumours of Mbeki being a CIA plant, the detention and murder of MK veteran Thami Zulu by the NAT and the bombing of the Andrews Motel in Lusaka to cover up corruption within NAT (among other incidents) made it apparent that the ANC was now no more than a collection of factions held together by the SACP. That October, Tambo declared that though the ANC/MK was willing to cause 'a lot of chaos' and were willing to see the death of 'many thousands', they stood no chance whatsoever of defeating the SADF. (In the same interview, he claimed that the ANC was not a Marxist party, which must have come as a hell of a surprise to Thabo Mbeki, SACP, who was sitting next to him).[509] Lord Thomas, the British historian to whom he vouchsafed this information, read the old fraud correctly from the outset; 'he is merely an attractive front for more dangerous forces.'[510] In a later Thames TV interview, Tambo waffled endlessly and unimpressively about the 'end being in sight' but 'not in sight', about 'uncontrolled violence' and sanctions, but only managed to project an image of a bumbling mission school teacher.[511] No-one could possibly mistake him for a leader.

*

The government's response to the failure of its constitutional reforms and the emergence of the UDF was rather more coherent than that of the ANC. Convinced that the UDF was an off-shoot of the ANC and convinced that it was co-ordinating its actions with MK – especially after a car bomb was exploded outside the SAAF HQ in May 1983 – the strategy of decapitation of the leadership (often by assassination), containment of rebellion and development to take away economic and social grievances, that had already served them so well was adopted and intensified and wielded into a single policy for deployment at home and abroad. The main innovation in what was a classic COIN approach was that whereas the standard practice, roughly speaking, was for intelligence agencies to acquire knowledge and then pass it for action to the police or army, from now on the two functions would be combined. So, for example, if a *Koevoet* unit caught a guerrilla, they would interrogate him themselves and then follow up on that intelligence themselves thus making the reaction time short and the response swift, nimble and deadly. Under Operation Barnacle, Special Forces units were deployed to the townships, while at Vaakplaas farm a facility was set up to 'turn' ANC operatives, torture the recalcitrant and train assassins. Just as RENAMO had been utilised as a 'contra-mobilisation' operation – mobilising one group of revolutionaries against another – the government also intended to make use of the tensions created by the UDF in the townships by supporting groups opposed to them. The most famous of these was Inkatha, who received training from the SADF in 1986 under Operation Marion. Operation Katzen in the Eastern Cape hoped to set up a Xhosa version of Inkatha but smaller vigilante groups were also supported in the petty rivalries and bloody feuds that characterised much of the violence in these years. The result was a low level civil war between different non-government groups from the mid-1980s onwards, brutal, bloody, terrifying and usually unsuccessful in whatever aims the antagonists set for themselves. The Midlands War between Inkatha and the UDF began in 1987 and lasted for three years.

Containment of the opposition at home remained difficult however, because, whatever the many excesses of 'comrades', *amaButho*, MK, ANC or the UDF, the fact was that in the townships there was a broadly based

---

[509] Lord Thomas Record of Conversation, 31st October 1985. https://www.margaretthatcher.org/document/150425
[510] Lord Thomas Record of Conversation, 31st October 1985. https://www.margaretthatcher.org/document/150425
[511] https://www.youtube.com/results?search_query=julius+nyerere+1985

opposition to Apartheid which was made worse by police tactics and responses. Riot squads deployed a variety of weapons against demonstrators including batons, dogs, armoured vehicles, CS gas, baton rounds, birdshot and ultimately bullets while actual Standing Orders for how to deal with political protests were often patchy or non-existent. Beatings, torture, electric shock treatment, simulated drownings and exposure to extremes of cold became depressingly frequent police tactics; deaths in custody were covered up with excuses so flimsy that it was a wonder the police bothered to think them up at all and, indeed, often they never did. Those who did come out of police cells were often maimed, had sustained injuries for life or collapsed into mental illness. All this tended towards an impression that the police were no longer serving and protecting the public but waging war upon them. Police figures for the period March-May 1985 reveal that 108 people were killed in the riots in Uitenhage-Port Elizabeth, of whom 68 were victims of the police and 40 those of the rioters,[512] and we may take the example of what happened there as fairly typical of very many other incidents.

Between 8-10th March, the police recorded 23 incidents of arson and 18 of stone-throwing which caused damage of R220,000 (for comparison, the average wage for black workers was R5,000 p.a. so in two days, the entire year's work of forty-four families was wiped out[513]). Six people were killed by the police. The following weekend, petrol bombs were thrown at the police; two policemen's houses were torched and another young man was shot in response; of those arrested, one was in the process of being tortured when Molly Blackburn of the Black Sash marched into the police station and stopped it. Police also ordered the funerals of those killed to be postponed, but the order was not widely understood and the funerals went ahead on 21st March. Police dispersed the crowd with gunfire, killing twenty and wounding at least twenty-seven more; because of orders to cut up rough, and believing that an attack on white people generally was on the way, the police had no other means of riot control at their disposal and so had little choice but to open fire or risk being lynched by the thousands of protestors. It was the finding of the TRC that although the police were actually justified in dispersing the crowd, they used 'grossly excessive'[514] means to achieve this, but the underlying story is really that all confidence in the police and judicial authorities evaporated because of incidents such as these.

And there is no really adequate way to tell the story of the suffering of activists in these years for they were legion. The truth is that the security forces declared war on their own people in these years, abandoned any semblance of law or restraint and committed one atrocity after another. Death squads routinely murdered suspects and then blew up their bodies with landmines to frame them as incompetent terrorists. Good people, like the lawyer Victoria Mxenge, were shot on their doorsteps or, like the 'Cradock Four', ambushed on lonely roads as they travelled from town to town. To go into a police cell risked the very real prospect of never coming out. Many never even got to the police station but were beaten, tortured and murdered, their bodies hastily buried in unmarked graves and their families left bereaved, without even the dignity of a funeral, for years. The TRC quite rightly picked out the case of Ms Phila Portia Ndwandwe whose body was exhumed in 1997, one of almost 250 people who had been killed in this way.

> 'She was held in a small concrete chamber on the edge of the small forest in which she was buried. According to information from those that killed her, she was held naked and interrogated in this chamber, for some time before her death. When we exhumed her, she was on her back in a foetal position, because the grave had not been dug long enough, and had a single bullet wound to the top of her head, indicating that she had been kneeling or squatting when she was killed. Her pelvis was clothed in a plastic packet, fashioned into a pair of panties indicating an attempt to protect her modesty.'[515]

It's always the detail that reveals the true nature of those who perpetrate such crimes. Not only did these bastards behave like animals towards this poor woman – they were too bloody lazy to dig a proper grave.

*

---

[512] TRC Vol.3 Ch.2 para.150
[513] Servaas van der Berg & Megan Louw, *Changing patterns of South African Income Distribution: Towards Time Series Estimates of Distribution of Income and Poverty* (University of Stellenbosch, 2003).
[514] TRC Vol.3 Ch.2 para.179.
[515] TRC Vol.2 Ch.6 p.543.

The business community both at home and abroad watched these developments with more than dismay. If a business and, as the economy is made up of businesses, an economy is going to continue to provide the necessary goods, services, jobs, profits and taxes to put food on the table and provide public services then it must be confident that an investment has a reasonable chance of seeing a return. Otherwise, the rational thing for an entrepreneur to do is sell up, liquidate the assets, let the workforce go and put the money realised into something less risky - under the mattress in extreme circumstances. So the maintenance of business confidence is vital.

Alongside this reality is the corresponding fact that governments can rarely raise enough revenue from taxation to satisfy their electorates' craving for ever higher public spending and ever lower taxes and so fill in the gap by borrowing on the international money markets. This is usually in the form of a loan or the issuing of bonds, which are promises to pay the loan back at a specific date along with some annual interest. The more confident lenders are in the ability of a government to repay loans and debts, the lower the interest rate charged. So, a government dents that confidence at its peril, for without the ability to borrow, a financial crisis immediately follows; if it cannot pay its bills, then public services are cut, public servants are sacked, taxes rise, consumption falls and private sector businesses crash. This is, of course, all music to the ears of the Left who believe that from the ashes of such a crash a revolutionary situation will arise and socialism will be born. What actually happens is that the quick, the smart and the wealthy get their money out while the poor, the workers and pensioners get shafted, socialism fails and then the socialists help themselves to whatever is left of the country's wealth and apply ruthless repression to those 'counter-revolutionary' forces who have the temerity to want to eat or get a job. Any decent government is therefore extremely careful to nurture business confidence and to reassure international lenders that they are good for anything they borrow. If you doubt this, compare the ease with which Britain or the USA finance their massive national debts with the attempts of Zimbabwe and Venezuela to borrow a couple of quid.

There had, of course, been campaigns to undermine confidence in the South African economy through sanctions but they had been no more effective in denting the financial standing of South Africa than the ludicrous campaigns to bring down Apartheid by preventing bat and ball games being played and banning disabled South African athletes from swimming competitions; 'little significant effect' was the judgement of the British Foreign Office on the grandstanding efforts of far-Left municipal socialists like Ken Livingstone and David Blunkett to pile sanction after sanction on South Africa.[516] As far as the British Foreign Office was concerned, the Commonwealth sporting boycott begun at Gleneagles in 1977, like the UN arms embargo and the expulsion of South Africa from the Olympics in 1970, was a useful way to divert attention from demands for more wide-ranging economic sanctions[517] and as we have seen, plenty of countries were willing to pay lip-service to sanctions against South Africa but very few were willing to actually carry them out; in 1979, Britain was negotiating to build a new power station in South Africa and feared that if she refused the contract, it would simply be snapped up by the Germans, thus achieving nothing but making British workers poorer.[518] There was also the possibility of South African retaliation in the form of restricting minerals vital to the British steel industry on which 300,000 jobs depended and, notwithstanding the fact that British investments in the rest of Africa at the time were three times those of investments in South Africa, the only other significant source of supply of those minerals was the Soviet Union;[519] in some cases, there was no other supplier than South Africa, especially for minerals vital to the aerospace and nuclear industries. In the case of oil, Iran happily sold the crude stuff to South Africa both before and after the Islamic revolution[520] and while the biggest source of the Soviet Union's hard currency - $500m p.a. – came from selling its diamonds through de Beers, it is hard to see why anyone would want to pay more than lip-service to an idea as bad as economic sanctions.

---

[516] FCO Briefing for Margaret Thatcher 31st May 1984, p.22 https://www.margaretthatcher.org/document/144540
[517] FCO Briefing for Margaret Thatcher 31st May 1984, p.37 https://www.margaretthatcher.org/document/144540
[518] Robert Armstrong to Margaret Thatcher, 2nd November1979. https://www.margaretthatcher.org/document/121049
[519] Cabinet Office Armstrong and Wade-Gery Note UK Interests in South Africa 19th September 1980.
https://www.margaretthatcher.org/document/116794
[520] FCO Minute to No.10 11th September 1985. https://www.margaretthatcher.org/document/145397

Again there was the staggering hypocrisy of black Africa to contend with too; in 1983, Kaunda of Zambia demanded of Margaret Thatcher that Britain should impose comprehensive and mandatory sanctions on South Africa, that the West should stop investing in South Africa, that the West should stop supporting South Africa 'militarily, morally and diplomatically', openly support the 'liberation movements' and 'strongly speak' against the South Africans[521] i.e. do virtually all the things that Zambia refused to do (bar the last; words are cheap; still, at least he had the good grace to thank her for the £4m loan that Britain gave him in the full knowledge that it would never be repaid). Margaret Thatcher's firm conviction was that 'the use of sanctions is never effective'[522] and in this she was supported by Foreign Secretary, Geoffrey Howe, who was of the equally firm conviction that it was in no-one's interests to 'provoke by drastic action a violent economic collapse.'[523] Veteran anti-Apartheid activist Helen Suzman agreed too, (as did Buthelezi, who spent four weeks in 1985 touring North America to speak against disinvestment[524]) dismissing them as ineffective, injurious and undermining the attempts of business to push back against the idiocies of Apartheid as well as impacting badly on those neighbouring states dependent on South African trade.[525] Industry, she told the French PM in 1985 'was the main force working against Apartheid.'[526]

Attempts to paint South Africa as an international pariah made good headlines at international conferences and good reading on placards outside the South African Embassy in Trafalgar Square (a demonstration that was roundly disapproved of by the ANC because the City Group Anti-Apartheid Movement backed the PAC[527]) but in international circles, pariah was a title for which there were many contenders; in the early 1980s, the focus was on the Ethiopian famine brought on by Soviet and Cuban backing for collectivisation programmes that resulted in the usual mass killings; the Soviet invasion of Afghanistan; also the only genuine spontaneous rising of the workers ever recorded – against the Soviet system in Poland; and, of course, the emerging UN investigations into that truly appalling experiment foisted on poor people by socialist intellectuals, the Cambodian killing fields, which saw off almost 5 million people from a population of 8 million, and thus broke yet another record for mass murder. Furthermore, there was a real fear that putting sanctions on South Africa would just drive the Afrikaaners into a laager from which it would be difficult to extricate them.[528]

What was spooking international investors was both the volatility and the continuing slide in the value of the Rand. In 1975, one US dollar was worth roughly R0.80c; in 1976, almost R0.90c; in 1980, R0.75c; in 1983, it went over parity to R1.20c; by the end of 1984, it was edging up to R2.0; by the end of 1985, it was trading at roughly R2.20c; in ten years, the Rand had fallen to a third of what it was once worth.[529] For Sterling, the story was the similar; in 1975, £1 bought R1.7c; in 1976, the dire financial situation brought on by Wilson and Callaghan's hopeless management of the UK economy gave the Rand a fillip and brought it up to R1.4c but by the end of 1977, it was back to R1.7c; by 1980, with the advent of effective financial management under Margaret Thatcher, the Rand slid to R1.85c despite high gold prices and a mini-boom; by 1982, it was touching the R2 mark but back down to R1.7c in 1983; by the end of 1984, it was trading at R2.3c and by the end of 1985, it had almost halved to R4; in ten years, against a currency as weak as Sterling was during the domestic upheavals of that period, the Rand had still lost almost half its value. Over the next five years, it would depreciate a further 20% to £1:R5 while the dollar rate would slip even further to $1:R2.6c. This meant that anything that South Africa wanted to buy from abroad was getting more and more expensive. South Africa, though still important, was also becoming less attractive as a market, slipping from being the ninth most important UK export market in 1975 to fifteenth in 1979,[530] while the value of British trade with Africa to the north was by 1984, roughly double what it was with Pretoria.[531] *That said*, as the economic incompetence of

---

[521] Kaunda to Thatcher, 5th May 1983. https://www.margaretthatcher.org/document/131857
[522] No.10 Record of Conversation with Dutch PM. https://www.margaretthatcher.org/document/126705
[523] G. Howe speech to The Royal Commonwealth Society, 14th Nov 1983. https://www.margaretthatcher.org/document/144501
[524] FCO Minute for Margaret Thatcher's meeting with Buthelezi, 31st July 1985. https://www.margaretthatcher.org/document/145283
[525] Helen Suzman speech to the European Democratic Group 10th July 1985. https://www.margaretthatcher.org/document/145348
[526] No.10 Record of a Conversation with M. Fabius. 1st August 1985. https://www.margaretthatcher.org/document/201030
[527] https://nonstopagainstapartheid.wordpress.com/2012/01/08/the-anc-the-kitsons-and-the-city-of-london-anti-apartheid-group-anc100years/
[528] British Consulate-General to FCO 1st April 1980. https://www.margaretthatcher.org/document/121061
[529] https://www.poundsterlinglive.com/bank-of-england-spot/historical-spot-exchange-rates/usd/USD-to-ZAR-1985
[530] Cabinet Office Armstrong and Wade-Gery Note UK Interests in South Africa 19th September 1980. https://www.margaretthatcher.org/document/116794
[531] FCO Briefing for Margaret Thatcher 31st May 1984. https://www.margaretthatcher.org/document/144540

black Africa worked its magic - $170 billion in debt by 1985 with $17 billion interest owing and nothing much to show for it[532] - South Africa retained its relative attractiveness in terms of investment and invisibles.[533]

None of this could mask the seriousness of the uncertainties though. In May 1984, the British Ambassador to South Africa, produced a devastating assessment of the South African economy which is worth quoting from at length as a fair guide to the problems facing the Botha government.

'The resources needed for the social and economic development of the non-white population, the economic and financial subsidies required to keep afloat economically unviable 'independent' homelands and to promote industrial decentralisation and the costs of staying in Namibia/SW Africa and the economic demands of rapprochement with Mozambique and other neighbours all increase the demands on the South African treasury. The consistent economic growth rates of the 1950s and 1960s have given way to negative growth rates....The population meanwhile has increased....a continuing drought, adverse trading conditions and a weakened gold price seem bound to depress the economy throughout 1984....The recent budget lacked credibility....Though very many blacks enjoy a high standard of living there are millions of South African blacks...who are on the same subsistence level as blacks elsewhere in Africa. The situation is unlikely to improve in the short term. White South Africans face a declining standard of living. Black economic aspirations have been disappointed.'[534]

All this was far more important than whether some South Africans played a bat and ball game with some Englishmen or New Zealanders, or whether a small British citizen brought up in South Africa called Zola Budd should be allowed to run in a race of longer or shorter duration. The real concern at the South African situation was driven by the hard-headed business notion that capitalism requires stable government to flourish and that increasingly P.W. Botha couldn't provide it. 'To allow the dogma of Apartheid to block the benign forces of the market place would be to the benefit of no-one,' declared the British Foreign Secretary in November 1983.[535] 'Seldom, if ever, since the end of the Second World War, has the South African economy been in such dire straits,' was the 1984 view of one bank.[536]

*

P.W. Botha was aware of the worsening economic situation but also aware that his triumph over Mozambique in 1984 had opened up some cracks in the diplomatic isolation that had been imposed on South Africa since the 1960s. Despite the spluttering protests of black Africa, many states had maintained regular diplomatic contacts of a greater or lesser extent with South Africa throughout the 1970s and into the early 1980s but the public nature of the Nkomati Accords blew away all the fig leaves of supposed non-contact; if Samora Machel could meet with the South Africans, went the thinking, then why not the Europeans or the Americans? In early 1984, the Portuguese had issued an invitation to the South Africans to visit Lisbon, which was promptly seized upon by the Germans who were slavering at the commercial possibilities presented by the South African electrification programme. Seeing which way the wind was blowing, the British quickly followed suit and offered lunch at Chequers.

This was a major opening for the South Africans for despite their love-hate relationship with the British (mostly the latter, among Afrikaaners), it was British recognition and involvement that they most craved - simply because they trusted the Americans even less. The British, went their reasoning, at least understood *something* about Africa while the Americans, they supposed, would be hard placed to find it on a map. They also grudgingly accepted that though they had no love for the British, Africa had been a whole lot more predictable when the Union Jack fluttered over it than it was under the various dictators, incompetents and Marxist ideologues that they now faced. Black Africa recognised to their horror that this was indeed an opening too; being for the most part increasingly dependent on the financial aid that the West extended and which the Soviets

[532] UKE Dar es Salaam to FCO 24th July 1985. https://www.margaretthatcher.org/document/145352
[533] FCO Briefing for Margaret Thatcher 31st May 1984. https://www.margaretthatcher.org/document/144540
[534] UKE to FCO 30th May 1984. https://www.margaretthatcher.org/document/144544
[535] G. Howe speech to The Royal Commonwealth Society, 14th Nov 1983. https://www.margaretthatcher.org/document/144501
[536] UKE Pretoria to FCO 1st August 1984. https://www.margaretthatcher.org/document/144488

were unwilling or unable to provide, they wondered just what would happen to their aid subsidies if the South Africans managed to pull off a rapprochement with Europe.[537]

A storm of protest was manufactured, the most remarkable of which came from the man who was busy starving half a million of his fellow citizens after having already murdered widely and indiscriminately; the Swedish representative of Save The Children reckoned that a thousand children had been killed by his militias and their bodies left out for the hyenas in 1977 alone; it was widely rumoured that he had had the body of the overthrown Emperor Haile Selassie buried under his toilet. So step forward that darling of Castro and the Soviet Union, (and recipient of Bob Geldof's formidable, admirable but naïve energy, which produced *Live Aid* and mobilised the largesse of British and American pop fans to feed his starving people, while he exported food and imported whisky and weapons), Mengistu Hailie Mariam of Ethiopia, Chairman of the Organisation of African Unity. His lambasting of P.W. Botha and Apartheid as 'obnoxious', condemning people to 'permanent slavery and undignified existence', 'brutal oppression and merciless oppression', a 'callous and criminal disregard for basic human values and democratic rights', 'wanton and systematic destruction of life and property' which made South Africa an 'international outlaw' stands as perhaps the most unedifying example of the pot calling the kettle black imaginable.[538]

In Britain, the Anti-Apartheid Movement, founded in 1959 and run by the SACP (as was its sister organisation, the International Defence Aid Fund, set up to channel funds to ANC defendants in 1956: it published Brian Bunting's *The Rise of the South African Reich*), had been steadily growing in strength and numbers – it's message was hardly a difficult sell – and quickly attracted support across the political spectrum. (Ironically, it was based in Selous Street, London). Unfortunately, at the behest of the Soviet Union and the OAU, it quickly took up the campaign to bring about economic sanctions and so lost much of the support and sympathy of those of a conservative disposition. This is not something that the AAM particularly regretted as it allowed them to occupy the moral high ground alone while demonising their conservative political opponents as supporters or dupes of Apartheid, which they were very definitely not. In 1964, they overplayed their hand by trying to force economic sanctions onto the Labour Party during the election campaign, only to be rebuffed by Harold Wilson once he had garnered their votes (300,000 steelworkers jobs depended on South African minerals; but no student grants or academic salaries). After that blind alley, they shifted to campaigning for an academic boycott in support of Jack Simons, the SACP ideologue, (who in 1984 was filling up young minds with Marxist drivel in the 'University of the South') and Frank Kitson, who had been arrested for MK activities. From then on there were the usual demonstrations, vigils undertaken by people whose minds were woollier than their hats, displays of comradely solidarity, letter writing campaigns, demands for disinvestment, boycotts of oranges, etc etc none of which had any effect at all but which were usually characterised by a visceral hatred for America and 'Maggie Fatcha', a blindness to the many outrages of the Soviet Union, an equally blind faith in the coming Marxist Utopia, faction fighting and a depressing social life in run down pubs among wimmin called Roz wearing leggings, combat boots and a permanent look of frustration and dissatisfaction. Indeed, during the 1980s, it was fashionable for students to sport a whole load of lapel badges proclaiming adherence to campaigns to 'Save the Whale', 'Free Nelson Mandela', 'Say No to Cruise and Trident', 'Troops Out' (of Northern Ireland), 'Nuclear Power – No Thanks' and 'The Miners United Will Never Be Defeated' (they weren't and they were) without this ever really impinging on the views of the general public who kept on voting for a Conservative government who agreed to items one and two of the agenda but resolutely opposed the others. The more cynical liked to wear badges that said 'Save the anti-nuclear whale, win a cruise and get a free Nelson Mandela' but when this spilled over into the relentlessly black humour of the Federation of Conservative Students' cry to 'Hang Nelson Mandela', the Conservative Central Office frowned and began to look for ways to shut the society down (which it did on trumped up charges of a riot at Loughborough University which never happened). The last thing the Conservatives wanted was to cede any more of the moral high ground; the Mount of Olives was crawling with enough orcs as it was. None of this stopped the deluded, old socialist windbag Barbara Castle MP claiming in 1999 that it was the AAM that brought down Apartheid South Africa though.[539]

---

[537] Colin Welch, *How Africa Could Have helped Mr Kinnock's Learning Processes,* The Spectator 3rd August 1985.
[538] Mengistu message to Margaret Thatcher 12th May 1984. https://www.margaretthatcher.org/document/144571
[539] The Anti-Apartheid Movement: a Forty Year Perspective. Symposium at South Africa House, London 25-26th June 1999. https://web.archive.org/web/20070509010117/http://www.anc.org.za/ancdocs/history/aam/symposium.html

(I once came across her in the Pack Horse Hotel, the best in Bolton - naturally - noisily demanding that the kitchens be opened and the chef brought back from home so that she could get something to eat; it was perhaps an urban legend that she never stayed in Blackburn, her own constituency, because there was nowhere good enough for her).

The British government's official position remained remarkably stable throughout the decolonisation period and when Margaret Thatcher came to power, she continued with it. Basically, the policy was one of gradual push to get South Africa to ameliorate and then end Apartheid without pushing so hard that the country collapsed in revolution and allowed the Russians, Cubans and East Germans to step in. There was also nuance; Black nationalism was not be confused automatically with communism and there was a recognition that what empty vessels like Julius Nyerere (an autodidact who had studied at the feet of a hopeless teacher) might say in public was usually quite different to both his private utterances and his actual actions and what went for him went for Machel, Kaunda and Dos Santos too; it was possible that both Mozambique and Angola could be tempted out of their Soviet inclinations. Sanctions, other than the symbolic arms and sporting embargoes, were to be avoided as economically damaging to the UK and causing unemployment in South Africa. Reagan's America followed a similar line, but saw things more firmly through the prism of the Cold War and appointed Chester Crocker as the point man in southern Africa to run a policy of 'constructive engagement' based on the view that;

> Apartheid... was not only morally indefensible but in the long run unsustainable. Change was inevitable but bloodshed and destruction would be a tragedy for all South Africans....The US could not influence people if it treated them like moral lepers.[540]

Abandoning President Carter's Human Rights babble, Crocker believed in practical dialogue and diplomacy to bring about an end to Apartheid, get the South Africans out of Namibia/SW Africa and so prevent the advance of Soviet and Cuban influence. Perhaps the main difference in policy was that while the Americans agreed with the linkage between Cuba pulling out of Angola in return for South Africa pulling out of Namibia/SW Africa, Britain didn't think it was so important but was prepared to go along with it.

At home, the main difference between Margaret Thatcher's policy and that of her domestic opposition was that she was prepared to deal with the problem rather than just rant about it – making things better rather than simply feeling good about oneself. The public position of the Conservative Party had long been to oppose Apartheid without letting the communists take over, (mixed with a less publicly stated huge and justified scepticism about the competence of Black Africa to actually govern a country). Conservative Central Office were absolutely in accord with too.

> We are, after all, the party that considers people not as classes, groups or races, but as individuals; each worthy of consideration; each equal before the law; each with a right to make their own decisions and bear the responsibility for their consequences. A Party founded on the principle of one nation cannot condone a constitution founded on the principle of a superior race. A Party dedicated in its opposition to the class war cannot accept a nation divided into two classes distinguished by the colour of their skins.[541]

Margaret Thatcher, as Arthur Scargill, one of her greatest opponents said of her, always said what she meant and always meant what she said and her attitude to those who opposed the proposed Botha visit might best be summed up as polite disdain. This was justified because they rarely listened to her when she said that she was opposed to Apartheid. It never occurred to them that a capitalist might be against racism because they had so often convinced themselves that Apartheid was capitalism writ large rather than a major obstacle to its proper operation, in the same way that they thought that the self-evident end of the British Empire in Africa was really just a cunning plot to maintain colonialism and imperialism. To the leaders of black Africa, she simply pointed out that if Machel and Kaunda could talk to the South Africans then so could she, and in this she was supported by Buthelezi[542] and Van Zyl Slabbert.[543] It would, considered the Foreign Office, provide an opportunity for

[540] UKE Washington to FCO 17th April, 1985. https://www.margaretthatcher.org/document/145316
[541] Extract from a speech by John Selwyn-Gummer 31st May 1984. https://www.margaretthatcher.org/document/144543
[542] FCO Minute to No.10 11th May 1984. https://www.margaretthatcher.org/document/144493
[543] No.10 Record of Conversation 7th November 1984. https://www.margaretthatcher.org/document/145261

some plain speaking.[544] Desmond Tutu offered a long winded whine that the world would be hoodwinked by P.W. Botha if she met him (*oh, please!*) and that merely talking to him would confer respectability on Apartheid (*really?*). This, despite the fact that he admitted trying to get a meeting with P.W. Botha himself[545] and that less than three months later, the UDF would be *demanding*, in what can only be described as grossly offensive terms, that Britain intervene with the South Africans.[546] A year later, Neil Kinnock MP, the leader of the opposition, would be rubbing shoulders with Mengistu in a new Addis Ababa conference centre built within the stench of the mass graves of Ethiopians starved to death; (the MP for Flannelli, as *Private Eye* named him, would later lecture Tanzanian students on development economics which, one commentator noted, was like a blind man describing Impressionist paintings to a deaf audience[547]).

Trevor Huddleston, the veteran anti-Apartheid campaigner was invited to Downing Street to discuss the visit and was told by Mrs. Thatcher in no uncertain terms that 'it was not necessary to attempt to convince her that Apartheid was wrong. That was knocking at an open door.'[548] This did not stop Huddleston betraying the characteristic deafness of the AAM by saying that she was 'ambiguous' in her opposition, that P.W. Botha never attempted to talk to African leaders in South Africa (which was wrong), that Nyerere was not guilty of his own forced removals in his 'villagisation' programme (he was) and made demands worthy of Monty Python's People's Front of Judea. Very patiently, she maintained her position and denied his charges that she was seeking to overthrow the existing sanctions – an article of faith among the more rabid sections of the Left – and reminded him, (which he had clearly forgotten), that it was her that had ended white rule in Rhodesia. Well, old Trevor was a decent old stick and honest with it and I suppose he realised that he was just a 'useful idiot' used by the SACP/ANC to get into Downing Street when Oliver Tambo and Joe Slovo stood no chance until they renounced violence. That said, the old hypocrite did have the cheek to reference Mengistu as one of 'those who are striving for freedom' in a public protest letter that fairly dripped innuendo and arrogance which the AAM got him to hand in to Chequers when the meeting with the South Africans went ahead.[549] He then sent a Personal and Confidential note congratulating Maggie on her generosity and patience and thanking her for the 'encouragement and hope' she had given him – 'it was really all I could hope for' - in the full knowledge that convention prevented her from publishing that personal note.[550] It comes as rather a surprise that Margaret Thatcher, despite her public image, was, at times, prepared to suffer fools gladly.

In 2014, very many of the documents concerning the South African visit were declassified and among them was the Botha visit Foreign Office Briefing notes provided for Margaret Thatcher. This remarkable 102 page document, which she read from cover to cover and marked up with her characteristic underlining, laid out the policy, rationale and aims of the visit for the British as well as a careful choreography of 'tete-a-tete', working lunch and press arrangements. Her grip of the material was evident throughout the subsequent meeting which she conducted with firm charm and without recourse to the handbagging she was accustomed to mete out and, by and large, the meeting was a success. This was in contrast to the harangue that the Portuguese President delivered and which had P.W. Botha looking at his watch and getting ready to walk out, which would have ended the dialogue then and there. Margaret Thatcher's way was much better in that P.W. Botha went away under no illusions that if the South Africans wanted the co-operation of the West, they would have to get out of Namibia/SW Africa, free ANC leaders, make ever more moves towards ending Apartheid, forge better relations with her neighbours and could not expect either the sporting or arms embargo to be lifted until she did. Requests to close the ANC offices in London were firmly rebuffed.

Although the South Africans were pleased just to be talking to the British and Europeans, it was clear that the message P.W. Botha received from them was discouraging; 'South Africa would never be able to evolve a system of government that would satisfy the Europeans,'[551] he declared to the National Party on his return,

---

[544] FCO Minute to No.10 13th April 1984. https://www.margaretthatcher.org/document/144577
[545] Bishop Tutu letter to Margaret Thatcher 25th May 1984. https://www.margaretthatcher.org/document/144530
[546] Yunus Mahommed to Margaret Thatcher 14th September 1984. https://www.margaretthatcher.org/document/144479
[547] Colin Welch, *How Africa Could Have helped Mr Kinnock's Learning Processes*, The Spectator 3rd August 1985.
[548] No.10 Record of a Conversation, Margaret Thatcher and Bishop Huddleston, 30th May 1984.
https://www.margaretthatcher.org/document/144545
[549] Bishop Huddleston's letter to Margaret Thatcher, 2nd June 1984. https://www.margaretthatcher.org/document/144536
[550] Bishop Huddleston's letter to Margaret Thatcher, 3rd June 1984. https://www.margaretthatcher.org/document/144534
[551] UKE Cape Town to FCO 3rd July 1984. https://www.margaretthatcher.org/document/144513

which was not strictly true; a liberal, non-racial democratic one would do. All attempts to justify Apartheid were met with steely rejection but it was also true that the FCO learned that a much more sophisticated approach was needed to understand the mechanics of the internal South African situation, rather than just dismissing it as black vs white issue. Perhaps the major result, thought the FCO, was that P.W. Botha had been drawn out of his laager and from that more promising things might flow. Particularly promising for black South Africans was that Margaret Thatcher had now opened a door through which she could (and did) badger P.W. Botha on all sorts of issues such as forced removals and cross-border raids. This was bound to have a greater effect on his thinking than banner waving Marxists and anything that the ever ineffectual ANC did. Indeed, 52 townships were spared forced removal in part due to Maggie's ear-bending.[552]

This was movement and 1985 opened with P.W. Botha bringing forward a series of measures which aimed at gradually abandoning Apartheid and extending political, economic and residential rights to urban blacks. These were frustratingly small and hedged about with so many qualifications and caveats designed to placate his increasingly suspicious Afrikaaner *Verkramptes* that they were widely dismissed and, at best, only cautiously welcomed.[553] Going forward at such a glacial speed produced a constant anxiety in Washington and London that Botha would frustrate their policy of constructive engagement by not seizing the moment and exploiting the political space that had been opened up for him. Indeed, although the level of township dissatisfaction remained high and clashes with the police continued to occur, the fact that neither the UDF, the trade unions nor anyone else could produce any effective leadership meant that P.W. Botha was able to go at his own chosen speed. However stretched the police were, the army was waiting in the wings, the ANC were nowhere and the Frontline States might fairly be renamed the REMF States. When, in July 1985, Botha introduced a State of Emergency for the disturbed areas, he could be sure of containing any more violence and thus had every opportunity for a great leap forward; but then in August, after declaring that South Africa had 'crossed the Rubicon' in its commitment to ending Apartheid, he failed to take the opportunity for a bold and sweeping programme while he still could. It seemed that he was ignoring the warnings coming from Washington and London.

There was, however, one thing that could not be ignored; economic sanctions. So far, they had been successfully resisted by both Thatcher and Reagan but the endless films of township violence flooding Western TV screens by journalists who simply could not resist signalling their virtue or revelling in the gore, resulted in more and more calls for economic sanctions that would bring down the Botha government. Continued political resistance to these demands meant the continued expenditure of political capital and this, the South Africans knew, would not continue forever. Looming ever closer on the horizon was the Commonwealth Heads of Government meeting due to take place in October where it was a virtual certainty that effective economic sanctions would be enacted, while in Washington and Europe a similar prospect was in the offing for the summer of 1985. These sanctions would not be fatal but they would be unwelcome. In the event, something far more damaging happened though; in 1985, Chase Manhattan bank took the decision not to roll over its loans to South Africa and thus signalled that Apartheid was not a sustainable business proposition. Then Harry Oppenheimer sent his men to Lusaka to open up direct talks with the ANC and from London came the blunt opinion of the Rothschilds, in a note terse to the point of contempt, that P.W. Botha should 'publicly state as a matter of urgency that you have decided (not "intend") to renounce apartheid, but in an orderly fashion.'[554] 'Admirably succinct', was how Margaret Thatcher described the message.[555]

Capitalism was coming to the rescue of the townships.

Now, as that is the sort of statement that makes the Left shudder, I'll qualify it by an extensive quotation from Vella Pillay, SACP, and leading light of the Anti-Apartheid Movement, whose opinion was informed by hindsight;

---

[552] UKE Cape Town to FCO 10th May 1985. https://www.margaretthatcher.org/document/145313
[553] NSC Comment on Botha letter to Reagan 8th February 1985. https://www.margaretthatcher.org/document/110536
[554] Lord Rothschild to President Botha 28th August 1985. https://www.margaretthatcher.org/document/145296
[555] FCO Minute for Norgrove. 30th August 1985. https://www.margaretthatcher.org/document/145297

It is my judgement that what broke the back of the apartheid regime… was the refusal of the international banks to renew South Africa's bank loans so that it could no longer raise funds abroad….

The State of Emergency which was declared in mid-1985 in South Africa was a further catalyst in this regard. Led by Chase Manhattan, the New York banking community refused to roll over the expiring loans to South Africa. With the de facto freeze of real investments from abroad, this development proved decisive in the sense that it led to a collapsing domestic economy, accompanied by sharp falls on the South African Stock Exchange and the heavy depreciation of the Rand. South Africa was forced to renege on repayments of its expiring loans and sought a three-year period of grace for repaying its outstanding international debts. The three-year moratorium was provided at a heavy cost, leading to a further deterioration in domestic economic stability. With the falling gold price, the financial crisis became overwhelming, leading the then President P W Botha to fly to Zurich to plead for fresh loans and later to visit London for a similar purpose. The failure of those visits proved to be a critical aspect of the process which led to the resignation of Botha and the opening of contacts with the ANC.[556]

Pillay claimed that it was he who persuaded the American banks to disengage, but such decisions are made on commercial grounds, not because of the tedious representations of a raddled old communist. (And Botha resigned because he had a stroke. And contacts with the ANC had been opened long before. Ho hum. Never mind. The gist of his view is correct). The reality was that South Africa still remained a decent business proposition and would continue to be one if something was done about the political situation and it was thus in the interests of both international finance, domestic business and black workers to see that something *was* done promptly.[557] On August 29th, 1985 a joint statement was issued by the South African Association of Chambers of Commerce, the Federated Chamber of Industries, the National African Federated Chambers of Commerce and Industries, and the Urban Foundation (an Oppenheimer organisation dedicated to improving black housing) calling for negotiations with black leaders, the end of the State of Emergency and the rapid dismantling of Apartheid.[558] Unlike the looting of a township bottle store or the necklacing of an innocent, these were protests that could not be ignored or dealt with by the army.

Chase Manhattan's decision came as something of a surprise to both the US and British governments who decided then and there that government sanctions were no longer necessary. This was not the view taken by the AAM, who hoped that even deeper sanctions would lead to a rapid collapse of the South African economy, closely followed by that of the government and so open the way to reason, racial harmony, peace, rainbows and unicorns. Nor was it a view taken by the Commonwealth, who started to pile on the pressure, or the US Congress, who in response to a noisy press campaign, brought legislation forward that threatened the necessity for a Presidential veto. Afraid that a bandwagon had started to roll, in September Margaret Thatcher called for a major government seminar on South African policy while Reagan in Washington opened up a 'public diplomacy' exercise to educate US public opinion on constructive engagement. Delaying tactics in Congress were also employed to slow down and water down any talk of economic sanctions. In the event, the Presidential veto was used in September alongside a face-saving package of largely meaningless 'sanctions' aimed at placating Congressional opposition; the clause that declared that no new loans to South Africa would be permitted unless they were for 'good' works (a term left undefined) was a particularly fine example. Something more would be required at the Commonwealth Heads of Government meeting, however.

It was always going to be a difficult meeting, given the determination of Margaret Thatcher to avoid economic sanctions and promote dialogue, and given the deep hypocrisy and utterly revolting nature of very many of the Commonwealth leaders. Rajiv Gandhi, pudgy, posturing and corrupt, was Prime Minister of India simply because he was not called Gupta, Smith or Patel; the blood of Matabeleland was still under the fingernails of Mugabe; Bob Hawke of Australia was rabidly anti-British and very rarely sober; Machel (though not in the

---

[556] Vella Pillay, *British and International Relations with Southern Africa 1959-1994*. The Anti-Apartheid Movement: a Forty Year Perspective. Symposium at South Africa House, London 25-26th June 1999.
https://web.archive.org/web/20070509010117/http://www.anc.org.za/ancdocs/history/aam/symposium.html
[557] MacFarlane to White House 29th August 1985. https://www.margaretthatcher.org/document/111640
[558] UKE Pretoria to FCO 30th August 1985. https://www.margaretthatcher.org/document/145365

Commonwealth) offered to accept the inevitable hit to the economy of Mozambique that sanctions would entail – if he got compensation of course;[559] Kaunda, like a broken record, repeated the cant that the Frontline States were ready to accept the hardships that sanctions would bring – it was an easy thing to promise from the luxurious surroundings of a Caribbean Cay, especially when none of those leaders present would be forced to give up their Rolls Royces. Perhaps the only glimmer of light on the horizon was that Margaret Thatcher would be spared having to listen to Nyerere's third rate student politics as he was unable to attend. There were forty-five leaders of the Commonwealth present at the meeting and rabid for sanctions - but she still outnumbered them.

'Their knowledge of the situation in South Africa seemed slim; and their drafting skills rudimentary,'[560] said Thatcher's private secretary, Charles Powell, when they tried to bounce her into a declaration on sanctions. Exchanges with Bob Hawke were acrimonious, a subsequent meeting full of harsh words alongside accusations that the UK preferred 'British jobs to black African lives,'[561] with several lectures on morality and human rights thrown in for good measure. Thatcher would later admit that the debate had been 'a highly unpleasant and bitter one' in which she had been handed 'a good deal of abuse.'[562] None of it made any difference though, simply because she pointed out their own considerable hypocrisy and double-standards 'in no uncertain terms'[563] and dismissed their demands as she had dismissed Nyerere's made before the conference;

> 'I am certainly not prepared to create unemployment in Britain in order to create worse unemployment and disruption in South Africa. I do not argue that full-scale economic sanctions would not damage the South African economy. They certainly would. But I disagree with you over whether such damage would promote reform.'[564]

Her aim, she stated, was to preserve the South African economy so that it would be inherited by a South Africa without Apartheid and to reward Botha each time he carried out a reform, rather than endlessly pillorying him and forcing him back into the laager. She wanted to persuade him into dialogue with black South Africans so that some arrangement could be made to their mutual satisfaction – and it was no business of anyone else's what that arrangement looked like because the complexities of race, tribe and nationality were entirely different there than anywhere else. In order to do this, all parties had to renounce violence if any sort of negotiations were to take place. And just how would sanctions help the business community who were, right now, campaigning for reform? And besides which, just how useful would sanctions be when considered against the judgement of the financial markets?[565] By the time the meeting was over, Thatcher had, by turns, shamed and handbagged them so hard that she succeeded in 'making them all feel perfectly rotten'.[566] More importantly, she made no substantial concessions and had persuaded them to open up a dialogue with South Africa in the form of a Commonwealth Eminent Persons Group.

Was she right?

Undoubtedly; it was a meeting with the Eminent Persons Group for whom Nelson Mandela was poured into a new suit a few months later.

*

Opening up a dialogue with black leaders was a lot harder than it sounded, largely because Botha's government was faced with the dilemma of 'how to promote dialogue with leading blacks when so many of them are either under arrest or frightened away by other blacks'.[567] During the Rhodesia settlement there had been any number to choose from but the National Party's decapitation strategy meant that the UDF leadership had been incarcerated before it had gained any sort of leadership experience or formal political legitimacy. Those leaders

[559] FCO Minute to No.10. 25th September 1985. https://www.margaretthatcher.org/document/145378
[560] Charles Powell Record of Conversation, 21st October 1985. https://www.margaretthatcher.org/document/150929
[561] Charles Powell Record of Conversation, 21st October 1985. https://www.margaretthatcher.org/document/150929
[562] Margaret Thatcher to PW Botha 31st October 1985. https://www.margaretthatcher.org/document/111650
[563] Charles Powell Record of Conversation, 21st October 1985. https://www.margaretthatcher.org/document/150929
[564] Thatcher to Nyerere, 10th October 1985. https://www.margaretthatcher.org/document/150404
[565] FCO Minute to Charles Powell 1st November 1985. https://www.margaretthatcher.org/document/150942
[566] Charles Powell Record of Conversation, 21st October 1985. https://www.margaretthatcher.org/document/150929
[567] UKE Pretoria to FCO 22nd July 1985. https://www.margaretthatcher.org/document/145349

in the urban areas who were prepared to co-operate had been branded as 'sell-outs', often intimidated and in more than one case, necklaced, while those who weren't were very often little more than thugs. The ANC on Robben Island were not much of a prospect because they had been out of contact with the people and situation for some decades, while those abroad, like Tambo and the SACP, could hardly be mistaken for leaders capable of delivering anything but their orders from Moscow. Furthermore, whereas Botha insisted that order be restored in the townships before any dialogue was opened, the view from the townships was that Botha should call off the police and the army and only then should dialogue be initiated. Many looked to Buthelezi but despite the fact that he represented a sensible, moderate non-Marxist alternative, he commanded very little support outside his Zulu constituency. The British hoped that someone might emerge from the trade union movement while the Frontline States continued to insist that the ANC to be recognised, but neither of these things were likely to happen in the immediate future, which left just Desmond Tutu.

Even this was problematical. Although he was recognised as second only in popularity to Mandela among wide swathes of black opinion, behind the extroverted and engaging public persona was a fiercely ambitious, often rather vain man with a background in Liberation theology (a toxic mix of Marxism and Christianity) and a somewhat ambivalent attitude to the use of violence. Given to grandstanding, a love of the limelight, and being in possession of a Cheshire cat smile and a manner that was simultaneously gratingly patronising and holier-than-thou unctious, he was also too quick to accuse white people of racism on no good grounds at all and beyond critical of the two people who were doing most to pressurise Botha into movement – Reagan and Thatcher. Constructive engagement, he dismissed as 'evil, immoral and un-Christian'.[568] Being an Anglican Archbishop and thus freed from any adverse consequences of economic sanctions, he enthusiastically called for disinvestment and demanded that those Western businesses that did remain should immediately dedicate themselves to providing housing, education and training for their black employees; this just pointed out how economically illiterate he was. He also entertained a visceral and entirely un-Christian loathing for Buthelezi. Clearly, someone better than this was needed. On top of this, he wasn't ANC and as the ANC represented themselves as the voice of the people, they were unlikely to accept Tutu as anything but an ally or an adjunct, so it was back to Mandela.

One of the people pushing for talks to be opened up with Mandela was Hendrik Coetsee, the Minister of Justice since 1980, who also had responsibility for prison conditions and thus the opportunity and cover to initiate those talks. In an indication of just how small the politically networked world was in South Africa, it came as a fortuitous coincidence that Coetsee's old pal from college was a small town solicitor by the name of Piet de Waal, who just happened to be the only solicitor in the small Free State town of Brandfort, to which Winnie Mandela was exiled in 1977. Reluctantly forced into handling her legal affairs, de Waal and his wife gradually struck up a friendship with the loud, flamboyant and theatrically defiant Winnie, allowing her to meet with various foreign journalists and visitors in their house while simultaneously badgering Coetsee to lift the banning order and get her off their hands. Like many other white people, it was their personal experience of the security police that turned them against the system and when Mrs de Waal was arrested for being in a black area without permission – she had been giving Winnie a lift home – from that point on, Piet de Waal started to lobby Coetsee to start the process of springing Nelson.[569] At the same time, Niels Barnard, head of the National Intelligence Service, was keen to start finding out just who Mandela was and just what he stood for.

The National Party government began seriously grooming Mandela in April 1982 when he and his immediate colleagues, Walter Sisulu, Raymond Mhlaba and Andrew Mlangeni, were moved from Robben Island to Pollsmoor prison outside Cape Town. For several years the amount of his contact with the outside world had been steadily increased but it was clear that something more was being prepared, especially when the four found themselves in what was relatively quite luxurious accommodation and given access to outside newspapers. In 1984, conditions were eased once more, with the introduction of 'contact' visits with his family; 'It had been twenty-one years since I had even touched my wife's hand,'[570] wrote Mandela, with great pathos. This was followed by an interview with Lord Bethell, anti-communist campaigner, member of the House of Lords,

[568] UKE Pretoria briefing to FCO 16th September 1985. https://www.margaretthatcher.org/document/150442
[569] Allister Sparks, *Tomorrow is Another Country*, (London 1995).
[570] N. Mandela, *Long Walk to Freedom* (London 1994), p. 616.

supporter of Soviet political prisoners and the man who brought Solzhenitsyn's work to the West. It was the first of several interviews permitted with foreign observers and journalists. This resulted in January 1985 with P.W. Botha offering Mandela's release on condition that he renounced violence. Mandela refused, which was probably a bad idea, but at least an opening had been made. The problem was that, afraid of being accused of selling out, Mandela had stuck to the official ANC line. The decision was taken, therefore, to isolate him from the other ANC prisoners at Pollsmoor, in order to give him more space to think and to perhaps develop an independent line without, at the same time, giving anyone an excuse to accuse him of being 'turned' or selling out. The opportunity came when he was admitted to hospital in November 1985 and Coetsee called on him to hint about opening up talks. When he went back to prison, he went back to his own suite of (damp) rooms.

The tactic worked. The information that Mandela had at his disposal led him to the conclusion that there was a stalemate between the ANC and the government and that it was up to him to break it. At the same time, Coetsee made sure that he was able to communicate clandestinely with the ANC in Lusaka through his Greek lawyer, George Bizos. At the end of February 1986, Bizos was able to tell Coetsee that both Mandela and Tambo were ready to start talking. Within a few short weeks, Mandela had written to Coetsee asking to open up talks and in the summer of 1986, Coetsee invited Mandela around to his house for the first of many informal talks. At Christmas of that year, Mandela's day trips out were started. His guide was a warder with the wonderfully ironic name of Marx, who was able to take him up to the beautiful fishing village of Paternoster (which resembles Greece in the 1960s and even today (2019) remains unspoiled), allowed him to walk down Paarl High Street and gave him fish and chips in a traffic jam in the Bains Kloof Pass without him ever being recognised. Contacts with Coetsee were maintained throughout 1987 with the full knowledge of P.W. Botha until in May 1988, after he had been moved to a pleasant villa in the grounds of Victor Verster prison outside Paarl, more formal talks began. The timeline is important because it wasn't until the State of Emergency had defeated the UDF and the SADF had defeated FAPLA in Angola that P.W. Botha pushed ahead with the talks, secure in the knowledge that he had achieved the position of strength he so desired.

In many ways, the talks were frustrating because they tracked over the same old ground repeatedly. Botha wanted Mandela to renounce violence as a precondition of his release; Mandela refused on the grounds that this would throw away the ANC's main negotiating card. This simply revealed how far Tambo in Lusaka was keeping him in ignorance of the true state of MK. This went for the question of communism too; Mandela held to the point that the ANC was not communist but the SACP had been such firm and loyal allies that there was no question of abandoning them. The main sticking point was that of black majority rule; here Botha could not believe that the ANC would not fall on the Afrikaaners with naked revenge if they gained power and Mandela could not convince him that the commitment to non-racial democracy was genuine. Until the dual issues of Mandela's credibility and the future shape of the constitution could be resolved, there could be little hope of resolution; but there were grounds for optimism in the fact that both sides were sitting down to discuss difficult issues as equals, with mutual respect, and without underestimating each other's sincerity.

Mandela's anxiousness not to get out of step with Tambo revealed just how little he knew about the SACP's virtual annexation of the ANC and just how little control Tambo had over either organisation and just how hopeless MK was. It is hard now not to believe that he was being deliberately kept in the dark about such things. At the same time, many elements of the ANC distrusted him because he was being less than candid with them about the nature and extent of the negotiations and given the routine paranoia of the ANC in exile and the endless nervousness of each faction at the prospect of missing out on a fair grab of the spoils of political victory, a great deal of suspicion was created. Under these difficult circumstances, there was no way that the National Party could risk releasing Mandela until they were convinced that he was actually able to control the ANC, otherwise it was all too easy to imagine a complete breakdown of law and order, a three or four way race war, the necklacing of whites, the general ruin of the economy, several refugee crises as whites ran for Europe and Indians ran for India, amid a litany of all the other evils that had befallen Africa to the north.

Alongside these officially unofficial but still pretty much official talks, another much more surprising dialogue was taking place. In 1983, the *Broederbond* had chosen Piet de Lange as its new head and Piet de Lange had a wholly new conception of Afrikaanerdom than his predecessors, the inventors of Apartheid, had. For de Lange and his *verligte* Afrikaaners, the future lay in coming to terms with black majority rule and preserving the cultural and linguistic identity of the *volk* through all that that entailed. In 1984, he was able to persuade the *Broederbond* to accept this vision and from then on began to impress it upon P.W. Botha during their regular meetings. This was a message which could not be ignored, delivered as it was by the High Priest of Afrikaanerdom, but Piet the Crocodile (whose favourite song, incredibly, was the anti-slavery hymn 'Amazing Grace'[571]) still had to be dragged, kicking and screaming, down that road. At a 1986 Ford Foundation conference in New York, de Lange met Thabo Mbeki and impressed upon him in turn the importance of Botha's reforms in preparing the way for a change in mindset of the majority of Afrikaaners. For blacks, the abolition of the Group Areas Act might seem cosmetic but for the government, argued de Lange, it was a way to convince whites that they didn't need it to feel safe and secure. They next day, he told Mbeki that he intended to devote the *Broederbond* to national reconciliation, which was something that probably made Mbeki swallow his pipe but he was, indeed, genuine.[572]

Mbeki had also been meeting with British business leaders in an attempt to win them over to the ANC's sanctions policy but without much success, largely because the credibility of unsuccessful black African guerrilla leaders, who simultaneously declared themselves to be members of the SACP but not really communists at all, was not particularly high among people with the relevant business skills, knowledge and experience. However, Andrew Young of Consolidated Goldfields preferred to take a longer view, he having previously served as an advisor on Rhodesia to Edward Heath, and asked Tambo what he could do to help. Tambo wanted to speak to some well-placed Afrikaaners so Young began to tap some of his South African contacts who eventually yielded up two ANC-inclined Stellenbosch academics by the name of Esterhuyse and Terreblanche. Niels Barnard got wind of this almost immediately but instead of scuppering it, as Botha was more or less inclined to do with all such private contacts with the ANC, he gave them the nod as long as he was kept fully informed; what this meant was that as well as talking to Mandela in jail, he was also talking to Tambo and Mbeki in exile and meetings were duly set up. One of the other Afrikaaners invited to be part of this was 'Wimpie' de Klerk, brother to the rising National Party star, F.W. de Klerk. Between November 1987 and May 1990, twelve meetings took place between Mbeki and a range of prominent Afrikaaners in conditions of complete secrecy facilitated by the remoteness of the venue - Mells Park House in Somerset; it's a stone's throw from Bath and though I've been back and forward through that picturesque if occasionally wet part of the world for twenty years and more, I'd never heard of it until now (2019). The importance of these contacts should not be understated because the people at these meetings were actually the movers and the shakers - business, church and political leaders who had the power to take decisions, set the tone and direction and deliver the right messages into the right ears at the right time and were thus far more important than the more visible student demonstrators or township mobs, or even the more publicised meetings with white opposition leaders in Dakar, 1987, and Lusaka, 1989. The discussions were wide ranging as each side explored the other's ideology and positions but at least one participant noticed a real change in the content during 1988 as the Afrikaaners began to move from 'where and why we are' to 'where are we going and what happens next'. This in itself was remarkable, given the legendary pig-headedness of the average *verkramptes* Afrikaaner.

The increasing willingness of the ANC to engage in dialogue was driven largely by military and political defeat both inside and outside the country. With tens of thousands of people banged up in jail, banned or murdered, the townships under military occupation, and the ever ineffectual MK witnessing the collapse of the FAPLA offensive on the Lomba in Angola, there was little else that the ANC could do. Their operatives inside South Africa had halved from roughly 500 in 1986 to 222 in 1988.[573] Facing almost certain death when they did manage to infiltrate successfully, once there, they had no means of communication, little in the way of command and control and even less in the way of arms or training. It was also the case that Tambo & Co had almost no understanding of what was going on inside the National Party beyond what they could glean from the newspapers and this meant that they were no better informed of the situation than anyone else, which, for a theoretical government in waiting, was unforgiveable. It's probably fair to say that most of the ANC still had dreams of riding into downtown Pretoria on top of a tank, but the more realistic among them, like Mbeki, realised that this was never, ever going to happen and that the future lay in negotiations. What was worse was

[571] PW Botha's interview with Cliff Saunders, SABC 2006 https://www.youtube.com/watch?v=BDD6OfLabOQ
[572] Allister Sparks, *Tomorrow is Another Country*, (London, 1995) pp.73-74.
[573] Stephen Ellis, *External Mission; the ANC in Exile 1960-1990* (Oxford, 2013) p. 225.

that when negotiations opened up in 1988-89 for the Cuban withdrawal from Angola and the South African withdrawal from Namibia/SW Africa, nobody bothered to tell the ANC, let alone consult them, and as a result, MK was expelled from its main base in Angola. Even the Quatro Gulag had to be relocated to Uganda.

Even more worrying was the fact that their main sponsor, the USSR, was beginning to push the ANC in the direction of compromise and, more worrying still, engaging with the South Africans over their heads. This had begun in 1986-87 with a series of Soviet sponsored academic papers proposing constitutional arrangements based on the protection of white minority rights which mirrored P.W. Botha's thinking much more than Tambo's. They also voiced a real scepticism about the usefulness of the armed struggle and an even deeper scepticism about the possibility of socialism succeeding in South Africa. This was a message that was so unwelcome that it drew a less than enthusiastic response from *The African Communist*, the mouthpiece of the SACP in London, but was repeated by President Gorbachev in August 1987. That Gorbachev was now in the market for change was enough to send Tambo winging off to Moscow for reassurance and *The African Communist* into full grovel mode. Still though, it was not enough to prevent Franz Josef Strauss, a rather obscure Bavarian politician arriving in South Africa in January 1988, hot foot from Moscow, bearing the news that Gorbachev was so sick of throwing good money after bad in southern Africa that he was prepared to negotiate with anyone – not just the ANC and quite possibly with both the NP and Buthelezi - to get a solution. The idea that the ANC might be supplanted by the UDF, Black Consciousness orientated trade unions, the Pan African Congress or Inkatha fed into the growing sense of panic that all those years in exile might end up with the ANC being bypassed and their stipends being cut; in May 1988, it was announced that the previously Chinese orientated PAC had been invited to Moscow for talks, with visits by Desmond Tutu and a number of white South Africans to follow. Equally terrifying was the realisation that the prospect of the Red Flag fluttering over Cape Town was now regarded with horror in Moscow simply because it would mean another socialist basket case joining the queue of Cuba, Vietnam, Laos, Kampuchea and Ethiopia coming cap in hand to Moscow for bailouts that it could not afford; that went for Namibia/SW Africa too, where Gorbachev backed the US/South African stance over the Cuban withdrawal – the Soviets were, after all, picking up Castro's tab there too. Tambo and Slovo began to twist in the wind, firstly assuring Moscow that they were not against a negotiated solution and then, back in Lusaka, insisting on the permanence of what they were still calling with a straight face, the 'people's war'[574] and then setting up a commission to draw up a constitution in case negotiations were suddenly forced on them.

It was the Angolan situation that opened up the opportunity for direct USSR-South Africa negotiations and in March 1988, Pik Botha met with the Soviet Deputy-minister for Foreign Affairs in Mozambique. By the end of the year, USSR-South Africa trade relations beyond the long standing de Beers connection were under review and Soviet policy towards South Africa was beginning to look identical to the constructive engagement of Britain and the USA. Amidst talk of diplomatic relations being re-opened, Tambo then got a very abrupt snub when in March 1989, he went to Moscow but could not get a meeting with anyone higher than a non-voting politburo member.[575] There could be no stronger signal that Moscow was sick to death of the incompetence and ineffectiveness of the ANC and the cessation of arms supplies to MK that followed in August 1989 indicated a growing reluctance to keep funding this expensive and useless organisation. It would take the ANC/SACP's support for the coup against Gorbachev mounted by the hard line Stalinists they always preferred for funding to finally be cut off, but the fact was that Gorbachev had threatened the ANC where they felt it hardest – in their pockets.[576] Defeat was staring the ANC in the face. In August 1989, amid much blustering camouflage about intensifying the liberation struggle, the ANC's Harare Declaration committed them to a policy of ending Apartheid through negotiation. This was nothing less than an admission that MK had lost the war.

It's possible that P.W. Botha might well have had cause to feel pretty satisfied with himself. His Total Strategy had got the Cubans out of Angola, ended the financial drain both of the war and supporting Namibia/SW Africa, beaten the Angolans and Mozambicans, defeated MK, got the ANC kicked out of just about every one of the Frontline States and had contained the UDF rebellion within the country. He could believe that he had got the

[574] Centre for Strategic and International Studies; Africa Notes No.89, Sept 1st 1988.
[575] John F. Burns, *Soviets in Shift, Press for Accord in South Africa*, New York Times, 16th March 1989.
[576] R.W. Johnson, *The Past and Future of the South African Communist Party*, London Review of Books Vol.13 No.20 October 1991.

ANC to the negotiating table pretty much on his own terms but this was not quite true. He had been brought to this point mainly by American and British pressure alongside the quiet but irresistible pressure of capitalist finance both at home, in the shape of the Oppenheimers and others, and internationally by the hidden hand of the capital markets. Those who thought that demonstrations, township rebellion or the condemnations of the UN and OAU were the driving force behind the process were deluding themselves.

The problem was that his reputation as an uncompromising *verkrampte* who was too ready to wield the sjambok combined with his sheer stubbornness and reluctance to actually go to the negotiating table where he would have to yield to black majority rule, however favourable the terms, meant that it would not be him who would do the negotiating. In February 1989, when he was recovering from a stroke, he decided to resign as leader of the National Party. This was followed on August 14th by a decision by the rest of the cabinet to remove him from his position of State President and replace him with the new leader of the National Party, F.W, de Klerk. During a stormy meeting, Botha finally decided to go and that night announced his resignation in a long, rambling, angry TV address. No-one really knows why he resigned but it was supposed that he had another scheme up his sleeve which was to push the idea of a confederation of racial states that he preferred to the non-racial unitary state that just about everyone else wanted; he could not stomach 'one man one vote', thought the rest of his cabinet were weak and refused to believe that blacks could govern; perhaps more important was the possibility that he did not want to be the man who oversaw the end of Afrikaanerdom; he was unrepentant to the end and died in 2006, still bad tempered and furious.[577]

That F.W. de Klerk and other leading Afrikaaners within the National Party were prepared to enter into serious negotiations was largely because the contacts that they had built up with Mandela in jail and with the ANC negotiators at Mells Park had helped to dispel many mutual misunderstandings. Foremost among these was the idea that the ANC was a wholly owned subsidiary of the SACP. This was largely due to Thabo Mbeki, who had always been ambivalent about communism since his time at the Lenin Institute in Moscow, despite very many utterances of more or less Marxist parentage which, it is possible to believe, were simply made to convince the SACP that he was still one of them and thus deserving of their continued patronage. He was often a target of distrust and manoeuvre by the likes of Slovo and Kasrils but, being brighter by several orders of magnitude than those murderous chuckle brothers, he was always able to shrug off their challenges. Mbeki emerges in this period as a key figure because he was able first, to convince many of the Afrikaaners that the influence of the SACP fellow travellers was less than it was imagined to be. It was possible to hold this line largely because during the later 1980s, Gorbachev's Soviet Union were indeed abandoning the SACP while Mandela insisted that they had been merely allies in the liberation struggle. Not only this, but Mbeki was a realist when it came to the efficacy of armed struggle; he knew first hand that Slovo and Kasrils were no soldiers and MK no army. He was, however, convinced that demographics and the underlying economic reality was on his side and, accepting that armed struggle was a non-starter, decided that persuasion was the only way to alleviate the fears of Afrikaaners facing a future as a minority it what they had previously considered to be *their* own country. He also liked to portray himself as urbane, intellectual, pragmatic which, with his pipe and fondness for late night talks over whisky, also helped to win over many Afrikaaners. More than one commentator called him 'the seducer'.[578]

There were several other factors adding both urgency and complexity to the talks and these were largely to do with a progressive splintering of South African society as the crisis came to a head. As rumour began to leak out about the National Party contacts with the ANC, very many senior members of the SADF, the police and special forces saw the writing on the wall and began to draw their own conclusions about the future. Very many of them had conducted operations that they knew to be illegal at worst and of questionable legality at best on the understanding that they would be protected by the government's policy of Total Strategy. That essential trust between the government and the security forces began to fray as they began to fear that their heads would be offered up to the ANC as part of the price of settlement. When F.W. de Klerk took over, one of his first acts was to quickly reduce the influence of the security forces, which in turn very quickly resulted in a welter of mutual recriminations among them and a virtual collapse in morale that went all the way through the ranks.

---

[577] PW Botha's interview with Cliff Saunders, SABC 2006 https://www.youtube.com/watch?v=BDD6OfLabOQ
[578] J.P. Brits, *Thabo Mbeki and the Afrikaaners 1986-2004* Historia 53,2 Nov.2008.

Eeben Barlow, who would soon become the leader of the mercenary outfit Executive Outcomes and was at that time a member of the rather shadowy Civil Co-Operation Bureau, refused to participate in the assassination of a suspected ANC operative in London; Ferdi Barnard, another CCB operator, was arrested in October 1989 for the murder of an anti-Apartheid activist and held under Section 29 – which meant detention without trial; in January 1990, several tons of security force and police files started to burn.[579] The sense of impending betrayal led other members of the security forces to begin thinking about armed resistance to whatever was coming, a process that would culminate in demands for a separate Afrikaaner Homeland and the formation of General Constand Viljoen's *Volksfront* militia. It would also produce the far more unpleasant *Afrikaaner Weerstandsbeweging* led by Eugene Terreblanche, a straightforward Nazi-style organisation led by a comically unpleasant, stereotypical backveldt boer. Still other members of the security forces started to approach the ANC with a view to making their peace privately; it was only during the closing stages of this game that the ANC's intelligence gathering Operation Vula made any gains worth mentioning in suborning the security forces.

It wasn't just the security forces that were splintering. The cut in funding imposed by the Soviet Union sharpened up more than a few minds in the ANC. Many of those who had spent their lives abroad on stipends provided by the Soviets or other donors began to realise that those days were now coming to an end and that they would need to earn a living in some other capacity. While it was reasonable to suppose that senior ANC exiles would be assigned a place at the table, there would have to be places made available for those who had made a name in the UDF and, no doubt, some others reserved for the senior National Party politicians but for those at the bottom of the pile with few marketable skills there was no guarantee of a long term future. This was especially the case for those who were SACP because the main funder of the ANC now became the USA. What this meant was that the patronage networks of senior ANC figures became ever more entrenched and with ever more insecurity, those members lower down in the network were more willing to engage in corrupt activities to provide wealth for their masters and gain favour for themselves. This was already a feature of ANC life; it would become one of the dominant features of the new South Africa.

Further consequences flowed from the ANC's practice of using criminal networks within South Africa to raise funds through drug-running and smuggling. The fact that liberation was at hand was really quite irrelevant to people engaged at the bottom end of this kind of trade and a democratic election was no guarantee that a new government would create more lucrative legal opportunities. Indeed, as the 'war' seemed to be coming to a close it became quite clear that new opportunities for criminal activity and association would soon arise, especially if the police were emasculated or discredited; especially if the criminals *became* the police themselves – Robert McBride, an ANC member who joined the police in the 1990s was subsequently arrested for gun-running in Mozambique. When allied to the practice of 'transactional leadership' (which means government officials handing out contracts in return for bribes) already common throughout the ANC, there can be little doubt that the fortunes that many leading members of the ANC suddenly acquired were acquired illegitimately. Joe Modise, whose role as MK commander in the struggle he chose to interpret as avoiding going anywhere near danger while running his lucrative drugs racket became internationally famous for his role as Defence Minister in a 1999 scandal-ridden arms deal. At the other end of this scale were people like Colin Chauke, ANC council member in Pretoria and armed robber; when Mandela came to power in 1994, some 60,000 members of ANC 'self-defence' organisations or MK were unaccounted for along with their weapons.[580]

To add to this chaotic background, what looked to be very much like the end of the Cold War in Europe was happening as East Europeans stormed westwards through the holes opening up almost every day in the Iron Curtain. It is to F.W. de Klerk's credit that he decided then and there that, as that equation was changing, then perhaps the South African one could change too. On October 15th 1989, he released Walter Sisulu and five other ANC lifers. Three weeks later, the Berlin Wall came down and not just the equation but the whole world changed. At the beginning of December, de Klerk told his cabinet that Apartheid was over and on 2nd February 1990 went to parliament to announce that decision. Nine days later, on 11th February 1990, Nelson Mandela walked out of jail. Apartheid was indeed over. Now the hard part would begin, for what South Africa needed was no less than the creation of a country that could do what looked like the impossible; put a bloody and

---

[579] E. Barlow, *Executive Outcomes*, (Alberton 2007), pp. 68-74.
[580] Stephen Ellis, *External Mission; the ANC in Exile 1960-1990* (Oxford, 2013) p.274.

unresolved past behind it and find a way into the future that was radically different from the one that Africa to the north had taken.

*

Conclusions

This is a good place to halt because from this point on History must begin to give way to political science, simply because the problems of records, the reliability and availability of sources and the lack of hindsight means that anything written from this point is provisional to the point of being merely speculative. This is not to say that there aren't some good books on the post-1989 period, but it *is* to say that no matter how well researched they are they cannot provide the historical overview that I have aimed at. Also, the revolution in journalism that began in the 1990s with the coming of satellite communications and the 24 hour news cycle which resulted in even more instances of journalists being plonked down in places they knew nothing about to cover issues they were equally ignorant of, means that many of the contemporary sources lack even the worth of immediacy. There are good people working out there, trying to understand what is happening and explaining it to an audience, but there are also plenty of internet charlatans, academics, politicians, spin doctors, axe-grinders, media managers and news outlets that have abandoned any commitment to any sort of objectivity and are trying full time to 'shape opinion' rather than report the news or properly inform the public. Personal experience so often contradicts what comes through a screen that really, you can only go off the evidence before your eyes to try to understand what has happened in the recent past and the chaotic present. Rejecting the given narrative and forming your own opinion does not make you a bad person - as long as you have formed it by consulting a range of sources.

So now, let me draw some conclusions about Apartheid and how it ended.

Firstly, although Apartheid grew out of some of the practices of segregation that were quite common during the 19th and early 20th Century, it was not a natural extension of them. Attempts to show that it was a system inherited in all but name from the British are wrong. Apartheid was a theory, a vision of Utopia that owed much more to the totalitarian visions of Socialism, Communism, Nazism and Fascism than it did to British notions of individual liberty, parliamentary democracy and free market capitalism. Where segregation existed in the British Empire, it rapidly declined and was progressively abandoned. In South Africa, Apartheid went far beyond the petty segregation of colour bars and was elevated into a system that was designed to maintain the separation of people of different races, whether they wanted it or not.

Secondly, Apartheid was not the handmaid of capitalism. Job reservation, the colour bar and all the other detritus of Apartheid was an active hindrance to the operation of the free market because it interfered with the free utilisation of labour, restricted competition, depressed demand and prevented entrepreneurs from entering the market. The origins of this accusation lie with those on the Left who hoped that the collapse of Apartheid would be preceded (or followed) by the destruction of the capitalist system across the world and the establishment of a worldwide socialist order led by the Soviet Union.

Thirdly, Apartheid was an overtly racist system that had its roots in Social Darwinist assumptions that had been largely abandoned by 1945 but racist ideas, behaviour and speech persisted and were widely accepted across South African society. It is also the case that many white South Africans rejected racism and that as time went on, the number of those rejecting racist notions and, indeed, the idea of Apartheid itself, grew from a significant minority into a large majority. Similarly, racism was not confined to white South African society but was prevalent in one form or another throughout Africa and indeed the world. The case of the Ugandan Asians is probably the most famous example of black racism but it is certainly not unique.

Fourthly, whatever the faults of Apartheid – and they were legion – black South Africans were not subjected to the kleptocracy, civil war, government incompetence, economic collapse, starvation and impoverishment that so many other Africans suffered under post-colonial government. Although the day to day humiliations of Apartheid were intolerable, there was still space for a black middle class to emerge and for a black working

185

class to keep body and soul together. In this respect, black South Africans were fortunate - in the same way that the East Germans were fortunate not to be citizens of the USSR and the citizens of Communist Vietnam were fortunate not to be citizens of Communist Cambodia. In the devil's arithmetic, it often comes down to a matter of degree.

In terms of what caused the collapse of Apartheid, a hierarchy of causes may be established. First and most important is the demography of the period. The rapid growth in population would overwhelm any social or economic system which denied or limited the aspirations of people to a decent standard of living and reasonable self-respect and so Apartheid was doomed because its anti-capitalist aspects restricted the ability of its economy to provide sufficient economic growth at sufficient speed to meet those aspirations. This remains a problem for South Africa today – indeed, virtually all Africa today. The experience of China since the 1980s is unequivocal in showing that unless free market capitalism is made the bedrock of economic policy, the aspirations of a growing population can *never* be met. The disturbances that began in Soweto in 1976 were a direct result of Apartheid's resistance to capitalism.

Second comes the opposition of employers and businesses, personified by but not limited to, the Oppenheimers. Their constant opposition to Apartheid on business grounds chipped away at its foundations by showing time and time again its business inefficiency. Employers and businesses also financed the opposition in parliament, in society, culture and, not least, the Mells Park talks in Britain. This was then made decisive by the conviction of the financial markets during the mid-1980s that unless Apartheid was dismantled, business confidence and thus access to investment and finance would rapidly diminish.

Third comes the intervention of Britain and the USA. Constructive engagement allowed effective pressure to be brought on the South African leadership without forcing it back into the laager. It also ensured that the ANC had a functioning state and economy to inherit. The key moments were Henry Kissinger's intervention with Vorster over Rhodesia, Margaret Thatcher's facing down of the movement for economic sanctions and Chester Crocker's diplomacy over Namibia. After this, the decision to cut the funding to the ANC by the Soviet Union was decisive in getting them to the negotiating table. Both the UN and Organisation of African Unity's campaigns achieved nothing.

The fourth factor is the popular discontent of the period 1976-1989. Although these protests were poorly directed and failed to make the country ungovernable outside the townships, the heavy repression directed against them convinced very many people that something other than Apartheid was needed for the country to function in a reasonable fashion. Those popular demonstrations that took place against Apartheid outside South Africa had no significant effect on policy or decision making.

Finally, we can assess the impact of the ANC. Incompetent in opposition, quickly decapitated and from then on ineffective in exile, its armed wing made no significant impression on the ability of the Apartheid state to defend itself. Only taken seriously after the financial shock of 1985, it was sought out as an interlocutor simply because there was no one else to talk to and because the mass of demonstrators adopted it as their flag of resistance because there was no-one else to follow. In this the ANC were fortunate in the extreme, for these things happened independently of any of their efforts and they did very little to deserve the keys of the kingdom that were handed to them on a plate. They were doubly fortunate in the persons of Nelson Mandela and Thabo Mbeki, who were able to provide effective leadership where none had existed since the 1960s.

And finally, finally, you will of course have picked up the underlying idea that this guide to the History of South Africa is not just a guide to the History of South Africa as billed, but also a challenge to that particular historical paradigm which divides things into 'Left/Good' and 'Right/Bad'. It seems to me that the division between Left and Right is redundant because the distinctions between those ideas characterised as 'Left/Good' and 'Right/Bad' simply do not exist in any meaningful form. Socialism, Communism, Nazism, Fascism and Apartheid have far more similarities than differences because they are each characterised by a vision of Utopia, an intolerance of dissent, and a determination to impose and maintain that vision regardless of its practicality or possibility of success, by any means, including unrestrained violence. These ideas should not be labelled 'Right' or 'Left' but understood in the more simple category of 'bad' because they are injurious to humanity in every case that they have been tried and in every case that they are likely to be tried. In opposition to that category of 'bad' are the virtues of individual liberty, parliamentary democracy, the rule of law and capitalism which we may put into the category of 'good' not because they are always in themselves successful but because they have demonstrably provided the best approximation of best outcomes for humanity in a flawed and uncertain world. That this is so is because within those virtues are contained the ability for mistakes to be corrected before they become disasters and because they allow people to live their lives, within the bounds of the law, in the way they see fit, rather than as the playthings of theorists of greater or lesser benevolence or, indeed, greater or lesser malevolence.

www.ingramcontent.com/pod-product-compliance
Lightning Source LLC
Chambersburg PA
CBHW051346280526
45784CB00007B/2831